Islam and the Russian Empire
Reform and Revolution in Central Asia

Islam and the Russian Empire

Reform and Revolution in Central Asia

HÉLÈNE CARRÈRE D'ENCAUSSE

Preface by Maxime Rodinson

Translated by Quintin Hoare

Comparative Studies on Muslim Societies, 8
Barbara D. Metcalf, Editor

University of California Press
Berkeley Los Angeles London

University of California Press
Berkeley and Los Angeles, California

Originally published in 1966 under the title *Reforme et Revolution chez les Musulmans de l'Empire russe*, c by the Presses de la Fondation Nationale des Sciences Politiques, Paris.

Library of Congress Cataloging in Publication Data

Carrère d'Encausse, Hélène.
    Islam and the Russian Empire.
    (Comparative studies on Muslim societies ; 8)
    Translation of: Réforme et révolution chez les
Musulmans de l'Empire russe.
    1. Muslims—Soviet Central Asia—History.
    2. Soviet Union—Foreign relations—Islamic countries.
    3. Islamic countries—Foreign relations—Soviet Union.
    4. Bukhara (Uzbek S.S.R.)—History. I.Title.
    II. Series.
    DK855.5.M8C3713   1988   327.47017671   88–14367
    ISBN 0–520–06504–2 (alk. paper)

Printed and bound in Great Britain by
Redwood Burn Limited, Trowbridge

In memory of my parents

Contents

Note on the transliteration of Persian and Turkish   viii

Publisher's Preface   ix

Preface   xi

Introduction   1

Part 1 The Origins of Reformism in Bukhara

   1 Bukhara on the Eve of the Russian Conquest   7

   2 The Russian Conquest: Bukhara Face-to-Face with Capitalism and the West   37

   3 Preambles to Reformism   54

Part 2 In Search of an Ideology, 1900–17

   4 National Awakening in Turkistan   71

   5 Beginnings of Reformation in Bukhara   78

   6 Era of the Secret Societies, 1910–14   89

Part 3 National Reconquest, 1917–24

   7 End of the Russian Empire: Bukhara Face-to-Face with War and Revolution   119

   8 The October Revolution. Alliance between the Jadids and the Bolsheviks   148

   9 The People's Republic of Bukhara   167

Conclusion   185

Appendix 1 Dynasties and Rulers of the Khanate of Bukhara   193

Appendix 2 Statutes of the Benevolent Society of Bukhara for the Dissemination of Knowledge among the Masses   194

Appendix 3 The Emir of Bukhara's Manifesto of 30 March 1917   197

Appendix 4 Reform Programme for Bukhara, drawn up by the Young Bukharan Party   199

Notes   207

Select Bibliography   237

Supplementary Select Bibliography   252

Glossary of Arabic, Persian and Turkish Terms   255

Index of Subjects   261

Index of Names   265

Note on the Transliteration of Persian and Turkish

The administrative language of nineteenth-century Bukhara was Persian, also spoken by the Tajik inhabitants of the Emirate. However, a majority of the population spoke Uzbek, a Turkic language. For the sake of simplicity, and to bypass the often impossible task of deciding whether particular terms or personal names — many of them common to both languages — should be rendered in Persian or Turkish fashion, the system of transliteration adopted in this book uses Arabized vowels. The exception is in the place names for which, to avoid confusion, the familiar vowels of contemporary Russianized spellings have been retained. References to books and articles in modern Turkish have been written in modern Turkish orthography. All diacriticals have been omitted, as have final *hamzas*.

Publisher's Preface

The Central Asian republics which form part of the USSR have attracted much interest in recent years. Mainly Muslim in religion and Turkic or Persian in language, their populations are increasing at a higher rate than the Russian, and so are coming to form an ever larger proportion of the total population of the USSR. In what seems to be a new political climate in the USSR, the relations of the republics with Moscow are likely to change in ways which are still difficult to predict. At the same time, the reassertion of Islamic identity which is taking place just across the frontier, in Iran and Afghanistan, cannot fail to have repercussions in Central Asia.

These problems of the present and future cannot be understood without some knowledge of the history of the Central Asian countries, of the ways in which they were incorporated into the Russian empire and their reactions to Russian rule. The Muslim societies of the region have a long tradition of settled life, high culture, and independent political existence. During the nineteenth century they were drawn into the orbit of Russia's expanding power; Russians settled among the indigenous population, and the economy and society of the region began to change. By the beginning of the First World War there were the first stirrings of nationalism among the Muslims, and also movements for religious and social reform. The Russian revolution of 1917 seemed for a moment to offer an opportunity for independence, and the new communist regime was only established after some years of struggle and confusion.

Among the Muslim principalities which were drawn into the Russian empire, that of Bukhara is of special importance. Hélène Carrère d'Encausse's study of the first half-century or so of its encounter with Russian power is of vital significance for those who wish to understand a subject of growing importance to a changing Soviet society.

Preface

I consider it an honour to have been asked to present this book to the public, because it is an important work.

It is important, first, as a work of so-called factual history; I shall not dwell on this aspect, however, since readers will soon discover it for themselves. A work that can guide non-specialists, in other words most of us, through every twist and turn of events and identify the fundamental axes of an epoch, on the basis of a vast mass of assorted documents, is useful and merits interest and respect. It must, of course, be done honestly and intelligently; in the case of Hélène Carrère d'Encausse's book, such qualities are undeniable. Readers will therefore find it provides them with a convenient and reliable source of information concerning the Central Asian state of the Khanate of Bukhara, as it was in the nineteenth and early twentieth centuries; concerning its history and structure; and concerning the shock Russian conquest and the penetration of a capitalist economy inflicted upon it, its masses, and its élites. From her book, we learn how a reformist ideology developed in the Muslim milieu, and about the vicissitudes of the Russian Revolution's encounter with that movement, spawned by one of the most archaic of societies. All this is an indubitable contribution, and one that must be appreciated to the full.

But this book also contributes something else. The author has not confined herself to uncovering the fabric of events, already a more than honourable task; she has striven to illuminate their motive forces and to reflect upon their interconnections and their articulation. So her book is one — rare enough in all truth — which shows us that human history is not mere sound and fury, dream or formless nightmare, haunted by vague shadows groping through darkness and headed for the night. Humanity, or at least human collectivities, weave their destinies around great problems, whose modalities are ceaselessly transformed but which nevertheless remain substantially identical throughout the centuries and the millennia. 'The future is more like the past than one drop of water is to another,' wrote the great Arab sociologist Ibn Khaldun in the fourteenth century, which is in one sense quite false but in another quite true; and that dimension of truth, alone, creates the possibility and the legitimacy of a reflection upon history. Contrary to what Valéry and others have thought of a reflection that is instructive, if not always encouraging, if lucidity is a quality for confronting the trials of individual and collective life, how is it to be acquired without recourse to history?

The history Hélène Carrère d'Encausse recounts is particularly rich in lessons, from this point of view, for the contemporary person, who will discover there — as the author's final reflections especially show — a first 'model', a first performance, of the crucial problems of today. And this performance was given in a theatre particularly interesting and typical. If we were to readopt the problematic that the fathers of the Christian Church borrowed from Philon of Alexandria — the conception according to which all the events of the New Law were prefigured in the Old and had already been 'performed'; every character at every moment having had a 'type' that prefigured him or her and having played his or her role a millennium earlier — we could say that in this forgotten region of Asia the prototypes of today's *dramatis personae* were already stirring, unobserved from the main stage of the world — today's and, no doubt in large measure, tomorrow's.

Allow me to develop somewhat, in my own fashion and upon my own responsibility, a few reflections flanking those of Hélène Carrère d'Encausse, or following in their wake. As she so well shows, the history of Bukhara in the period that concerns her revolves entirely around the clash of two ideologies. The effects of this clash are evident half a century later on a far wider scale — that of the entire so-called Third World. On the one hand, a universalist ideology had captured Russia spiritually before dominating it politically: an ideology of social progress accomplished uniformly, through the agency of class struggle, everywhere; an ideology whose bourgeois forms saw themselves as applicable to the problems of dependent countries and whose proletarian form saw itself, proclaimed itself, and theorized itself as having to play that role. On the other hand, an ideology existed — still at that time imprecise, clumsy, not theorized, and often borrowing its intellectual scaffolding from the previous universalist ideological movement in those areas — namely Islam. This ideology was incomparably strong by virtue of a thousand implicit feelings, which were barely outlined and scarcely venturing to formulate or to define themselves, yet were implanted in the depths of every heart by daily life; by the warmth of the paternal hearth; by the emotions of childhood; and by the triumphs, griefs, and bitternesses of maturity. The time had not yet come for the former, universalist ideology and for precise plans polished by economists and engineers: it was still the phase of ideals, whose appeal was all the greater for their being ill defined; their existential resonance, all the greater; and their clashes, all the fiercer.

In the nineteenth century, for the European Bukhara was the very exemplar of stagnation. The Danish traveller Olufsen, who visited Bukhara at the beginning of the twentieth century, was delighted to have seen 'all the features of the country at a time when it and its population are still the same as in Tamerlane's day'. He was delighted (in 1911!) because the Russians had established their power only indirectly, eliminating only 'the most serious abuses of power and the brutal influence of ancient superstition':

> Thus Bukhara is still assured for a good while of not being decked out in European attire, and it will be a long time before its original Oriental stamp disappears. The Emir of Bukhara still lives as in the days of yore, behind his high, crenellated walls, and his vassal kings, the Begs, still maintain their antiquated courts in gloomy romantic castles. The winding streets with their terraced houses of clay, the mosques and the *madrasas*, are not yet disturbed by houses in the European style. The mullas, the dervishes, the *qalandars* and the *divanas* (beggars of feeble mind) still throng the sanctuaries as they did centuries ago. Slowly and calmly the caravan with its camels crosses the vast deserts and the steppes, the *araba* on its two wheels jolts forward along harsh tracks and the donkey, laden from ears to tail, walks patiently on its short legs as thin as drumsticks; the dogs jostle in the Muslim cemeteries and the vultures circle over the carcasses of camels. The 'Allah Akbar' of the muezzin, accompanied by the braying of donkeys and the cooing of doves, still echoes across the orchards and the rice-fields of the oases. The mystique of enclosure prevails everywhere: the gates of the towns are shut at night, the doors of the houses are bolted against intruders and the aversion to intimate contact with those Christian dogs is the same as in the Middle Ages. It is force not desire which has brought the Muslims into contact with Europeans. Probably only the rollers, perched in rows on the telegraph wires, have anything to do voluntarily with one of the acoustic devices of European civilization.

This idyllic picture resembles those that all the romantic spirits of the Western world were then wont to paint of the Muslim world, with equal parts of somewhat suspect tenderness and somewhat self-interested myopia. The explanation was not far removed from the description; such a lazy explanation is still widespread today in terms of the good and bad qualities of peoples: 'nowhere did Turkish supremacy show itself more incapable of guiding a country onto the path of civilization, despite many other fortunate qualities of the Turks.'

The romantic spirits were as usual mistaken; they were unable to discern either the mud in the millpool or the hellfire in the forge. The Turks of Bukhara were humans, after all. In the gloomy romantic castles, the winding streets, the houses of clay, the mosques, and the *madrasas*, on the jolting *arabas*; and across orchards and rice-fields — there one could hear, provided one had a sharp ear and understood Uzbek, something other than the braying of donkeys and the cooing of doves. One could hear human voices, reacting as humans normally should react everywhere and always. Struggles for power and control over people and goods had never ceased; stagnation had never been complete. But the strength of monarchic power — compared with that which any conceivable social opposition could have mustered — was so great, the hopes for success of a reform movement were so slender, and the alternative solutions so hard to see that resignation had overcome everyone. Tsarism, for Europe, might represent a despotic régime verging on barbarism. To the Bukharans and all the Muslim peoples of Central Asia it brought a new model, an alternative. They knew that another way of life was possible, perceived through the window to Europe that the Russian presence furnished, even if the Russian model was not sufficiently appealing. That world involved at least customary limits to the supreme ruler's arbitrary power, at least participation of the élites controlling persons and goods. Moreover, that new practice seemed linked in organic fashion to a constant progress along the road of power and prosperity.

The appeal of that European model was general and unconquerable — and on a worldwide scale — despite all counter-factors. That crude but evident fact should be enough to silence those fond of twaddle about the irreducible originality of peoples or about the imperviousness of certain civilizations to certain stimulants. But our culture, like every other, has a right to its share of nonsense.

In Turkistan this appeal (in the broad sense) took the form of the movement of Jadids (innovators or modernists, from the Arabic *jadid*, meaning 'new') — a movement whose development in Bukhara Hélène Carrère d'Encausse portrays with accuracy and intelligence and on the basis of an impressive documentation. With few exceptions, the Jadids remained Muslims. In some cases that meant a stubborn attachment to the existential values transmitted by Islam. In all cases it meant a wish to remain themselves and not be detached from the people whence they had sprung — a fidelity to an identity handed down and accepted. Here, again and already, was revealed the fundamental ambiguity of the reference to Islam, as is the case with the reference to any ideology whatsoever, once a certain stage is passed. The traditionalists, the reactionaries, and the supporters of the old (*qadim*) likewise invoked Islam. But for them Islam was the world of thought, values, and customs in which they had always lived and which had been effectively rendered sacred by religion, even if the origin of each element was alien to Islam and had imposed itself or been imposed upon it by some Jadid movement in the past.

The tragedy is that the masses often recognized themselves more readily in the traditionalists than in the innovators. The slaves of antiquity, the proletarians of the capitalist world, were sufficiently excluded from the city and its values to welcome with joy anything that could shake the world of oppression; or to recognize themselves in Eunus, Spartacus, and Jesus or in Marx, Bakunin, and Lenin. But traditional Muslim society gives the poor person a place, recognizes the human's eminent value in God's eyes and the right to holy alms, welcomes a man into its brotherhoods and guilds, and can make of that man a guide and a saint. It makes holy and sanctifies human filth and destitution. It seems at first sight to the poor person that the innovator wants to topple him or her from the ideal throne. And what does the innovator offer in recompense? Nothing.

Marxist authors of the institutional kind, Soviet ones especially, have taken it as axiomatic that any movement of thought which assailed the traditional values of an oppressive society was one which met with the assent and support of the oppressed. No idea, however, could be more frequently refuted by history. The thinkers who initially attacked tradition had sprung from the privileged classes; the masses, stupefied by conformism, could inspire them only with contempt, and contempt in turn engendered envy and hatred. The masses always prefer ideological cadres born of, and close to, themselves to theorizing innovators, who are proud of their knowledge and intellectual originality, and bent on destroying the world of certainty off which the masses live. This can be observed even today in the ideological movement of Communism. The Jadids advocated orientation towards a way of life to which, at least for the foreseeable future, the poverty of the masses barred them from aspiring, whatever political reforms might be adopted. The Jadids already partly conformed to the way of life of the foreigner and the unbeliever; they already enjoyed a culture inaccessible to the masses and were largely recruited from the relatively well-off strata. The hatred that at least a section of the suffering masses turned upon them can be explained far more easily by these factors than by any innate propensity of Muslims (or Orientals) to fanaticism and xenophobia. The reaction is not essentially different from that of proletarians breaking machines or of Renaissance pietist movements throwing the paintings of aristocratic and enlightened artists into the flames.

These are problems the victorious Bolsheviks discovered before too long in their own field of experience. The texts Lenin drafted between his triumph and his death overflow with bitter allusions to the barbarism and backwardness of the muzhiks. Like the French democrats of 1848, fighting to postpone the date of the elections that would make the real people into the true judge of democracy, the Jadids of Bukhara and the Bolsheviks of Moscow were obliged to make the masses happy despite themselves; otherwise they would perish. A new, but by no means unusual, meaning was given to the 1793 watchword 'liberty, equality, fraternity, or death'.

Confronted with the masses they wished to drag towards happiness, the Russian Bolsheviks were in the same situation as the Uzbek Jadids at a different stage; and to some extent this was to condition the clash between those two forces, each being linked to its people. The Jadids won a clientele also among those most deprived and least integrated into traditional society, among such victims of that society as dispossessed peasants. But that clientele was fickle and its leaders had to follow it. Since social reforms were envisaged only timidly by leaders, often of relatively privileged origin and terrorized at the prospect of destroying a coherent structure without any real idea of what to put in its place, the masses demanded at least (or above all) intransigence in the national domain. The Russian Bolsheviks were able with some difficulty — by utilizing barbaric methods to fight barbarism, as the celebrated formula put it — to subjugate their own people to the vision they entertained of its happiness. They were able temporarily to appear to the restive muzhiks as new oppressors, awesome reincarnations of Antichrist or of Ivan the Terrible. In the eyes of the Uzbeks, however, they appeared first as foreigners. They had initially been appreciated as friends — without consideration for their social doctrines, which were a matter for themselves alone — because they proclaimed their intention of renouncing the nationally oppressive policies of the Tsars. But people soon perceived that it was not so easy for them to change their behaviour towards the non-Russians.

The Bolsheviks, following Lenin and Wilson, might have inscribed on their banner the right of peoples to dispose of themselves — and that with the greatest sincerity. Nevertheless, in practice, leaving the Muslim peoples to choose their own social order meant yielding power, in the best of cases, to somewhat visionary reformists with no great practical experience, who before too long would be duped by a traditionalist native bourgeoisie, which draped in the folds of the green flag of Islam its defence of its own privileges and its contempt for and exploitation of the masses. It meant the fairly likely prospect, in all truth, of an imminent appeal by that bourgeoisie — or even by the landed aristocracy with which it would reach an accommodation — to the anti-Communist imperialist powers. It would be easy enough also to sanctify that appeal by Islam for help from the infidel! What this at once entailed was establishing the enemy (class enemy and national enemy) within the confines of the Russian empire so lately deceased. It meant giving the enemy gratuitously — for purely quixotic motives and without any benefit accruing to the indigenous masses — access routes across the Urals, Siberia, and the lower Volga towards the nerve centres of the proletarian revolution; an opportunity to help the revolution's foes effectively; and a means of pressure upon the revolution.

It is understandable that the Bolsheviks should have shrunk from this prospect. But the other horn of the dilemma was also perilous. In the decision to keep those Muslim provinces within the Soviet orbit, who can say which was stronger — the determination not to endanger the revolution, or Russian reluctance to give up land conquered by Russians? But that is a matter for only the psychoanalyst or lay confessor. There was no longer any God in glory at the summit of the Kremlin to probe the innermost hearts of the Soviet leaders; there was worse: the officials, the soldiers, the policemen — in a word, the cadres — who were to be entrusted with the implementation of those measures, might not all be Bolsheviks; but they would all be Russians or Russified. In practice, they would inevitably tend to have the reactions of Russians, of Europeans, who would subdue backward natives incapable of understanding for themselves what was good for them, namely the proletarian dictatorship, because to them it had formerly been the autocracy of the white tsar. And the natives would certainly see them above all as Russians — as oppressive, impious foreigners deciding on the natives' behalf and seeking to impose upon them devilish Russian customs and reckless transformations of an order hallowed by centuries, hence by Allah, praised be his name. Thus was reconstituted the traditional situation of tension between dominator and dominated, in a climate that had been modified but that in many ways strongly recalled that past which the aim had been to transcend.

The same dilemma appeared once again in the colonies, where the dominators had less justification, however, than the Bolsheviks for claiming to bring new and effective solutions to the social calamities weighing down the masses. But above all, in a modified guise, this dilemma underlies the current problems of the Third World. Since the accession to independence of almost all Asiatic and African countries, in each an indigenous ruling élite has undertaken to lead its people towards progress. Some are sincere and some hypocritical; some open to the future; and some attached to the past; some rigid and some flexible; some intelligent and some limited. They may be linked to one or another layer of the population, or they may constitute a specific layer with its own selfish interests. But almost everywhere, whether for pure or for self-interested motives, at the prospect of the eventual overturn of traditional society they seem to experience the same terror that seized the Jadids of Bukhara in 1920. We must grant it is genuinely hard for them to entrust the illiterate masses immediately with responsibility for deciding their own destinies, determining investment quotas, or settling the most serious political and economic questions. They cannot but readopt the attitude of the Russian Bolsheviks, albeit with the incomparable advantage of being indigenous, but also with the notable handicap of not being linked organically to a progressive ideology and erected against their own shortcomings (on that path of social progress alone!) by a doctrinal and organizational framework.

Over and against them, almost everywhere, alternative élites already exist, on the lookout for breaches in the protecting walls; and these in certain respects also repeat the position of the Bolsheviks. They put less emphasis on the national character of their projects, since the national position of the groups in power is generally not easy to contest. But it is simple, and perhaps will become increasingly so, to denounce the social compromises of those who rule; their attachment to their economic and political privileges; and their slowness in ensuring some benefit from the fruits of development for the masses, who will be increasingly less unsuited to receive it, or from sharing their power and their advantages. Over and against those who, by a traditional process, will find an excuse in exalting national values, those who will brandish the standard of social struggles, the red or black flag of the claims of the oppressed, will increasingly rise up (whereas in the Communist world, perhaps, oppositions will on the contrary take the national emblem as a rallying sign).

All these perspectives were barely taking shape in the years after 1917 in the old Uzbek khanate, in the shadow of the glowering fortress of the Arg, when everyone still trembled before the sinister 'Emir of the Night'. But the germ was there and this book, which I am about to let speak for itself, helps us to discern it. In Arab works you may read the following quotation regarding Bukhara from Ibn Balkhi, a local geographer who lived in the tenth century:

> I have never seen and I have never learnt that there exists in the lands of Islam a town superior to Bukhara for the charm of its surroundings. For if you climb to the summit of its citadel, wheresoever your eyes may wander they will alight only on greenery whose colour mingles with the green of the sky. You would say the sky was a green lid that has been upturned over a green vase, the castles glitter in the midst like sparks, the fields around the villages depending on them seem to have been polished like a mirror.

The book you are about to read will present you with a less poetic but more instructive view of the Bukharan lands — of Bukhara, mirror not of the sky but of the earth.

Maxime Rodinson

Introduction

Situated in the heart of Turkistan,[1] the Emirate of Bukhara was, on the eve of the Russian conquest, a closed country, hard to reach, and protected in the east by very high mountains and on every other side by the vast deserts of Qizil Kum and Qara Kum.[2] The state was made up of two quite distinct parts, which every factor helped to separate and counterpose. In western Bukhara, life had always been organized in the plains flanking the great rivers: the Zarafshan, the golden river celebrated in history and legend;[3] and the Amu Darya,[4] the Oxus of the ancient Greeks. In eastern Bukhara, land of mountains and domain of cold and death, humans had taken refuge in the narrow valleys accompanying the rivers and streams on their capricious courses. Everywhere, in the rich oases and in the mountain valleys, humans have always had to struggle against two implacable enemies: the limitless sands, whence humans have torn their oases; and the wind, which ceaselessly carries the sands back over those oases and erases all life there during a storm. Each oasis and each river constitutes a living island in a hostile nature; and the continuous labour of the emirate's sovereigns has been an attempt to group these isolated centres of life together and weld them into a unified state.

The effort was all the more considerable in that Bukhara harbours very disparate peoples, who in the course of centuries have ended up there as the result of invasion, rapine, or the transit of caravans. In the early 1920s half the population of the Emirate was Uzbek, 31 per cent was Tajik, 10 per cent was Turkmen, 6–7 per cent Kirghiz, and the rest made up of Arabs, Persians, Hindus, and Jews.[5]

The unifying factor around which these peoples coalesced was Islam, which was introduced into Bukhara by Qutayba b. Muslim [6] between 705 and 715 A.D. With Islam also began the age of the great invasions. From this history, so fertile in tragic events, the Uzbek state of Bukhara that arose in the sixteenth century inherited a number of elements: Islam, Iranian, and Turkish civiliza-

1

tion; and the memory of two quite extraordinary revolts, which, from many points of view, prefigure the crisis of the twentieth century and the accounts of which were to haunt popular consciousness when similar problems arose at the time of the Protectorate. The first of these revolts took place at the beginning of the thirteenth century, when the Gurkhans ruled in Bukhara. The urban population, led by an artisan who was to take the name of Malik Sinjar, rose simultaneously against the domination of the Gurkhans and against local property-owners, who were treated with the most extreme cruelty and stripped of their goods. The second revolt took place during 1238–9: unlike the former, it began not from the towns, but from the rural areas; but like the former, it mobilized the dispossessed both against the Mongol invaders and against the rich, whose goods the rebels intended to distribute to the whole people in accordance with the principles of strict justice.

Despite the recurrence of invasion, destruction, and revolt, until the sixteenth century Bukhara was not only in certain periods an important political centre, but also an incomparable centre of religious and cultural life — above all, a city whose greatness and splendour were noted by historians and travellers. Did Marco Polo not say that Bukhara in the thirteenth century was 'the best city in all Persia'?

A new period opened up for Bukhara when in 1500 A.D. Shaybani Khan[7] ensured the victory of the Uzbeks and founded the Uzbek empire, over which he ruled as first sovereign of the Shaybanid dynasty. For almost two centuries that empire, whose real capital was Bukhara, was powerful and renowned.

With the Ashtarkhanids or Janids, who succeeded the heirs of Shaybani Khan, began the decadence of the Uzbek state and its division. Its power was first impaired by the desire for independence of the nomads, who considered the territory over which they roamed to be their absolute property and who refused to submit to the authority of a state less and less capable of imposing it. Power thus gradually passed from the sovereign to the chiefs of the major tribes. This crisis of local power was not specific to Bukhara; it affected all the neighbouring states and was aggravated by the fact that Central Asia at that time lost all its economic importance. The maritime route had definitively ousted the age-old caravan road, and local unrest had served only to accelerate this process: apart from the constant threat that raids by the ill-controlled tribes posed to the lives and property of merchants venturing onto the desert routes, the sovereigns themselves, weakened and isolated, also multiplied customs' impositions for their own profit.

Under the Manghits, successors of the Ashtarkhanids, and above all from the reign of Emir Nasrallah (1827-60) onwards, there began the work of reinforcing and regrouping the state. To restore central power, Emir Nasrallah took on the aristocracy of the Uzbek clans: he eliminated feudal chieftains from the administration and replaced them by functionaries of more humble origin; and for the army of Uzbek tribes raised by each tribal chief, he substituted a permanent army of which he was the sole master and which he utilized for his external conquests.

His successor Muzaffar al-Din (1860–85) had to confront the Russian conquest. For the second time since its conversion to Islam, Bukhara was destined to be dominated by infidels and brought face-to-face with the outside world. This problem was not specific to Bukhara; it affected all Islamic countries in the nineteenth century, and the crisis of the Bukharan Muslims in that period belonged to the general crisis of Islam. It was just one aspect of it, assuredly, but it had its own specific features — hence its destiny would be exceptional.

Part I

The Origins of Reformism in Bukhara

1

Bukhara on the Eve of the Russian Conquest

Just what, in the second half of the nineteenth century, was Bukhara — a state whose name was holy for the entire Muslim Orient and of which it was commonly said, 'though everywhere in the world light is shed upon the earth from above, in Bukhara the light proceeds from the earth itself'?

The travellers who visited it and left detailed memoirs (Meiendorff and Eversmann in 1820, Buterroff in 1840, Vambéry and Hanykov around 1850–60; and later Logofet, Sneysareff, Olufsen, and many others); the victorious Russian authorities; and finally the historians — all delivered their judgements and left an image of the emirate in which the prevalent impression was of an extraordinary lag behind the world of the nineteenth century, indeed of total immobility.

Arminius Vambéry, who visited Bukhara with the eyes of a European but in the guise of a *hajji*, delivered an unqualified judgement upon the emirate. He noted the extreme tyranny of the Manghit sovereigns, the omnipotence of a repressive and unscrupulous administration, the wretched state of the people, and the degradation of the state.[1] The Danish traveller Olufsen, to whom we owe one of the first accounts in which scientific concerns continually surface and from which an excellent ethnographic view emerges, is no less severe. For him, nowhere in the world were the Turks so incapable of guiding a country's destiny; he saw the Russian conquest as necessary to wrest the country from its age-old backwardness.[2]

Nevertheless, in the same period a certain dynamism of Bukharan society and its elements stood in seeming contrast to the immobility of the dominant structures. The main feature of Bukhara on the eve of the Russian conquest seems to have been this contradiction between the obstinately hidebound and conservative character of the structures of the state, and the slow evolution of society.

7

Factors of Evolution

Land

Life in Bukhara during the nineteenth century was entirely organized around the land, for 90 per cent of the population lived from agriculture: the agrarian organization of the emirate continued forms already known in the sixteenth century. The agrarian system of Muslim Central Asia was dominated by the fundamental idea that the land belongs to the state and is placed at the disposal of the ruler of the state, who wields simultaneous spiritual and temporal power. The process of concentration of landed property and the evolution of its forms have not followed a straight line. What is constant is the pre-eminence of state over private property.

Various elements constantly limited the development of a system of private property and assured the pre-eminence of state property. Settlement and the transition to agricultural activities brought about a decomposition of the clan community and replacement of the relations it had implied by ones of a new type. But, above all, one problem necessitated state intervention — that of water. In Bukhara an artificial irrigation system was indispensable; this necessity influenced the political future of not only the state, but also social and economic relations. Creating an irrigation system over an extended territory presupposes considerable resources in money and people and a collective effort at the level of the state, and transcends by far the possibilities of a tribe or an isolated landowner. The fundamental problem seems thus to be one of authority. Mustering individual people concerned with their own or with local interests for a long-term, large-scale effort requires a strong central power. The necessity of irrigation implied the necessity of central power.

Because they were strong enough to impose their power, the sovereigns were transformed into overseers of works. To complete those works they reinforced, developed, and justified their power. Moreover, the irrigated areas belonged quite naturally to the state, whence the sovereign derived a new power. This was particularly obvious in Khiva, where the whole economy of the country was ruled by a unique system of irrigation, that of the Amu Darya; and where the importance of state lands was far greater than anywhere else in Central Asia. Thus in Bukhara, as often in the Orient, irrigation appears as one of the principal functions of state power, its justification in a sense.

But once the irrigation system was installed, its maintenance still had to be ensured. The land was then given to individuals, so that they would cultivate it and take part in the upkeep of canals and wells. In this way, the need for irrigation in Bukhara brought about, in a first stage, the statization of land and, in a second, the creation of parcellized holdings.[3]

In the absence of statistics, it is scarcely possible to put forward exact figures; but it appears that the land was divided more or less as follows, according to the historian Gafurov:[4] 12.2 per cent of the land, personal property of the emir; 55.8 per cent belonging to the state; 24.2 per cent *vaqf* land; and 7.8 per cent belonging to the population. The land system of Bukhara allows us to understand how such a concentration was achieved. In theory, in Bukhara as throughout the Muslim Orient, the true owner of the land was the state — the political form of the community, whose temporal leader the emir disposed of it. Once this general principle had evolved, three categories of land emerged: state property, private holdings, and *vaqf* lands.

State holdings or *amlak* represented more than half the land in the emirate. By definition, all dead holdings — those that were not cultivated, whatever the reasons might be for their abandoned state (for example, lack of water or material difficulties) — were *amlak*. The emir, as supreme guardian of the land, could recuperate them, irrigate them, restore them and then bestow them upon private individuals, who had the right to use and bequeath them in return for payment of a tax. In this case, *amlak* land passed over into the category of private land. The tax on such land, the *amlakana*, was higher than that on the *kharaj* lands said to have been taken in earlier times by the Muslim conquerors and placed by them at the disposal of the subjugated population.

The *amlakana* was levied either in kind or in cash; but in the last years of the nineteenth century collection in cash became predominant. The amount depended on the area of the holding, the quantity of water necessary for its irrigation, and the harvest (in principle, the tax represented a sum between one fifth and half of the harvest). Collection of the *amlakana* was the task of the *amlakdar*. The state pool of *amlak* land was perpetually renewed by the recuperation and restoration of dead lands, by the appropriation of irrigated lands, and by the acquisition of lands as a result either of deals or of confiscation for various reasons.[5] *Amlak* lands could be bought back, and they would then become genuine private holdings. Their special characteristic, in legal terms, was that they could not be given as *vaqf*, other than by the sovereign.

Finally, the emirs used to withdraw land from the state pool and offer it on special conditions: such gifts bore the name *tankhvah*.[7]

The *tankhvah* evolved in both form and appellation during the various phases of Central Asia's economic development, but as a general rule it always expressed the desire of the rulers to secure the loyalty of the beneficiaries. For a long while, such gifts were made to the begs, representing the aristocracy of the nomadic tribes they led. When a beg was appointed, the emir would give him as *tankhvah* lands occupied or even cultivated by his fellow-tribesmen. However, this institution was soon perverted by the contradiction that existed between the personal character of the *tankhvah* and the hereditary power of the tribal chieftains. In practice, *tankhvah* lands passed automatically from father to son and took the form of hereditary property, even though their jurid-ical form remained theoretically unchanged. In exchange for such gifts, the begs committed themselves to place at the emir's disposal troops (*qara-chirik*) raised from their tribes or on their lands. These troops, maintained by a special tax called *jul*, were an element of extraordinary power for the begs. The sovereigns, who by means of *tankhvah* gifts were seeking to acquire the loyalty of the tribal chieftains, were in fact giving the chieftains the means to oppose them. Thanks to the *tankhvah*, the begs disposed of an organized military force and a new economic power.[7]

Aware of this contradiction, the Manghit Emir Nasrallah fun-damentally reformed the institution of *tankhvah*. Confiscated lands swelled the *amlak* pool and were redistributed in the form of *tankhvah* to supporters of the central power. However, Emir Nasrallah stipulated that henceforth *tankhvah* would be assigned on an individual basis and for a specified period, that is, no longer on a hereditary basis.[8] Furthermore, whereas, formerly, as *tank-hvah* emirs had given villages or even whole regions with their inhabitants, who in certain areas were absolute slaves,[9] with Emir Nasrallah the *tankhvah* became territorially limited and relations with the peasants living on *tankhvah* lands strictly organized. The emir used this system to secure the services of an army that would belong to him[10] and allow him to avoid recourse to the armies of the begs, his recompense for *tankhvah* in its old form.

The situation of the peasants living on *tankhvah* lands was very unstable and sometimes tragic. As long as the land they worked was *amlak*, they were dependent on the state and paid *amlakana*. When the land became *tankhvah*, they became dependent on the beneficiary or *tankhvadar*, and the *amlak* tax was replaced by the tribute they had to pay to him. Often, when land passed from one category to another, both parties demanded taxes and tribute. On the eve of the Russian conquest, the situation of these peasants was aggravated by the transformation of economic relations in Bukhara. With the appearance of capitalism the towns developed.[11] The large feudal owners left their lands to live in the capital at the emir's court. Since their financial needs were thereby increased, they demanded increasingly more from the peasants. At the same time, being now separated from them, they delegated to an intermediary, the *musta'jir*, the task of collecting the taxes. The *musta'jir's* office was very profitable, since he committed himself in advance to make a lump payment to the owner, who thereafter lost interest in the precise total of his impositions. Veritable *musta'jir* portfolios were created and assigned, and the owners entrusted the management of their affairs to whichever *musta'jir* bid highest.

Private holdings (*milk*) had increased at the expense of state lands in the late eighteenth and nineteenth centuries, thanks to the struggle the tribal chieftains ceaselessly waged against the centralizing power for ownership of the land.[12] The problem of *milk* land is extremely complicated, since little is known about its distribution and the extent of its holdings. Barthold asserted that *milk* holdings did not constitute large domains;[13] Ivanov, that they did not have any great importance for the country's economy, since the important holdings, of which there were as many as 36,000 under Haydar, were constituted by *tankhvah* land.[14]

Milk holdings were subdivided into several categories:
(1) The majority were *milk-i kharaj* whose occupants had to pay a tax related to the volume of the harvest. However, even within this group certain differentiations existed. *Milk-i kharaj* holdings proper were subjected to a tax in kind not only of one-fifth of the harvest (*mushtibar*) and to a cash levy fixed in relation to the *mushtibar*, but also in relation to the quality of the land and various other criteria, depending basically on the subjective assessment of the official charged with evaluating it. Certain *kharaj* lands became *milk-i nim kharaji* (that is, lands subjected to a tax smaller by roughly a half than the pure *kharaj*) because the owner had partly bought back the *kharaj* — done so only in part, either because he did not have the means to do so in full or because the emir, for some reason, had been against freeing the land in question fully from the *kharaj*. A third group of *kharaj* holdings were *milk-i kharaj-i sulhi* lands, freed from the classic impositions and

subjected to a tax fixed annually by the two parties on an amicable basis.

(2) Very close to the *kharaj* lands were holdings subjected to the 'tithe' (*milk-i 'ushri*), which were likewise lands the Muslim invader conquered and ceded back to the population that had voluntarily rallied to him and the Islamic faith.

(3) Finally, certain *milk* lands called *milk-i hurr-i khalis* (lands free of taxes) were given by the sovereign, but were distinguished from the *tankhvah* in that the gift had a definitive character.[15] These were naturally the most coveted, since their privilege persisted through all transactions. Their owners were nonetheless subject to the obligation to take part in collective corvée duties (*hashar*), basically for the upkeep of the irrigation system. These tax-free lands were rarely the property of small peasants; they were to be found in the hands of large landowners, who levied all possible taxes on the peasants attached to such land for their own profit. The only beneficiaries of such exemptions were thus the big landowners. The same was true for the partially free *kharaj* holdings, whose owners still collected the full range of taxes from the peasants.

It must be noted that the owners of *tankhvah* lands strove by all means to have them treated as *milk* lands, which gave such owners definitive ownership of them. This ambition is the source of a great deal of confusion and makes it hard to assess with accuracy the extent of land in the two categories, respectively.

Vaqf holdings[16] were properties in mortmain, inalienable — whose revenues were destined for some charitable foundation, or else for the descendants of the endower. Such lands were partly gifts from the sovereign, but mainly gifts from individuals; and they were totally exempt from taxes. In Bukhara there were two kinds of *vaqf* land. The *vaqf-i mutlaq*, or absolute endowment, was given for eternity: such land belonged to the establishment or order that had received it, while its management was entrusted to a powerful individual entitled the *mutavalli*; all revenue from such land obviously went to the beneficiaries. Other forms of *vaqf* were only partial gifts, made up of a specified fraction of the revenues of an estate that the donor was transforming into *vaqf*. Here, the land was not exempt from taxes, and the donor, who retained ownership of it, bore a double burden — the taxes pertaining to it and the share to be remitted to the *vaqf*. Such lands could be bequeathed and sold, but the obligation to hand over a precise share of the revenue to a religious order or establishment remained.

Their exploitation was entrusted to share-croppers (*yarmichi*), who contributed their labour and their own means of production and had to hand over half the harvest to the owner (for example, the *madrasa*). Like peasants in the service of owners of *milk* land, share-croppers attached to *vaqfs* lived in a state bordering on slavery: their dependence was total, for as a general rule they were given together with the land and could not leave it.[17] On the other hand, if they did not maintain payment of their taxes, the religious authorities on whom they depended, like the owners of the *milk* lands, could dismiss them summarily.[18]

From the years 1840–50 on, the development of *milk* and *vaqf*[19] lands at the expense of *amlak* lands accelerated, at the same time as the land was increasingly the object of commercial transactions, whereas previously it had been the object of gifts. The emir and the state followed this trend, to the extent that the financial needs of the state had increased.

Another characteristic of this period was the transformation in Bukhara — as throughout Central Asia, and notably at Khoqand — of laws governing inheritance. On the eve of the conquest,[20] Bukhara was living under the system of Muslim inheritance law based on the primacy accorded to the paternal line, within which precise shares were assigned to heirs determined according to a strict order (descendants, ancestors, collateral relatives).[21] This law organized a complete and complicated division of property and led to its fragmentation. To counter such fragmentation various ways of getting round the law existed, notably through the institution of *vaqf*. The land became the object of equitable division among all heirs, whatever the line of their descent. The will became an important element in the division; in other words, an inheritance law came into being that favoured bourgeois ownership of land. All that was needed to complete this process was the development of commercial exchanges, a greater interpenetration of commerce and agriculture, i.e. the commercialization of farming — in short, the opening up of Central Asia to the capitalist economy and the whole upheaval brought about by the conquest. But from the middle of the nineteenth century on, Bukhara was maturing continuously in that direction.

At the end of the nineteenth century the landowning system which culminated in the concentration of a considerable part of the land in the hands of large owners[22] — emir, state, *tankhvadar*, tribal chiefs — proved to be defective in economic terms. Logofet, when he surveyed Bukhara, grew indignant at the contradiction that existed between the extraordinary agrarian potential of the emirate and the misery that prevailed there,[23] especially in the rural areas. He observed that local resources were immense, both for stock-rearing and for agriculture; and that, nevertheless, abandoned holdings everywhere gave the country a desolate image — everywhere the population was ravaged by famine.   Bukhara suffered, among other misfortunes, from natural calamities of two kinds: first, periodic floods, which, far from solving the water problem, blocked the irrigation systems and made them temporarily unusable (the Zarafshan floods were particularly tragic); and second, swarms of locusts that periodically destroyed the crops. To guard against this plague of locusts, the peasants took precautions by burying part of each year's harvest, so that in case of catastrophe they would be able both to survive and to sow next year's crop. If the harvest was good, the buried reserves came out of their hiding-places, a bit the worse for wear; and crafty merchants mixed them with the fresh grain, which Logofet indicates gave the whole harvest a pronounced flavour of mould and rot.[24]

Above all, Bukharan agriculture suffered from its technical backwardness and from the scant interest the big landowners showed in these problems. The peasants who cultivated the land with their own means, like all their brethren throughout Turkistan, had only primitive tools, mentioned in the most ancient sources; and these tools necessitated a large labour-force. The most common implements of cultivation were the *amaj* and the *ketmen*. The former, called *supar* in Tajik areas, was a simple wooden plough, with an iron ploughshare but no mouldboard. A pair of oxen, horses, or camels was harnessed to a long yoke. This plough was economical in terms of cost, but inefficient, having to be supplemented by repeated harrowings (from four to ten, or even fifteen). The *ketmen* was a hand tool universally employed to replace the plough, make vegetable beds, and dig irrigation canals. To harrow the land the *amaj* was turned on its side. For harvesting cereals and alfalfa, there was a wooden-handled billhook with a straight blade, used like a knife: the *uraq* (*das* in Tajik areas). This implement was also used to cut down the thorny plants, which were the country's fuel. Threshing took place on floors cleared in the fields, with the help of oxen or horses, which had to trample the sheaves of corn. When the grain was free of the ear, the straw was removed with a wooden pitchfork or *panjah* and winnowing was carried out with wooden shovels. To transport grain or manure, in the plain regions they used a large-wheeled cart called an *araba*, while in the mountains they employed a primitive sledge, the *chigin*.[25]

Badly cultivated, the land also suffered from the defects of the irrigation system, which during the period 1850–70 the officials, too busy collecting taxes, barely improved.[26] The organization of collective corvée duties for maintenance of the irrigation canals played a particularly deleterious role, since the interest of the officials supervising the corvée contradicted the actual execution of corvée labour. These officials were paid out of the fines imposed on hamlets (*qishlaq*[27]) or landowners failing to participate in the corvée — no fines, no salaries.

Nor was badly irrigated land protected at that time against the advance of the sands, which the administration made no effort to stem. Badly cultivated, parched, and invaded by the desert, the land was less and less adequate to feed the peasants, whom owners and officials nevertheless required to pay in full taxes that no longer corresponded to any real production. Moreover, this degradation of the soil was proceeding at the same time that the financial needs of the state were growing, primarily because of increasing internal insecurity.

Insecurity increased in the second half of the nineteenth century, when the emirate once again suffered from the ill that Emir Nasrallah had endeavoured to overcome — the constant insurgency of the more distant regions — to which was added around 1850 the threat of raids by Afghan tribes.[28] The emir had simultaneously to defend his frontiers and to try and maintain his authority over the totality of his possessions — tasks that required increased resources and an ever more numerous body of officials.

In Bukhara the land problem was thus posed in complex terms. On the one hand, the system of land ownership had undeniably evolved, especially between 1840 and 1870, and had gradually become oriented towards forms of ownership closer to capitalist society than had been the case in the past. On the other hand, during the same period exploitation of the land had changed neither in its forms nor in its social relations. Worse still, the product of the land, the main source of income in the emirate, was declining, while the emirate was gradually opening up to the modern world, and its financial needs were increasing.

Social forces

To conjure up the men and peoples who lived in the emirate,

figures are lacking. Only the accounts of travellers allow us to have some idea of their number. In the nineteenth century Khanykov, having noted the absence of any serious local evidence, estimated that the population totalled between 2 and 2.5 million inhabitants.[29] Masal'skii gave a similar figure (2.5 million), but pointed out that this was an approximation.[30] Logofet arrived at 3 million.[31] The non-Russian Orientalists who visited the emirate sometimes gave higher figures. Though Vambéry reckoned that the emirate had 2.5 million citizens,[32] Olufsen put their number at 3 or 3.5 million.[33] The censuses carried out after the October Revolution in the People's Republic of Bukhara, whose territory corresponded to that of the emirate in the years 1880–1900, give a far smaller total than those just mentioned: 1,531,015.[34] A Soviet author has estimated that, if allowance is made for the human losses from revolution, insurrections, population movements, famine, and epidemics, this figure should be increased by 25 per cent in order to assess, with any degree of accuracy, the population of Bukhara before the revolution — that is, 2 million,[35] a figure for which it seems reasonable to settle.

Although it is quite hard to give statistical information concerning the inhabitants of Bukhara, it is still harder to provide a social description of them. It is hardly possible to portray accurately Bukharan society at the end of the nineteenth century without taking account of the ethnic, religious, and tribal factors — which introduced supplementary systems of differentiation within it. At the end of the nineteenth century Bukharan society was not really stratified; thus, one should be cautious about accepting certain seductive portrayals that give a clear, precise, and organized image of a society then in full evolution.

Since the sixteenth century, Bukhara had been an Uzbek kingdom, and the Uzbeks who were Sunnis represented the largest group in the emirate (778,000 inhabitants in 1920, or 50.7 per cent of the population).[36] With the accession to the throne of the Manghits, who came from a major Uzbek tribe, the Uzbek élite became the mainstay of power, and struggles for power itself merged with age-old tribal struggles. Thus, the Beg of Shahrisabz's opposition to the emir overlaid the traditional opposition of the two great rival Uzbek tribes, the Manghits and the Kenegesh. On the one hand, the Uzbeks' progressive movement from a nomadic life to a settled one did not really modify this state of affairs, since nomads who settled preserved in their village the name of their tribe or tribal fraction and brought to their settled life the structures of the organization to which they had belonged. Recent sociological work has demonstrated the extraordinary strength of such transfers.[37] On the other hand, Barthold has noted that settlement in Bukhara — unlike in Khiva where it took place by whole clans — was confined to tribal fractions or sub-fractions, though here too it was never a question of isolated families. Clan organization always appeared at every stage of the great social mutations.

This persistence of clan organization was even more marked among the Tajiks living in the eastern part of the emirate.[38]

Clan organization was also marked in the Panj mountains where the old order was almost wholly preserved at the end of the nineteenth century. At that time, the Rushan mountain-tribesmen were led by a shah whose genealogy, true or mythical,[39] went back to Nasir Khusraw and who was the 'family head' of all his fellow-tribesmen. A contemporary author wrote of the situation in the Darvaz and in the Qarategin thus: 'The mountain-tribesmen have absolutely no knowledge of the conjugal family or the division of inheritance.' Describing Bukharan society at the beginning of the nineteenth century, Ivanov certified that the Uzbek tribal élite was also the ruling class of the emirate.[40] This judgement was repeated by Khanykov, who said that the upper class of the state, 'were Uzbeks, and in general those who belonged to a class whose ancestors had served the Emirate well'.[41] Khanykov also noted that this class stood in opposition to the Tajiks, the Persians, the freedmen, and in general to all people of common extraction.[42]

In the second half of the nineteenth century, the situation had changed somewhat; the ruling class was no longer so clearly attached to the Uzbek tribes. Various authors testify to this,[43] especially the Orientalist Semenov, who writes that 'the personnel of the régime in Bukhara for the most part had been drawn from the intelligentsia (Uzbeks, Tajiks, Arabs,[44] and others)' and that the majority of high-ranking officials were *khvaja* and Persian slaves.[45]

By the end of the nineteenth century the sovereign of Bukhara, who had borne the title emir (*amir*) since the accession to the throne of Muhammad Rahim, wielded absolute power.[46] This was due to the efforts of the Manghits, who had imposed it despite continual challenges and unrest. The Manghits traced their genealogy to the Prophet and, as such, bore the title of *sayyid*,[47] to which 'Alim Khan, the last ruler, added that of Caliph.[48] The Manghits claimed Chingiz Khan as source of their legitimacy.[49] Their absolute power, limited only by the prescriptions of Muslim canonical law, was surrounded by a pomp commented on by travellers;[50] this seems to have increased with the later rulers, since Vambéry at least had particularly noted the great simplicity of Emir Muzaffar.[51] As ruler of Bukhara, the emir was also a big landowner and important capitalist. Though their domains were not extraordinarily extensive,[52] since the land belonged primarily to the state, the last two emirs owned a number of cotton-cleaning factories; moreover, exporting astrakhan worth 15 million roubles a year, as individuals they ranked third in the world astrakhan trade.[53]

Concerning the ranks and responsibilities of Bukhara's ruling stratum, as a general rule every member of the class that governed the emirate's destiny occupied a particular grade or rank (equivalent to the Russian *chin*), allocated by the emir or, for the lower cadres, by his regional representatives.[54] The totality of individuals belonging to these ranks were designated by the term *sipah* (which seems to indicate that they were originally military ranks),[55] and each of them was known as *'amaldar* (possessor of an *'amal* or responsibility). The hierarchy of ranks and responsibilities developed during the nineteenth century, until by its latter half according to Semenov, 'Bukhara experienced the same evolution as the Russian Empire, in which ranks in no way corresponded to specific responsibilities.'[56]

Semenov indicates that there were fifteen such ranks divided into three categories. The lowest were known as *mubarizat-panah* (refuge of power) and, moving from the bottom upwards were designated as follows: *bahadur, chihra-aghasi-bashi, mirza-bashi, jibachi, qaravul-begi, mirakhur, tuqsaba,* and *ishik-aghasi-bashi.* The next five were collectively known as *imarat-panah: bay, dadkhvah, inaq, parvanachi,* and *divan-begi.* The last two ranks, known as *vizarat-panah*, were at the tip of the hierarchy: *qul-i qush-begi*[57] and *ataliq* (major-domo).

Vambéry[58] indicates a slightly different hierarchy from that given by Semenov. Using military terms, he divides the ruling class into three hierarchical groups: *'kette sipahi'* (lower), *'orta sipahi'* (middle), and *'ashaghi sipahi'* (upper).

This civilian hierarchy was complemented by a hierarchy of military leaders comprising five grades[59] and, above all, by a religious hierarchy whose importance was considerable. The clergy had come originally from privileged groups — the *sayyid*, the *khvaja*, and the *mir*.[60] Many of them were *'ulama* from father to son — in other words, scholars and experts on the *shari'at* — and as such they carried out multiple responsibilities, for example, as judges, commentators on the law, or teachers. The hierarchy of religious grades (collectively designated as *'ulama*) comprised three levels: *uraq, sudur,* and *sadr*.[61] A *mulla*, after leaving a *madrasa*, could ascend through these levels and, once he was a *sadr*, aspire to the highest religious functions (whose significance will be discussed later): *qazi-kalan, mufti, 'alim,* and *akhund*.

These ranks, and possibly the responsibilities that corresponded to them, brought their owners numerous advantages: first and foremost, that of obtaining *tankhvah* lands from the sovereign. Thus, the governing class often merged with that of the land-owners; it possessed land and a certain power. Throughout the nineteenth century this privileged layer would increasingly set off for the capital and towns of the emirate; it would thereby come into greater contrast with the peasant masses than in the past, losing almost all its links with them.

Concerning other layers in society, one of the important social facts in nineteenth-century Bukhara was the development of various intermediate groups between the governing class and the masses. The most prominent of these were the minor clergy and petty officials.

Madrasas were numerous in Bukhara,[62] as were students, consequently all could not aspire to high office. At the end of their studies many became schoolmasters or scribes and, together with certain of the poorer *mullas* (students), formed a kind of intelligentsia. These were joined by officials of lowly rank, such as the *mirza* (scribes or secretaries, at all levels of the administration) or the village *nawkar* (for example, messengers or policemen, who exercised the most varied functions and whose great privilege was to be exempted from taxation on the revenues of their land). Similarly exempt from taxation were craftsmen and smiths rendering services to the collectivity; and the *du'akhvan*, a term designating minor clerics, 'those who say the prayers'.

In the nineteenth century these intermediate classes were swelled by elements whose development was linked to new political and economic conditions: the commercial bourgeoisie and the *bays*. The commercial bourgeoisie began to appear only in about the 1850s and essentially was composed of a few merchants and all kinds of middlemen — for example, agents of commercial firms and banks or representatives of foreign companies that had penetrated as far as Bukhara. In so far as it did not have its source or basis in land, this bourgeoisie had few financial means of its own and had to seek resources outside. Even before the Russian conquest, this stratum fostered relations with the European powers and was curious about the outside world and hungry for progress. It was also aware of what limited its development: the inward-looking organization of the emirate itself and the fanatical refusal of all progress, for which the bourgeoisie held the clergy responsible.[63] The *bays*, owners of farms exceeding twenty *desiatins* of land — often exempted from taxation on their production, but not on the sale of their products — likewise became detached from the mass of the peasantry and came to swell the intermediate groups. The number of *bays* and the extent of their lands were on the increase throughout the nineteenth century.

Lastly, certain 'infidel' groups (Jews, Hindus, Gypsies, and a few Christians) have to be included here, whose status was very strict and who did not participate in public affairs. All these infidels were obliged to pay a poll tax (*jizya*) in return for their right to retain their respective religions in an Islamic state. Of these, the most inconvenienced were the Hindus and Jews, who were penned into reserved quarters and had to dress in black and wear a cord in place of a belt (the mark of an unbeliever). In the towns they could not move around on horseback, and outside the towns the only mount they were allowed was a donkey. Even then, if they crossed a Muslim's path they had to dismount and let him go by before continuing on their way.[64]

The Hindus (around 500) were dispersed between the capital and the provinces, nowhere did they form a significant group. They had concentrated all disposable capital in their hands, and they were present as usurers at all markets and fairs[65] — hence the hostility directed at them by the Muslims, who were convinced of their rapacity and particular skill at duping all their interlocutors. Little is known about the origin of these Hindus. Olufsen says that they had a red, black, or white cross — or a round spot — painted on their foreheads and that they were known by the name of *multani*. Vambéry on two occasions asserts that they were 'worshippers of Vishnu'[66] and this statement can seemingly be accepted as true.

The Jews, numerous in the towns (more than 4,000 in Bukhara), spoke Tajik and were mainly employed in silk-dying. Always in a position of inequality *vis-à-vis* the faithful, who were humiliated by them, they nevertheless communicated with their co-religionists in Damascus and the Syrian provinces by way of the *hajji* (pilgrims) going to Mecca, whom they entrusted with dispatches addressed to their brethren. Vambéry notes that the only privilege the Jews enjoyed in the emirate derived from the aversion that they inspired among the inhabitants of Bukhara, for they alone were never threatened with being reduced to the condition of slaves, since they were deemed unworthy even of that.[67]

The mass of peasants and nomads was collectively designated by the term *fuqara*, in contradistinction to the *sipah*, whereas a specific place was allocated to nomadic and semi-nomadic groups still retaining their differentiations, who were known as *ilat*. It is hard to establish precisely the relations between the settled, semi-settled, and nomadic populations. Settlement continued uninterruptedly throughout the nineteenth century, though the process was a slow one since the irrigated land was insufficient to receive the nomads (despite the efforts of a number of diligent rulers like Shah Murad). The regions suitable for farming were to some extent overpopulated, while the others were too unappealing. The population often found itself halfway between two ways of life. Thus, around 1850 many Uzbeks from the Zarafshan were semi-nomadic and semi-settled. No longer having enough stock to lead a nomadic existence and unable to obtain enough land to settle down definitively, they spent the winter in mud huts and moved to new pastures relatively nearby in the spring and summer. The number of nomads was estimated at almost one million around 1820, but by roughly 1860 their number was already much reduced:[68] Ivanov writes that there were then no more nomads strictly speaking, only settled transhumants.[69]

It is estimated that at least 25 per cent of the rural population of Bukhara was totally without land and forced to lead a wandering life[70] and to hire out their services for the most pitiful yearly wage.[71] There were various categories of peasants (*dihqan*). Above the landless peasants and agricultural workers — *charakar, yarmichi,* and *kushachi*), whose condition was all the more tragic in that the scantiness of their wages barred them from any hope of ever acquiring the few patches of land that would make them independent — there were the smallholders. Their farms were very tiny, somewhere between one and three *desiatins* in the irrigated regions and approximately five *desiatins* in naturally watered areas.[72] Very few reached fifteen or twenty *desiatins*; this category of peasants accounted for about 50 per cent, or more perhaps, of the rural population.[73] Depending on the region, the inadequacy of the holdings was compounded by an inequitable distribution. In general, the regions where nomadism was prevalent had enough land, whereas the settled regions were tragically short of it. Thus, in the Shirabad region, where nomadism predominated, all the households in certain hamlets possessed between four and ten *desiatins* of land. Further off, in a settled area poor in stock, the holdings were on average made up as follows: Qishlaq Kushman-Ariq — 1.8 *desiatins* of land, 1 head of cattle, 4 sheep, one-tenth of a horse, and one-fifth of a camel for each household; and Qishlaq Ur Tut Ariq — 1.5 *desiatins* of land, 4 head of cattle, one-fifth of a horse, two-fifths of a camel, and 15 sheep per household.[74] Taking the country as a whole, the problem was as follows: of eight *qishlaq*, two had enough land to enable the population to live (albeit without real profits), two were below a decent average, and four did not have the minimum of land necessary for survival.[75]

A Russian author, L. Klimovich, has described what the life of these small peasants was like at the end of the nineteenth century.[76] The details he provides highlight the condition of the masses, who represented more than half the emirate's population. A smallholder (five-person family) disposed of about three *desiatins* of cultivable land, two oxen, two cows, and ten sheep: three-eighths of the land was given over to the cultivation of wheat; two-eighths, to that of cotton; one-eighth, to various crops; one-eighth, to fodder; and one-eighth, to the vegetable plot (see Table 1.1).

Table 1.1
The Smallholders' Annual Harvest

Annual harvest	Money value	Taxes	Money value
Cereals 110 puds	110 roubles	Various to public funds	52 roubles
Cotton 20 puds	100 roubles	Tax for upkeep of officials	33 roubles
Various crops 8 puds	8 roubles	Tax on sales at market	3 roubles

Source: L. Klimovich, *Islam v Tsarskoi Rossii*, p. 193.

Thus, 88 roubles out of 218 — that is, more than one-third of this family's income — were absorbed by various taxes. In reality, this figure is a minimum — always surpassed — since the administrative assessment of income applied to production, not to the real product of its sale, and was always carried out at a rate higher than the market one. So almost half of a family's income actually went in regular taxes and exceptional expenses (participation with raw materials in collective corvée duties), and in religious contribution.

Artisanal activities expanded in this period, but mainly in the countryside. In the absence of a developed industry, the landless peasants could not leave to work in the towns: offers of employment were extremely rare there and increased very little during the nineteenth century. In the towns the great mass of craftsmen, even organized into guilds, never had the means to achieve acceptable working conditions. A traveller described the organization of artisanal work in this period as follows: 'The capitalist distributes the work to families whom he knows: to some the whitening of the cotton, to others the task of spinning it, to others that of dying — which allows him to ignore entirely the problems of material organization, of instruments of labour, and also saves'him from paying the craftsmen when they are not working.' In these conditions, should one be astonished if, in 1868, a craftsman in Bukhara used to earn, by working non-stop, barely ten copecks a day? Even so, it was primarily female and child labour that was sought, which was paid even worse.

The urban population, not very large, was grouped into a few large centres (Bukhara; Samarqand, with its 20,000 inhabitants; Qarshi, whose economic role was considerable; Kermine; Katta Qurghan; and Charju'i[77]), where, besides the craftsmen and the commercial bourgeoisie, there existed an urban semi-proletariat — hard to incorporate in the framework of precise definitions. There was not actually any industry, and hence no real proletariat existed; but in that period in the towns there were some 10,000 persons — such as drivers, water-carriers, and shoemakers — exercising badly rewarded activities.[78]

At the bottom of the social hierarchy in Bukhara were over 20,000 slaves according to Vambéry's testimony,[79] and more according to other authors,[80] who put the figure at more than 10,000 in the Samarqand region, at a time when slavery was in principle less developed than at the time of Vambéry's voyage. These slaves (or *zarkharid*) were mostly Iranians captured by the Turkmens, who raided the Khurasan and then sold their captives on the marketplaces of Central Asia.[81] Among the slaves there were also (though in smaller numbers) Kalmyks, Afghans, people who had come from Kafiristan and the regions near to the Pamir, and Russians captured on the Kazakh steppes and the fishing-grounds of the Caspian.[82] These slaves were generally employed in agricultural labour, and Vambéry writes that the price of wheat was a function not only of the level of water in the Amu Darya, but also 'of the greater or lesser number of slaves obtained in the course of the year'.[83] Considered as a kind of 'outward sign' of wealth and power, the slaves were much sought after by the propertied strata. Vambéry also notes that Hakim Bay — *qush-begi* to the Emir Haydar and then to Nasrallah — owned 'more than 1,000 slaves who worked on his estates'.[84] They were also set to watch herds in particularly inhospitable regions.[85] Lastly, they often served in the army as *sarbaz* (infantrymen). One particularly remarkable fact was that, despite their very humble position, slaves could in certain cases attain the highest state posts.[86]

All in all, society in the Emirate in the second half of the nineteenth century seems fairly hard to describe in terms of classical criteria. Slow economic and social transformations were becoming clear. These mutations were not peculiar to Bukhara, they were common to all the states of Central Asia.

Society and the system of landownership were *de facto* evolving. A process of division of the land existed within the family — a process in the plains regions due to the development of monetary relations and in the mountain regions to disintegration of the structures of patriarchal society. Everywhere, on the plains and in the mountains, people were growing accustomed to the appropriation and to the commercialization of land. This had the effect of concentrating it in the hands of a feudal class, whose power was increasing, and of handing over to the feudal owners a peasant mass swollen by settlement and whose difficulties were likewise growing.

Between the feudal and peasant classes, middle strata were also developing, formed in part by officials, whose proliferation was due in the second half of the nineteenth century to the centralizing effort; and in part also by that bourgeoisie of merchants and middlemen, a layer still ill defined and which could not develop further in the confined and closed framework of the emirate prior to the Russian protectorate.

Whatever level of Bukharan society one examines during this period, one can see it progressively change: differentiations sharpen and conflicts become clearer.

Immutable Structures: the Bukharan State

Central Asia in 1850 was no longer, as it had been in the preceding century, a mosaic of little, rival feudal principalities. Through a slow process of centralization and regroupment, the sovereigns of Bukhara, Khiva, and Khoqand had imposed their domination upon the innumerable tribal chieftains nurturing their own claims to sovereignty. But this effort at political consolidation was far from being completed: a great number of regions, nominally attached to one or another of the three states, were living in a situation of almost total independence or constant rebellion; and the effort of the Central Asian khanates was perpetually directed at these untamed elements. Sometimes they clashed among themselves during their attempts at conquest. At the same time that they were carrying out this drive towards centralization, the three sovereigns of Central Asia were striving to extend their sway over the peripheral zone of nomadism. However, while Khiva and Khoqand were gradually managing to absorb the neighbouring nomadic areas, the territory of Bukhara was shrinking.

The task of unification began with Emir Nasrallah. He had to struggle tirelessly (as did his successors after him) against the rebellion of the tribal chieftains; and to succeed he had continuously to increase his power, the power that was exerted from the capital. The instrument of this power was a heavy and complex administration, divided into four domains (political, financial, juridical, and religious[87]) and organized at three levels (the capital, the main towns, and the population centres).

The political authorities assumed considerable importance throughout the period of unification, since they allowed the emir in his capital Bukhara to be the omnipresent sovereign he needed to become. To administer from a capital a territory of almost 250,000 sq. km., of which many regions were either always or in certain seasons inaccessible, seemed an impossible enterprise. The complexity of the emirate's administrative apparatus was of the greatest assistance.

In Bukhara at the apex of this hierarchy stood the *qush-begi*, first official of the emirate, who in the sovereign's absence exercised power on his behalf.[88] Under the last Manghits, he became in a sense the prime minister. The *qush-begi* was by right *mir* (governor) of the *vilayat* (region) of Bukhara and, as such, in authority over all governors in the emirate[89] — this personage's most important characteristic. The emirate was divided administratively into regions, whose number seems to have varied from twenty-five to twenty-eight,[90] with between 50,000 and 300,000 inhabitants in each and which were run by *mirs* or begs subordinate to the principal among them, the *mir* of Bukhara. The power of the begs (outside Bukhara, this term was usually preferred) was more extensive the farther away they were from the *qush-begi*; as a general rule it was fairly unlimited, provided they handed over punctually to the central authorities the taxes that they were responsible for collecting.

The *vilayats* were themselves subdivided into *amlakdaris* (from three to twenty-five per *vilayat*), run by *amlakdars* who had towards the begs the same obligations to collect and hand over taxes that the latter had towards the emir.[91] The *amlakdaris* were further divided into hamlets or villages (*qishlaqs*), run by *aqsaqals* (elders); several hamlets or villages were grouped under the authority of a *min-bashi* (a leader of 1,000). Finally, the nomads had an *il-begi* at the head of each tribe, responsible for representing them in relation to the *amlakdar*. The *aqsaqals, min-bashis,* and *il-begis* were chosen or elected by the people they had to represent; they were elected for life, except in the event of a serious misdemeanour, and constituted an element of permanent contact between the central power and its subjects — a stable point of reference, but without real effectiveness since their role remained purely representative, except when the centrifugal forces shaking the emirate caused them to escape the control of the central power.[92]

In Bukhara there were thus two administrative systems juxtaposed: a representative system, emanating from below and inherited from the political traditions anterior to the Uzbek state; and a system of political administration, emanating from above and formed by state cadres under the authority of the *qush-begi*, who imposed themselves upon the traditional democratic cadres.

Financial administration obeyed the same laws. At its head stood the *divan-begi,* who in Bukhara played the dual role of finance minister and controller of the entire system of tax collection. For the people of Bukhara, the *divan-begi* was more simply the *qush-begi* of 'down-below' because, hierarchically subordinated to the *qush-begi*, he lived at the foot of the Arg or citadel. The administration over which he presided coincided in territorial terms with the system described previously. While the *divan-begi* ruled in Bukhara, in the *vilayats* he had under him *zakatchi* or collectors of *zakat*. Certain particularly large *vilayats* (notably,

Charju'i and Hisar) possessed their own *divan-begis,* subordinated to the *divan-begi* of Bukhara. At the level of the *amlakdars,* the lower-ranking *zakatchis* came under the *zakatchis* of the *vilayats.* All these officials, working in a precise territorial framework, were strictly subordinated to the authorities of their hierarchy and independent of the local political authorities, in particular the begs.[93] Abuses resulted on a considerable scale and in almost continuous conflicts, with the citizenry usually being the victims.

Public order, for its part, was ensured by the army and police, whose organization had changed little over the centuries. The Bukharan army, theoretically made up of volunteers,[94] was put under the orders of the *tupchi-bashi-yi lashkar* (or commander of artillery), who was simultaneously a kind of army minister and commandant of the Bukharan garrison. Under his command were placed both regular troops (*'askariyya*) and temporary levies (*nawkar*) or even militiamen.[95] When the Russians arrived, the regular army had 13,000 infantrymen, some 500 horse-soldiers and 620 artillerymen, divided among five garrisons: Bukhara 8,000 men; Shirbudun (the emir's country residence, five kilometres from Bukhara) 2,000; Shahrisabz 1,000; Qulab 1,000; and Baljuan 1,000.[96] The artillery was entirely concentrated in Bukhara, under the orders of the *tupchi-bashi.*

The soldiers were poorly paid; and since they could not manage on their pay alone, they engaged in activities far removed from their profession, by cultivating the land (they received *tankhvah* holdings) or entering trade; often they even traded with their weapons. The begs were obliged, in certain circumstances, to place troops at the emir's disposal, whose upkeep remained their responsibility and whom they had to levy as they pleased from their territory.[97] The result of this system was to give the begs a considerable military power, which they used in their conflicts with the emir.

In addition to the army, there was a police force of some 2,000 men,[98] placed under the command of the *mirshab* or head of the night police, who was simultaneously head of the capital's police and the hierarchical superior of all other *mirshabs* in the emirate.[99] After sunset, Bukhara belonged to the police and once the bazaar was closed nobody ventured outside: 'The nearest of neighbours do not have the right to visit each other and the sick are in severe peril of dying for want of doctors, the emir having declared that the *mirshabs* might arrest even himself if they were to meet him walking out during the forbidden hours.'[100]

The system of public administration evidently resulted in the juxtaposition of several hierarchies of officials, totally independent of each other at all levels and in principle supposed to restrain one another mutually through constant supervision. This apparatus, extremely burdensome,[101] was estimated in the last decades of the nineteenth century at about 30,000 men,[102] not including the army — a figure that would continue to grow, since in 1910 Logofet reckoned that it should be put at over 50,000, with the army still being excluded from the calculation.[103]

This apparatus displayed three principal characteristics. First, no member of it received a regular salary paid out of the public purse, except for the soldiers. High-ranking officials (for example, begs, *zakatchis,* and *amlakdars*) had no fixed salary and themselves deducted sums — which they arrived at, in principle, according to certain vague general rules; in practice, as they wished — from the taxes that it was their responsibility to collect. These sums also covered the salaries — whose level was likewise arbitrary — of the minor officials subject to their orders. Naturally, the total of the taxes they extracted from the population grew in proportion to their needs. For their part, the always ill-paid minor officials used, likewise, to increase the sums they collected.[104]

Another feature of the system was the condition of strict dependence in which the lower levels of each hierarchy found themselves by comparison with the leading cadres. Each official had his own little staff, which would follow him from post to post (the begs, for example, had a whole administrative apparatus stretching from *amlakdars* to the humblest of scribes). The prestige of each official was tightly linked to the number of inferiors who were attached to him, and each multiplied his assistants as he liked. The element of stability, basically, was represented on the local level by the elected *aqsaqals, min-bashis,* and *il-begis,* who were not supposed to deduct anything and who cost their fellow-citizens nothing.

The final characteristic feature of the Bukharan administration was the actual origin of the officials. The first Manghits had summoned Uzbeks, especially fellow tribesmen, to assist them at all levels. With Emir Nasrallah the situation changed, since even if he kept Manghits in the administration, he nevertheless got rid of all representatives of Uzbek tribes hostile to his power, because he could thereby weaken their resistance in the provinces by depriving them of the support of their fellow tribesmen in the capital. He then called in Tajik, Turkoman, or Arabs; thereafter this tradition was continued.

In the middle of the nineteenth century two elements neverthe-less dominated the administration: Persian slaves and *khvaja ju'ibari.* In the case of the slaves, it is remarkable that they should sometimes have attained very elevated positions without ever hav-ing been restored juridically to the condition of free persons.[105] The *khvajas* of Ju'ibar,[106] who according to some authors claimed to be descended from the pious Caliphs,[107] likewise held a sizeable share of court posts.[108]

Thus the administration of Bukhara in the second half of the nineteenth century appeared as an apparatus of centralization in which all the authorities of the capital, acting in lieu of actual ministers, presided over a highly differentiated hierarchy whose roots extended to the furthest corners of the emirate — an ex-traordinarily centralized system, yet one that bore within it the germs of decentralization and dislocation, in so far as it coexisted with an almost uncontrollable power of the local authorities. What also characterized this administrative apparatus was that it had passed through the centuries from Nadir Shah to the Russian conquest without the least structural modification,[109] whereas the emirate was continually evolving in the direction of a growing centralism.

To consolidate the unity of the territory or striving simply to secure it, the emir relied on an administration in which officials of every rank proliferated. To pay these non-salaried officials and also to swell the public exchequer, only one source of income existed — taxes. The economic and fiscal system of Bukhara was complicated from two points of view: in terms of (1) the means mobilized to levy taxes and (2) the multiplicity of the taxes. Even though the administrative hierarchy made it seem that a financial apparatus existed, levying taxes was the business of all servants of the state at all levels, according to the following principle: the begs were endowed with a considerable independence in the adminis-tration of their *vilayat,* on condition that each year they handed over to the central authorities certain sums, which in theory were fixed invariably and which went into the public purse together with the taxes collected by the financial officials. Because the begs had to pay both 'their officials' and themselves, they increased the sums imposed for the exchequer by whatever amounts they needed. Furthermore, they entrusted the material responsibility for collecting the various taxes to subordinates, on condition that these subordinates handed over to them a sum determined in relation to the demands of the exchequer and their own needs. The sum initially fixed was thus advanced from one rung to the next and bore only a distant relationship with the theoretical level of taxation. The limits upon such increases lay in the capacity of the population — that is, in the value of the harvest; nevertheless, the energy of the officials often pushed back those limits.

Another complicating factor was the multiplicity of taxes levied in Bukhara at the end of the nineteenth century. There were so many of them that the authors who studied the emirate's fiscal system became lost.[110]

The Koran sanctioned two taxes: the *jizya* or poll tax on unbelievers, the only one that Shah Murad accepted to maintain his exchequer,[111] and the *zakat* or tax on property levied for purposes laid down in the Koran.[112] Murad's successors relied primarily on the *zakat* and the *kharaj*.[113] The *kharaj* or land tax was levied on agricultural production; in principle, it supposed the payment of one-tenth of the harvest on artificially irrigated land and one-sixth of the harvest on naturally irrigated land.[114] The amount of the *zakat* was thus fixed in a precise manner; but in practice all was arbitrary here, as well. These taxes were levied increasingly often during the nineteenth century, in cash rather than in kind; and determination of the rate was subject to the most astonishing variations and to constant abuses. These impositions were supplemented by the obligatory *aminana*, or bazaar tax.

Upon these basic taxes were grafted a multitude of levies whose purpose was to recompense all the local officials.[115] The *zakat-shakan* hit the wretched individuals who escaped the *zakat* because of their extreme poverty; the entire product of the *zakat-shakan* went into the personal coffers of the begs. The *khish-puli* — a tax on draught animals counted in pairs, levied in the spring before the working season began and determined in proportion to the area of a holding — went the same way, as did the *yak-shira*, which supplemented the *khish-puli* and made single animals taxable too. The *qafshan*, a tax in kind, contributed to the private wealth of the *amlakdars*. The *miraban* made it possible to recompense the *mirab*, the official responsible for distributing water; the *kafshan darhgua* rewarded the *darhgua,* another official with an ill-defined role but who abounded in the emirate and settled the amount of exactions through 'friendly arrangement' with the owners of land. The *tanaf-puli* and *alaf-puli* were taxes on vegetable plots, orchards, and alfalfa fields. Also noteworthy were the *kupruk-puli*, or bridge toll; the *baj*, a customs duty that was exacted sporadically at the begs' whim (for example, to cross from Hisar into Baljuan); and a host of other taxes — from one on housing, another on people in transit, to yet another on the weighing of goods in the bazaar. Sadr al-Din 'Ayni concluded his analysis of the Bukharan fiscal system by the following hardly encouraging statement: 'The air alone is not yet taxed in Bukhara.'[116]

The citizen, taxed in this way from all sides, was not thereby free of further obligation towards the government. He still had to participate in collective corvée duties. Another form of physical corvée, perhaps convertible into a tax, was participation in the armies of the begs. Given that the taxpayer had also to participate in the upkeep of religious institutions and bear the burden of judicial expenses, his situation can easily be imagined.[117] Moreover, this worsened continuously throughout the nineteenth century as a result of centralization: because the emir was constantly reinforcing his administrative apparatus to extend better his power, which necessitated more and more money; and because the begs, in their will for independence, were developing their own power, by levying troops and a body of functionaries devoted to them.

Islam

Over and above men and the régime, Islam furnished a meeting-place and a catalyst for all the forces that were either shaking or immobilizing the emirate. There are few Islamic countries in which during the nineteenth century the role of religion was so fundamental; for it was simultaneously the basis of the state and the only force that stood apart from the emir's power and might possibly serve as a counterweight to him — a force that transcended all others and participated, at all levels, in the life of both rulers and masses.

The majority of Bukhara's population were adherents of Sunni Islam; only a minority, mainly composed of Turkish and Persian speakers incorporated into the emirate after the capture of Marv in the eighteenth century, were Shi'a. I shall, therefore, be dealing essentially with Sunni organization.

The religious hierarchy represented a considerable force,[118] since it played a spiritual, judicial, and cultural role. At the spiritual level, its organization was based on the same territorial principle as the emirate's other hierarchies. At the apex stood the *qazi-kalan*, who in the religious sphere benefited, like the *qush-*

begi, from the decadence of the *shaykh al-islam*.[119] The *qazi-kalan* (guardian of religious law) ensured the control of the *madrasas*, the *maktabs*, and the mosques. Beneath him, in the *vilayats* and *amlakdaris*, there was a hierarchy of *ra'is*: the *ra'is* of Bukhara bore the title *ishan-ra'is* and assumed simultaneously spiritual functions and those of prefect of police, and the *ishan-ra'is* had to be chosen from among the *sayyids*.[120] Clerics made up 3 per cent of the emirate's population,[121] and enjoyed a prestige all the greater, in that their religious culture was famous throughout the Muslim world.[122]

Through the mediation of the *muftis*, the clerics played a political-al role. Fourteen in number — initially appointed by the emir but towards the end of the century by the *qazi-kalan*, the *muftis*, chosen from among the best legal experts of all Islam — formed an assembly of wise men responsible for drawing up the *rivayats* (conclusions regarding the conformity of an action or decision with the *shari'at*), which had to be confirmed by the first *mufti* or *'alim*. Thus, the authority of the Islamic clerics extended far beyond the religious domain into that of government.

In the juridical domain, the role of the clerics was likewise fundamental. The organization of justice in Bukhara was based on the *shari'at* as it had been defined by Abu Hanifa, founder of one of the first juridical schools of Islam. At the same time, *'adat* (custom) retained a certain force in the emirate, especially among the nomads.[123] This organization was characterized by a reduction of formality to the extreme, a swift oral procedure, and the absence of collegiate jurisdictions and of any machinery for appeal or annulment. At the apex of the system there stood once again the *qazi-kalan*, who was here the equal of the *qush-begi*. He was assisted by a judge chosen by himself and bearing the title of *vakil*. At the level of the *vilayat*, justice was handed down by judges or *qazis*, appointed for life by the emir, unless embezzlement brought about their downfall. These *qazis* (one for each *vilayat*, except where the latter was particularly large) were, like the *zakatchis*, independent of the begs and controlled the *qazis* of lower rank to be found in the *amlakdaris*. Independent from the administrative hierarchy, the *qazis* supervised it and were supervised by it. Judicial cases were tried at the local level, unless they were serious or unless the defendant could, in turn, lodge a complaint against his judge: the problem was then referred to the *qazi-kalan*; to the *'ulama*; or, in the last resort, to the emir, who alone wielded the power of life and death. In the common run of less important judicial cases, personal connections and relations between plaintiffs and defendants played a considerable role and generally influenced the judgements handed down. These were moderate in all money disputes, especially in the light of Koranic prescriptions forbidding usurious lending.[124]

On the level of culture the clergy of Bukhara could take most pride in its past, its traditions, and the power that it represented. Those in charge of the emirate's countless mosques[125] were formed in some 150 *madrasas* (advanced religious schools),[126] which contained more than 20,000 students.[127] These *madrasas* figured among the oldest in the Muslim world.[128] Up to the sixteenth century, natural sciences were taught in them and there was debate over interpretation of the Koran. Under the aegis of the *mudarris* Mirzashah Mawlana Shirazi, the teaching moved much closer to a strict orthodoxy; nonetheless, its reputation remained such that it continued to attract Muslims from the entire world.[129] Finally, the clergy had a monopoly of primary education thanks to its 2,000 or so *maktabs*.[130]

Fanatical in the extreme, doctrinally rigid, proud of Bukhara's religious position in the world of Islam, the clergy had great influence both on mass consciousness and on the secular authorities. Independent of these authorities (even though the emir did have the right to oversee certain offices), it had available an enormously powerful means of pressure upon them: its influence over the students, whose agitation and whose demands it orchestrated. These were divided into two political groupings: the *tullab-i tumani* (or students of Bukhara) and the *tullab-i kuhistani* (or disciples of the *madrasas* of eastern Bukhara). Often they used to clash in supporting the candidature — especially to the post of *qazi-kalan* — of clerics from one part of the emirate or the other.[131]

But these representatives of official Islam were not the only ones to wield a religious power. The Sufi brotherhoods developed widely in the emirate over the centuries and reached all layers of the population. Of all the Sufi orders, the most widespread was that of the Naqshbandi, whose main centres in the period under consideration were Bukhara and Samarqand. The order of the Qadiriyya, although oriented more towards Ferghana, also recruited disciples in the emirate, as did the Kubrawiyya, which had its centre in Khvarazm. The nomads were attracted more by the appeals of the Yassawiyya, who introduced them to Islam. From the sixteenth century on, Bukhara was the chosen ground of the order of Khvajagan,[132] to which the *khvajas* of Ju'ibar primarily belonged. All these orders were similarly dominated by the true or mythical descendants of their founders, while each of their communities was placed under the authority of an *ishan*. The *murids* (members of the order) would place themselves entirely in the hands of their *ishan,* 'like a body in the hands of the washer of corpses', and were totally obedient to him. In general, the brotherhoods contained two kinds of members: the regular *murids*, who lived the life of the order and depended on its resources; and the far more numerous secular *murids*, who lived a worldly life and turned to the order for the *zikr* and *namaz*. When the *murids* arrived they brought gifts in money or in kind, which swelled the order's resources.[133]

Although it is hardly possible to calculate the size of these orders, some idea can be given from the fact that the funeral of the most renowned *ishan* of the Naqshbandis at the end of the nineteenth century was attended by at least 15,000 *murids*. Sufism was also widespread among women, who attended the *zikr,* generally presided over by the wife of an *ishan*. The patronage of Baha al-Din Naqshband was also claimed by the mendicant dervishes (*qalandars*) who lived in closed communities and whose calling was hereditary. This order was presided over by the *tura*, descendant of Shaykh Safa of Samarqand who had founded it in the seventeenth century. The *qalandars* replaced the *zikr* by morning prayer meetings in the *tura*'s house and were directed by the *tura*.[134]

Finally, at the extreme limit of the Sufi brotherhoods, there was Shamanism, whose external forms sometimes approximated Sufi rites. The function of the *shaman* — essentially a seer, healer, and heir to the priest of the old pre-Islamic animist religion of the nomads — was to heal by casting out demons through ceremonies of individual or collective exorcism, characterized by dancing or animal sacrifices. These rites, going back to the most distant animist past, had become strongly Islamicized; and this Islamic coloration had helped to attract believers. The role of the *shamans* was extremely important; and the masses, by having recourse to them — whereas they refused the services of the few doctors who ventured into the emirate — still had the conviction that they were participating in the life of Islam. Alongside the *shamans* in Bukhara there were also a considerable number of fortune-tellers (*falbin*), hypnotists and snake-charmers, even in the most remote villages, where their presence and prestige recalled how close India was.[135]

This many-faceted religious force which dominated the entire life of the emirate, even if it sometimes came into conflict with the ruler on specific points, nevertheless gave unconditional support to the religiously-based and absolute power of the emir. From this point of view, Bukhara was a prestigious centre of the Muslim world: the emir, after the caliph, was the second personage of the world Islamic community; and all the representatives of Islam in the emirate were the pillars of that Muslim state and helped to preserve for the community the face that history had forged for it and that gave it that central place.

Popular Revolts

Crushed by a powerful, centralizing, and rapacious state, the peasant masses, even while believing that all was in the order prescribed by God, reacted spontaneously in a sporadic manner against that situation.

Throughout the nineteenth century popular uprisings wracked the emirate — uprisings provoked for the most part by the fiscal demands of the authorities. They took a particularly acute turn in the last third of the century. Already in 1800 the Turkmens of Marv had risen against the excesses of the Bukharan *zakatchis*; in 1801 the revolt reached Kerki and brought a bloody intervention by the army. From 1821 to 1825 the Khitay-Qipchaq unleashed a veritable civil war that reached Samarqand,[136] because the emir wanted without the least compensation to levy troops intended to renew the Marv garrison, and to collect the taxes in advance. Twenty years later all Khoqand rose against Emir Nasrallah, who was seeking to superimpose his own taxes upon those of Khoqand and to take a quarter of the Khoqand harvest. The strength of the rebellion was such that the Bukharan officials took flight and Khoqand thereby regained its independence, which dealt a definitive blow to the old dream of the emirs to unify Central Asia round Bukhara. In 1855, Emir Muzaffar, who was seeking to take advantage of a good harvest to catch up on the fiscal backlog of the lean years, saw all Baljuan rise up against him under the leadership of a poor peasant, 'Abd al-Vasi, whose rage made no distinction between administration and clergy. Defeated and executed at Shahrisabz, 'Abd al-Vasi long remained a hero of Bukharan legend, whose memory the masses used to invoke as the symbol of anticipated salvation.

As a general rule, until 1870 peasant anger exploded against the official whose task was to collect the taxes[137] — an anger pitilessly repressed.[138] The important fact remains that on the eve of the Russian conquest, the anxiety and malaise caused by the fundamental contradiction of Bukhara — the dynamism of its society and the rigidity of its structures — expressed themselves primarily in these outbursts by the rural masses; these were anticipatory signs of the movements of ideas that were subsequently to reflect these problems clearly.

2

The Russian Conquest: Bukhara Face-to-Face with Capitalism and the West

The diplomatic and economic relations between Bukhara and Russia which had been maintained since the sixteenth century[1] were given fresh impetus at the end of the eighteenth century with the development of capitalist relations in Russia and British penetration of India.[2]

Establishment of the Protectorate

The Crimean War temporarily restricted Russia's relations with the emirate; but once the war was over, Russia was free to turn anew towards Asia, where external threats were taking clear shape. Having consolidated its positions in India, Britain was extending its presence in Afghanistan, and British envoys were multiplying in the Central Asian khanates. Meanwhile, the Afghan ruler Dust Muhammad had just taken Balkh and was extending his control over the entire region to the south of the Amu Darya.[3] It became urgent for the Russian government to re-establish friendly links with the rulers of Central Asia, primarily with Bukhara, which was the object of the strongest Anglo-Afghan pressure.

The solution to the problem was the conquest of Turkistan, initiated in 1864 and facilitated by the war then raging between Bukhara and Khoqand. Emir Muzaffar was first invited by the Russian government, anxious to placate him,[4] to associate himself with the conquest. However, when General Chernaev proposed to him a partition of Khoqand along an east-west line, with the emir occupying the southern part and the Russians the northern, the mistrustful emir rejected the offer because he was determined to conquer Khojend and Uratube, on his own.[5] So the capture in 1866 of Khojend, Uratube, and then Jizakh by Russian troops brought the emir into direct conflict with Russia. In the spring of 1868 the conquest of the emirate began:[6] in May Samarqand was taken, and then it was the turn of Katta Qurghan.

The scale of these defeats was such that in Bukhara there was ever-increasing talk of an abdication of the ruler in favour of the heir. To avoid this, Muzaffar sued for peace, which was signed on 23 June 1868. The treaty gave Russia all the conquered territories (Khojend, Uratube, Jizakh, Samarqand, and Katta Qurghan) and great commercial advantages (taxes on Russian goods reduced to 2.5 per cent, free passage across the khanate for Russian merchants, and creation of commercial agencies[7]) — in other words, everything that for almost three centuries Russia's envoys had been unable to obtain. The emirate became a vassal state of Russia.[8]

But fighting resumed shortly afterwards, in 1869, in the untamed mountain regions of eastern Bukhara. At first it seemed to be directed mainly against the emir. Seeing how anxious the Russian authorities were becoming as a result of these events, Muzaffar asked Kaufman, the governor-general of Turkistan, to help him pacify the mountains.[9] At the same time, however, he proclaimed a *ghazavat* (holy war) against the Russian infidel and assured the chieftains of the rebel tribes that he would grant them independence if they drove the invader out of the emirate.[10] The rebels were commanded by 'Abd al-Malik Khan, Jora Beg, and Baba Beg; the latter two, feudal lords of Hisar and Shahrisabz, waged the holy war in the hope of being freed from the emir's authority. The emir stood by as Russian troops under General Abramov attacked the rebels. The 1873 treaty rewarded his neutrality and his calculations by placing under his authority eastern Bukhara, which he had previously been unable to pacify on his own.[11] The push towards centralization that Emir Nasrallah initiated thus found its conclusion in the treaty that made Bukhara a protectorate; the treaty that put an end to the emirate's independence was, nevertheless, relatively favourable to it, since it also gave it the right bank of the Amu Darya, following the defeat of Khiva.[12]

The 1873 agreement treated Bukhara infinitely more generously than it did the other khanates, though they had scarcely suffered any worse defeat.[13] While the Emirate of Khoqand was suppressed and while the Khan of Khiva, dispossessed of part of his territory, had to call himself 'the docile servant of the Emperor of all the Russias';[14] the 1873 treaty was expressly termed a 'friendship treaty' and the emir could communicate directly with the Russian government (whereas the Khan of Khiva had to go through the intermediary of the administrative hierarchy). Barthold explains that Bukhara, despite its defeat, had retained an immense prestige in Central Asia because Russian troops had never entered its capital.[15]

By avoiding a political presence in Bukhara, Russia was able to ask Britain to observe a similar attitude in Afghanistan. Bukhara was an important factor in the division of Russian and British spheres of influence in Asia. Its privileged status initially found expression in its political situation. Bukhara's external relations came under the Russian ministry of foreign affairs, while Turkistan was placed under the supervision of the ministry of war.[16] Russia was represented in Bukhara by a 'political agent', who acted like an ambassador and came under the foreign ministry;[17] this gave Bukhara a semblance of quasi-independence which contributed to the external prestige of the emir.

Capitalist Penetration

The first consequence of the conquest was the opening of Central Asia and Bukhara to capitalist penetration, especially after the construction of the Trans-Caspian railway. This project, undertaken for military purposes, profoundly altered the entire economic life of Central Asia. Begun in 1881 with the section from the Gulf of Mikhailovsky to Qizil Arvat, the line reached Ashkhabad four years later, Marv in 1886, Charju'i and the Amu Darya across the deserts of Qara-Kum at the end of 1886, and Samarqand in 1888. In 1894 the point of departure was shifted to Krasnovodsk; in 1898 the Marv–Kushki branchline was built; and in 1899 appeared a new line from Samarqand to Andijan, with branches to Tashkent and Novy-Margelan. The main line from Krasnovodsk to Tashkent thus stretched for 1,748 versts.[18]

So the Emirate of Bukhara was reached by the railroad very early on, with the Ashkhabad–Samarqand link via Charju'i and Bukhara being accomplished between 1885 and 1888. The line crossed the rich plain of the Zarafshan, whose already considerable economic role in the emirate was further enhanced. This plain had always been the great commercial route connecting Bukhara with the outside world. The caravans used to go from Bukhara to Orenburg, to Samarqand and to Tashkent; via Balkh they went to Kabul and to Herat, and thereafter to Qandahar and to Mashhad.

The railroad did not strip Bukhara of its central role, but connected the city to Moscow and to Nizhny-Novgorod. And whereas the carriage of a pud (or 16.38 kg.) of goods by caravan from Bukhara to Orenburg would cost as much as three roubles, the railway brought the cost down (carriage guaranteed and insured as far as Moscow) to 70 copecks per pud, which considerably improved the situation of the local merchants.

In 1895, Bukhara having entered the Russian customs system, customs posts were established at Kerki, Kelif, Pata-Hisar, Ayvaje, Saray, Chubak, and Bogaran; checkpoints were placed at regular intervals along the Amu Darya, the Panj, and the Qizilsu; and in this way, the customs frontier of the Russian empire was pushed out to the borders of Afghanistan.[19] The inclusion of Bukhara in the empire's customs system had the effect of developing considerably Russo-Bukharan economic relations: in 1865 Bukhara's exports to Russia totalled 3,306,000 roubles and its imports 1,913,000 roubles;[20] by 1913 exports had risen to 31 million roubles and imports to 35 million.[21]

From 1873 on, Russians began to arrive in Bukhara, brought there to construct roads or the railway, to establish garrisons and customs posts, to staff the Amu Darya flotilla, or to study commercial possibilities. The 1896 census counted 12,150 Russian subjects living in Bukhara, to whom almost 8,000 soldiers could be added.[22] At the start of the First World War the Russian population of the emirate was put at almost 50,000, excluding military personnel.[23] Russian colonies thus grew up at the end of the nineteenth century, especially along the railroad and the Amu Darya.

Some of these settlements produced colonial-type towns, like Charju'i, Novaya Bukhara (Kagan), Kerki, and Termez/Pata-Hisar. The population of these towns was heterogeneous: in addition to Russians there were Armenians, Jews, Tatars, and Persians; and the families of officials and soldiers, merchants, craftsmen, workers, railwaymen. The Russian presence was confined to the towns; the idea was never entertained of making Bukhara a place of rural colonization, both because of the shortage of irrigated land and because of the hostility of the native population. Various decrees[24] regulated the organization and planning of the Russian towns and villages, and even the size of holding that could be bought by Russians in Bukhara, whether from the government or from individuals.[25]

Charju'i was the first to be established, near the old town of

Chorzoy, in December 1886, at the same time that the railway was forging ahead; shortly thereafter, barracks and then houses were built in the neighbourhood. The town developed rapidly because of its privileged position at the junction of the railway and the Amu Darya. In 1913 it had 15,000 inhabitants, ten factories, railway and riverboat repair yards. In 1888, 12 kilometres from the capital, Novaya Bukhara sprang up to provide a site for the Russian Agency. Factories appeared, then an agency of the Russian State Bank in 1894 and a printworks; and the population soon reached 12,000.

In 1899 border difficulties with Afghanistan prompted the Russian authorities to establish a fortified post near the old town of Kerki, on the caravan road linking Bukhara with Afghanistan. Subsequently, that post became a town of 6,000 inhabitants, an important economic and industrial centre where the cotton products, wool, and carpets of eastern Bukhara were sold. The business handled at Kerki amounted to some 22 million roubles, and the agency of the Russo-Asiatic Bank saw between 70,000 and 80,000 roubles pass through each year.[26]

Finally, in December 1894, again in response to the need to settle the border problem with neighbouring Afghanistan, the Russian authorities in Turkistan sent units of the Thirty-First Amu Darya Brigade to the frontier and these were stationed in the little village of Pata-Hisar, close to ancient Termez. The village became an important fortress, to which were added 9,074 *desiatins* of non-irrigated land ceded by the emir. An irrigation system was realized and Termez, because of its key position on the Amu Darya, became the main centre for trade between Russia, Afghanistan, and north-eastern India. Navigation on the Amu Darya was extended to there. A mail route linked Samarqand with the Russian fortress: its construction was to require the (unremunerated) participation of the neighbouring Bukharan peasants, who harboured bitter resentment about it.[27] Eventually, in 1916, a railway from Kagan to Termez definitively attached this faraway centre to Bukhara and, beyond it, to all of Turkistan.

Although these towns, whose economic development was rapid, were originally populated mainly by Russians, the opportunities for work that their industries and later the construction of railway repair yards offered attracted a few natives, often destitute peasants who found some means of survival there.[28] The Russian concessions thus played a certain role in the slow transformation of local society, though the small number of natives integrated in this way limited their importance.

The Russian presence in Bukhara and the opening of the Trans-Caspian railway profoundly altered the basis of the local economy and gave pride of place to the emirate's cotton resources, although cotton exports had begun well before the conquest (in 1850–60 60,000 puds of cotton were exported annually). But from the 1880s on, the demand for cotton grew and pushed the peasantry to practise an intensive cultivation. In this respect, the place Bukhara held on the Central Asian market was a considerable one, since on the eve of the revolution the area sown with cotton in Bukhara extended over 110,000 *desiatins* (against 530,000 *desiatins* for Turkistan as a whole).[29] During that period, Bukhara was producing 2 million puds of cotton a year, almost entirely exported, which represented 40 per cent of its total exports and 13 per cent of the cotton exported by Central Asia as a whole.[30]

Production similarly developed of astrakhan (*karakul*), wool, silk, and carpets. From the beginning of the twentieth century on, raw materials and semi-manufactured products represented 93 per cent of Bukhara's total exports. Conversely, Russia sent the emirate increasingly more manufactured products, which, to a considerable extent, came to compete with the production of such traditional crafts as silkwork. (See Table 2.1.)

Table 2.1
Bukhara's Export and Import of Manufactured Products
in Roubles and Puds

	1849	1867	1880	1913
Exports (Bukharan manufactures)	303[a]	265[a]	—	3[b]
Imports (Russian manufactures)	142.7[a]	1,139[a]	43[b]	265[b]
		38.9[b]		

Note: a = millions of roubles; b = thousands of puds
Source: M. N., 'Pod znakom Islam', p. 78.

Several Russian banks opened branches in Bukhara at the beginning of the century: the State Bank, the Russian Foreign Trade Bank, the Russo-Asiatic Bank, the Azov and Don Commercial Bank, the Siberian Commercial Bank, and the Volga and Kama Commercial Bank.[31] Each of these banks had a veritable monopoly on one sector of local economic life: the Russo-Asiatic Bank signed an agreement with the emir for the construction of the emirate's railways; the Azov and Don Bank served as intermediary for the cotton trade between Bukhara and Russia; the Russian Foreign Trade Bank was primarily interested in the astrakhan trade; and the Siberian Commercial Bank focused on cotton purchases and imports of manufactured goods.

The bankers who had opened branches in Bukhara loaned commercial enterprises almost 40 million roubles every year. The banks, oriented primarily towards cotton production and processing, financed the establishments (factories, firms) which were involved in it, not directly but through a series of native intermediaries, like the *tarazudar* (weigher of cotton in the marketplaces) and the *pakhtakash* (small buyer, an agent of the foregoing).[32] So the price of cotton was fixed, not on the basis of supply and demand, but under conditions suiting the buyer, who organized the entire purchasing network in his own way. A complex hierarchy placed the producer under the absolute domination of purchasers-cum-retailers, who in turn were dominated by the Russian banks, since the cotton-purchasing firms received loans of the order of 90 per cent from the banks to carry out their operations. Russian-Bukharan trade was organized, controlled, and run by ten firms of middlemen, fifty or so commercial enterprises and four transport companies.[33]

At the same time, there appeared the beginnings of an industrial capitalism; but its activities remained limited, since the doctrine of the Russian empire regarding the emirate, and all of Central Asia, was to retain a market in raw materials for Russian industry and a selling area free from competition for Russian manufactured goods.[34] The basis of this embryonic industry in which capital was invested was a cotton-processing industry. On the eve of the First World War, Bukhara had twenty-six factories of this kind, but almost all were located on the Russian concession and belonged to the Russian bourgeoisie, when they were not quite simply branches of Moscow or Lodz factories.[35] A few other Russian industries installed themselves at the same time.[36] Nobel opened a number of oil depots, in Bukhara, Charju'i, Kerki, Termez, and Saray.[37] The gold-bearing sands of the Panj and its tributaries (the Bahsu, the Qizilsu, the Qulab-Darya, the Yaksu, and the Nubi) attracted Russians,[38] Englishmen, and even Frenchmen. But it was mainly the Russians who organized local exploitation, based on archaic techniques and hampered by similarly ancient regulations.[39] Finally, railway repair shops, concentrated on the Russian concessions, attracted a staff of Russian workers, often highly skilled, whose subsequent political role was considerable.

The Social Consequences of Capitalist Penetration

The reinforcement and enlargement of the emirate's relations with Russia; railway construction; industrial development, however limited; the growth of towns;[40] and the intervention of Russian capital in rural production — all these had the effect of developing capitalist relations in the emirate. The social consequences were considerable: traditional rural ownership was destroyed and class differentiation accelerated in the villages; agrarian production took on a commercial character; and the peasantry's specialization in cotton cultivation brought about a progressive adaptation of other sectors of the economy. The Bukharan peasantry felt the effects of these changes, which resulted in its pauperization. Above all, the extension of cotton cultivation led to reduced production of foodstuffs, which then had to be imported from Russia.[41]

But at that time the fundamental problem of the Bukharan countryside, as for all Turkistan, was the problem of credit. Loans were originally advances on cotton production given to the peasants by the commercial houses, through the intermediary of the *tarazudars*; these advances, called *bunak,* were given in April, the period when the peasants felt the lack of money most cruelly. The peasant pledged himself — in writing and before the *qazi* — to hand over his produce to the *tarazudar* at the price fixed by the latter at the moment when the advance was paid (a price fixed on the basis of the previous year's rate, taking no account of any increase and, in any case, always below the market rate).[42] The loan was secured by the harvest and then by the peasant's land and all his goods. It was not given entirely in cash — far from it — but partly in kind: for example, manufactured goods, tea, soap, and paraffin — all products whose value the *tarazudar* boosted by at least 25 per cent. In addition, the *bunak* was accompanied by substantial interest, since for a three-month loan of fifteen roubles, the interest was three roubles, so that by the end of a year interest would total 80 per cent.[43] At the start of the twentieth century, 75 per cent of Bukharan cotton was bought under such conditions by the *tarazudars*.

The astonishing docility of the peasants in the face of such practices may be explained by a socio-religious cause. Islam formally forbids usurious lending, and practices of the *bunak* type did not exist in Bukharan Islamic society before the penetration of Russian capitalism. Although the Hindus were active usurers in the emirate well before 1867,[44] their activity was limited; the loans they accorded were of no great size and, in the event of conflict, justice was indulgent towards the debtors because of the Koranic prescriptions.[45] When an advance on their crops was proposed to the peasants of Bukhara, they never imagined that someone would one day come and demand both the loan itself (whose value, for the reasons indicated, was already far greater than the product of the harvest) and interest upon it. Their inability to comprehend the full implications of the usurious loan — legally non-existent in Muslim society — led the entire peasantry of Bukhara to deliver itself bound hand-and-foot to the middlemen. When the moment of repayment came, the peasants, unable to settle their debts, borrowed anew. From one loan to another they ended up losing their land, sometimes even finished in prison.[46]

In this complicated system whereby at each stage, from the peasant to the merchant, all had to repay loans on interest, the victim was always Mustafa or 'Ali, the poor peasant of Bukhara. Against such odds, what could he do? He could take a job as an agricultural worker, who was a semi-slave; look for work in industry, whether in the Russian concessions or in the guberniya; or leave a land that no longer belonged to him and take refuge in the mountains, where he could lead a semi-nomadic life supplemented by the growing banditry of those decades.[47] Finally, when his exasperation grew too strong, he could rebel — and there was no shortage of unrest.

At the same time that the appearance of capitalism in Bukhara brought with it a tragic crisis for the peasantry, and to a lesser degree for the artisans, there was as a corollary a social phenomenon: the development and consolidation of a national bourgeoisie. Although all the control levers of the emirate's economy had been concentrated in the hands of the Russians, the Russians needed interlocutors and intermediaries on the spot. Here the Bukharan bourgeoisie found a role and a means to develop; its members served as agents for Russian commercial enterprises in the purchase of raw materials and as intermediaries in the sale of Russian goods on the domestic market.[48] At the apex of this class stood some extremely wealthy men whom Russian capitalism greatly benefited: these included the Khodzhaevs, whose annual turnover reached a million roubles at the beginning of the century; the Vazhaev brothers, who owned eleven factories and managed twenty others; the Arapov brothers, who held a considerable slice of the astrakhan market; and the big bankers Mir

Salih and Mansurov, who went in for the lucrative activity of financing the *bunak*.[49] As it developed and its resources increased, this commercial bourgeoisie — which depended directly on Russian capitalism — gradually thought of playing an economic role of its own; however, it then discovered the disadvantages of Russian competition.

Finally, despite the appearance of a small industry, it would not be possible to speak of the existence of a conscious working class in this period. The workers who came to work in the newly created factories were mainly Russians. The few natives among them were usually ruined peasants, were not only haunted by their memories and the desire to return to the land, but also too influenced by the clergy to be able to form the embryo of a national proletariat endowed with class consciousness.[50] For these uprooted elements, the countryside remained their universe and their *raison d'être*. Because Russia was firmly opposed to the creation of an industry indigenous to the countries of Central Asia, the necessary conditions for the formation or development of a proletariat did not exist in Bukhara until the Russian Revolution. Thus the appearance of capitalism in Bukhara not only radically altered the life and economic structure of the emirate, but also undermined its society. Although the changes were very slow, they were grafted onto a process that had begun even before the conquest.

Political Forms of the Russian Presence

The presence of Russia in the emirate constituted an important factor in the emirate's evolution, in so far as it assumed, despite the moderate character of the 1873 agreements, a colonial hue.

In 1885 in Bukhara the Russian government created a Russian Imperial Political Agency, which was not an embassy of the kind that sovereign countries exchange but a unilateral official representation. The political agent was the intermediary in relations between St Petersburg or Tashkent and the government of Bukhara; he also had the task of controlling the situation on the Russo-Afghan frontier. The organization of the Political Agency corresponded to three Russian concerns: first, to establish a certain control over the emir and his government; second, to oversee the Russian concessions; and third, to defend Russia's industrial and commercial interests on the spot. The political agent had overall control of the Russian concessions; by virtue of this, he belonged under the Guberniya of Turkistan, and hence under the minister of war. His mission was also to protect on the territory of the emirate not only Russian subjects but also foreigners of the Christian religion.

Within a few years the imperial power, whose presence had begun with the introduction of a few Russian troops and a few technicians, succeeded in modifying profoundly the status of the protectorate and in creating veritable concessions there, totally immune from the common law of the emirate. Theoretically, Russia intervened neither in the customs nor in the laws of the emirate. But under the pretext of organizing Russian settlement zones, the government in St Petersburg created in Bukhara an apparatus that allowed it to control that faraway possession and its 2 or 3 million inhabitants: the political agent exercised a certain control over the local government; Russian trade enjoyed a privileged status; and the Russian judicial system separated Russian subjects from the common rule and placed all Bukhara's relations with Russia within a system, structures, and a psychic universe that were purely Russian.

The Russian Conquest and Local Consciousness

Here we come to the difficult question of how the Bukharan authorities and people respectively interpreted the actual nature of the Russian presence and how each reacted to that presence. From 1873 the emir and the Bukharan masses adopted fundamentally opposed positions in this respect. For the emir, the Russian presence was initially — despite the defeat suffered (whose relatively unhumiliating character has already been noted) — a blessing, in so far as it allowed him finally to enforce his authority in uncontested fashion over the restless *vilayats* of the eastern part of the emirate, with their dreams of independence. Though his power tottered during the ill-starred campaigns of the years between 1868 and 1873, it emerged strengthened from the conflict. In comparison with the conditions imposed on Khoqand and Khiva, the favourable character of the protectorate treaty could not but add to the ruler's prestige.

In the space of a few years the emir of Bukhara had at all events managed to progress from being a ruler whose power was disputed and who was then demoted and subjected to the authority of a governor-general, to one who headed a strong centralized state and exercised an absolute power no longer limited, as in the past, by constant local revolts. Regarding the Russian authorities in

Turkistan, the emir progressively compelled recognition, and the titles they granted him testify to this astonishing recovery. In 1873 Emir Muzaffar was merely 'Your Excellency' to General Kaufmann, and his son 'Abd al-Ahad was called 'Majesty';[51] so he naturally found himself above the governor-general of Turkistan, and his relations with the Russian authorities were thereby modified.

During the protectorate, the Russian authorities at every level of the hierarchy, convinced of the emir's fabulous wealth,[52] made constant calls upon it. The emir was invited to take part in various Russian projects in Central Asia. He had the Tashkent *Realschule* built at his own expense and constantly subsidized the schools and charitable bodies of the guberniya. In addition, he acquired the habit of marking all the important events of the Russian empire by personal gifts and for the tsar's birthday, a sumptuous gift was always sent to St Petersburg. In 1905 his generosity reached a climax with the gift of a battleship, which was named the 'Emir of Bukhara'. At the beginning of the twentieth century, the emir's largesse to Russia was of the order of a million roubles a year.[53] Added to this were disbursements made within the confines of the emirate, where every Russian was magnificently welcomed and laden with gifts by the begs and their subordinates as well as the emir. News of these acts of generosity soon spread throughout both Turkistan and Russia, so that numerous officials would seek some pretext or other to pay a visit to this cornucopia.[54]

The emir derived a twofold advantage from this state of affairs. On the one hand, it was difficult for the Russian authorities, especially those in Turkistan whose job it was to exercise a certain control over the emir, not to take his largesse into account. And the best way of doing so, also the way of having constant recourse to his coffers, was to appeal to his self-esteem, hence to build up his prestige. On the other hand, the respect with which the emir was surrounded, at least formally; the aid he gave the Russian conqueror; and facts like the existence of a Russian battleship bearing his name — all these made an extremely strong impression outside Bukhara, first in Turkistan and then in all the neighbouring countries of the Orient.

This circumstance was to give traditionalist Islam its power; for, from the viewpoint of the Muslim community, Bukhara was the most important spot in all of Central Asia. Khoqand had vanished before the infidel; Khiva was stagnating, reduced to a humbled state; but Bukhara testified to the resistance of the Muslim world to Russia. Yet the emirate had been no better armed against the conquest than the other two khanates; on the contrary, it had succeeded less well than they in its attempts at territorial expansion, and it was more torn than they by internal dissent. The notion that the resistance of Islam to European conquest was stronger where Islam was practised best was still only embryonic during the last years of the nineteenth century. But the awareness that existed outside of the emir's prestige and growing power helped to develop it, to anchor it in people's minds, and to transform it into an important element in the Muslim ideological debate in Bukhara.

However, the emir did not confine himself to distributing gifts to the Russians; he used them also to establish his authority more and more firmly within the emirate, especially in its eastern part. The worsening condition of the peasantry provoked a renewed crop of rebellions at the end of the nineteenth century. The Bukharan authorities acquired the habit of appealing to the Russians to put them down; this appeal was all the more justified, in that disorders that became transformed into local riots — in which all the old spirit of separatism was reborn — led to massacres of which the officials were the first victims.[55]

Sometimes the situation was complicated by murders of a few Russian subjects by the insurgents. To the protests of the Russian authorities, the emir used to reply that 'in spite of his very keen desire to remedy the situation, he did not have the means to do it, so heavy was the task of keeping watch over the population and over his frontiers'.[56] Even more frequently, he used to warn the political agent that if Russia wanted to see order reign in Bukhara and to protect her subjects, it would have to intervene itself and use, for that purpose, the troops stationed on the emirate's territory.

Similarly, the emir acquired the habit of invoking the authority of the Russians to cover all the excesses of the fiscal system, and in this he was followed by the entire financial hierarchy of the emirate. Whenever there was a protest against the levying of taxes and whenever there was an increase in taxation, the official responsible for collecting the taxes would imperturbably explain that the government was conscious of the exorbitant demands of the tax system, but that the Russians wanted it that way;[57] the emir's contributions to the life of the Russian empire were invoked as justification to the masses from whom, under this pretext, ever larger sums were being extorted. It was the same story with the corvée labour in which the peasants had to take part: from the 1880s on, such obligations were all explained and justified by Russian requirements, even if they bore only the remotest relation to the Russians, or no relation whatsoever. Finally, the water problem was one further reason for invoking the malevolence of the conquerors: at the end of the nineteenth century the irrigation system was scarcely improved, and in drought years water distribution was closely supervised and a high price paid for it. Here again, peasant discontent was directed against the Russians, since the emir could opportunely recall that he was no longer master of the Zarafshan and that the Russian authorities in Samarqand were subjecting him to constant pressure.[58]

The people, for their part, reacted simultaneously against the emir and against the Russian presence. The emir's ingenuity in using the Russians to consolidate his state was not viewed in the same way in Bukhara as it was outside the city. For the tribes in revolt against the emir's domination, the Russian conquest was simultaneously a personal defeat for the emir at the hands of the Russian armies and, in so far as it signalled the end of their aspirations for autonomy, a defeat for themselves. For certain peoples of eastern Bukhara, attachment to Russia would have been preferable to attachment to the emirate;[59] once Russia had placed them under the emir's authority, they bore a grudge against both. So, in their bouts of revolt they massacred Bukharan officials and Russian subjects indiscriminately; this provoked intervention by the Russian garrisons and, as an indirect consequence, lent a certain credit to the Bukharan version of the exactions ordered by 'the infidel'. Nevertheless, the emir did not win much prestige in his own country by always invoking the obligation to satisfy Russia, for the masses held it against him. Within the emirate, everything appeared to them a sign of the government's weakness and of the collapse of traditional authority. Thus, all the positive sides of the Russian presence were effaced in the minds of the masses, even when it deserved their effective support. This was particularly clear in two matters: the struggle against locusts, and efforts in the domain of public health.

Locusts were a permanent nightmare for the peasants of Bukhara. Already burdened with taxation and debts, working on insufficient and inadequately irrigated land, in some years they would see the entire fruit of their labours annihilated by invasions of locusts. Until 1873 their main means of defence against such plagues consisted in burying in the ground each year reserves of grain for the following year. The Russians suggested the adoption of more positive — albeit still primitive — methods of struggle: digging a ditch not far from the spot where the young locusts, as yet incapable of flight, were to be found, then pushing them towards the ditch and burying them in it.[60] The method had the major disadvantage of demanding a sizeable human input; but having proposed it, the Russian authorities saw it as only natural that the peasants directly interested in the struggle should be obliged to take part in the work, and this was in addition to their existing corvée impositions.[61] So the anti-locust campaign was unpopular, especially since the peasants did not believe that it was efficacious or that the absence of locusts in certain places was at all connected with the measures taken. Since the peasants displayed a total lack of good will, the application of the measures was neither systematic nor general, and thus locusts continued to proliferate.[62] Hence, every invitation to take part in the anti-locust campaign provokes a veritable explosion of peasant fury; and for local officials, being put in charge of organizing the work was tantamount to a certain sentence of violent death.

Under the two last emirs, anti-locust expeditions became the signal for jacqueries; all the main revolts of those years were seen to coincide with such health campaigns.[63] The government of Bukhara, becoming aware of the consequences of Russian aid — consequences that threatened the entire hierarchy of power and also provoked reactions in Russia that might lead to ending the protectorate and attaching the emirate to the guberniya[64] — also grew hostile to it. Emir 'Abd al-Ahad grew abruptly indignant at the idea — which could have been conceived only in the minds of infidels — of 'destroying locusts sent by God'.[65] So, progressively, a certain change began to appear in public opinion, with the régime aligning itself with the masses against the Russians, out of fidelity to the teachings of the Prophet. Between the holy war unleashed in 1858 and 'Abd al-Ahad's protestations of piety, a long distance had been travelled and culminated in a generalized rejection of progress in its Russian guise, in the name of the most varied interests or principles — from respect for the will of God to the refusal to work without wages.

In like manner, peasants refused to take part in the construction of dykes designed to protect those living along the banks of certain particularly unruly rivers (like the Kafirnigan and the Vahsh) from sudden floods that destroyed their crops and swept away their homes.[66] The reluctance of the peasants to take part in works

designed to dam the course of the rivers also reflected local super-
stitions. The strength of these rivers and their ravages could be
explained and accepted only if they had a significance that transcended the human. Aquatic *jinns* were invoked (the *jinn vahsh*,
protector of all streams and waterways, being placed in the river of
that name),[67] and it was believed that to oppose the rages of these
jinns would expose those responsible to reprisals infinitely more
serious than the periodic overflowing of the rivers.

There was a similar reaction in the domain of public health. The
Russian authorities — frightened by the scale of epidemics (in
1897 an epidemic wiped out half the population of Hisar)[68] and
appealed to by the local administration — sent in health missions.
These were at first relatively well received,[69] but soon the population refused to accept medical care or consult doctors. Among the
direct causes of this turnaround were the clumsiness of the Russian
authorities and their misunderstanding of life in Islamic countries.
A mission sent to the *vilayat* of Kerki in 1898 included a woman
doctor, who was amazed that the men of a neighbouring tribe
refused to come into contact with her.[70] An additional factor was
the intervention, not only of the clergy but also of all the healers
and *shamans* who proliferated in Bukhara and whose influence
over the peasant and nomad masses was considerable. Logofet
notes that the period following the establishment of the protectorate was marked by an increase in the authority of *falbins* (fortune-
tellers, sorcerers).[71] Here again, the position of the Bukharan
government was changeable and ambiguous: having demanded
medical aid from Russia, at the local level it sought to convince the
Russian authorities that the population of Bukhara was too backward to accept putting itself in the hands of Russian doctors, so
that the best course was to abandon it to its fate and to the *falbins*
to whom it had for centuries had recourse. From then on, the
Russian doctors also recorded the difficulties placed by the local
authorities in the way of their least freedom of movement, and
gradually any effort at public health improvements disappeared.[72]

It thus seems that on the level of the psychological consequences
of the Russian presence in the emirate, two phases must be distinguished in the period lasting from 1873 to 1905. At first, the arrival
of the Russians barely made any impression on the peasant masses. The Russians were infidels against whom the standard of the
ghazavat had been raised; but the peasants, crushed by their
hardships, rarely saw further than their immediate oppressors,
who were the officials responsible for collecting taxes, distributing

water or organizing forced labour; or, again, the owner of their land. The result at first was a real indifference, and in certain cases a curiosity about the Russian initiatives.

The situation changed little by little as the condition of the masses worsened visibly in certain domains[73] and as the local authorities channelled popular discontent against the Russian empire. This had the great advantage of bringing discontent into conflict with a power external to the Islamic community and hence did not call into question a power of divine origin. Hitherto, everything had been simple and inevitable. The wretchedness of the people's condition was part of an order guaranteed by the authority of clergy and ruler. However wretched and oppressed, the lowest illiterate peasant in Bukhara knew that things had to be that way because they were inscribed in an order of divine origin and because they were part of God's plan. Islamic society was an ideal society; whatever the material conditions of their existence Muslims had an absolute loyalty towards their community. Suddenly the very people who spoke in God's name were telling the masses that the prevailing order, which for them was even more oppressive than it had been in the past, was external to the community. There was a popular realization that something radically new was beginning and that a rupture with the past had been effected. The history of Bukhara, like that of every country, has experienced many ruptures and transformations; in the case of Bukhara, the difference was the changed nature of the phenomenon: this was a qualitative rupture. Evolution was for the first time consciously felt, even if only in a rudimentary way.

This reaction of consciousness at the base of society probably would not have gone beyond the stage of popular discontent and sporadic revolts had it not found the native bourgeoisie, which was developing with the infiltration of capitalism, to channel it and give it form.

3

Preambles to Reformism

The anxiety that the popular masses confusedly felt in Bukhara is important because it was not an isolated phenomenon: it formed part of a general current that, in elaborated and idealized forms, subsequently questioned the evolution of the Muslim community; and, beyond it, of the colonial world as a whole. Here I shall confine my discussion to the specific crisis of the Muslim world, because even though it belongs to a wider movement, it nonetheless has its own characteristics and features and evolution, which are closely bound up with the bases of the Islamic faith and the history of Islam.

Elements of the Crisis of Islam

For the Muslim world, history — its history — began in 622: a fundamental date, since it constitutes one of the elements of the problem of modern Islam. The year 622 is not that of the Prophet's birth, nor is it that in which he received the Revelation. It is a sociological and political year: the birth of the Islamic community as a real force. On that date the Prophet and his followers arrived in Medina, where they established their community, free from any constraint external to Islam. And this community — indistinguishably a social group and a religious body, the terrestrial projection of an ideology — was first characterized by a feeling of unity. The divergences that emerged around the Prophet's succession, the separation between Sunnis and Shi'a, remained primarily on the level of events rather than on that of theory. Whatever theological discussions Islam may have known, scarcely any fundamental debate occurred that questioned the existence of the community.

For centuries, the fate of that community found its guarantee in the course of history. The conquests of early Islam allowed it to create its own society and order. The temporal empire which subjugated the Persian empire and a considerable part of the Roman empire, and which stretched from the Pyrenees to the

Himalayas, was enriched by the civilization of the conquered peoples. Islam then gave society its cohesion and dynamism. Islamic law created the unity of the peoples who formed part of that empire. Early Islam found great strength in the fact that it was the religion of a ruling, conquering, and active class — the religion of power. Although the distance was great from the conquests of early Islam to the later retreats and history seemed to turn its back on the community, to get through the difficult period separating the fall of Baghdad (1258) from the taking of Constantinople (1453), the community found the remedy of Sufism. After the Mongol conquest it also discovered that defeat did not prevent Islam from advancing, sometimes even through the proselytism of the conquerors who rallied to it.

The second victorious period of Islam — with the Ottoman empire, the Safavid empire, the Moguls — was already revealing the first symptoms of decline, despite the territorial extension during this period. The Islamic faith, deeply marked by Sufism, was more indifferent to the successes of history; and already a certain divergence made its appearance between religious power and political power. Although there was no question as yet of a secular power, religion was perhaps no longer entirely the crucible from which emanated and in which were fused the various aspects of life: it was tending imperceptibly to become one of those elements.[1]

With the eighteenth century, decline had set in: military, political, commercial, economic, and in particular intellectual. And this retreat was all the more evident in that, at that moment, Europe was becoming a conquering, exuberant force — a force which was destined to dominate the new weakness of the Muslim world. With the nineteenth century, the rule of the West was extended progressively to all the Islamic regions, which, since Islam had existed, had lived under their own order.

From that time on, the fundamental crisis of the Muslim community began. Until then, the constant success — despite the halt of the Middle Ages — of Islam's terrestrial undertaking had provided blinding confirmation of the validity of the whole edifice. Religion was guaranteed by history. With the decline of the eighteenth century and the European conquest, religion was no longer travelling in the same direction as a history that God nevertheless controlled. The Islamic crisis of the nineteenth and twentieth centuries was, therefore, fundamentally a spiritual crisis; and its original aspect was that it was entirely conscious. Henceforth the essential problem for Muslims was to seek out the path of regeneration.

Reformist Tendencies in Islam[2]

The first exploration in this direction took place on the spot where Islam was born, in eighteenth-century Arabia: this was the Wahhabi movement,[3] born in reaction against an internal degeneration of Islam, which the movement viewed as the cause of its global decline. To counter this degeneration, it preached a pure and simple return to early Islam — purged of all medieval accretions, mystical wanderings, the alien intellectualism that had corrupted philosophy and theology, and all deviations, including Shi'ism. Truth resided in the Law, such as it had been preserved in the Hanbalite version — in principle, also stripped of all its historical accretions. The source of reform was the Koran and the pure *sunna*. Though in its specific form Wahhabism remained limited, the Wahhabi call for a return to early Islam and a rejection of historical errors found an echo in other countries, where similar tendencies emerged, related to the specific conditions and historical development of each of them.

India saw similar quests, to which the political degeneration of the community gave an additional argument and a fresh dimension. The movement was organized in two directions: first, it was a struggle within the community to purify and regenerate the Islamic faith — as was also the case, by other routes, in Arabia; and, at the same time, the foreign presence gave India's reformist movement its second dimension, that of struggle against the infidel oppressor — in other words, a liberation movement. The two aspects of the Islamic reaction to the crisis of the nineteenth century were thus represented in Indian reformism, and these two aspects were subsequently to be found everywhere: spiritual struggle for regeneration within Islam; political struggle for liberation externally.

The man who, in the nineteenth century, gave a unity to this quest of the Muslims to escape from the crisis in which they felt they were foundering was Jamal al-Din al-Afghani, an astonishing figure the profundity of whose thought — and the precise degree of whose sincerity — no one can work out. Claiming to draw his inspiration both from the Sunni orthodoxy and from Sufi mysticism, preaching reconciliation with Shi'ism, and tied to England yet struggling against her — these factors make al-Afghani appear less an original thinker than a remarkable agitator.[4] His great merit was to pose clearly the elements of Islam's problem in the nineteenth century and to make those elements accessible to the consciousness of all. He was the first to speak of Islam and the West as antagonistic concepts and to show that their clash is a historical phenomenon whose elements are inseparable. What now seems obvious was made explicit and clearly grasped only with al-Afghani. He added a third dimension to internal reform and external liberation, one which appeared only in a confused manner among the inhabitants of India: nostalgia for the past greatness of the Muslim community. He saw the West not only as the enemy and conqueror of Islam, but also as a model to follow in order to acquire a new strength, which would lead to liberation and the rebirth of a strong community. To attain this, human, conscious action was crucial. He never wearied of stressing that Muslims bore the responsibility for their own fate; and he did so by invoking the verse of the Koran: 'In truth, God does not change a people's condition, if that people does not change its own condition.'[5]

In this way — through the searchings of the Wahhabis, the Indian reformists, and Jamal al-Din al-Afghani — the Islamic understanding of the crisis of the modern world was illuminated. This crisis could be resolved only by a twofold struggle, which every Muslim must wage, against internal degradation and against the non-Muslim world. The more clearly the elements of the problem were defined, the more clearly it was seen how great was the rupture with the past. The evolution was conscious and the fundamental element in the change, from that period onwards, was knowledge. All mutations were to be the deed of the community and of every individual within the community.

Engendered by these fundamental tendencies, movements emerged in the Muslim countries at the end of the nineteenth century and in the first years of the twentieth that were linked with the specific problem of each group but simultaneously partook of this general concern. The one upon which it is perhaps most worth dwelling is the movement of the Sanusis, originating in mid nineteenth-century Libya.[6] In contrast to the preaching of al-Afghani, who sought to integrate elements of the West in the struggle that Islam was to wage for its regeneration, the Sanusis rejected any compromise with the West. The movement sacrificed theoretical reflection in favour of clear, comprehensible action: a total struggle carried through to the bitter end, whose object was eviction of the infidel. Each Sanusi considered himself the natural rallying-point of all popular resistance to foreign oppression.

In the general crisis, modern Turkey held a role that merits careful attention, in so far as it was one of the essential supports for reformist thought among the Muslims of the Russian empire, though the meditation of the Turkish reformers coincided with that of the Muslim world as a whole. Basing themselves on the decadence of society and the need to halt the advance of the infidel, many Turkish thinkers, from Ibrahim Muteferriqa (1674–1745) to Namiq Kemal (1840–88), oriented themselves towards spiritual reform. Yet in the most recent centuries the Turkish destiny had diverged from that of the other Muslim peoples, and this perhaps produced a different reaction to the general problem. Turkey did not experience the crisis of Islam and it escaped foreign dependence. Confronted with the degradation of the Muslim world, to which it remained external, Turkey sought an attitude of its own that was more political than spiritual, more Turkish than Islamic: this was fundamentally an adaptation of Turkish society to the modern world.[7]

The first solution was Ottomanism, which seemed to oppose pan-Islamism. 'Unity and Progress' formally condemned pan-Islamism. After the Balkan Wars, which dealt a fatal blow to Ottomanism, there was a development towards pan-Turkism, which was far removed from pan-Islamism or which was a purely Turkish version of it. Nevertheless, these two distinct tendencies, which characterized the positions of Islamic society at the dawn of the twentieth century, were both jointly at the origin of reformist thought among the Muslims of Russia.

Pan-Islamism and Pan-Turkism in Russia

Reformist ideas were first introduced and clarified in the Russian empire by Tatars and for a time, Bukhara was the geographical centre for the elaboration of their thought. The links between the Tatars and Central Asia were constant throughout history, and this had considerable repercussions upon ideology. For one thing, the Tatar ruling classes considered Central Asia as their private commercial domain; for another, it was in Central Asia, especially in the *madrasas* of the Khanate of Bukhara, that the Tatar youth was educated. The Russian conquest of Central Asia put an end to the privileged situation of Tatar commerce in the region. To survive, the Tatar bourgeoisie had to break completely with the past and to enter the modern world, where Western values were then dominant.[8] The religious authorities opposed this; and to overcome their opposition, any attempt at reform had first to situate itself upon the religious plane.

As early as the beginning of the nineteenth century the need for religious renewal was advocated by the Tatar Abu Nasr Kursavi (1783–1813),[9] a scholar who resided for much of his life in Bukhara. Kursavi's criticism of the ossified forms of Muslim scholasticism and the degradation of mysticism was, perhaps, premature. It did not in any case correspond to any generalized social awareness and during his lifetime his movement remained limited. However, his work provided the basis for all the Muslim reformist thought elaborated thereafter, in particular by Shihab al-Din Marjani (1818–99).[10] Arsharuni and Gabidullin write that Marjani was the representative of 'the growing contradictions of the Tatar commercial bourgeoisie',[11] whose existence had been reflected in Kursavi's work. Without going so far as to assert, like certain Soviet authors,[12] that the social basis for reformist thought among the Muslims of Russia in those first years was a class whose interests had been threatened by competition from emergent Russian capitalism, we should accept that its role was very great. The fundamental problem was the choice between maintaining the traditional way and breaking with it.

In his programme,[13] Marjani made six proposals:

1 Freedom of *ijtihad* or interpretation of religious law: individuals must make their own responses to every question, based on their own understanding of the Koran.
2 Abandonment of blind submission to the traditional authorities (*taqlid*).
3 Rejection by the *madrasas* of books of scholastic, conservative philosophy.
4 Introduction into the *madrasas* of teaching of the Koran, the Hadith and the history of Islam.
5 Introduction into the *madrasas* of teaching of science and the Russian language.
6 Return to Islamic culture and the purity of early Islam.

Arsharuni and Gabidullin, who reproduce this programme, insist on its contradictory character. On the one hand, Marjani demanded a new orientation appropriate to the conditions of the modern world: rejection of dated scholasticism, study of science, and study of the Russian language. At the same time, he called for a return to the sources of early Islam. The contradiction was only apparent: despite his modernism, Marjani shared the confidence of the Wahhabis in the virtues of early Islam and believed with other reformers that Islam declined as it evolved. Originally, it was pure, dynamic, and open to everything; but was turned from its original form by the fanaticism and exclusivism of ensuing periods.

The true father of religious revival, and of pan-Turkism in Russia, was a third Tatar, Isma'il Bay Gaspirali (Gasprinski, 1851–1914),[14] who welded reformist thought, previously diffuse, into a coherent ideology. In 1883 Gasprinski founded the newspaper *Tarjuman* (The Interpreter), and used it as an organ for the propagation of his ideas about the reform of religious education, and pan-Turkism. He advocated that the Turkish peoples of the empire should unite first around a common literary language (to be created) and a common culture, then in political organizations working for their national recognition. Gasprinski identified the roots of the crisis of Islam as internal ossification and external oppression, denouncing two adversaries: the traditional Muslim clergy, fanatical and authoritarian, and the tsarist régime. The most urgent thing, he believed, was to strike down the former through a reform of education. Like al-Afghani, moreover, Gasprinski considered that relations between the West and Islam could not remain entirely negative and sterile; Islam should borrow from the West, even rely on it, in its own struggle against its internal weaknesses.

Gasprinski's pan-Turkist ideas suffered initially from a conflict with Ottomanism, then widespread in Turkey,[15] which denied any unity other than religious and vaguely linguistic between the Turks of Turkey and the peoples of Turkish origin scattered across the Russian empire. With the ebbing of Ottomanism, however, Russian pan-Turkism found much support in Turkey. By the beginning of the twentieth century it flourished and around Gasprinski there had developed a pan-Turkist movement which flanked *Tarjuman* with a whole series of organs propagating pan-Turkist ideas.[16] So much so that, according to an Okhrana report,[17] in the newspapers and programmes of Russia's Muslim peoples there was little pan-Islamism and a great deal of pan-Turkism.

The reformist movement in Bukhara had, however, a character of its own. To understand this it is necessary to consider the whole region of Central Asia to which Bukhara belongs, whose dismemberment was consummated by the military events of the nineteenth century. Though separated by administrative frontiers, the people of the area never ceased to recall that they formed part of a single, identical Turkistan. And this awareness — albeit highly confused — of a unity transcending alike the present state of separation and past historical disputes among the local potentates resurfaced in the anxiety common to all the peoples of Central Asia and in the explorations undertaken in common by the élite, even if divergent tendencies did emerge among them subsequently.

It is impossible to study the first manifestations of reformism in Bukhara without also considering Turkistan as a whole. A twofold influence weighed upon the formulation, in that region, of the anxiety that agitated the local masses as intensely as other Muslims. First, the Tatars were historically tributaries of the culture of Central Asia, and during those years of renewal they breathed into it part of the spirit of criticism and lucidity that was then animating all the lands of Islam. This kind of spiritual restitution, effected at the end of a long process, was not peculiar to the Tatars alone. Their influence was accompanied by that of Turkey, all the more prestigious in so far as it remained a great sovereign power; and in Bukhara itself the influence of India, Iran, and Afghanistan was noteworthy.

Here again, contact was made via the traditional path of the *madrasas*. For centuries the education provided in Bukhara had attracted young students, often the sons of wealthy merchants, to come there from those neighbouring countries. Through them not only were commercial relations initially established, but also there arrived, at the end of the nineteenth century, echoes of the movements of thought then troubling their countries, especially India (the ideas of Shah Valiallah and of Ahmad Barelawi were passionately embraced in Bukhara[18]) and Afghanistan. Furthermore, the political problem of Bukhara was a specific one — a problem less of the emirate's independence than of how to re-establish the independence of the rest of Turkistan. So, even while reformism as an articulated body of thought did not yet exist in Bukhara, a vague notion seemed to take hold of the minds of its rulers that it was incumbent upon their state, so miraculously protected in the terrible period of Western triumph, to assume a liberating role on behalf of those which had succumbed. This awareness on the part of the Bukharan authorities of having a saviour's role to play was significant, in so far as it also fitted into the line of reformist tendencies. Subsequently, it also influenced relations between the reformists and the régime.

After Kursavi and Marjani had so harshly questioned all forms of religious life in Bukhara, people were never again to find their former peace of mind. The travails of the populace and the élite's awareness of a fundamental conflict between Islamic society and the West were expressed by Ahmad Makhdum Danish (1827–97), one of the true intellectual pioneers of nineteenth-century Central Asia and the precursor of all strictly Turkistani reformists.[19] Three journeys through Russia between 1850 and 1870 — in the years in which the empire was extending its power over Turkistan and while the Central Asian khanates were struggling amid insoluble internal difficulties — allowed him to observe not only that a difference prevailed between Russia's blossoming and the collapse of the ancient Muslim states, but also that the wars of conquest, so costly for Central Asia, seemed easy for Russia, which was simultaneously pursuing its external expansion and its internal evolution. From one journey to the next, Danish could see the progress accomplished in Russia. He also familiarized himself with the representatives of Russian liberal thought[20] and learned about the 1825 revolution. He contrasted the development of a state in which liberal ideas, albeit forbidden, proliferated with the decline of his own country, where any thought that diverged in the slightest from the settled framework was branded as 'infidel'.[21]

So gradually a philosophical, scientific, social, and political thought formed which later served as a point of reference for all the reformists of Turkistan.[22] Danish sought to detect the seeds of death first within Bukhara itself, in the life of the community. Analysing the degradation of power, he saw its origin in the excessive appropriation of wealth — an idea that, however tentatively formulated, sounded somewhat revolutionary. He questioned the entire social order when he wrote: 'All that goes beyond the necessary minimum is a rope round the neck of the people and can lead only to death.'[23]

Thus, even as he clung to classical scholasticism, Danish was nonetheless marked by the rationalist and democratic thought he had come to know in Russia. Vaguely and without any great assurance, Danish also took up a personal position on the difficult question of the relations between divine will and human initiative. Although recognizing the importance of divine will and the weakness of human destiny in relation to that will, he rejected the notion that human will was not a fundamental element in human destiny. He condemned blind submission to a transcendent design, asserting that the human being must fashion his or her existence.[24]

Together with Danish's passionate interest in the exact sciences and with the conclusions to which he was led by his study of astronomy,[25] these important discussions made him suspect to the religious and civic authorities. Both were aware that his ideas led to a condemnation of the established order and of their own power, first and foremost. Similarly, the religious authorities of Bukhara discovered with horror that in his cell Danish was accumulating maps and globes in which he claimed to see a representation of the world — a world in movement, in which the earth and countless planets had a destiny independent from that of human beings and from that of the Islamic community. In the land of Ulug Beg, at the end of the nineteenth century, astronomy was thought of as a body of ideas inspired by the Evil One.

Danish added a positive element to this critique of prevailing philosophical education, to this constant recourse to science, and to his indictment of the authorities. Like other thinkers of the same epoch, he wanted to replace his country's decadence with a return to past greatness; but unlike some, he did not have to denounce foreign enemies on its soil. Hence he could appeal to the qualities of the West and to the factors that constituted its strength more easily than, say, Gasprinski, who belonged to a people which did not enjoy national independence.

Brought into contact both with the liberal spirit in Russia and with its temporal power, it was of Russia that Danish thought first when he denounced the narrowly restricted knowledge of his compatriots and their refusal to know anything that was alien to them. He thus advocated that the people of Bukhara should study the Russian language in order to gain access to the dynamic culture and material achievements of Europe. Gasprinski came to the same conclusion much later and went further than Danish by proposing concrete methods for the new education; but perhaps to a greater extent than Gasprinski, Danish reflected upon the movement of ideas then beginning to convulse Europe rather than upon Islam alone. Meditating upon his country's weakness, he sought replies not only in traditional philosophy but also in the utopian socialism that flourished in Russia during the 1860s; in the preaching of men like Herzen, Belinskii, Chernyshevskii and Dobrolyubov.

The contribution of Danish to the Muslim reformist movement would have been more concrete, more immediately obvious, had he limited his quest to the destiny of the Muslim community. But, perhaps unintentionally, he opened breaches onto a problem of a quite different dimension — that of the human condition within a certain economic and social framework — and was the first to do so in Central Asia. Hence Danish was a precursor, blazing a trail for all the movements of ideas that burgeoned after him. In many respects, his spiritual kinship with Jamal al-Din al-Afghani was remarkable: though a contemporary of al-Afghani, he had apparently not met him and was not familiar with his ideas when he formulated the essence of his own work. The figure and *oeuvre* of Danish are still poorly known; yet, one day it will be necessary to accord him the place he deserves, an essential place, in the history of Muslim reformist thought in the nineteenth century.

Simultaneously, in a certain fashion two other writers placed themselves in this perspective, but without ever attaining the depth of thought or the originality of Danish: Furqat (1858–1909) and Muqimiy (1850–1903). In the already critical climate of a Khoqand conquered by Russia, Zakirjan Furqat[26] analysed the reasons for this downfall in a quite considerable poetic *oeuvre*. Like Danish in Bukhara, Furqat indicted the régime of the former emirs, their excesses, and their exploitation of the masses; and proposed that his people, in order to bring its genius into line with the contemporary world, should draw its inspiration from victorious Russia. Actually, after the Russo-Japanese War — and although, on that occasion, Furqat violently assailed the excesses of English colonialism regarding India — Russia disappointed him; and this disappointment was to grow until his death. Nevertheless, at no time — either in the period of enthusiasm for and faith in Russia, or in the period of disenchantment when Furqat realized he no longer had a country other than the soles of his feet or a house other than ruins — did he broach the fundamental problems that Danish was already posing or call into question the actual bases of the community whose state of degradation he was judging. The debate, however poetic, had already been opened by others; but the solutions advocated (study of the Russian language and profound educational reform) justify citing Furqat among the minds who opened up Turkistan to the spirit of reform.

Such was also the case with Muqimiy (Muhammad 'Ali Khvaja Mirzakhvaja),[27] in whose popular poems denunciation of all past literary forms figured prominently. Through this criticism, Muqimiy concluded that the traditional Muslim world should be over-turned in its entirety.

As the first signs of reformism appeared in Turkistan towards the end of the century, the Tatar bourgeoisie long established in that region gave a real impetus to such vague tendencies, at first under cover of a movement in favour of a modernized, European-ized education. But in Turkistan Gasprinski and his disciples did not confine themselves to an educational activity: through their efforts, pan-Turkism also reached the region. Shortly after the Turkish revolution of 1876, Gasprinski published his famous pamphlet *Russkoe Musul'manstvo — mysli, zametki, o nablyudeniyakh Musul'manina*[28] (Russian Islam — thoughts and notes on a Muslim's observations), which really launched the Tatar reformist movement. This pamphlet was widely distributed, especially in Tashkent, Samarqand, and Bukhara. Similarly, during those years people in those towns read attentively various works by authors inspired by pan-Turkism — such as *Makhomet kak prorok* (Muhammad as the Prophet) by Devlet Kil'deev,[29] or *Otnoshenie Islama k nauke i k inovertsam* (The attitude of Islam towards science and the infidels) by *mudarris* Bajazitov[30] — which defended Muhammad and his teaching and asserted that far from being an inert force, it was a dynamic one that could move in the direction of history and progress.

But above all it was Gasprinski's paper *Tarjuman* that in this period overturned Turkistan's traditional structures of thought. In a report to the police department, the military governor of the Sir Darya noted how widely *Tarjuman* had penetrated throughout his region. He added that its diffusion was ensured both by Tatars living there and by the journeyings of Gasprinski, who carefully fostered his relations with the local bourgeoisie. Similar reports emanated from those in charge of the other regions of Turkistan; all were agreed in asserting that, in the absence of Turkistani publications of the same order, those administered by them (especially the merchants) felt considerable interest in the intellectual currents of which *Tarjuman* was the vehicle,[31] notably in the idea of pan-Turkism. Among other themes, *Tarjuman* advocated unification of all the Turkish peoples of Russia into a single nation; renunciation of the phonetic specificities of the languages of those peoples; extensive study of Arabic; a renewal of faith and even rejection of a certain religious formalism; the widest possible borrowings from European culture. Even before 1905, the links between Turkey and the Muslims of Russia were reinforced and the emergent bourgeoisie of Tashkent, Samarqand and Bukhara acquired the habit of turning towards that powerful Muslim country, where so many ideas appealing to the Turks under Russian dominance were freely expressed.

In Bukhara, the climate was somewhat different. The ideas of

Gasprinski and those arriving from Turkey were complemented by other external influences, among which that of Jamal al-Din al-Afghani was foremost. The Persian review *Qanun* (The Law), which he helped to found, made its way into Bukhara by the most varied routes.[32] On the one hand, pan-Islamism evoked a response in the emirate all the stronger in that it chimed with the aspirations of the authorities to assert the ruler's pre-eminent role in Islam. On the other hand, the ideas of pan-Turkism developed by Gasprinski were less seductive in Bukhara than elsewhere, for several reasons: Bukhara's sovereignty had survived the Russian advance; a national majority existed there, endowed with a pre-eminent role in the state; and, finally, the régime, mindful of its quasi-independent position and the humbled condition of the other Turkish peoples of Russia, viewed the notion of a fusion of all of them in its own particular way. At the end of the nineteenth century, the emir of Bukhara still considered himself 'the protector of the Muslims of Russia'; subsequently, he too would move towards a kind of pan-Turkism, but one based on Bukhara. What dominated people's minds in the emirate, then, was the preaching of Jamal al-Din al-Afghani: the idea of a rallying and regeneration of Muslims throughout the world.

One event helped to accentuate this orientation, specific to Bukhara, within the Muslim movement in Russia: the Andijan revolt in 1898. Ever since the conquest, anti-Russian agitation had sporadically made its appearance in Central Asia. It was almost always a question of religious movements which, going well beyond a precise territorial framework, appeared as did so many protests of the entire Muslim community against the infidel installed in the *dar al-islam*. Towards 1880 the Ferghana region was thus unsettled by religious elements known as *jeti-khans*. In 1885 the districts of Osh, Margelan, and Andijan were led to revolt by Darvish Khan Tura, a big landowner and official of the deposed khan, and it took a full-scale military expedition to crush the movement — whose leader was never captured. Subsequently, a relative calm was established, broken in 1895 by the arrest of a Naqshbandi *ishan* from Andijan, Isma'il Khan Tura, who while visiting his *murids* in Aulie-Ata was collecting funds to finance the holy war (*ghazavat*). He was released soon afterwards for lack of evidence and disappeared.

Finally, on 18 May 1898, the Andijan rebellion broke out and quickly spread to the districts of Osh, Namangan and Margelan. Once again, a Naqshbandi *ishan,* Muhammad 'Ali, headed the rebellion; he proclaimed the *ghazavat* and with 2,000 men marched upon Andijan, where he was routed by the Twentieth Turkistan Infantry Battalion. Muhammad 'Ali and his devotees were hanged; others sent to Siberia; and 546 conspirators stood trial. Muhammad 'Ali had enjoyed considerable popular support, the masses of Turkistan having rallied spontaneously to the slogan of re-establishment of the khanate of Khoqand and, above all, to the summons to a *ghazavat* against the infidel. As Terent'ev reports,[33] the aim was 'to drive the Russians out of Turkistan'.

During the trial of the leaders of the rebellion, the prosecution's principal objective was to make the defendants admit that, by proclaiming the *ghazavat* against the Russians, Muhammad 'Ali was 'executing the will of the Turkish Sultan, who by virtue of his spiritual authority over all Muslims throughout the world had to be obeyed'. In reality, however, what emerged from the proceedings went far beyond the Turkish plots that the prosecution wanted to establish. The *ghazavat* was not some dark conspiracy but a sacred obligation — of which the faithful had been reminded by Mohammad 'Ali's propaganda to rise up against the forces of the *dar al-harb* (land of war) which had penetrated the *dar al-islam* (land of Islam). In Bukhara the Andijan revolt met with a response that was all the greater because the emir, to oppose the Russians at the moment of the conquest, had already proclaimed the *ghazavat*.

For the ruler of Bukhara, for the spiritual authorities who surrounded him, and for the people, Muhammad 'Ali's struggle was merely a continuation of the one they had waged. In the emirate, already gravely troubled by awareness of a historic break, this virtually spontaneous revolt was viewed as an extension of the 1867 conflict, a reminder of the situation created since the infidels' invasion of Turkistan, and a summons to Turkistani and Islamic solidarity — a summons that carried special weight because Bukhara alone, having remained sovereign[34] and retained its social structures, could assume leadership of the movement taking shape around it.

Hastened perhaps by the Andijan crisis, the problem of the confrontation between Islam and the modern world was posed for the traditional authorities in Bukhara. The emir, whose external prestige and distance from the Russians were growing, thought it was in the emirate that a liberation of Turkistan should be effected.[35] He thus sought to preserve that which in his view gave the emirate its privileged position among the Islamic territories of Russia: its traditional social and political structures. Supported by the clergy, Emir 'Abd al-Ahad, albeit more liberal than his father, made himself the defender of an absolute conservatism, a conservatism in all domains: religious (where the position of the *qadimis* or traditionalists was not very different from that of the Wahhabis, in their pure and simple rejection of freedom of the *ijtihad*); political; and even social. All the tendencies to a reinforcement of despotism and social stratification, which had appeared at the time of the conquest, were now accentuated.

Despite these difficulties and a gnawing concern which elsewhere (Andijan, for example) were expressed by spontaneous explosions, the masses failed to react, since the *qadimi*'s beliefs had very solid popular roots.[36] Accustomed to respect traditional Islam, the masses in Bukhara paid more attention to the Andijan revolt than they did to the first attempts at reform (confined to the educational field), which appeared in Bukhara at the turn of the century. Although they failed, these attempts nevertheless produced some remarkable effects. In the *madrasas* the discussions which had broken out after Kursavi was sentenced to death, and which Danish had subsequently revived, now continued actively, with every attempt to open a reformed *maktab* meeting with a passionate response.[37] Among the mullas themselves appeared a number of advocates of religious educational reform. But, in the first years of the twentieth century important events convulsed the internal and external life of Russia and had deep repercussions upon the Muslim peoples of the tsarist empire. Because of these events, the crisis of conscience through which Bukhara was passing finally assumed a definite form. The reformist tendencies came together in a movement founded upon a social base, with leaders, an ideology, objectives, and supporters.

Part II

In Search of an Ideology, 1900–17

4

National Awakening
in Turkistan

The years 1904 and 1905 were exceptionally difficult for the Russian empire. In 1904 the empire, apparently strong and victorious, was defeated by Japan. This defeat was significant not only for Russia, but also the world: it was the first time for many centuries that a conquering power from the Christian West had collapsed before a non-white people. This event was experienced as a true revenge by all colonial peoples, then just becoming aware of their humiliation. Throughout the Orient, news of the Russian defeat was passed from mouth to mouth, commented upon, and surrounded with hopes.[1] The Muslims within the Russian empire followed the event even more passionately, since it concerned their own conqueror. Ostroumov observed how all the admiration felt by Turkistani schoolchildren visiting the empire's capital disappeared, as soon as the Russian military disasters were announced.[2] A few years later, an observer noted that what had decisively marked the political awakening of Bukhara's Uzbek tribes, far removed as they were from all outside influences, was the Russo-Japanese War.[3]

From that moment on, Russia's Muslims envisaged a possible end to colonial domination. All the rancours and problems which racked the empire's Muslim periphery were linked to the dream that was suddenly taking shape: the dream of independence. The 1905 revolution further accelerated this awakening of national consciousness among Russia's Muslims. The hopes it aroused and the liberal ideas that then circulated for two years changed everything in the Muslim periphery. Ideas of political and social reform developed and gave new force to the aspirations of the native intelligentsia. When the hour of reaction came in Russia, it was doubly felt by Muslims: it assailed not only liberal ideas but also their own national awakening; but by doing so it gave this awakening a new impetus.

71

The 1905 Revolution in Turkistan

The indigenous Turkistani population took no part in the revolutionary unrest of the years 1905–7, though in the guberniya this
took the form of extremely violent clashes. In Turkistan, revolutionary developments were helped by the presence of deported
Russian social-democrats. According to very incomplete information,[4] in 1903 there were 59 political deportees in the
guberniya, and by 1906 this figure had risen to 377. A number of
these were social-democrats who, from the moment they arrived,
entered into contact with working-class circles, especially railwaymen and printers.

In Turkistan the revolution was an undeniably Russian phenomenon: almost everywhere, except in Azarbayjan, Russia's
Muslims remained outside the revolution. But in Turkistan —
which seemed isolated from the movement of liberal ideas,
whether those of the 1905 Russian Revolution or those which
inspired attempts to unite the empire's Muslims — this apparent
indifference to the revolution was particularly striking. At all
events, it strongly impressed the Russian authorities;[5] they concluded it had to be a result of weak development of the spirit of
reform, and to the traditional spirit of the *maktabs* and *madrasas,*
that the native masses and intelligentsia were so uninterested in
events taking place on their own soil.[6]

Peasant Movements after 1905

For all this, the one non-Russian region upon which the 1905
Russian Revolution left a really deep impression it was Turkistan,
where, from then on, growing unrest was to penetrate the way of
life of the peasantry and foster national and reformist ideas. The
peasant movements of the late nineteenth century received an
abrupt stimulus from the 1905 Revolution, while their form was
modified. The sporadic risings of the nineteenth century gave way
to organized banditry in the twentieth. By 1905 bands of brigands
had appeared almost everywhere in Turkistan. Their attacks multiplied until 1908, increasing by 83 per cent in the year 1905 alone,
though subsequently they did diminish somewhat. Some of these
groups were organically linked to the rural population (the villages
seem to have delegated members occasionally for operations of
this kind); others were made up of individuals who 'took to the
hills' and joined quite organized groups. To this last category

belonged the legendary Namaz,[7] who plundered the Samarqand region in the years 1906–7. With paid informers everywhere, since his coffers were bulging, he was warned immediately of any troop movement, of any convoy of money or goods, and of any threat to him that might be impending. Namaz was the object of approval: he had the reputation of being a protector of the weak; a disinterested robber who redistributed the wealth he 'confiscated' to the poor; a dispenser of justice; and a national hero.[8]

Whether closely linked to peasant life or separate from it, these bands of brigands had in common (as the authorities saw it) an astonishing ability to merge with the population. The archives of the guberniya testify to this:[9]

> We may comb the entire Ferghana and nowhere find the least band of brigands; yet since 1905 banditry is endemic there. In the reports from the authorities in the *uezds*, it is a striking fact that neither the leaders nor the members of these bands are ever found. Once the attack has been committed, the band disperses and mingles with the surrounding population. Before long, another attack occurs and there is no sign that the same band is involved; on the contrary, these attacks seem to have no connection with one another.

Little was known of these bands, made up usually of between four and six members. However, some interesting information is available about their social origin. A document from the guberniya archives — where a great deal of anxious attention was paid to this problem — was explicit:[10] 'The fundamental cause of banditry lies, in all probability, in the growth of a landless proletariat.' What was the case in Bukhara was true for Turkistan as a whole: Russian penetration had, in effect, brought about a concentration of holdings in the hands of rich usurers or, in some regions, Russian farmers; deprived of their plots of land, however small these might be, the poorest peasants banded together and became brigands.

But this solution, far from excluding them from the community, kept them within it by conferring upon them a certain prestige. These impoverished peasants — who at first, as in the extreme case of Namaz, represented the protest of the dispossessed and, albeit confusedly, expressed the general aspiration to a certain social justice — subsequently made up the popular base of the Basmachi movement. For their protest, which was quite naturally voiced against the Russians who appeared to be responsible for the situation that had produced them,[11] quickly took on the character of a protest that was not only social, but also national. This is why the closest attention must be paid to those forms of spontaneous, unorganized protest by the peasant masses of Turkistan after 1905. Whereas in the years 1905–16 this peasant movement seems totally independent from the reformist ideology, which the Turkistani intelligentsia was to discover, in the years of the revolution the two currents were to re-merge, the peasant protest movement furnishing troops for the national demands of the intelligentsia. Tables 4.1 and 4.2 illustrate the bonds that existed between banditry and the political evolution of the Russian empire.[12]

Table 4.1
Bandit Attacks by Region in Turkistan, 1899–1917

Year	Ferghana	Samarqand	Trans-Caspia	Sir-Darya	Semirechye	Total
1899	16	9		6	19	50
1900	39	8		14	14	75
1901	45	22		10	18	95
1902	51	33		24	12	121
1903	49	37		9	13	108
1904	71	31	7	17	4	130
1905	144	34	18	30	9	235
1906	111	59	24	33	5	232
1907	135	90	41	57	23	346
1908	161	101	77	52	9	400
1909	213	75	31	19	21	359
1910	151	124	27	24	8	334
1911	107	56	42	25	7	237
1912	136	35	59	31	39	300
1913	150	39	66	27	22	304
1914	103	98	64	12	18	295
1915	109	166	69	8	20	372
1916	104	151	79	[e]	18	382
1917	324[a]	47[b]	171[c]	[e]	5[d]	547
Total	2,249	1,215	775	398	285	4,922

Notes: [a] Obtained in the first eight months of 1917.
[b] Figures correspond to only four months.
[c] For only ten and a half months.
[d] For the two first months.
[e] No figures available.
Source: Galuzo, Turkestan, Koloniya, p. 93.

In the years 1905–16, however, what was involved was still an unorganized movement, independent of the ideas then spreading through Turkistan. The peasants who rose up were protesting against their poverty and against the Russian administration.[12] Table 4.2 outlines the development of these conflicts with the administration:[13]

Table 4.2
Clashes with the Administration, 1901–15

	1901–5	1906–10	1911–15	Total
Bloody clashes with authorities	17	40	30	87
Russian officials attacked	19	44	55	118
wounded	6	16	25	47
killed	10	18	10	38
unhurt	3	10	20	33
Mass operations	3	2	8	13

Source: See Table 4.1.

In 1899 a single, harmless instance of a clash between native peasants and administrators had been recorded; in 1900, none; after that there were no further years without their quota. These apparently low figures are very remarkable if two circumstances are taken into account: first, Table 4.1 (bandit operations) and 4.2 (clashes with the administration) should be added together; and second, in both cases the Russian administration did not take ordinary criminal acts into account, but merely operations that struck it as being of an unusual nature and connected with a recent transformation of social relations in Turkistan. As the Palen Commission had stressed,[14] it was a question of new phenomena arising out of the dispossession of the peasants. Two other things are highlighted by these tables: on the one hand (Table 4.1), the scale of the movement in Ferghana, where the Basmachi movement developed after the 1917 Revolution; on the other hand, the increase in mass operations against the administration and the proliferation of attacks on officials in the years preceding the 1916 revolt. Both of these are solid indications of the increasingly emphatic refusal of the native peasant masses to bow to Russian demands. The archives of the guberniya bulge with reports that illuminate the essential features of these events.[15]

Sometimes it was a question of refusing some external mark of respect for the Russian authorities, sometimes of protesting against excessive taxes, and often of opposing the settlement of Russian colonists. Sometimes, learning that colonists were about to settle on confiscated irrigated land, the peasants would collect armed with sticks to drive them away; settlement of the colonists generally had to be postponed to such time as a good escort was available.[16] All such explosions, like the attacks, were included under the single heading of 'crimes against public order'. Although in Bukhara there were no grounds for protesting against a Russian administration, the discontent of the peasants was no less nor were the sporadic revolts less frequent. Unfortunately such revolts were scarcely catalogued, but the political agent's reports suggested that they followed more or less the same graph as in Turkistan.[17] In the eastern part of the emirate, dispossessed peasants often went off to join bands in the guberniya.[18] In the years 1905–10, the political agent's reports referred constantly to bloody explosions in the provinces of Sujnan, Rushan, and Vakhan; and to the local authorities' pleas to the Russian forces to crush those explosions.[19] As a result of these frequent interventions of the Russian forces against the peasants of Bukhara, the two important peasant risings that were to shake the emirate on the eve of the 1916 revolt (the Shirabad rising in 1915 and the Qishlaq Ayvaj rising in 1916) were organized immediately and directed clearly against the Russians.[20]

The Russian authorities considered this constant agitation with growing mistrust and, in 1908, concluded that an emergency situation prevailed in Turkistan, tantamount to a state of war.

First Political Experiences

Although Turkistan's parliamentary experience was short-lived and limited — here again the Turkistanis remained effectively apart from the political activity of Russia's Muslims — it was nonetheless important, in that at first it aroused great hopes for change, now that the Turkistanis had the possibility of making their voice heard — frustrated hopes, however, since they were absent from the first Duma.[21] In the Second Duma, Turkistan had five representatives,[22] all conservatives with the exception of Mulla 'Abd al-Qari (Kariev); they contented themselves with supporting unquestioningly the positions of the Muslim majority that came from the *Ittifaq al-Muslimin* (Muslim Union), allied to the Constitutional-Democrats.[23] At the same time as he dissolved the Second Duma on 3 June 1907, Nicholas II published a manifesto modifying the existing electoral laws. As a result of its turbulence — the 'state of war' that prevailed there — Turkistan was deprived of all representation.[24]

This brief experience of parliament, however, was coupled with the experience of an organized national demand, which the Turkistanis made on their own and which was likewise the fruit of the 1905 Revolution. After the imperial message of 17 October 1905, representatives of the privileged classes of Turkistan (ecclesiastics, intellectuals, and big bourgeois living in the vicinity of the Russian administration) decided to launch a joint action aimed at winning recognition of equal rights for Turkistanis and Russians. In March 1906 a meeting took place in Tashkent, during which the following demands were formulated: religious freedom; inviolability of land ownership; the restoration of pastures to expropriated nomads; and, above all, the creation of a Muslim religious administration (*Musulman Dini Idarasi*) in Tashkent.[25] These demands remained a dead letter; but the Turkistanis had begun, somewhat belatedly, to take part in an organized manner in the demands of the empire's other Muslims.

Thus, the years marked by the Russo-Japanese War and the 1905 Revolution had, all in all, modified the situation in Turkistan. At the margin of the activity of Russia's Muslims, Turkistan gradually came to experience the upheavals that characterized the empire's Muslims.

In Bukhara the repercussions of this were great, since Turkistan's experience of parliament had also engendered a parliamentary dream there. The idea that gradually took hold of the emirate's intelligentsia was one of participating in power by way of some representation, however limited; of going beyond the restricted limits of the *'ulama* council.[26] Furthermore, popular reactions in the emirate were reinforced by the existence of similar reactions in Russia and by the realization that Russian power could no longer entirely control them.

5

Beginnings of Reformism
in Bukhara

Describing his homeland as it was in 1905, Fayzallah Khvaja-ughli (Khodzhaev), who became one of the main leaders of Bukhara's reform movement, wrote:

> Bukhara was a living anachronism. A land situated in the depths of Central Asia, away from the communication routes of the modern world, but at the hub of the great routes of Antiquity; with an illiterate population, but one which was everywhere confronted by traces of the prestigious Arabo-Persian civilization that was now only a memory; anachronistic too were the despotism of the Emir and all the structures of tyranny artificially preserved and protected by Russian bayonets. That was the Emirate of Bukhara for you.

Not coincidentally, Khodzhaev 'photographed' the emirate in 1905, at the exact moment when Bukhara discovered modern reformism. As everywhere in the Muslim world, reformism there was primarily an expression of the general anxiety about Islam's inability to confront the problems of the modern world. Religious reform and reform of education — such were the first undertakings upon which the movement embarked in Bukhara, where it took the name Jadid (from *usul-i jadid*, 'new method [of teaching]'), which shows how fundamental the issue of schooling initially was. But the Jadids quickly realized that the crisis of Islam in the twentieth century was a crisis of Islamic society as a whole, the solution to which demanded a total recasting of social, and consequently political, relations. The Jadids then became the Young Bukharans, for whom the model was Turkey. Until 1909 the reformist movement of Bukhara was inspired by the Tatars, who there, as throughout Turkistan, furnished the new ideas.

The Central Asian Press in the Emirate

For some years, the emirate's intelligentsia had been reading and commenting on Gasprinski's newspaper *Tarjuman*. Accustomed to receiving liberal ideas from the Tatars, in the wake of 1905 it quite naturally imported other organs published by the Tatars in Russia: *Ulfat* (Reconciliation) from St Petersburg, *Yulduz* (The Star) from Kazan, and *Irshad* (The Guide) from Baku. But its attention was soon drawn to newspapers published in Turkistan (first by Tatars, then by Uzbeks), which in Bukhara had a wide audience among the intellectual élite, though the masses, who scarcely read any papers, indignantly termed them 'babi newspapers' and accused their readers of turning to Babism.

The earliest of these papers was *Taraqqi* (Progress),[2] founded in 1906 at Tashkent by a Tatar Socialist-Revolutionary, Isma'il 'Abidi, who with the aid of the Russian Orientalists Vyatkin and Nalivkin, produced a paper that was highly critical of the tsarist administration, demanding reforms and defending the idea of the national unity of Turkistan. A Jadid organ, but also close to the ideas of the Socialist-Revolutionaries, *Taraqqi* disappeared after seventeen issues, the government having judged it to be seditious.[3] Stimulated by this example, Uzbek Jadids also published three newspapers in this period: *Khurshid, Shuhrat,* and *Tujjar.*

Khurshid (The Sun), founded by Munavvar Qari 'Abd al-Rashid Khan-ughli (Abdurrashidov) in 1906,[4] bore on its masthead the following information: 'Organ of the Muslims published twice- or thrice-weekly in the Turkish language, a scientifico-literary and politico-social organ.' In fact, it was published fairly irregularly and disappeared in November 1906. Munavvar Qari replaced it by *Shuhrat* (Glory), which appeared from the end of 1907 to the spring of 1908 with the same staff; and when this was banned he substituted for it an organ whose name alone was different — *Asiya* (Asia) — which had five issues.

Tujjar (Merchants) was the creation of one of the wealthiest men in Tashkent, Mir Sayyid 'Azimbay (Azimbaev),[5] who devoted a large part of his activity and his fortune to an attempt to interest the Russian authorities in the transformation of the intellectual and social structures of Turkistan. His newspaper, 'appearing two or three times a week in an Islamic language, a political and social national organ', soon disappeared for want of readers.[6]

So, within a short while, there was no Turkistani press left. Nevertheless, however ephemeral and irregular it may have been, it existed for long enough to bring to Turkistan echoes of the 1905 Russian Revolution and its liberal ideas. Furthermore, it had the merit of gathering a concrete enterprise of men who felt themselves united by the same, still confused, national aspirations and who felt obliged to set out, clarify, and coordinate their ideas. In the light of the activity in those years of men like Munavvar Qari, Bihbudi, or Azimbaev, it is impossible to accept unreservedly the following judgement of Barthold: 'The Turkistan press existed for only two years (1906–8) and was entirely in the hands of Volga Tatars'.[7]

These newspapers defended more or less the same ideas. The evolution of their demands between 1905 and 1908 was an exact reflection of the degradation of the liberal climate in Russia in the same years. If *Taraqqi,* the first of them, had been able to combat both tsarist power and the conservatism of the Muslim religious authorities, *Khurshid* was already more prudent on this last point; for, in the meantime, the Russian authorities in the guberniya had given the Muslim hierarchy of Central Asia credit for its followers' calm attitude during the revolutionary days, after which it became hard to attack it. In its sixth issue, dated 11 October 1906,[8] *Khurshid* published under Bihbudi's signature a real programme for the Jadids of Turkistan: this advocated joining the Muslim Union (*Ittifaq al-Muslimin*) and eventual support for the Constitutional-Democratic Party; it also attacked the Russian autocracy and its colonial policy. But with the ebb of revolution, freedom of expression was constantly reduced and the Jadid organs clung desperately to the sole possibility still accorded them to exist politically in the empire: the Duma. When *Khurshid* was banned, Munavvar Qari wrote to the governor-general of Turkistan as follows: 'The aim of our organ was simply to make the native population understand the Duma's activity, and its significance; also, in a reasonable way, to prepare the population for the coming elections . . . My intention was not to propagate any kind of anti-governmental idea, but to strive with all my power to calm electoral passions, to prepare serene and useful elections.'[9]

Shuhrat also followed this line and demanded, within the confines of the Muslim community, that spiritual purity be preserved by educating the high clergy away from all compromise with the West (*Shuhrat* advocated sending students to Bukhara, Istanbul, Cairo, and Alexandria because these were relatively independent Islamic lands). Concerning relations with Russia, *Shuhrat* not only placed high hopes in the legal possibilities for action that the Duma opened, but also expected much from the possibility of the Russian presence (from the Russian schools, basically) transforming Turkistan.

The position of *Tujjar* was different, since Sayyid Azimbaev unreservedly advocated cooperation with Russia; but the result was disappointing for him. The Russian authorities still suspected him of wanting to play too important a personal role,[10] while his paper lacked Uzbek readers, perhaps because he did not sufficiently respond to their national aspirations.

This passionate interest in the Duma and the possibilities for legal action found a considerable echo in Bukhara, among still barely formed groups of intellectuals, who had no means in the emirate of expressing their demands or of participating, even from afar, in the transformation they desired.

Finally, an additional theme was present everywhere in the publications of Turkistan: reform of Islam. Criticism of the ossified, scholastic Islam of the first years of the twentieth century was aimed primarily at Bukhara, the great spiritual centre. This deeply affected all those in the emirate who felt the need for a change in the ways of thinking of Islam. On this point, the Russian authorities helped to bring the Jadids into conflict with the conservative Muslim authorities through a brutal intervention favouring the conservatives. The reformers in Turkistan always attempted to win over the entire Muslim clergy for their struggle; but the warnings of the Russian authorities against any attack aimed at the clergy — warnings that were echoed in the Jadid newspapers — made a poor impression upon the conservative clergy, especially in Bukhara.

When, in 1908, the Turkistani newspapers disappeared — and the suppression of Turkistani seats in the Duma gave the Russian authorities an excellent pretext for banning papers that linked the justification of their existence to the parliamentary representation of Turkistan — the political vision of the intelligentsia and to a lesser degree the masses was no longer the same. These papers had carried discussion of a reform of Islam outside the confined circle of the *madrasas*. They had established clearly that all their endeavour was carried out within and for the community, to restore it to its past greatness and independence. They had brought to the attention of a broader audience not only the ideas of the reformers, but also those of Russian liberals and the echo of the revolution. They had expressed the general hope for political reform: the stress placed by them upon the Duma had engendered, or developed, the idea both of a representation of the élites in the ruling order and of a place accorded to the non-Russian nations in the empire that had conquered them. Having first aroused a popular political consciousness, these newspapers had given a resonance to the 30 June 1907 law depriving Turkistan of its representatives, which, without them, it would perhaps not have had. Public opinion in Bukhara shared the general emotion: after all, it was the Turkistanis who were frustrated and Bukhara was the heart of Turkistan.[11] Finally, these newspapers raised issues of educational reform throughout the emirate, which had the effect of giving the backing of an organized movement to the reformist idea.

The First Reformed Schools

The reform of Muslim education in Russia was the work of the Tatar Isma'il Bay Gasprinski. First, Gasprinski advocated adopting the system of phonetic reading and introducing secular subjects into school curricula. Since he had opened a reformed *maktab* (primary school) at the end of the nineteenth century at Baghchesaray, the issue of transforming and adapting the traditional pedagogy was posed for all the Russian empire's Muslims. The Tatars played an important role: in the last years of the nineteenth century, they began to open a number of reformed *maktabs* for their children in Central Asia (Andijan, 1897; and Samarqand and Tokmak, 1898[12]). In 1900 Munavvar Qari Abdurrashidov, who had studied in Turkey, opened the first Uzbek reformed school at Tashkent and accepted young Uzbeks and no longer Tatars.[13]

In Bukhara there was no school reform until 1900. The first attempts were the work of Tatars, Russian subjects settled in the emirate, and were intended for their children. In 1900, Mulla Jora Bay thus opened a school in the village of Pustinduzan, near the capital. He announced that he was certain his pupils would make spectacular progress within four or five months; but this hope was disappointed, since in a few months the school found itself entirely deserted; and having no pupils, it closed its gates.[14] Yet the idea that a reform of education was necessary was catching on. Two years later, in the Russian town of Novaya Bukhara, a Tatar called Kaypov, who ran a traditional *maktab* frequented by Tatar children, transformed it into a reformed school.[15] He too failed; but his successors — Mulla Niyaz Sabir-ughli (Sabitov) and Burnash-ughli (Burnashev), also Tatars — were luckier in 1907: still in Novaya Bukhara (extra-territorial status made things much easier), they opened a reformed school where teaching was in the Tatar language.

The following year in Bukhara, Sabitov and Burnashev opened a new reformed *maktab* and, with Gasprinski, who had come to study the problem in the emirate's capital, envisaged admitting young Uzbeks. They wanted to ask the emir for official assistance and, above all, for suitable premises. Its founders wished to call this school Isma'iliyya, in honour of Gasprinski; but Gasprinski suggested, diplomatically, dedicating it to the emir's late father; accordingly, Gasprinski negotiated for the establishment of the Muzaffariyya in personal interviews with Emir 'Abd al-Ahad, who was said to be attracted by these new schools.[16] Eventually, however, after long hesitation, the emir gave Gasprinski a negative response. In the meantime, the *'ulama* had presented the *qush-begi* with a *rivayat* in which they opposed the creation of such a school, which was contrary, in their opinion, to the *shari'at*. But this *rivayat* had been approved by only a fairly slender majority of the *'ulama*, since their assembly was divided on the issue. Burnashev eventually established the school in his home, but admitted only a few Uzbek pupils.

The project of Burnashev and Sabitov to extend the new education to the children of the emirate was not their own; it was based on a wish recently expressed by the local mercantile bourgeoisie. From the reformist newspapers it had been reading for two years, this bourgeoisie had come to know the aims, methods, and evolution of the reformed education and wished such schools to be established for its own children. After the events of the years 1905–7, it began to feel an urgent need for changes in this domain; it had followed with interest the attempt to create Tatar reformed schools; and the projects of Sabitov and Burnashev had brought it high hopes.[17] Though disappointed by the refusal which 'Abd al-Ahad had meted out to Gasprinski, this bourgeoisie had not renounced that idea; indeed its pressure, along with divisions among the religious authorities, led the emir to alter his decision.[18]

Perhaps there was also an intervention in this direction by the Russian political agent. Although in Turkistan the Russian authorities — seeing in them the germ of ideas hostile to Russia (liberal and pan-Turk) and believing in the politically conservative value of the traditional education — were hostile to the reformed schools, [19] in Bukhara the problem was posed in different terms. The Russian authorities considered that the Bukharan clergy was extremely fanatical and that it was setting the Muslims against them. So they were not hostile to anything that might weaken it. Just as they had thought it a good idea to develop a quality education in Russian Turkistan to compete with the clergy of Bukhara, so too the reformed schools seemed to them capable perhaps of playing this role in the emirate. The place accorded to the Russian language in certain reformed establishments also seemed to them a way of weakening 'fanaticism', a term which the political agent applied to any anti-Russian manifestation.

So, under these various pressures, Emir 'Abd al-Ahad in October 1908 authorized the opening of a reformed school for the children of his subjects, where the teaching took place in Persian.[20] Run by an untried master, Mirza 'Abd al-Vahidov, who with Sabitov's help quickly improved his teaching, the reformed school was soon able to bear comparison with the Tatar school. In the spring of 1909, the Tatar school organized public examinations to show the effectiveness of its methods. The representatives of the Bukharan authorities who attended recognized this and in recognition of its high level, it finally received larger premises; but it remained reserved for Tatar children only.

Galvanized by this example, in the autumn of 1909 Mirza 'Abd al-Vahidov also organized public examinations, to which he invited all the spiritual and civil authorities of the emirate: the *qush-begi* and *qazi-kalan* were represented by their closest collaborators; but the high clergy of Bukhara was conspicuous by its absence. The only religious dignitary present was an enthusiastic partisan of reform, Damulla Ikram,[21] who loudly proclaimed the virtues of the new education and the high level of the pupils of the first Bukharan reformed *maktab*. Damulla Ikram asserted that the instruction given in these *maktabs* was not contrary to the Prophet's teaching and that no objection to its development was valid in religious terms.

The previous year, when the muftis had discussed the problem of the reformed school and had produced the *rivayat* that put an end to Gasprinski's endeavours, the debate had taken place only among the most eminent clerics. After the public examinations of October 1909 and the declarations of Damulla Ikram, the debate was broadened and was carried on wherever the Bukharan intelligentsia congregated; in this way, it had a considerable resonance. Two tendencies were ranged against one another. On the one hand, the demonstration by Mirza 'Abd al-Vahidov was conclusive that his method should be adopted without delay; new reformed *maktabs* should be created; or, better still, existing *maktabs* should be reformed. On the other hand, the traditionalist clergy, seeing its educational work indicted in this way, reacted against the threat to its positions by accusing the new school of being a challenge to the *shari'at* and its defenders of being bad Muslims. An extraordinary attack was launched against Damulla Ikram, because he favoured using paraffin lighting in mosques. Was the author of such a heresy entitled to maintain the conformity or non-conformity of the reformed teaching with the *shari'at*?[22] The argument was brought before the emir, who once again took the side of the conservatives and ordered the school to be closed.

Feelings ran high in the Uzbek bourgeoisie and the enrolments flooded in daily to the banned school. The Tatar school then decided to accept fifty Uzbek children enrolled in Mirza 'Abd al-Vahidov's school, but this arrangement was greeted with indignation by the conservatives[23] and did nothing to enhance Tatar influence. This influence was then experiencing a certain decline in Bukhara, whose intelligentsia was turning its eyes, in those last months of 1909, towards a Turkey in which the Young Turks had installed a new order. The closure of the Tatar school seems to have been demanded at this moment by the whole clergy. The *qush-begi* Astanqul Bay had no difficulty in obtaining the agreement of the emir, who at the time was grappling with the bloody dispute between Sunnis and Shi'a: the school was closed. The Tatar masters and a few Bukharan intellectuals close to them appealed to Gasprinski, who broadened the dispute by publishing in *Tarjuman* an article entitled 'Appeal to the mullas of Bukhara', while *Mulla Nasr al-Din*[24] filled its pages with caricatures of those 'reactionaries'.

Thus, during the period in which reformist ideas penetrated Bukhara, the specific role of the local intelligentsia was limited. It may be judged that the impetus was provided by Tatars and favoured by the existence of Russian enclaves where the Tatars could more freely introduce the press of Central Asia and establish a school. Nevertheless, quite early on, reformism assumed certain particular features in Bukhara and developed there swiftly. In order to understand it, the reformed *maktabs* must be examined more closely.

The first peculiarity of reformed education in Bukhara was linguistic. In principle, by contrast with the traditional *maktabs* in which teaching took place in Arabic, the reformed education was based on the use of the native tongue. But in practice, since the Tatars were the first to implement this kind of education and were numerous in Central Asia and since their language was more or less accessible to most of the inhabitants, they gained recognition as teachers; and in Central Asia the reformed education was initially in the Tatar language. The same was true in Bukhara in the first schools. When the problem arose of creating a reformed school for Uzbek children, use of the emirate's language of civilization, Persian, was envisaged: in Mirza 'Abd al-Vahidov's school, teaching took place in this language.[25]

The hostility of the *qadimi* clergy to the new education was based not only on this linguistic aspect. The dispute between Damulla Ikram and the traditionalists led by Damulla 'Abd al-Rafiq showed that the reformed education constituted an indictment as much of the organization of schooling as of its content. The first argument of the *qadimis* against the reformed education was its 'non-Islamic' form, on the Russian or European model. The children suddenly found themselves on benches, in front of desks, and reading and writing all together. For centuries, the Muslim child, seated on the ground, had received an individual tuition.[26] According to the *qadimis* of Bukhara, the new forms borrowed from Europe, like the use of the phonetic method, were real infringements of the integrity of the rules of Islam. The second point in the traditionalist critique was that the religious teaching given in the reformed *maktabs* was a deformation of the true teaching of religion; furthermore, the presence in the curriculum of certain profane notions — such as arithmetic, geography, and above all the natural sciences — was absolutely contrary to the Muslim tradition and order.

In fact, the education given in the reformed *maktabs* was far from representing a common curriculum. In the schools of the Crimea, Kazan, Ufa, or Orenburg, alongside purely religious subjects, the study of profane disciplines came close to what it was in Russian institutions. In Turkistan, this was not the case. The reformed *maktabs* gave pride of place to religion, followed by the study of subjects necessary to economic relations with Europe, especially Russia (arithmetic, reading and writing in the Uzbek or Persian language, geography, and a few elements of physics and chemistry). The most thoroughgoing of the reformed schools of Central Asia, that of Munavvar Qari Abdurrashidov, illustrates that, despite the anxieties expressed by the *qadimis*, religion lost none of its rights there. In the fifth year of study, for instance, the distribution of lessons was as follows: eleven hours (or 44 per cent of the total timetable), were devoted to purely religious subjects; and nine hours to reading and copying works dealing with Muslim ethics. Only the five remaining hours (from a weekly timetable of twenty-five) were divided between arithmetic (two hours), geography (two hours), and the exact sciences (one hour); this last hour did not include natural science and had no proper textbook.

In Bukhara, of course, the innovators were even less free than Munavvar Qari; secular education was consequently even more limited. In the course of time, the *maktabs* of Turkistan evolved like the Tatar *maktabs* in the direction of according a larger place to secular education (in 1915 Munavvar Qari added the study of Arabic and Persian grammar). But those in charge of Bukhara's schools were still so closely supervised by the *qadimis* that any progress in this direction was practically impossible for them. This perhaps explains the fact that, whereas in the guberniya the leaders of the reformist movement often remained, up to the revolution, attached to the task of educational reform, in Bukhara their equivalents moved increasingly over to political action and were convinced by the obvious truths that the structures of the emirate hampered any development; that it was not enough to train an élite better adapted to the world of the twentieth century; and that, in any case, in the existing intellectual framework and political structures such a training could in itself resolve nothing.

The problem of school textbooks had very great consequences for the future of the reformist movement in Bukhara, because of the solution that was given it. Often, in the reformed *maktabs* of Russia, use was made of Tatar textbooks translated and adapted from Russian; or again, as Munavvar Qari did, of the manuals prepared by Gramenickii for Russo-native schools.[27] So, in the reading primers and textbooks used in these schools, phrases could be found of which the Russian authorities obviously approved, such as 'Fear God, respect the Tsar'; 'The Tsar's will is an obligation for all his subjects'; 'Our Tsar of Russia is more powerful than many other tsars'.[28]

In Bukhara, in the only non-Tatar reformed *maktab* that existed before 1910, such propositions were hardly thinkable, so the printing of textbooks had to be organized. For this purpose, some representatives of the Bukharan intelligentsia, who felt the need for a regroupment, founded the association *Shirkat-i Bukhara-yi Sharif* (Union of Bukhara the Noble) which had the aim of procuring books for the reformed schools. On that day, reformism took a giant step forward in Bukhara. Until then, it had been the product of Tatar initiatives or else of isolated ones.[29] By joining together in this grouping, with its still modest aims, men like 'Usman Khvaja-ughli (Khodzhaev), Ahmadjan Makhdum, Mirza 'Abd al-Vahidov,

Hajji Rafiq, Sadr al-Din 'Ayni, the millionaire Mansurov, and the no less wealthy Fazl al-Din Makhdum gave an organized framework to the still barely articulated reformist aspirations. They thus laid the foundations of the subsequently organized party of Young Bukharans.

The leaders of *Shirkat-i Bukhara-yi Sharif* were concerned above all to have textbooks printed on the presses of the newspaper *Vaqt* (The Time) in Orenburg and to send missions to obtain information outside concerning the methods of the reformed education, its advances, and the evolution of reformist ideas in general. Hamid Khodzhaev Mihri and 'Usman Khodzhaev went first to Baghche-saray — to visit Gasprinski's school and discuss with him — then to Constantinople. 'Ayni and Ahmad Makhdum travelled to Samarqand to see Munavvar Qari and visited Bihbudi, one of the intellectual guides of Turkistani reformism.[30] Though on a voyage of enquiry, these travellers also proclaimed to the outside world that in the emirate there now existed an organized group within which the reformist spirit found expression.

Infinitely more belated than Russia's other reformist movements, within a short space of time it became the best organized and structured. Like their brethren from Kazan or Turkistan, the Jadids of Bukhara had the luck to have among them some very rich merchants, who took care of the movement's material life. Mansurov especially, whose children were among the first to be enrolled in Mirza 'Abd al-Vahidov's school, placed his substantial fortune at their disposal.

The existence of an organized group, however small, gave a considerable force and concrete character to ideas that were still ill-formed. This group was created at the moment when, outside Bukhara, two events helped to orient the Jadids, consolidate them, and give them support. Iran and especially Turkey had made revolutions whose aims were those for which the Jadids were fighting. Although the language of culture in Bukhara was still Persian at that time, it was nevertheless towards Turkey that the Jadids turned for a model and for assistance. A Muslim and Turkish country had realized their dream of reform. Previously hesitant, having difficulty in formulating their aspirations, not going beyond the confines of educational reform, and trailing in the wake of their Tatar masters, the Jadids in 1909 turned resolutely towards Turkey and took the Young Turks as a model. The page of their gropings was slowly being turned; the history of the Young Bukharans was about to begin.[31]

6

Era of the Secret
Societies, 1910–14

The Religious Conflict of 1910

The year 1910 opened in Bukhara with a tragedy: a clash between the two main religious groups of the emirate, the Sunnis and the Shi'a. This tragedy had the effect of propelling the reformist movement, then being organized, to the front of the stage. The events were simple: during the Shi'i ceremonies of the *shahsay-vahsay* in Kagan,[1] some students from Bukhara invaded the site of the commemoration, made jokes of various kinds,[2] and mocked the martyr and his devotees. The outraged worshippers seized and manhandled the students; one of them was killed. This was the signal for a general massacre of Shi'a in and outside the capital, in every region where Sunnis were in a majority, that is, throughout western Bukhara. Emir 'Abd al-Ahad was away from Bukhara at the time and absolutely refused to return and intervene in the conflict. It was Russian troops under General Lilienthal who re-established order.[3]

What was the real cause of these events? Until the beginning of the twentieth century, Shi'a and Sunnis had lived in peace in the main towns of the emirate. Sunnis often attended Shi'i ceremonies, especially on the occasion of the commemoration of Husayn's martyrdom,[4] and never had this event aroused hostility or jibes. In the first years of the century, relations between Sunnis and Shi'a turned sour for political reasons. Emir 'Abd al-Ahad, concerned like his predecessors Nasrallah and Muzaffar to undermine the authority of the great Uzbek tribal chieftains, persisted in eliminating Uzbeks from the administration and in giving an increasingly important role in it to Persian slaves. These slaves obviously maintained more extensive relations with their Shi'i brethren than with the Sunnis and were soon accused of favouring members of their own community.[5] The resentment against them was considerable in various layers of society. The Uzbek feudal class was vexed to see power slipping from its grasp. The students in the *madrasas*, a good many of whom were aiming for an administrative post, reacted in the same way. Moreover, the masses — convinced by their spiritual leaders that abuses of power could be ascribed not only to the Russians, but also to the Shi'a in office, representatives of a devilish heresy[6] — were beginning to turn their resentment against them too. So in the peasant upheavals of the years 1909–10 numerous Shi'a figured among the officials massacred.[7]

The 1910 massacres and the harsh repression which followed them outraged the Russian authorities, alerted by the political agent[8] and even by certain Muslims alien to the emirate.[9] The events of January 1910 had drawn the attention of the entire empire to the despotic character of the emir's power and to the social problems which peasant participation in the riots betrayed. The governor-general of Turkistan made himself the spokesman for Russian public opinion by reaffirming at this juncture the conclusions of Logofet's investigation;[10] namely, that Bukhara should be annexed to Russia without further delay.[11] Stolypin's reform gave force to this idea, since Bukhara's abandoned lands, once irrigated, would have been good for Russian peasants. Considerations of international politics temporarily deflected Russia from this project, but Emir 'Alim Khan ascended a throne severely shaken by such a threat.

To remedy these difficulties, the emir announced in a manifesto that the old order, condemned by all and responsible for the emirate's recent misfortunes, was now a thing of the past. Although the new ruler's promises were modest, he was nevertheless tackling one of the great problems of his state, the problem of administration. Four points stood out from his manifesto, all of them designed to eliminate the most serious abuses:[12] (1) he sought to put an end to the corruption prevalent at all levels of the hierarchy, by forbidding the presentation of gifts by anyone whatsoever to officials, to court dignitaries, or to himself; (2) he forbade officials of lesser rank to impose taxes of any kind, with the possible exception of travel expenses, but even these were regulated and strictly calculated, which was a considerable innovation; (3) along the same line of thinking, he banned the *qazis* from fixing the price of legal deeds at will; (4) to give all these provisions force of law, he promised that real salaries would be granted to all servants of the state, to prevent them from collecting the sums they needed to survive from their fellow-citizens. These promises were enthusiastically received in the emirate; they opened an era of trust and, for a few months, 'Alim Khan was 'the emir of all hopes'.[13] Students wrote to him, denouncing the state of the *madrasas,* their excesses, and the narrowness of mind that prevailed in them.[14] Still haunted by the Russian threat and perhaps also drawn like his father by the idea of a spiritual reform, 'Alim Khan at first replied favourably to these appeals and invited the *qazi-kalan* to prepare the transformation. But then matters returned to the old terrain of the conflict between reformism and the *qadimis.* The *qazi-kalan,* a declared supporter of the traditional order, passed on 'Alim Khan's invitation to the authorities of the *madrasas;* they ignored it — already the traditionalists were busy trying to win back the lost ground. The supporters of reform, on the other hand, emboldened by promises and by the organization which the reformist movement had recently given itself, and exasperated by the prevarications, were demonstrating their opposition. In the countryside the peasants, roused no doubt by their mullas, were beginning to threaten again.[15]

Imperceptibly the emir weakened. With Russia showing itself in no great hurry to end the scandal of the protectorate, the main problem became that of pacifying the clergy — the clergy that his father had managed to dominate only by running away from it. 'Alim Khan annulled the reform of the *madrasas.*[16] As for the promises in the manifesto, they were never implemented. Gifts poured in to officials and high dignitaries, who in turn surrounded the emir with similar marks of affection; besides, the emir had begun even before his accession to the throne to amass an immense personal fortune;[17] and he found it hard to resist the attractions of the gifts forbidden by his manifesto. Barely a few months from the time he mounted the throne, his plans were already returning to the firmament of pure ideas. Meanwhile, the first secret reformist organization was born.

The Jadid Organizations

This secret organization corresponded to needs of which Bukharan society was becoming confusedly aware. The disappointment provoked by 'Alim Khan's unkept promises had deeply marked both the peasant masses[18] and the bourgeoisie of Bukhara:[19] the disillusionment of the young mullas, who in their *madrasas* had believed in an imminent reform; and the disillusionment of the commercial bourgeoisie, whose links with Russia had been strengthened after

1905 (the cotton orientation of the country's economy accelerated in 1910)[20] and which, to secure its future and that of its children, was anxious to see recognized an education better adapted to the emirate's new economic orientation. The bourgeoisie's anxiety found an echo in certain individual consciences which, some years before, had sufficiently identified with the spirit of reform to found the very innocent Union of Bukhara the Noble. The neighbouring revolutions in Iran and Turkey, moreover, provided an example to those who wished to act.[21]

On 2 December 1910 a secret society was created, *Jam'iyat-i Tarbiyat-i Atfal* (Society for the Education of Youth),[22] headed by the main leaders of *Shirkat-i Bukhara-yi Sharif* (which, in practice, merged with the underground organization): Mirza 'Abd al-Vahidov, 'Usman Khodzhaev, Ahmad Makhdum, Hamid Khodzhaev Mihri, and a few others. Almost as soon as it was created *Jam'iyat-i Tarbiyat-i Atfal* united under its authority all the pre-existing groups and gave a new force to their scattered action. The Bukharan émigrés in Constantinople, notably 'Abd al-Ra'uf Fitrat, had shortly before created a 'Society for disseminating knowledge among the masses' whose initial aim was to send students to Turkey.[23]

From its inception the secret society became indistinguishable from the society for propagating knowledge. Moreover, for still greater effectiveness, it subsequently provided itself with two branches. The first, *Ma'rifat,* under the management of Fitrat and 'Usman Khodzhaev, undertook to carry the spirit of reform among the masses by organizing the distribution of books and newspapers and the establishment of political clubs;[24] to serve these ambitious plans, it was necessary to find books and papers. A second branch, concealed beneath the reassuring features of the commercial importing firm *Barakat,* undertook to import from abroad all the necessary material for mass education and propaganda.[25] The financing of this underground organization was wholly guaranteed by a few rich merchants in the emirate:[26] in the first instance, by the millionaires Mansurov and Jaqubov.

The organization — created by a few men impelled by a current of demands, disappointments, and hopes; and born from the evolution of a society constantly moulded by new economic tendencies — was the only structured association established by reformists in Russia.[27] It is remarkable, moreover, that the Jadid movement in Bukhara, formed much later than the other reformist movements of Russia, should have been the only one capable of really organizing itself and confronting the problems of the Russian revolution as a structured body.

The life of the secret society was far from easy. In 1911 it was not some more or less tolerated official group, but a genuinely clandestine association which came up against the absolute hostility of the *qadimi* circles, then very close to the ruler. To avoid any indiscretion, it was organized according to strict rules and with an initiation ceremony influenced by the initiation rites of guilds, of the Young Turk organization and of heterodox Islamic sects, particularly Babism.

Admissions were subjected to an extremely rigorous control and followed a complicated procedure. Every candidate had to be introduced by a member of the organization, who would refer his case to a small committee of three members; this would study the candidate's character, comb through his past, and examine the circles in which he moved. It was necessary to be sure of the purity of his morals,[28] his temperance, and his strength of character (members of the society were expressly forbidden not only to drink, but even to be present at a meeting where alcoholic drinks were served[29]). The case would then be examined in a plenary assembly, in which every member was invited to express himself; the opposition of a single member was enough to have the candidature rejected. Given acceptance by the assembly, the second stage of this complex procedure would involve a direct meeting between the candidate and the committee. During this interview, the candidate would be told it was a question of setting the society up (the secret was so well kept that apparently no one suspected the trick); he would then have to expound his conception of the supposed association to be founded, and of the role he would himself be ready to assume in the work of establishing it. His replies would be submitted to the plenary assembly, with a prior recommendation from the committee. Finally, the assembly would rule.[30]

The candidate who had victoriously surmounted all these trials found himself face-to-face with the society of whose existence, somewhat to his amazement, he was just learning. This revelation was made in civil terms, while profuse apologies were made for the lies that had been told him.[31] Then the admission ceremony began, marked by the swearing of the oath and a fairly elaborate ritual, whereafter the newly promoted candidate would become a 'Brother'.

The secret society was far from being a mass organization.

Before the First World War its membership amounted at most to a few dozen. Samoilovich puts it at around twenty,[32] basing himself on the memoirs of 'Ayni.[33] According to Fayzallah Khodzhaev,[34] who like 'Ayni lived through the Jadid adventure from its earliest days, the movement spread like wildfire in certain *vilayats* and by 1915 already included ten clandestine organizations.[35] The actual number of members is of little importance, since the organization's activity went far beyond the narrow circle of its affiliates. These affiliates used to meet as rarely as possible, for security reasons, and observed the rules common to all secret associations — namely, that outside of meetings there would be as little contact as possible, and only through strictly organized channels, to avoid police infiltration.[36] The plenary meetings took place twice monthly, generally in the home of one of the members. The participants went there in the half-hour interval separating the summons to the last prayer of the day from the prayer itself and remained until the summons to morning prayer echoed across the sleeping city.[37] During the night the city was the domain of the *mirshab* (nightwatchman), and no one could venture onto the streets.

The *raison d'être* for the secret association is to be found in its programme, which had the following five tasks:[38]

1   To educate the population and, in order to do so, to create schools and a press and procure books for the masses.
2   To struggle against clerical reaction, first, through a reform of the *madrasas*, a reform of the Muslim mind.
3   To struggle against corruption in the administration.
4   To contribute towards the transformation of Bukhara into a modern state. In these terms, its first concern was to transform the state's financial system, by first securing a clear separation between the public exchequer and the ruler's private coffers.
5   To put an end to the hostility between the religious communities, which meant defeating the fanaticism of the Sunni religious authorities in the emirate.

So in Bukhara, from 1910 on, the religious and educational reform that preoccupied all Russia's reformists was coupled with a demand for thorough reform of the state. The traditional society's failure to adapt to the transformations introduced by the economy was no longer denounced solely at the level of thought; the political structures of the old theocratic state were called into question. Perhaps this modification has to do with the fact that the association was a grouping of elements representing the new layers that were gradually emerging from the mutations of Bukharan society.

Who constituted the secret society? The relatively imprecise available descriptions all agree. For instance, Fayzallah Khodzhaev writes:

> The Association was recruited essentially in the urban milieu. Most of its members came from the petty bourgeoisie of the towns, averagely endowed in material terms and even frequently very poorly endowed. But this petty bourgeoisie, in intellectual terms, was the richest part of the emirate's population: students from the religious schools, petty merchants anxious to know better the world they were entering, minor officials.[39]

Although around the association there were a few prestigious names and fortunes, like that of the Mansurovs, Khodzhaev adds, 'they were mainly present financially'. 'Ayni confirms this picture;[40] besides, the personality of the best known members makes it plausible that it corresponds to reality. 'Ayni himself, the son of peasants, had studied in one of the capital's *madrasas*;[41] 'Abd al-Ra'uf Fitrat was the son of a petty merchant,[42] 'Usman Khodzhaev the son of a mulla, and 'Abd al-Rashid Burhan (Burkhanov) a minor official like his father.[43] Around them the Jadids encountered considerable hostility, but also the sympathy of certain clerics attracted by their religious demands and the verbal support even of Mufti Ikram: we have already seen with what interest he had followed the attempts at educational reform. In fact, even if the Jadids were not very numerous in terms of actual members of the organization, they were the spokesmen for so many demands and real problems that they may be deemed truly representative of the needs of a section of Bukhara society between 1910 and 1914. Those who had banded together in the secret society, those whose names history has handed down to us, were probably the emirate's freest spirits.

One interesting feature of this society was that the Jadid grouping was initially leaderless. In associations based on ideology, one often finds a thinker, a person of action, or a person who is both of these at the same time. His drive creates the movement; his character, his antecedents, and the psychic universe to which he belongs give the movement a specific nature. Although such a person or such people respond to an initial situation and specific social needs, through them the movement is oriented in one direction or another. In Bukhara before 1910 there was no such leadership. The Jadids carried on referring to the master vanished since the end of the nineteenth century, Ahmad Danish.[44] Even when the secret society was being founded, the Jadids still had no ideology of their own. They no longer referred to their Tatar masters. Moreover, Gasprinski's name scarcely figures in the memoirs of 'Ayni, Khodzhaev or even Fitrat,[45] although almost all were teachers in reformed *maktabs*. His name is not mentioned either by Samoilovich.[46]

In 1910 the Jadids of Bukhara were clinging determinedly to their own past, that is to Danish or to the ideologues of the Young Turk movement. It is also the case that already in 1910 their problems did not coincide with those of the empire's Muslims. For them, there was the problem of the Bukharan state and its independence. Still lacking an intellectual guide, they did not have a person of action either to rally them. The meeting of 2 December 1910 brought together a few men conscious of the same problems, who wished to attempt jointly to resolve one of these: the educational problem.[47] In a way that was initially wholly empirical, from one day to the next, they devised solutions and carried on an action which developed and took shape in contact with reality. It was in action, and face-to-face with the problems posed by it, that an ideologue made his appearance: 'Abd al-Ra'uf Fitrat, whose ideas dominated the life and activity of the movement from 1913 on.

The Clandestine Struggle

The activity of the Jadids was at first oriented towards the problem of the reformed education, which for several years had never ceased to trouble the emirate.

Schools

Grouped clandestinely, the Jadids also organized a clandestine education. People have written subsequently that the success of the Jadid education in Bukhara after 1910 was due to Russian aid.[48] It appears, however, that before 1912–13, far from benefiting from any Russian help, the Jadids were the object of a deep mistrust on the part of the Russian authorities, who suspected them of acting under Turkish influence and of being, within the empire, the fount of Turkish propaganda among the Muslims of Russia.[49] This opinion had a real basis: the ceaseless movement of Young Turks arriving more or less officially in the emirate, and above all of students and Jadids going off to Constantinople. The links between the Constantinople organization and that of Bukhara — about which little was known but whose existence was sensed by the political agent,[50] — however discreet they might be, were hard to dissimulate entirely. It was known that liberals from Bukhara, in reality members of the secret society, were sitting on the provincial committees of the Young Turk Party.[51] So it is hardly likely that the Russian government, through the political agent and the governor-general of Turkistan, exerted any serious pressure on the emir in favour of the Jadids. In any event, the emir, in so far as he felt the threat of annexation was receding, took his distance once more with respect to the governor-general of Turkistan.[52]

It seems the success of the Jadids' educational efforts in the years 1911–13 can reasonably be attributed only to themselves, because their activity corresponded to a need intensely felt in certain milieux. At the start of the year 1911, Mukammil al-Din Makhdum opened a clandestine school at Bukhara in his home, which accepted a number of children.[53] The Jadids were aware of the possibilities offered by this clandestine education, which was hard to uncover, in that its secrecy was strictly guarded by the families; in which the timetable and school day were irregular; and in which the school often used to move from the masters' homes to those of the pupils.[54] The number of pupils increased steadily, the number of schools likewise. Umnyakov claims that in 1912 the school of Mukammil al-Din Makhdum boasted almost fifty pupils.[55] In the same period, an editor of *Turan* (one of Bukhara's first Jadid organs, which will be discussed later) was likewise opening a school in the capital; Usman Khodzhaev did the same and is said to have had many pupils, as did Ishan Hamid Khodzhaev.[56] These schools were Sunni, and the teaching was in Persian. To the list of the emirate's Sunni establishments, we should add also the one opened — again clandestinely — by Mulla Vafa, which differed fundamentally from the others because the teaching of Russian figured very largely in it and Mulla Vafa used Gramenickii's textbooks.[57]

The period of strict clandestinity, which began shortly after the accession to the throne of 'Alim Khan, was marked inside the Jadid movement by a rapprochement between the representatives of the warring communities of 1910. Shi'a seem to have been quite numerous in the movement and, like the Sunnis, they organized clandestine schools. The capital had two of these, run by Shaykh

'Abd al-Qasim and Shaykh Mirza Habib.[58] The movement also spread outside the capital. In about 1912, a Tatar named Qari Yuldash Pulatov opened an illegal school at Kerki. At Shahrisabz, Islamqul Tuqsaba founded a school in his home, for which he brought in teachers from Tashkent and Samarqand. Islamqul Tuqsaba belonged to the tribe of the Kenegesh, whose rivalry with the Manghit had dominated Bukhara's history since the Manghit were in power. In this *vilayat,* which had always accepted the Manghit domination reluctantly, old tribal disputes were combined with the spirit of reform. The success of the school was for that reason all the greater; likewise, the success of the secret society, which opened a branch there in 1913.[59] At Qarakul, the *amlakdar* himself, Ghulam Qadiri, became the promoter of the educational reform and organized a school with Qazi Ikram. In Gijuvan, finally, a similar school was opened by Muhammad 'Azim and, when he was prevented by the authorities from pursuing his teaching, a Tatar at once succeeded him.

These reformed *maktabs* did not, to be sure, have any great number of pupils. The figures alluded to by Umnyakov, who asserts that at times they taught from 100 to 200 children, or 'Ayni who puts at eighty the number of Mulla Vafa's pupils, seem excessive.[60] It was nevertheless these schools that, in the hard years following the communal clash of 1910, bore the hopes of all groups aware of the need for such an evolution. In any case, not only did children attend the schools, but also their parents would meet with the teachers there and their conversations would then turn to politics.[61] In about 1913 the reformed education benefited from a certain relaxation in domestic politics. The emir and his collaborators were subjected at this time to strong pressure from public opinion. In the *madrasas,* debates on the issue had taken a passionate turn, and the *qadimis* stopped attacking their adversaries head on.[62] The return to the capital of Damulla Ikram, exiled to the *vilayat* of Ziandan after publishing in about 1910 an extremely violent pamphlet against the Bukharan clergy, was a serious sign of relaxation. The reformed *maktabs* had the right to a quasi-official existence and multiplied at a rapid rate. This period, however, was shortlived. On one Friday in early July 1914, the *qazi-kalan* Burhan al-Din and the *qadimi* mullas of the capital waited for the emir near the gate of the great mosque, at the hour of the *salat,* to hand him a petition demanding the definitive closure of the reformed *maktabs.* On 5 July the emir announced that the era of 'liberal excesses' was ended, primarily that of the new *maktabs*; and that the most renowned teachers were exiled to distant *vilayats*, notably Mulla Vafa, who was put under house arrest in eastern Bukhara.[63] Those who escaped the *ra'is* — Fitrat, Ata Khvaja-ughli (Khodzhaev), Fayzallah Khodzhaev and a few others — took refuge in the eastern part of the emirate where, buttressed by the support of a populace traditionally hostile to the ruler, they reopened their schools.[64]

Certain Bukharan merchants then turned towards the political agent, demanding the opening of an improved elementary school: a four-class school, the cost of which they said they were prepared to bear. Their request, written in Persian, contains interesting indications as to their state of mind:[65]

> You know, that the reformed schools in which our children were rapidly learning to read and write have been closed as a result of the complaints of a few mullas. Since then our children, instead of going to school, are roaming the streets. You are not unaware that we are for the most part merchants and craftsmen. There are only a few educated persons among us. It is, therefore, necessary that our children should be able to read, so that we may entrust our business to them. We have spent seven or eight years in the schools which they are seeking to impose upon us and we know nothing. We therefore beg you, have the reformed schools opened.

But at the time when this request was reaching the political agent, war was breaking out. Russia's attention was fixed elsewhere, and the emir certainly felt freer to settle the issue in his own way.[66] In the last phase of the school struggle, it is clear that the development of the Jadid schools was not closely linked, as has been written, to Russian intervention in their favour. The emir banned the reformed establishments just when the Duma was studying the possibility of annexing the emirate;[67] and it was not after the war started, but before it that he enacted harsh measures striking at the reformists.

The approach to the political agent essayed by a number of Bukharan merchants, when the reform enterprise was harmed in this way, poses the question of the movement's social support. From which layers were its pupils recruited in that period, and who backed the movement? In Sunni circles the advocates of reform seemed always to belong to the urban bourgeoisie, basically mercantile; and the rural population — far more distant from the disputes provoked by the spirit of reform within the religious hierarchy itself — was almost wholly shielded from it. In the towns, there were initially few conscious supporters of the Jadids;

but their number increased, in order to bring its ideas to the notice of the public, as a consequence of the activity of the clandestine organization.

In Shi'i circles the situation was quite different, as can be seen by reading the description of the reformed *maktabs* in 'Ayni's works.[68] There were hardly any children of prominent people, but there were children from the poorest milieux. Instead of falling on the families, the costs of the schools were borne by the spiritual authorities, favourable from the outset to the movement, perhaps partly as a reaction against the attitude of the *qadimi*-influenced Sunnis. This explains why after 1914 in eastern Bukhara the Shi'i population was numerous and the success of the clandestine schools was greatest. This success was based on a conspiracy between the Jadids, the Shi'i clerics, and a populace hostile to the régime for reasons that were half-religious, half-social.

The reformed school thus experienced a continuous success in Bukhara between 1910 and 1914, despite the bans and persecution. The reformists did not content themselves with organizing elementary education. They were haunted by the wish to send young men to study outside the stifling, sterile atmosphere of the emirate. Since the Young Turk revolution, they reckoned that the country to which it would be most advantageous to send their youth was Turkey.[69] This was one of the essential tasks assigned to the Constantinople organization, and its efforts in this domain were constant. In 1911 there were fifteen Bukharan students in Constantinople; two years later, the association managed to bring in thirty of them.[70] Only the war halted this movement, which despite these derisory figures had considerable importance. In Constantinople the young students from Bukhara lived permanently in an atmosphere of hostility towards Russia and of reformism. These sojourns certainly had the effect of developing in them a keen national feeling and a deep sense of humiliation. In Young Turk milieux the emir of Bukhara's concessions to Russia were judged severely,[71] and on their return home the young students were not inclined to view the Russians as their natural protectors.

Press

At the beginning of 1912 the reformists judged that in the interests of internal relaxation the moment had come to attempt a more public action.[72] To found a newspaper, the first in the emirate, was for technical reasons no easy matter. They had the idea of calling upon the Russian political agent for support, by using a trick, for which he apparently fell. Two members of the secret association first negotiated with the owners of the Levin printworks in Novaya Bukhara, who agreed to print a newspaper. Fortified by these material assurances, they went to see the political agent — they had assured both alike that they were liberals attracted by Russian greatness — and put to him the idea, which they said was shared by the Russian printer and themselves, of a native newspaper that would make Russia known to the people of Bukhara.[73] Thus, what the reformists were proposing to the political agent was basically a means of propagating theses favourable to Russia, in the educated circles from which the devotees of pan-Turkism were recruited.

Interested in the idea, the agent urged it upon the emir, who, though not very convinced, nevertheless eventually yielded and granted permission to publish a newspaper. The political agent, whose responsibility it was to supervise it, delegated the task to his interpreter Haydar Khvaja Mirbedelev.[74] A Persian-language paper was first established, *Bukhara-yi Sharif,* for which an editor was brought in from Baku, Mirza Chalal Yusufzada; and from 11 March 1912 *Bukhara-yi Sharif* appeared daily for four months. In the summer, the reformists decided to add a publication in the Uzbek language;[75] this was *Turan,* which appeared for the first time on 14 July 1912, edited by the same team as *Bukhara-yi Sharif.*[76] Since *Turan* came out twice weekly, *Bukhara-yi Sharif* was reduced to four issues per week, so that everything would proceed as if there were only one newspaper.

Though widely read, these papers proved commercially unsuccessful.[77] Subscribers did not flood in. The political agent and the printer saw that the content of the papers had nothing in common with what had been proposed to them; but they did not dare admit they had been tricked. They stressed the financial difficulties, and Levin threatened to suppress the two papers; but the Jadids laboured away to save their creation. One of their patrons, probably Mansurov, took on the material cost of the two papers, which were reorganized and limited to two weekly editions. Isham al-Din Makhdum Husni, a Bukharan who had studied in Constantinople, became editor of *Turan*; while for *Bukhara-yi Sharif,* Husayn Ibragimov was summoned from Samarqand to replace Mirbedelev as editor-in-chief.

Since the pretext chosen to suppress these papers was financial, Mansurov's intervention saved them for a short while. Nevertheless, they were doomed; on 2 January 1913 they were banned and for years had no successors. *Bukhara-yi Sharif* had had 153 issues; *Turan,* 49.

Jadid Circles

The reformists, who voluntarily restricted the meetings of their secret association to preserve its clandestinity, nevertheless organized meetings with sympathizers on a wide scale. These were known as 'discussion and education meetings' and they took place in various places: schools,[78] the houses where lessons were given in periods of clandestinity,[79] or in tea houses.[80] The activity of the Jadids was tireless and their clandestine meetings, often held at night, drew a large number of sympathizers. Who used to attend them? Though no minutes exist, Galuzo has given valuable information about the lists drawn up by the police of the Turkistan Guberniya, not only for the territory it controlled but also for Bukhara. We thus find that out of a list of 170 individuals classified as 'pan-Islamists' during the years 1911–13, the police had indicated the social origin of forty-four: 'seven merchants; three religious personages; six Bukhara notables; three intellectuals; two factors; four *qazis*; four notables from Turkistan; one *zakatchi*; two native officials in Russian service (interpreters, etc.); one goldsmith; one commercial agent of the emir; one Muslim scholar (*'ulama*); six "very wealthy" men; one tea house owner; one cotton exporter; one schoolteacher'.[81]

These 'public' meetings were attended, in the first place, by the parents of the reformists' pupils, since this was the channel whereby the reformists made contact with public opinion.[82] Participants' accounts make clear the nature of these meetings: they were small groups, in which everybody turned the discussion towards the problems that interested them. The Jadids would reply to everything; above all, they would organize readings, for people read a vast amount in these groups, newspapers first of all and most of them foreign: from Turkey, *Sirat-i Mustaqim*;[83] from India, *Habl al-Matin*;[84] and shortly before the First World War, from Afghanistan, *Siraj al-Akhbar*,[85] published by Mahmud Tarzi (who was later King Amanallah's minister of foreign affairs), appearing with the explosive headline 'Asia for the Asians', and widely read in the emirate. Even in the most remote *qishlaqs,* the Jadids used to read and comment on it, as they did with *Qanun.* During their brief period of existence, *Bukhara-yi Sharif* and *Turan* were also read in these meetings; they thus had a circulation which bore no relation to their sales figures.

Books were also read, and the most interesting or explosive pages (if not the entire work, as with certain articles) were copied, disseminated on the sly, distributed, and thus pursued a clandestine path whose route is hard to trace but whose effect on people's minds increasingly made itself felt. The first works brought to public notice appeared at the same time as the secret organization itself. Shortly after the Iranian Revolution, the liberal bourgeois of Bukhara went wild over a little book,[86] written in Persian by Zayn al-'Abidin Maragha'i: *Siyahatnama-i Ibrahim Beg* (The Travel Diary of Ibrahim Beg).[87] In this work, which can be reckoned an important creation of modern Persian literature,[88] the hero who gives his name to the book is describing Iran. The social order, upon which he dwells at length, reminded Bukharan intellectuals of their own society and their own structures. In Iran, however, a revolution had occurred, putting an end to the scandal. So this book seemed at once to describe an order that Bukhara still knew and to prefigure another destiny.

The author most widely read, and who soon emerged as the ideologue of the movement, was Fitrat. Almost unknown in his country before 1909, by 1914 numerous Jadids knew his key works by heart, as they were known by certain representatives of the embryonic bourgeois class desirous of reforms. Fitrat's main works — *Munazara* (The Discussion) first published in Persian in 1909,[89] *Bayanat-i sayyah-i hindi* (Tales of an Indian traveller) published in 1919,[90] a collection of poems entitled *Sayha* (The Cry) published in 1910[91] and *Rahbar-i nijat* (The guide to salvation) — were copied and distributed in the emirate and throughout Turkistan.[92]

Such circles did not exist only in Bukhara. Everywhere in the guberniya little discussion groups multiplied before the First World War. Police reports (in Bukhara, those of the political agent) could only register the fact,[93] since it was difficult to ban people from an activity which had the external appearance of a family or social gathering. In all the larger towns of Turkistan, such groups emerged, equipped with, for example, lending libraries and mutual help associations. It was not easy, however, to have books and newspapers, especially in the emirate of Bukhara because almost everything was forbidden there. But in this respect the sister-firms *Mar'ifat* and *Barakat* were extraordinarily effective. They introduced into the emirate foreign papers and books printed in Constantinople.[94] There were other ways, moreover, of bringing in newspapers. The Afghan and Indian students or merchants who came to Bukhara used to bring their papers, and these were widely distributed in the groups.[95] Thus, the reformist and sometimes revolutionary thought of the Afghans and Indians penetrated directly into the *madrasas* themselves, even though these were fiefs of *qadimi* influence. Turkey's contribution was also great.

Theatre

In the years 1908–10, a few theatre companies appeared in Turkistan. At first these were companies of amateurs, who acted plays by Tatar or Azari authors (for example, Galiaskar Kamalov and Vezirov) in front of restricted audiences; and then professional troupes arrived, and the Turkistani public began to become really interested in the theatre. The Jadids, aware that here they had a means of disseminating their ideas, set about writing plays; reading them in public; acting them; and showing in their newspapers, during their brief period of existence, how important the theatre was for culture.

The work best known to audiences at the time was *Pidarkush*,[96] by Mufti Bihbudi, which was presented in all the towns of Central Asia.[97] The thesis of this piece was that the liberation of the Muslim peoples depended upon the prior formation of a national intelligentsia. This had to be recruited from the young bourgeoisie that had sprung up in the course of the nineteenth century, which, forming as it did a bridge between the old feudal society and the new world, was best prepared to supply these dynamic cadres. Educated abroad — preferably in Turkey, France, and America (the pan-Turk ideal and the appeal of liberal ideas were mingled in this programme) — this national intelligentsia, intensely Muslim, would be able progressively to penetrate the administrative apparatus of Russian power and, by so doing, to eliminate Russia from Turkistan.

This play had a considerable success.[98] It was staged right up to the First World War, despite the hostility of the *qadimis*, who condemned the theatre because it was proving to be a powerful weapon in the hands of their adversaries. They claimed it was hardly in conformity with the *shari'at,* and waxed indignant at the degradation of morals that it reflected: the presence of unveiled women on the stage, acting side-by-side with male actors and in front of essentially masculine audiences, seemed to them to threaten the whole of Muslim society. But these criticisms had little effect and audiences continued to pour in. Besides, it was not the theatre itself which the *qadimis* were seeking to get at, but the ideology it was expressing — the ideology of the Jadids, which was emerging gradually in the years before the First World War and which eventually became linked with the name of 'Abd al-Ra'uf Fitrat.[99]

The Ideological Leader: 'Abd al-Ra'uf Fitrat

Though the work of 'Abd al-Ra'uf Fitrat is well known to us, the same cannot be said for his origins, his life or even his personality. Fitrat's name rarely figures in textbooks and articles devoted to the recent history of Turkistan.[100] The only information we possess about him comes from a few articles written *a posteriori* by his comrades in struggle.[101] From these, we know that he belonged to a family of small Bukharan merchants and that he was a schoolteacher.[102] According to these sources, in about 1908–10 he was a young man by comparison with such elders as 'Ayni,[103] which allows us to infer that he was born in the last ten or fifteen years of the nineteenth century. The work of 'Abd al-Ra'uf Fitrat was entirely devoted to the crisis of the Muslim world. He studied the elements of this crisis in his own country, Bukhara, but his thought transcended this narrow framework and led him to reflect on the fundamental problems of the entire Islamic community.

For Fitrat, as for all the reformists, the crisis of Islam in the twentieth century was primarily the collapse of the society of the old Islamic state: a spiritual collapse within; a temporal collapse reflected in the victory of the infidels and the yoke imposed upon Bukhara. In anguished pages Fitrat described Bukhara's glorious past: 'O unhappy Bukhara, thou who hast known such spirits as Abu 'Ali Sina al-'Arabi (Aviccena), in these days of distress thou art bereft of motion. Yet this is the same Bukhara that, in the past, through the prestige of its knowledge and its faith, won recognition for its exceptional dignity. How low hast thou fallen?' He describes Bukhara's 'enslaved and humbled' condition and envisages for it a still worse end: the total disappearance of Islam.[104] He states that it is a question not only of Bukhara, but of a general and irreversible evolution of the lands of Islam, whose temporal decadence began when Andalusia, after 450 years of fidelity to Islam, was torn from the community of believers.[105]

Fitrat vigorously denounces all the inner signs of this collapse of
the power of the Islamic states. The strong state of yore no longer
exists; all is compromise and corruption. The régime, in the person
of its servants, is a source of constant abuse and violence. Moreover, while dedicating itself to the exploitation of a particularly
wretched people, it has allowed the entire patrimony bequeathed
by former powerful rulers to be destroyed.[106] The neglect in
which the roads built by 'Abd al-Ahad are left; the destruction of
the caravanserais and wells that he had installed to encourage
trade across his country and assist its prosperity; and the deteriora-
tion of the land — for Fitrat, these are so many tokens of and so
many reasons for his country's decline.[107] With the decline of
material civilization, civilization as a whole regresses; and in
Bukhara, civilization is Islam. Here Fitrat no longer contents
himself with describing; he analyses minutely the causes of decline.

Those responsible are, first, the clergy, who have replaced the
faith of the Prophet by a religion of their own — an ossified
religion, immobile, and hostile to all dynamism and all progress.
Turks questioned about the meaning of the reforms enacted in
Turkey after 1921 used to say the following: 'There are three
Islams: the religion of the Koran, the religion of the 'ulama, and
the religion of the masses. The last is a superstition, an obscurant-
ism, and a fetishism. The second is hampered by all the weight of
an outdated legalism.'[108] Such are also the main lines of Fitrat's
analysis: like all the reformers, he denounces taqlid, or servile
respect for religious authority;[109] This is the reason for the Muslim
world's isolation from the modern world in general[110] and its
enclosure in a total immobility.

Bukhara has for centuries been famous for the virtues of its
education. What has become of it? Fitrat describes the degeneration of that education in the madrasas where clerics are formed.
Concerning the material state of the madrasas, the disorder and
permanent bad example that reign in them, and the actual quality
of education, Fitrat's works are richly informative. Munazara,
which is a debate between a modernist and a supporter of tradition, is entirely centred on this theme. The modernist (here, a
European) realizes during his conversation with the mudarris that
Bukharan education, after thirty-nine years of study, produces
absolute ignorance, even regarding the subjects studied; for, his
interlocutor shows himself entirely incapable of understanding the
Arabic to which he has devoted so much effort and which he

thought he knew 'better than the Arabs themselves'.[111]

In *Tales of an Indian Traveller,* an inhabitant of Bukhara describes the situation to his Indian guest:[112]

There lies Noble Bukhara, which formed 400,000 scholars and sent them throughout the world. Formerly, she was mistress of such spiritual forces . . . now, alas! I must unhappily concede that this bright star of learning, this paradise of the human world, this centre of the world's learning, this centre of knowledge for the entire world, has become a country surrounded by mountains of stupidity and fettered by chains of contempt. This source of life for all the Orient, knowing so many paths to the other world, has allowed death to seize it by the throat. What is so astonishing? These happy lands endowed with vast resources have become the refuge for a handful of usurpers who know not God; who have brought the pot of duplicity and rottenness of a little company of gluttons to the boil . . .

Yes we have 200 *madrasas* . . . yes we have libraries, but where are the books? All the books have been taken by the scholars who keep them. As for the empty premises endowed by *vaqfs,* they are entrusted to the son of some *qazi* or *mufti* who does not yet deserve the title of *mudarris;* who, in other words, has no education. This respectable person uses for his own benefit the library's yearly subvention and rents out the premises to some young student, on condition that the student gives him lessons so that one day he may be recognized as able to teach and given the title of *mudarris.*

We have at least 300 schools for beginners, but they are no longer anything but useless establishments run by ignorant masters. O God! What a surprising country, the most surprising in the whole world. Intelligent people create schools to eliminate theft, coarseness, evil actions, and poverty; and when a school opens in their towns, they hurl their caps to the sky in joy. We have more than 300 schools and in them our children learn only to steal, to be rowdy and to beg. We have schools devoted specially to reading the Koran, yet there is not a man here who instead of the holy name of Allah does not say *'avah'* or *'ablah'.*

For this spiritual decline of Bukhara, Fitrat accuses the clerics and denounces their corrupt practices,[113] their debauchery,[114] and their utter lack of religion.[115] He reproaches them with having deliberately held the people of Bukhara in ignorance to preserve their privileges[116] and the better to dominate it.[117] He reproaches them with having entirely turned their backs on the modern world and with having ignored all branches of knowledge, through both idleness[118] and an aberrant interpretation of the rules of Islam.

But Fitrat indicts the clerics not only of having caused the spiritual decline of their country, but also of having weakened the Muslim community by dividing it:

> If you had not divided the strong and united Muslim nation into Shi'a, Sunnis, Zaydis, and Wahhabis, and had not ranged them against one another . . .[119] The infidels have found before them only this community rent by internal disputes and bereft of all means of military defence, because there too the clerics in their hatred of progress have prohibited it from making any effort to protect itself. If you had not limited our entire war equipment to blades and twisted bows, if you had not kept in your army wretches of up to seventy years old, if you had not banned the manufacture of cannon, rifles, bombs, dynamite, etc. . . . Islam would not be where it is.'[120]

But, for want of soldiers and weapons, the clergy gave Bukhara other defenders: the tombs of the saints. Here Fitrat's anger knows no restraint and he writes in *Munazara* that, once the clergy entrusted their country's destiny to Baha al-Din — whose role it was, they said, to defend them — Bukhara was conquered just as the Andalusian kingdom, Egypt, and India had been conquered.[121] And he asks, 'Have the Russians taken Bukhara or not? If they have not taken it, why does the emir receive the Emperor's directives each day, and the *qush-begi* those of the political agent? Let us say that these directives have a friendly character: well then, I ask why the emir does not in exchange give directives to the Russian government? If Bukhara is occupied by the Russians, why then does Baha al-Din not drive them out?'[122] This argument levelled by Fitrat against the clergy, so trusting in their saints that they had handed their country over to Russia, was expressed in a similar guise in Cairo by the review *al-Manar* of Rashid Rida and Muhammad 'Abduh, which attacked all those who sheltered under the protection of their saints instead of fighting to defend Muslim soil: 'What did the inhabitants of Bukhara do against the Russians?'[123]

Like the two Cairo masters, Fitrat is here making war upon the brotherhoods and all aberrant forms of religious sentiment. The problem was all the more serious in Bukhara because in the emirate the brotherhoods had links with broad layers of the rural and urban population, upon whom their influence was considerable. In his *Tales of an Indian Traveller,*[124] Fitrat offers the reader a picturesque account — full of humour — of a pilgrimage to the mausoleum of Baha al-Din Naqshband. The supposed Indian traveller describes with delight the tricks of the *shaykh* who guards the mausoleum, and is amazed by the naivety of the pilgrims, who festoon with their votive offerings 'a stick which was initially supposed to mark the site of the mausoleum, but which was never the same'. An account which the sham dervish Vambéry would not have disowned.[125]

This idea regarding the superstitious, obscurantist faith of the masses of Bukhara is expressed above all in a strange tale, *Qiyamat* (The Resurrection),[126] in which Fitrat recounts the temporary journey to the other world of a simple, devout Muslim — but devout in the manner of the uneducated masses. Clearly, the vision of the other world and the last judgement of the tale's hero Puchamir have more to do with superstition than with the teaching of the Islamic religion; yet Puchamir himself, back on earth after his experience, concludes that this other world 'is worthless'.[127]

To show his contempt both for miracle-working healers and for the dignitaries of Islam, Fitrat recounts — through the lips of the Indian traveller — how he fell ill one day in Bukhara. Not content with having sent packing all the 'holy men and healers who arrived at his bedside', he turns for help to a Russian practitioner, to whom he suggests that one of the emirate's *madrasas* be transformed into a school of medicine in which Europeans would teach: 'That is not contrary to the *shari'at* . . . The prophet said: Go seek knowledge even in China, if that is where it is to be found.'[128]

But — and this is remarkable in Fitrat's work — he not only tackles the clergy and those who wield authority, but also indicts the wretched, oppressed populace of Bukhara; and, by so doing, he calls into question the entire social order of the emirate. In his *Tales of an Indian Traveller*, Fitrat sets forth his thinking clearly: if Bukhara has been able to attain such a degree of spiritual and temporal misery, this is because the clergy and rulers have forgotten Islam in favour of their own selfish interests; but, it is also because the masses have blindly followed their rulers and submitted to them without discernment, in the name of Islam.[129] These shapeless masses, Fitrat says, have followed the ruling classes like a flock of sheep, whereas everything in the Koranic teaching forbids such submission on their part: man's destiny is his own, and God has given him the possibility of dominating all about him, starting with nature;[130] how can this man — stronger than nature and the best of the creatures God has created — be dominant or dominated, since all men are similar and equal?[131] It is thus contrary to the Koran that the masses should be transformed into 'flocks of sheep', when they are made up of God's creatures, of individuals, each one of whom has an inestimable value in God's eyes. The entire effort of the clergy, for more than two centuries, has been designed to falsify the Koran's teaching on this crucial point, because religion has been taught from the angle and according to the interests of a privileged class.

Though criticism occupies a considerable place in it, Fitrat's work is not solely destructive. Just as he scrupulously analyses the various aspects of Muslim decadence on every level (spiritual, social, and national) he similarly investigates the ways in which his country and the entire Islamic community can escape from this crisis and restore God's kingdom on earth. In this quest for salvation, common to all the lucid minds of his generation, Fitrat seems to represent the two fundamental aspects of Muslim renewal: he was both a reformer or an educator, and a politician whose thought was broadly revolutionary. For him, the point of departure for any reform was action upon the inner being of the people. Loyal to his first vocation as an educator, he thought no regeneration of the Muslim community was possible unless individuals were prepared and formed and unless the meaning and understanding of Islam were regenerated in each of them. Fitrat never ceased to insist on the value of the individual and on his role in the community. It was thus normal that he should have been particularly sensitive to the idea that the reform of Islam passed first by way of the personal reform that was the absolute precondition for it.

One of the important features of Fitrat's thought was his conception of knowledge. What he deemed to be a knowledge worthy of human endeavour was one that was useful not only to man's salvation, but also to his terrestrial existence. It was also a knowledge that could be acquired in a reasonable lapse of time, leaving a person the opportunity to use it for the good of humanity.[132] Consequently, he opposed the conservation of a scholasticism that was of no assistance to humans in the modern world, demanding that all knowledge should be subjected to intellectual criticism and not accepted blindly.

In the domain of education Fitrat, while recognizing the need to search out knowledge wherever it was, denied that Islam needed to borrow anything whatsoever from the West — either to draw inspiration from it or to imitate it; for, all that has made the temporal greatness of the West comes from Islam.[133] To reinforce his view, he referred to the French historian Seignobos, who reportedly had written that in the eleventh century — when Islam was powerful and prosperous, and its culture shone with incomparable splendour while the West was wretched — the encounter between these two universes had set the Europeans on the path of progress.[134] Fitrat concluded that it was necessary only to take back from the West 'our lost culture and civilization, thanks to which the West has been able to overtake us and conquer us'.[135]

But Fitrat did not think that the salvation of the Muslim community would come just from below, from a regeneration of all Muslims. For him, there was also another undertaking to be accomplished: the transformation of Muslim society by way of its apex. Here the political thinker emerged. Though he condemned the controllers of the state and the wealthy,[136] he nevertheless thought that the transformation should be made under the aegis of the ruler of Bukhara, whom he addressed in the epilogue to *Munazara*[137] as the 'Father of Bukhara'. In his writings he frequently insists that the ruler's counsellors were corrupt and evil,[138] whereas the ruler himself was worthy of respect. Here Fitrat's moderate position — moderate in relation to the revolutionary character of the remainder of his work — is at first surprising. But it must be remembered that in 1910 the Emir of Bukhara, whatever his faults, was the sole Muslim ruler in the Russian Empire who had managed to maintain himself in a quite strong position after the conquest and who had constantly consolidated this position since then.

Apart from the ruler, however, no dignitary or structure was spared in Fitrat's political programme. To save Bukhara, it was necessary to overturn the established order, the structures, and the nature of the régime: such is the theme of *Sayha* (The Cry). In *Rahbar-i Nijat* (The guide to salvation), he analysed the economic and social foundations of the régime and clearly separated spiritual requirements from natural ones, judging that natural conditions have primacy in the behaviour of human beings. To recognize in this way the primacy of economic and social conditions over spiritual requirements in the organization of the political order — for this is what Fitrat's argument came down to — represented a remarkable progress. Without attaining a clear separation between the spiritual and the temporal, Fitrat indicated that the solutions to the problems of Islam's adaptation to the modern world had to be sought in this orientation.

Another equally important orientation had to do with the introduction into society of relations of a new type. *'A'ila* (The Family) is devoted to a study of the reform to be applied to family relations. The reform Fitrat defined was not a compromise between the structures of Islamic society and those of Western society, but a radical option involving a break with the past and a total recasting of family relations. In this perspective, Fitrat allotted an important place to the evolution of women, hence to the education that should be given to women. He believed their role in social change to be considerable, since the individual is first heir to what his or her mother has inculcated into him during his or her childhood.[139]

In reality, for Fitrat, the inner regeneration of the Muslim community could be realized only by a twofold process: a spiritual renewal, involving the education of all individuals; and a political and social revolution, which would allow nothing to survive of the concepts, structures, and human relations of the period of ossification and which would give birth to a modern society and state. This inner regeneration was indispensable to guarantee external liberation, which was another of Fitrat's permanent preoccupations. For him, the salvation of Islam implied the end of foreign domination, which was a consequence of Islam's degradation. The struggle for liberation did not follow the work of inner regeneration, but it was one of its aspects.

Fitrat linked two notions closely: that of the good Muslim and that of the patriot.[140] But the nationalism that appears on every page of his writings did not exclude a broader vision, of the Islamic community as a whole. For Fitrat, reconciliation of all Muslims and pan-Islamism were the outcome of the whole reformist enterprise, and he showed this clearly by ending his major work *Munazara* on this theme. After enumerating the conditions for salvation, he wrote as follows: 'The second way is unity with the entire Muslim community. This means considering as Muslims all those whose creed is 'there is no God but God and Muhammad is his prophet', to whatever sect they may belong. Put an end to the disputes between Shi'a and Sunnis! Those who keep them going are enemies of Islam . . .' And Fitrat appealed to 'all his brethren in the faith'.[141]

Through all these pages it can be seen how much Fitrat had come under the influence of the masters of reformism, especially Jamal al-Din al-Afghani. Like him, Fitrat preached reconciliation between Shi'a and Sunnis, hardly managing to comprehend the meaning of the community's traditional divisions. Like al-Afghani, Fitrat experienced the wretched state of the community with painful intensity, and thought that the rebirth of Islam must come from the Muslims themselves. The incitement to action — the rejection of passivity, quietude or irresponsibility — that had so strongly marked the work of Jamal al-Din also marked Fitrat's work in the same way. Fitrat also followed the trail blazed by al-Afghani in placing the temporal history of Islam in the foreground. This is probably why his work was concerned more with defining the means for a new vitality than with redefining the content — or even just methods — of the faith.[142]

What was original in Fitrat was the revolutionary tone of his reformism and pan-Islamism, and his refusal to compromise with the West, even temporarily. In this respect it is not surprising that he should have been quite different from Muhammad 'Abduh, though they resembled each other in the importance they attached to pedagogical activity; or, to a lesser extent, from al-Afghani. Both 'Abduh and al-Afghani had died before a non-white people had defeated a great empire and before the revolutionary spirit of 1905 had blown, whereas Fitrat lived through these events. But he diverged also from another of his masters, the Tatar Isma'il Bay Gasprinski, who, rather than envisaging fundamental upheavals, felt that in certain circumstances Russia could help a structural transformation.[143]

He also went far beyond the other Jadids of Turkistan, who scarcely expressed any aspiration towards a fundamental overturn of the social and political order. Yet no one in Bukhara seems to have disowned Fitrat's extremism; and men whose destiny diverged as totally as Fayzallah Khodzhaev and 'Ayni both asserted in their memoirs that Fitrat was truly the thinker who had proved capable of formulating a theory of the emirate's situation and their aspirations.

If Fitrat and the Jadids were seeking to understand the crisis of the Muslim world and define a doctrine of salvation, can it be concluded that they were alone in considering these problems? Must it be conceded that this conflict between Jadids and *qadimis* pitted those who saw the new needs of society against those who were unaware of them? This is what the Jadids themselves sought to maintain,[144] and the books read in Bukhara's Jadid circles at the time bear witness to this state of mind. In reality, it does not seem possible to draw so sharp a line between the respective attitudes of each in the face of a problem of which all were certainly conscious. What were these Jadids before 1914? According to Khodzhaev, they were 'a little group of intellectuals and petty bourgeois which initially managed to reach only very limited layers of the population'.[145] However, the ruling strata — the followers of the *qadimis* came from the upper class of the emirate, the class which for generations had been accustomed to shoulder its problems —

was undoubtedly aware of the transformation of society and the new needs it implied. The sporadic explosions of popular anger and despair were a sure sign of them. The last emirs of Bukhara sought in their own fashion to resolve this crisis, as soon as the premonitory signs of it became clear, by limited measures of adaptation.

Thus, at the beginning of his reign 'Abd al-Ahad sought to adopt a more liberal approach than his father, at times authorizing a reformed education. 'Alim Khan's manifesto expressed not only a wish to avoid annexation, but also an intention to recognize the new situation and resolve it. The freedoms which the ruler granted in pedagogic matters in the years 1912–14 should be seen in the same light. The last emir of Bukhara did not, any more than his predecessor, correspond to the stereotyped image of an authoritarian despot hostile to all progress. 'Alim Khan, throughout his reign — which was the most unsettled and tragic of the Manghit dynasty — tried constantly to associate himself with the solutions put forward to resolve the crisis of Islam. The Jadids recognized this: even while attacking him, right up to 1917 they placed all their activity under the patronage of the 'Father of Bukhara'.

'Alim Khan was open also to pan-Islamic ideas, even if he interpreted them in a sense that was favourable to him personally. In 1911, after numerous interviews with Gasprinski, he tried to win acceptance as 'the rallier of all Muslims' — if not in Russia, then at least in Turkistan. He then suggested to the Russian government that it should unite eastern or Chinese Turkistan with Russian Turkistan beneath his sceptre, in such a way as 'finally to unify greater and lesser Bukhara'.[146] He made himself the interpreter of a purely Turkistani national feeling, which ran like a thread through all manifestations of Jadid thought in Turkistan. In their years of struggle, the Jadids never wearied of repeating Yassawi's motto 'My name is Ahmad, my fatherland is Turkistan', or that of 'Ali Shir Nava'i: 'It is easy to understand that, for as long as a man lives, he never stops fighting for his fatherland'.

The emir's attitude on certain points thus tended to coincide with that of the Jadids; but these attempts at convergence were only sporadic and soon failed. One is tempted, as the Jadids were, to accuse the *qadimis* of having exerted an influence on the ruler in the other direction, just as they fought against the Jadids to retain their influence over the masses. Here again, it is necessary to refrain from hasty judgements. In the ruling caste there were men like Damulla Ikram who supported the Jadids. If the *qadimis* were constantly hostile to the reformers and constantly opposed to any least modification in the structures and relations of society, this was not just because of a sterile conservative bias. By its religious fundamentalism, by its conservatism, and even at times by its fanatical stance, Bukhara's ruling caste — which was largely made up of *qadimi* clerics — could think it was defending the integrity of a Muslim Turkistan.

Over the centuries Turkistan had been invaded by various peoples, and its recent past had been no less turbulent. In the seventeenth century it had had to defend itself against the Kalmyks; at the beginning of the eighteenth, against the Dungans; and then the Russians had arrived. The traditionalists thought that their firmness had blocked the invaders' assimilationist endeavours. At the end of the nineteenth century and at the start of the twentieth, they judged that the crucial problem for the Muslim community, confronted with the modern Western world, was how to safeguard its integrity; and they advocated the path of salvation rather than the initiatives of the reformists (who, in sharp contrast, favoured a spiritual penetration by the West). So all was not negative in the refusal of the traditionalists to take account of new problems and requirements. Their attitude had the effect of perpetuating all that was immutable in the structures of society, and they persisted in this all the more as dynamic forces emerged; but this attitude was inspired by a certain conception of the Muslim community.

Caught between the reformists' appeals and the intransigence of the traditionalists, before 1914 the emir went from one to the other, sometimes seeking to recognize society's aspirations for renewal, sometimes denying them. From 1912 on, he seemed to move in the direction of recognizing those aspirations, but the First World War subsequently put an end to his liberal leanings. The emir retracted all his concessions. Those Jadids who had not been deported had no alternative but flight. Like Fitrat or Fayzallah Khodzhaev, they took refuge in neighbouring Turkistan, where they rejoined Jadids arriving from Turkey to continue the struggle they had undertaken with their brethren in the guberniya. In leaving Bukhara, however, the Jadids did not vanish from its stage entirely; the ideas they had sown proceeded on their way.

During the first fifteen years of the twentieth century, Bukhara evolved considerably. Until 1900, its society's needs and aspirations were reflected in explosions of anger from the masses and in the works of a few isolated intellectuals, without the anger of the masses or the meditation of the intellectuals ever coming together.

On the eve of the First World War, the situation of society and its problems were clarified, explained, and theorized. Popular disquiet found its expression in the reformist ideology and the Jadid organization. This rapid evolution, which contrasts with the immobility of the past centuries, was encouraged and hastened by four external events which caused the established order to be called into question, both within the state of Bukhara and in its relations with the empire.

First, there was 1904 and the collapse of all-powerful Russia before Japan. With this event, the Bukharan intelligentsia's dreams of past greatness and the popular resentments came to merge with the anti-Western current then sweeping across the subject peoples. The 1905 Revolution, closely linked with that defeat, was a second vital factor of change in Bukhara. The momentary triumph of liberal ideas in Russia, the possibility afforded these ideas to find expression and circulate, affected Bukhara all the more, in that freedom came to a halt at its frontiers. The despotic character of the régime and its refusal to consider the difficulties besetting society were felt particularly acutely, when outside Bukhara the effects of the revolution were visible. When, after 1907, revolution gave way to reaction, its effects persisted outside the empire's frontiers: Turkey and Iran each in turn offered a model to the subject Muslim peoples.[147] The revolutions that had occurred in these two countries corresponded to their dreams of renewal and brought them positive examples: constitutional régimes realizing the failed parliamentary hopes of the 1905 Russian Revolution.

Emancipation from Western tutelage, destruction of despotism at home, and construction of liberal régimes capable of meeting the needs of society and safeguarding the greatness of the national community — such were the milestone events that occurred between 1904 and 1914; and such would also be the essential lines of Jadid thought, and first that of Fitrat. Until the First World War, the Jadid movement of Bukhara had thus developed under the same conditions as other reformist movements in colonial countries. With the First World War and the Russian Revolution, it found itself grappling with new problems. These would be no longer only those of the colonial world to which it belonged, but those of the West from which it wished to detach itself.

Part III

National Reconquest, 1917–24

7

End of the Russian Empire: Bukhara Face-to-Face with War and Revolution

World War and the National Movement in Turkistan

The 1914 war, which seemed to interest only the society and order of Europe, was in fact crucial for the 'backward' regions of the Russian empire — and primarily for the most backward of all, Bukhara. This conflict, which concerned neither Bukhara nor Russia's Muslims, was nevertheless the motive element which gave concrete meaning to the ideas that until then had been slowly maturing, an impetus to the forces that were emerging. The structures of the empire, which had withstood the events of the years 1904–5, were threatened. The first almost imperceptible cracks, initially at the centre, swiftly reached the Turkistani periphery. Encouraged by intensive German propaganda centred on Bukhara[1] and by the state of effervescence that had been growing uninterruptedly for several years, the region's reformists thought the moment had arrived when they could display their aspirations openly. From 1916 on, all Turkistan — emirate and guberniya alike — found itself in a state of declared revolt against Russia: a revolt that ranged from limited protests to demands for total independence, with Bukhara's spokespersons representing the most extreme demands. Two facts testify to this effervescence, which contrasts with the calm demonstrated during the First World War by the Muslims of the empire's other regions:[2] the Lausanne Conference and the 1916 revolt.

From the start of the War, Russia's Muslim émigrés in Constantinople had engaged in intensive activity to draw the attention of world public opinion to their problems. Organized into a 'Committee for Defence of the Rights of the Muslim Peoples of Russia',[3] they had entered into relations with the 'Union of Nations',[4] which finally provided them with a platform from which to expound their demands publicly. The Third Congress of the Union of Nations, held at Lausanne from 27 to 29 June 1916 — a congress convened by a body theoretically favourable to the Entente — saw a veritable arraignment of Russia as an oppressing power. The representatives of the empire's subject nationalities gave an international dimension to their demands, but these were varied. The maximum demands were presented by the representatives of Bukhara and Finland, at one in calling for total independence.

The great nomad revolt which broke out in 1916 was provoked by the decision of the Russian authorities to mobilize Muslims exempted from military obligations into an agricultural service at the front.[5] The news, published by a Russian newspaper in Turkistan, *Turkestanskie Vedemosti*,[6] caused considerable local feeling. The leaders of the Turkistani reformist movement came out resolutely against the decision. In May 1916 a secret meeting was held in Bihbudi's apartment in Samarqand attended by Munavvar Qari Abdurrashidov, Pahlavan Niyaz,[7] 'Usman Khodzhaev (one of the most active leaders of the Jadid movement in Bukhara), Abijan Mahmud,[8] and Qari Kamil.[9] After discussing the possibility of Turkistani mobilization, they decided to provoke an armed uprising if this eventuality came to pass.[10]

Not all who took this decision had the same reasons for acting. The representatives of the Kazakh-Kirghiz nomads wanted restitution of their confiscated lands, in relation to which exemption from military obligations appeared an extremely limited kind of recompense. Bihbudi and Munavvar Qari thought Muslims should not be conscripted, since they did not enjoy the same rights as Russians. 'Usman Khodzhaev, on the other hand, was clearly interested in the possibility of a general uprising against the Russians that would lead to a break-up of the empire. On 25 June 1916 the mobilization order[11] provoked considerable feeling among the Turkistani masses. General Kuropatkin, analysing the events,[12] wrote that the rising was facilitated by the highly confused character of the text, very badly drafted, which made it extremely hard to know which individuals and which age categories were affected by the measures. The entire male population of Turkistan aged between nineteen and forty-five felt threatened. Soon the most alarming rumours were abroad, fuelled by the reformists, by 'German and Turkish agents', by various pamphlets, and so on.

A few days later armed risings broke out, and on 13 July Jizakh was the site of extremely violent incidents. The rioters attacked the Russians and their installations, sabotaged the railroad, uprooted telegraph posts and burnt fuel depots. The agitation spread. At Samarqand, eighty-three Russians were killed and seventy taken hostage. There was a succession of burnings and rapes, and the insurgents proclaimed a *ghazavat* (holy war) against the infidel. The governor-general of Turkistan, however, sent troops from Samarqand and Tashkent and within a week the revolt was broken. Sporadic outbreaks occurred for a few days longer in some parts of Central Asia, but the organized insurrection was defeated, at least at the level of the guberniya (though farther away, in the steppes, the Kazakh-Kirghiz maintained an armed opposition until the February Revolution. The drama, which in Turkistan lasted only a few weeks, had a considerable impact. The mobilization order of 25 June 1916 had allowed the leaders of the reformist movement to raise publicly a number of issues closely bound to Russian colonization. Together with legal inequality, rural colonization and peasant hardship had been the arguments advanced from the beginning of the insurrection; since they re-flected the difficulties of the Turkistani masses, the masses had been only too ready to listen to the leaders' call. But very soon, beyond immediate concerns, the summons to holy war challenged the Russian presence as a whole. The 1916 uprising then became — especially in the minds of the reformists and masses of Bukhara and to a lesser extent all Turkistan — a logical sequel to the resistance of 1867-8.

The February Revolution

The February Revolution met an extremely favourable response in Turkistan, since the régime, challenged there for months, had at times been totally rejected and excitement ran high. The First World War had highlighted, and facilitated a deeper understand-ing of, all the region's problems. As the February Revolution dawned, nationalist demands, which had gradually crystallized from aspirations for religious reform, were brought to the fore. What reform was the new régime going to institute here? What solutions could it provide for the problems of all the empire's nationalities?

The Provisional Government installed on the ruins of the monarchy was very divided and uncertain about what solutions might settle the national problem.[13] It was also hampered in its choice by the determination shared by all the February leaders to continue the war. It quickly discovered how much easier it was to defend oppressed nations when doing so was a weapon against imperial power than it was to settle their fate in a liberal manner once it was itself in power. It postponed any solution until such time as a constituent assembly could decide on it and contented itself with offering the non-Russians a declaration of rights, on 19 March. This accorded equal rights to individuals but avoided the national question itself. Thus, inequality between individuals was abolished for non-Russians, as for Russians — that is, the revolution was extended throughout the former empire at the individual level — but inequality between nations continued.

The population of Central Asia welcomed the February Revolution with contradictory feelings, which gave a specific character to the régime installed there until the October Revolution. For the local people, bruised and shattered by the repression of 1916, the prevailing feeling was one of relief. They took no part in events because the traces of coercion were too deep in their memories for them to dare intervene, but the fall of a detested régime, responsible for so much suffering and blood, filled them with hope.

For the Russians (prelates, officials, and settlers) the reaction was just as unanimous: what was necessary was to save Russian power in Central Asia, save the positions Russia had acquired, and prevent a Russian revolution from degenerating into a native revolt. The attitude of Kuropatkin, the governor-general, expressed this general feeling extremely well: as soon as he learned of the Petrograd events, he declared that he was entering the service of the revolution and proposed to the Tashkent soviet plans to organize defence 'against a native rising'. The Provisional Government supported him, since one of its first decrees had been enacted to order 'officials and soldiers to remain in their positions'.[14] This order was obeyed, particularly in Turkistan, where the first soviets set up in March gave a minimal place to the local population, but where a number of former Russian military leaders sat who had taken part in the repression of all the revolts that had drenched Central Asia in blood over the past twenty years.

Only in April 1917 did the representatives of the old order give way to new political cadres. The Provisional Government replaced the authority of the former governor-general of Turkistan by a 'provisional executive committee'. Kuropatkin was arrested in his home, and on 7 April the 'Turkistani Committee of the Provisional Government' was established,[15] presided over by Schepkin, a former Constitutional-Democratic deputy. This included not only Russians (Preobrazhenskii, Lyapovskii, Elpatiev, and Shkapskii), but also four Muslims (General Davlechin, Sadri Maksudov, Muhammad Tanyshbaev, and 'Alikhan Bukeykhanov). A sizeable number of the council members belonged to the Constitutional-Democratic party, which did not help to consolidate the committee's authority over the soviets then being established, notably the Tashkent Soviet. As early as 22 April, the committee was attacked by the soviet at Jizakh, which reproached it with being a product of the former régime's leaders. In May, the regional soviet elected by the first congress of Turkistan soviets (7–15 April 1917) removed Schepkin and some of his collaborators from power; the Orientalist Nalivkin assumed the presidency of the committee.[16]

Parallel with this legal power, a soviet power was established from the first days. On 12 March, while making the official announcement of the revolution, Kuropatkin granted Russian parties the right to organize:[17] the Social-Democrats formed a Council of Worker Deputies of Tashkent, which contained only Russians; the Socialist-Revolutionaries, presided over by Brojdo, formed a Council of Soldier Deputies,[18] and the Constitutional-Democrats grouped themselves into a Council of Political Organizations. On 17 March these three groups, which contained only Russians in their ranks, fused into the Soviet of Worker and Soldier Deputies, which was presided over by Brojdo and dominated by Socialist-Revolutionaries and Mensheviks up to the revolution.

During this entire period, which dawned with an immediate if temporary alliance among all Russian tendencies, the conflict that was increasingly to develop between the committee and the soviets[19] — and to culminate in the committee being routed[20] — was a Russian affair that did not concern the Muslims at all. From the outset, too, victory for the soviets appeared inexorably certain.[21] Excluded from the revolution, the Muslims strove to organize themselves. From March onwards the *Shawra-yi Islam* (Muslim Council) grouped liberal intellectuals and numerous Jadids who demanded a democratic and federal constitution, under which the peoples of Turkistan would enjoy equal rights with the Russians.[22] The Muslim clergy of Turkistan was organized into the *Jam'iyat-i 'Ulama*, presided over by Shir 'Ali Lapin, whose monarchist and conservative positions were miles away from those of the reformists. Eventually the reformists grouped around an organization that they dominated, *Turkistan Musulman Markazi Shawrasi,* which was joined by Bihbudi, Mustafa Chokay-ughli and 'Ubaydallah Khodzhaev.

Lastly, a Muslim Socialist Movement (MSM) made a timid

appearance, but it was not very representative. It was paralysed, moreover, by innumerable divisions; the Union of Muslim Workers of the Ferghana and a similar group in Samarqand were the most effective of the groups that sprang from the MSM. All had in common the fact of being dominated by Socialist-Revolutionaries and Mensheviks. In reality, the Muslims of Turkistan had little latitude for action on the morrow of the revolution. This is why the interest of the most advanced (the Jadids) turned towards Bukhara, where the situation at first appeared favourable to change.

In Bukhara the Russian Revolution was learned of on 4 March 1917 and provoked intense excitement and hope there. The news arrived at a juncture when the situation in the emirate was particularly difficult. This was true, first, in political terms: with the advent of the First World War the ruler had re-established an authority demanded by the *qadimis*; that is, he had reversed the liberal measures put through in the educational sphere, giving the reformists a choice between flight and clandestine activity. The effect of this had been to displease the bourgeoisie considerably and to spread the Jadid endeavours into the ever restless eastern part of the emirate.

Second, Bukhara's economic life was seriously unsettled. During the war, Russian imports of essential foodstuffs — indispensable since Bukhara had oriented itself towards intensive production of cotton — had dwindled, creating from the end of 1916 on conditions of semi-famine in the emirate. Furthermore, the price of products imported from Russia increased rapidly during the war, whereas the market-price of cotton, stable until 1915, subsequently declined. Between 1914 and 1917, the buying-power of the Bukharan peasant was reduced by 50 or 60 per cent, on a normal cotton harvest.[23] Given how low it was already before the war, one can easily imagine what poverty prevailed in the emirate. As misfortune would have it, the year 1916–17 was also characterized by a drought of exceptional severity: the harvest was very bad. At the beginning of 1917 the population of Bukhara was thus suffering from a serious famine and from a drop in its income, as a result of the poor cotton harvest. This last point had tragic consequences,[24] because of the system of buying cotton 'uncut', through advances to the producer, which had been developing continuously since the nineteenth century.

That year the peasants were unable to deliver the cotton for which they had already been paid. Since their debts were considerable, the number of peasants dispossessed of their land by moneylenders increased sharply. A mass of idle wretches wandered from town to town in search of employment; increasingly they congregated round the Russian cities, alone possibly in a position to offer them a job. The family unit, formerly very strong, was thus shattered; the departure of the men to find means of support elsewhere altered the physiognomy of the villages, and on their return, the men brought with them the vision of new horizons and new ideas. For these families, dislocated and driven to desperation by poverty, the authority of the traditional clergy no longer provided the same certainties as in the past.

As soon as the revolution was known in Bukhara, unrest broke out in the Russian towns.[25] Even if there existed no organized proletariat among the indigenous population, the situation was different with the Russians of Charju'i, Novaya Bukhara, Kerki, and Termez: out of 50,000 individuals,[26] a high proportion of railwaymen and textile workers constituted a true proletariat, subjected since 1905 to continuous propaganda from the Social-Democrats.[27] On 8 March 1917 a meeting organized by the railwaymen of Novaya Bukhara drew more than 6,000 people.

The Bolshevik Poltoracky,[28] who had organized it, proclaimed that the February Revolution, bourgeois though it might be, should be extended to Bukhara as soon as possible. The Russian political agent, Miller, who had scarcely any knowledge of the situation in the empire[29] and was there as an observer, was taken to task and enjoined to intervene with the Provisional Government in order to get it to transform radically the emirate's institutions. Miller, who knew nothing of the Provisional Government's intentions, tried in the days that followed to calm people down. But his moderate attitude was viewed as a betrayal and led from the outset to a virtual rupture between the tsar's former representative, who had now become the official representative of the new government, and the Russians of the emirate. Russian workers disarmed the police in Novaya Bukhara, invaded the prisons and freed the inmates. Miller summed up the situation as follows in a cable addressed to Kuropatkin,[30] still governor of Turkistan: 'Very large numbers of Russian textile workers and the clerks and workers of the Central Asian and Bukharan railways are establishing organizations designed to replace the local Russian police and, it seems, our other organs.' Worried about the actions of those subject to his authority, Miller also saw that the unrest was reaching the local people. In a secret cable to the Provisional

Government,[31] he mentioned that the spirit of rebellion and disorder had spread 'to the Bukharan Jews, to certain merchants and to the Shi'a'.

The Jadids and the Struggle for Reforms

In the event, Miller proved himself to be a poor observer, as he was to remain throughout this difficult period. Right from the beginning of March 1917, the unrest extended far beyond the emirate's minority groups and the liberal merchants. Those who listened with most enthusiasm to the inflamed harangues of the Russian meetings were the uprooted and dispossessed peasants waiting for work in the towns; they hardly found any work, since the Russians' own activities slowed down. But they heard the echo of the revolution and the calls for a transformation of Bukhara. What they retained was the demand 'The land to the peasants' advanced by the Bolsheviks. And they returned to their land, in order not to miss the distribution, which they thought should occur. They brought back with them the revolutionary spirit of the Russian towns, the demand for a political transformation, and the immense hope — but soon disappointed — for ownership of the land that provoked in them a rebellious sentiment greater than in the past. Until 1916–17, the ideas of spiritual, political, and social reform were the prerogative of the urban bourgeoisie. After March 1917, thanks to the Russian proletariat in the emirate, the call for social justice and revolt reached the furthest depths of the countryside, where it was heard by those wretched masses who had never ceased to revolt spontaneously and who suddenly found ideas and a movement to which they might attach their revolt. If the Provisional Government and the Russians of the emirate could not offer these masses definite hopes, the reformists for their part were going to channel their aspirations and give them an outlet.

During the war and under clandestine conditions, the Jadids had made great progress in organizational terms. Two tendencies had gradually emerged within the movement. The moderates, dubbed 'the old men', defended a programme of limited reforms: civic freedoms, lowering and strict control of taxation, and suppression of fanaticism. Over against them, the left wing of the Jadids demanded radical transformations, wanted a reform like that of the Young Turks, and demanded that the ruler's power be strictly organized and limited.[32] Around this demand, the most radical elements of the Jadid group and the secret organization had in

1916 organized themselves into a party of Young Bukharans (*Mlado-Bukhartsy*). The February Revolution allowed them to emerge from their clandestine status and establish themselves in a semilegal existence, in which the party was transformed, opened, and developed.

The Central Committee was enlarged[33] to make room for personalities whose fame transcended the narrow circle of the initiated. Alongside 'Abd al-Vahid Burhan (Burkhanov) as president,[34] Fitrat as secretary, 'Usman Khodzhaev as treasurer, three new members were seated: Muhitdin Rafat, Musa Saizhanov, and Ata Khodzhaev.[35] The party organization was likewise taking shape. According to the pyramidal system of 'twelves',[36] each member of the Central Committee exercised authority over twelve individuals, each of whom was responsible in turn for twelve other individuals. Fifty organizations of this type were established in Bukhara as soon as the revolution occurred.

The revolution did not seem to have changed the ruler's attitude very much. When he heard the news, fearing lest the new government might have annexationist intentions towards him,[37] he hastened to assure it of his friendship and wish to maintain the links which had always united him with Russia. What had encouraged him in this attitude was a certain continuity of the Russian political personnel in Bukhara. Indeed, as in Turkistan where governor-general Kuropatkin had kept his functions, in the emirate the Russian February Revolution was at first marked by a simple change of title and place: Miller was transmuted into a 'Resident'[38] and moved his offices from Novaya Bukhara into the capital.

From the emir's attitude in the first days of the revolution the Young Bukharans concluded that they could hardly hope to see him embark on the path Russia followed. They needed support in prosecuting their demands, and they turned towards the Provisional Government — an understandable choice. Although the men grouped together in the new party were all hostile to Russia and to cooperation with the Russians, as they had always said and written, the Russians in the emirate were demanding that reforms of which the Jadids had dreamed should be carried out. In deriving support from wherever it was available, the Jadids were true to themselves. Had Fitrat not written that it was necessary to 'seek progress wherever it may be found, be it in China or even in Hell'? They were entering the hell of the infidels, but of infidels who were proclaiming the end of the imperialist régime and 'equality of all the empire's peoples'.[39] What the Young Bukharans did not yet know at the time was that Kuropatkin would find himself in agreement with Kerenskii, when the latter said that 'on no account should equal rights be established in Turkistan'.[40]

Trusting in the promises of the Provisional Government, in March 1917 the Young Bukharans sent the government a cable setting out the situation in the emirate and asking it to intervene in favour of an institutional reform whose two main points were the organization of a parliament (*majlis*) limiting the ruler's power and the establishment of a system of control over the local authorities in Bukhara, especially those representing the financial hierarchy.[41] The Provisional Government, alerted by Miller's cables to the unrest that was developing in Bukhara, replied to the Jadids that it was supporting their demands by interceding with the emir, while it advised the emir to satisfy the demands of the 'liberals'.

In any case, the Provisional Government knew nothing at all about the Emirate of Bukhara or about the Young Bukharan Party.[42] Kuropatkin's diary conveys some idea of the government's ignorance regarding the emirate. Recording an interview with Kerenskii on the subject of Bukhara, he wrote: 'Kerenskii, who is reputed to be a specialist in Asian questions, declared himself in favour of broadening the scope of the Manifesto, indicating the need to suppress slavery! Klem had to get things straight again and point out that slavery had been suppressed in Bukhara ages ago.'[43]

The official instructions to Miller to support the Young Bukharans were, because of this lack of knowledge, extremely vague. In particular, it seems Petrograd never suspected that application of the Young Bukharans' programme might encounter any opposition in the emirate. The cables arriving from the capital opined that, in view of the unrest reported by Miller, such measures would probably restore calm. No one seems to have envisaged the possibility that the emir might have other plans and that around him there might exist a conservative party hostile to any transformation of the emirate's political structures.

When the government's intercession produced little effect, Fayzallah Khodzhaev, Fitrat, and Musa Saizhanov sent via Samarqand a second appeal to Petrograd. Then a delegation made up of Fitrat and 'Usman Khodzhaev set off to plead the reformist cause. They got no further than Orenburg, since there they learnt of the departure for Bukhara of Russian envoys charged with settling the problem directly. Fitrat and Khodzhaev made haste to regain the capital, so that they might be present during the negotiations with the emir.[44]

The Russian delegation brought to Bukhara proposals as confused as those contained in the earlier telegram to the emir. Moreover, it sought to ignore entirely both the Young Bukharans and the ruler's conservative entourage; its intention was to settle the problem solely with the emir and the Russian resident. The proposals it was intending confused the issue of reforms with more general organizational plans, which amounted to a quasi-annexation. Kuropatkin wrote thus: 'It strikes me as a good idea to introduce into Bukhara, with appropriate modifications, the same military Commissariat organization that I intend to install in Khiva.'[45] To which Miller replied: 'Adoption for Bukhara of the same kind of military Commissariat as in Khiva is impossible, in the first place because of the existence of an organized liberal group which must be given the chance to express itself . . . It must also be given the chance to find a compromise with the conservative Party under the Resident's authority.'[46]

Once he had managed to bury Kuropatkin's proposals, Miller took upon himself the task of advocating reforms to the emir, stressing that in the event of his refusing he ran a considerable risk of seeing the governor of Turkistan's annexationist plan succeed.[47] The emir yielded and Miller, whose wish to play a personal role in this affair seems to have outweighed by far any political ideas or sense of consistency he may have had, took responsibility for drafting the manifesto in which the emir announced the reforms.[48]

In a cable to the Russian minister of foreign affairs, Miller indicated his conception of the manifesto:[49] 'A policy of reforms is indispensable, but under certain conditions. It must not run counter to the *shari'at* or to the religious sentiment of the Bukharan masses; it must not destroy Bukharan autonomy; above all, it must be effected under the supervision and guidance of the Russian authorities.'

Miller spelled out the most urgent reforms, those which the Jadids were demanding:

1 Establishment of a budget and a regular fiscal system.
2 Control over the local governors (begs).
3 Control over the emir's civil list.
4 Establishment of an autonomous administration of the capital and perhaps of other towns in the khanate.
5 Improvement of education, especially in the *madrasas*.
6 Finally, with respect to the Russian institutions, an expansion

of the postal and telegraphic network, the road network, and cultural institutions.

Elsewhere,[50] Miller instanced the reforms the emir had already undertaken since the start of the unrest — reduction of sentences and even amnesty measures for certain criminals; arrangements for the establishment of a printing-works in Bukhara, and publication of a joint Russo-Bukharan newspaper — and reported that the emir was discussing with him administrative autonomy for the capital.

During the preparation of the manifesto, Miller consulted the Young Bukharans on one occasion. In the course of an interview he asked certain of their representatives, including 'Usman Khodzhaev and 'Abd al-Vahid Burkhanov, to express their wishes and indicate to him by what means they might be realized. Fayzallah Khodzhaev, the most reliable witness to this interview, wrote that each of the Young Bukharans took care to reply in a way that avoided over-committing the party.[51] Their demands were as follows:

1 Establishment of a twofold popular representation to the emir and to the begs, this representation having in particular the power to improve and control the central and local administration.
2 Suppression of all taxes that were not authorized by the shari'at.
3 Total freedom for education, publishing and the press.
4 Modification of the emir's cabinet, by excluding all fanatical and reactionary ministers.

Despite the extreme prudence of the Jadids, their demands went much further than the plans Miller had outlined to the minister of foreign affairs.

Miller took no more notice of the conservatives' opinions; yet he knew that the emir's entourage, beginning with his qush-begi Nasrallah and the qadimi high clergy, was keeping a watchful eye on his plan, ready to display its hostility. This group derived considerable strength from the emir's own attitude. He had yielded to Miller's representations — though not, he made clear, to those of the Young Bukharans — but he pretended to stand outside the whole business by leaving Miller the task of preparing the manifesto. For this reason, in the eyes of the conservative group the whole reform plan appeared as a Russian initiative and an intolerable external intervention in the life of the emirate.

Meanwhile, the manifesto drafted by Miller was submitted first to the governor-general of Turkistan and then to the minister of foreign affairs,[52] who was slow to react. Petrograd's silence embarrassed Miller considerably. He multiplied his appeals to the minister, describing the trouble this silence was causing: 'The absence to date of comments upon the manifesto already approved by the governor-general is creating a tense situation here, dangerous to our interests in the khanate.'[53] He spelled out the dangers in question on numerous occasions:

> An extremist group of advocates of reform has established relations with the Muslims of Samarqand in an attempt to wrest from the emir the batch of reforms already proposed and in addition to present the government of Bukhara with its own demands . . . There are active contacts with Afghanistan here. Persistent rumours are afoot of preparations for a massacre and the elimination of Russians from the emirate.[54]

Milyukov's approval arrived at last, accompanied with a significant caveat: 'The said reforms should be enacted only in so far as is felt to be necessary.'[55] On the morning of 6 April, Miller could at last take the manifesto to the emir, who signed the two texts, Russian and Persian, without reading them, and only enquired as to their conformity with the *shari'at*. Reassured by Miller, he declared that 'he was ready to act for the good of his people by following, without hesitation, all instructions that Russia, protector of the emirate, might give him to this end.'[56]

The text of the manifesto did eventually contain Milyukov's procrastinatory advice. But thanks to a decoding error the term 'reform' had been replaced by 'autonomy', something which escaped Miller, the manifesto's author; the emir, who was signing it; and the personalities invited to attend its proclamation. This occurred on 30 March at the emir's palace, in the presence of religious personalities, ministers, high officials, Miller's colleagues Shulga and Vvedenskii, delegates from the Kagan and Samarqand soviets, Mahmud Khvaja, Isakharov, and a mulla — these last three representing the 'progressive' element.[57] Some 200 persons had been invited to hear the stand-in for the *qazi-kalan* read the text, which contrary to custom was not made public in the bazaars.

This manifesto proclaimed very modest reforms.[58] The emir promised, but in an extremely vague manner, that an assembly would be convened; a fiscal and judicial reform would be promulgated; the administration would be purged; and a printing-works would be established in the emirate. When? How would these reforms be put into practice? That remained unclear and the Jadids could say, 'The manifesto speaks of everything and of nothing.'[59]

Scarcely had the manifesto been proclaimed than the opposition to it erupted. The conservatives and *qadimi* clergy, who had at no stage of the drafting been consulted and were now invited to register a *fait accompli,* exploded. For the first time in the history of the state of Bukhara, reform measures had been taken without consultation with the religious authorities. Worse still, these measures, supposedly in conformity with the *shari'at,* had been drafted by the Russian resident. In the religious domain, the judgement of an infidel was substituted for that of the *'ulama!* Above all, behind the juridical and religious opposition, the *qadimi* clergy saw the chance to regain sway over the masses. The people of Bukhara, who contrary to established traditions in the emirate had not been given the manifesto to read, were tempted to investigate what this departure might mean. The *qadimis* set about explaining, first in the capital and then outside, that the text of the manifesto had been kept hidden from the masses because, being the work of a Russian, it bore no relation to the social demands of the people of Bukhara, but provided for reforms contrary to the law of Islam and, in particular, 'the introduction of Christianity into the emirate'.[60] The emir's silence was interpreted as a token of disapproval. A prisoner of the Russians, he had not wished — said the *qadimis* — to give them any support, in order to avoid leading his people into error. This position was all the stronger inasmuch as Miller had made the mistake of excluding also the Young Bukharans from the proclamation of the manifesto.

The Young Bukharans now decided to act to impose, this time without Russian help, the immediate application of all the reforms provided for in the manifesto. In this way, the reforms would not vanish into the firmament of pure ideas, and they would themselves be able to regain sway over the population, which was turning towards the *qadimis.* To realize this plan, two conditions had to be fulfilled: it was necessary to make the emirate's population understand what the manifesto was; and the emir had to be shown that he could implement it with the help of the Jadids — shown, if need be, that under their pressure and that of the popular masses he must implement it. For this, it was necessary to enter into direct contact with the population; the best way was certainly to organize a popular demonstration, which would prove to the emir the power of popular demands and to both the emir and the Russians the Jadids' influence over public opinion.

On 7 April the Young Bukharans held a meeting in the house of one of their supporters, Ahmad Naim,[61] in the presence of Turkistani Jadids, including Mufti Bihbudi, who played a decisive role there.[62] The discussion threw up two tendencies. The temporizers, that is, the majority of the original Jadids grouped around 'Abd al-Vahid Burkhanov, wanted the party to organize itself first on solid foundations rather than launch upon an adventure that would undoubtedly alienate the emir and provoke a rapprochement between the régime and the conservatives — between whom relations had been strained ever since the emir had accepted reforms. The 'revolutionaries' of the left wing reckoned, like Bihbudi, that whatever happened they would sooner or later come into conflict with the emir. The big disadvantage of the planned demonstration was perhaps that it would bring the moment of conflict closer. Its compensating advantages, however, were manifold: as Fayzallah Khodzhaev wrote,[63] it would enable the Jadids to count their troops; enter into contact with the masses; make real propaganda for the first time; and, in the event of failure, rid the party of fainthearts and provocateurs. Even if defeated, the Young Bukharans would emerge from this trial wreathed in sympathy, having shown their vitality and courage. The most ardent defenders of this viewpoint were Fitrat, 'Usman Khodzhaev, and Fayzallah Khodzhaev.

The demonstration took place on 8 April. From eight o'clock in the morning, the Young Bukharans mustered almost 1,000 sympathizers, among whom, according to Fayzallah Khodzhaev,[64] were 'numerous members of the Jewish, Persian, Shi'i, and Lezghin minorities, who had come to applaud the manifesto that would ensure them equal rights with the emir's other subjects' — a view the *qadimis* could not accept. Bearing red banners inscribed with the slogans 'Long Live the Liberator Emir', 'Long Live the Reform', and 'Long Live Freedom', the demonstrators marched on the Rigistan[65] and gathered new recruits on their way. Fayzallah Khodzhaev asserts that, on its arrival at the Rigistan, the column contained almost 5,000 people.[66] There it encountered a crowd of 7,000 or 8,000 counter-demonstrators — mobilized and marshalled by the *qadimi* mullas and students from the *madrasas* — who tirelessly proclaimed, 'We have no need of a new faith, we will die for the emir and the *shari'at*'. The Jadids could not explain to this crowd that the *shari'at* was not in question; so, to avoid a bloody clash with the fanatical mob, 'Abd al-Vahid Burkhanov ordered the demonstrators to disperse.

As the crowd shouted outside, the emir, shut up in his palace, listened to the *qadimis* advising him to be firm in the name of the popular will that had been expressed against the reforms and against the Young Bukharans; the failure of the demonstration, they said, testified to this. Until this moment, the emir's position had never been clear. He had accepted that reforms should be implemented, but at no time had he taken part in the preparation of such reforms. Faced with the opposition of the *qadimis*, he yielded to their demands and decided that the liquidation of the reformist movement would resolve all the other problems. He took immediate measures against the Jadids. Those who had not had time to flee — like 'Ayni, Mirza Sahbabe, or the three deputies sent to the *qush-begi* to assure him of the Young Bukharans' peaceful intentions (Ata Khodzhaev, Mir Baba, and Yusufzada) were arrested. While, on the emir's express orders, unrestrained beatings were being administered in the prisons ('Ayni, for example, received seventy-five strokes of the cane), Fayzallah Khodzhaev was advising the Jewish leaders to flee to Kagan, where 'Abd al-Vahid Burkhanov, fearing a massacre, had asked the Russians for asylum on behalf of the Young Bukharans. With a few friends Khodzhaev himself took refuge at Novaya Bukhara, and the Russian towns of the emirate henceforth became the centre of Jadid activity.

Despite the failure suffered on 8 April and the emir's abrupt volte-face, the Young Bukharans could not forget that they had always wanted changes in Bukhara to respect its structures, its past, and its traditions. In any case, the reaction of the masses, over whom it had been possible for the *qadimis* to regain control, proved that any other way would have been impossible, in so far as such changes needed to be based upon public opinion. The masses, who had no political education, had a poor understanding of grand ideas. After the upheaval of the first days, provoked by the impact of the February Revolution, they found the traditional religious and political cadres reassuring. Furthermore, one feeling was rooted in the people — perhaps the only conscious feeling it had — hostility to Russia. The reforms had failed precisely because they came from the Russians, who had ignored the traditional authorities and forms.

The Young Bukharans decided, on the morrow of their collapse, that it was still necessary, despite everything, to try to reform the state under the authority of its sovereign. However, they were not alone in wishing to act. While they strove to relocate their effort within the framework of the national community, Miller intervened to save the Provisional Government's authority in the emirate and strengthen the position of Petrograd's representatives in Turkistan. The power of these representatives was increasingly discredited. They were accused of having managed to achieve nothing. The success of a reform in Bukhara would have been a justification of their activity: a favourable point, belated perhaps, but one which they could have adduced to parry criticism from the soviets.

For all these reasons Miller, whose personal position was also increasingly insecure, on 10 April organized a meeting at the palace, attended by V. L. Vyat'kin,[67] the members of the Samarqand executive committee, those of the Novaya Bukhara soviet, and General Kolchanov, who had brought military reinforcements to Bukhara two days earlier. At this meeting, he obtained a twofold success:[68] he obliged Isakharov, a member of the Samarqand executive committee, to admit before the emir that he had encouraged and helped the demonstration of 8 April; and he got the emir to declare in the presence of the members of the executive committee, over whom for a long time he had had no authority, 'his intention of implementing reforms in full accordance with the views of the Russian government, whose directives he would always follow'. Miller reported these statements to Milyukov, indicating that an alliance between the Provisional Government and the emir was henceforth indispensable, since the Young Bukharans were turning more and more towards the soviets.

Miller's intervention with the emir had the effect of showing the Jadids, outlawed from the capital, how ambiguous his role was. Taking refuge in Novaya Bukhara and Samarqand, they then sought backing from the resident's enemies, that is, from the Samarqand Committee. Miller wrote the following to Milyukov:[69] 'The agitation of the Young Bukharans is growing, thanks to the provocations of the Muslims and Russians of Samarqand and Novaya Bukhara, who are urging them to present categorical demands directly to the government. They are convinced that its inability to respond to these will bring about an armed intervention by us, and that is precisely what they want.'

The new friendship between the Young Bukharans and the Samarqand Committee was translated into joint actions, in which it was hard to know who was involving whom. Together, they organized a solemn funeral for 'the first victim of the Bukhara liberation movement', the Muslim Nurallah Gafur. Also together, they cabled Milyukov, to ask him to support implementation of the reform and the initiative they were going to take *vis-à-vis* the emir.[70] Learning of the existence of this cable, Miller sent a message of his own to Milyukov in which for the first time he opposed any reform or support for the Jadids and asserted that the hour for reforms had passed and that it was necessary to avoid a rupture between the government of Bukhara and Russia and the general massacre of Russians that the enraged population was preparing. To that end, said Miller, it was necessary to support the ruler and his reactionary entourage: 'The adversaries of reform are, as I have already said, all classes of the Bukharan population; its only supporters are the Young Bukharans, of whom there are about 200.'

By adopting the opposite position to that which he had previously advocated, Miller was demonstrating a certain realism. Over the three or four days which followed the abortive Young Bukharan demonstration, the state of ferment in the capital had heightened considerably. The population of Bukhara was swollen by countless workless peasants arriving from the neighbouring countryside to take part in the 'movement', though they were not too sure which one — some still believed it was the revolution; others, a defence of the *shari'at* and the land of Bukhara. Although the reasons that brought these people to Bukhara appeared confused, since early March the entire population of the emirate was still filled first with an immense hope, then with a terrible anger; and it remained available, ready to respond to any call. It was all the more available at the beginning of April, inasmuch as this was the moment when agents would normally be travelling through the countryside to buy the summer harvest and paying out advances. Amid the unrest of spring 1917, nobody was venturing into the countryside and the peasants, who had spent an exceptionally hard winter in expectation of April's advances, discovered there were probably not going to be any.

They were ready, after that, to rush off wherever an organized movement might emerge, irrespective of its programme. In the space of a few weeks they learned to mistrust promises and programmes. Throughout the emirate, peasant troops led by their mullas were setting off for the capital, where some event was going on. From now on, the problem of Bukhara was to know who would control and use this mass, ready for any adventure.

The anger of the masses having been deflected by the *qadimis* onto the Young Bukharans and their Russian friends, it is easy to understand Miller's fear of plunging the entire emirate into chaos — and into a bloodbath whose first victims would be Russian citizens — if the *qadimis* were further enraged. Less lucid perhaps than the resident and haunted by their anxiety to reconquer those masses who had so swiftly escaped them, the Young Bukharans wanted to make one more attempt to impose reforms — in which for the moment (Miller in his message was right) nobody except themselves any longer believed. A last interview with the emir was granted the Jadids, but the conditions in which this took place indicate that ruler and resident had decided in advance to destroy the Jadids' position once and for all.

On 14 April a delegation of Young Bukharans who had taken refuge in the Russian zone arrived in Bukhara,[71] where a remarkable reception had been prepared by the emir's collaborators. From the station to the imperial palace, the delegates were conducted in an open carriage through the bazaar and the Rigistan, where a vast crowd was assembled. It was a Friday, at the exact hour when the congregation was emerging from the *salat*. The crowd, which the priests in charge of the service had just been preparing for this encounter, hurled itself upon the carriages, showering the Young Bukharans with abuse and stones.[72] When, after a very rough passage, they finally reached the throne-room, the emir's collaborators had divided those present into two groups: on one side, the Young Bukharans and the Russians (Miller, Shulga, Vvedenskii, and four members of the Novaya Bukhara executive committee); opposite them, high clerical dignitaries, officials, and the new *divan-begi* Nizam al-Din Khvaja, who 'in order to calm everyone down' had replaced a supporter of reform after the 8 April demonstrations.[73] Abused by those present, who called them traitors to their country, the Young Bukharans did not succeed in speaking. Mansurov's first sentence was interrupted by shouts of 'Death to them!'

The emir then intervened to assert that 'everything must remain as in the past',[74] whereupon he left the room and did not come back. At this moment the mob, still led by the mullas, arrived at the palace gates where it shouted loudly for the Young Bukharans to be handed over to it. The troops that Miller had arranged to be brought from Samarqand were 'forgotten' at Bukhara's railway-station; so, unaware of what was going on at the palace gates, they could not come to the help of those under siege. Realizing that they had fallen into a trap laid for them by the emir and Miller together,[75] the Jadids clung to the presence of the members of the Kagan Committee, which was their only safeguard and which Miller attempted to persuade to leave. Late that evening, the troops left at the station managed to come and free them and helped them flee to Novaya Bukhara. Thus ended, in a desperate flight, the activity of the reformists in Bukhara; here too came to a halt the attempts at reform in the emirate. Until the October Revolution, nothing was to be changed there.

Collapse of the Provisional Government's Representatives

After the 14 April interview, the Young Bukharans found themselves definitively rejected by the Bukharan community, as much by the masses as by the ruler. The anti-Russian, pro-emir position,[76] which they had maintained for so long despite bans and persecution, collapsed. If they were not, as certain historians have written,[77] Bolsheviks from the start, after their break with the emir they turned determinedly towards the Russians, towards the Bukhara soviets.

These soviets had steadily been growing stronger and asserted their authority *vis-à-vis* the Provisional Government's executive committees and according an ever-increasing place to the Bolsheviks. In the most important of these soviets, established by Poltoracky among the railwaymen of Novaya Bukhara, the Bolsheviks were in a majority from the outset. Natives working in the Russian cities sometimes took part in the soviets ('Abdallah Khvaja Tura),[78] but in Bukhara as in Turkistan the executive committees remained closed to the natives. Thus, from the outset the Bolsheviks seemed more liberal than the Provisional Government in recognizing national aspirations.

The executive committees and the resident at first attempted to resist the rise of the soviets. But they soon felt overwhelmed by them and relapsed definitively into inactivity, while the soviets displayed continuous energy. In April the Charju'i soviet founded a bulletin for demands and propaganda, *Chardzhuiskii Listok*, which appeared uninterruptedly until October and also reached the native population of the emirate's towns. On 9 May 1917 the first Social-Democratic organization was established in the emirate; one month later it had thirty-nine members. The soviets were concerned above all to weaken the Provisional Government and its representative.

On the morrow of the 14 April events, in possession at last of a serious subject for polemic, they threw themselves into an extremely violent campaign from which it emerged that Miller's blatant support for the *qadimis* and reaction was not fortuitous, but in conformity with his government's whole policy. In this campaign, the soviets solved two tactical problems at one time. In the first place, by positing a stance in favour of the Young Bukharans, who had hitherto ranged themselves under the protection of the Provisional Government's organs, they thereby opened the way for them to cooperate with the Bolsheviks. The slide of the Jadid party towards the Social-Democrats was thus precipitated by this action on the part of the local soviets. However, the line followed by the soviets on the morrow of 14 April had a second consequence too: it proved not only to the Provisional Government, but also to the local authorities and the Jadid opposition, that the soviets' hour had struck and the government henceforth had to take their wishes into consideration.

Not satisfied, in fact, with underlining that the resident was a reactionary and an agent of the overthrown régime, the soviets launched an attack on the residency[79] and arrested Miller.[80] The Turkistan Committee, increasingly outmatched on the spot by the soviets, which had undertaken to reorganize it,[81] sent a mission to Bukhara to reassert the resident's authority. The mission (Preobrazhenskii and Davlechin) wrote to Schepkin[82] that nothing justified such great alarm; nevertheless, it was unable to obtain the soviets' agreement to Miller's reinstatement.[83] Miller was replaced by Chirkin[84] (like him an imperial official) and Vvedenskii[85] (the ousted resident's deputy). So from April 1917 on, in the first important conflict between themselves and the Provisional Government, the soviets of the emirate had succeeded in imposing their will.

From that time on the activity of the soviets developed unchecked. At the beginning of May the first regional congress of soviets of the emirate's Russian towns met in Novaya Bukhara, and decided to intervene in 'the Bukharan question'. The congress then addressed a message to the legal authorities of Turkistan, demanding, on the one hand, a right of supervision over the 'bourgeois' resident and, on the other, the preparation of a reform that would this time not be proposed to the emir by the Russian authorities, but imposed upon him.[86] This initiative, regarding which the Provisional Government's representatives would prove incapable of taking up a position,[87] nevertheless provoked a conflict between the local soviets and the Turkistan Soviet (*Turkestanskii Kraevoi Sovet rabochikh i soldatskikh deputatov*) which, annoyed by this act of insubordination on the part of soviets that it intended to dominate, on 11 May 1917 ordered the local soviets not to intervene in the affairs of the residency or the emirate. In spite of this, a Committee for Bukharan Affairs (*Komitet po Bukharskim voprosam*) was created by the regional soviets and grouped the representatives of the soviets, Young Bukharans, and even a delegate of the Provisional Government.

The collapse of the Provisional Government had another effect: the ruler, who had hitherto seemed to be Petrograd's docile ally, gradually embarked upon a path that would lead him to break totally with Russia. Once rid of the Jadids, 'Alim Khan wanted to enact part of the reforms the manifesto promised. He sought to convince the *qadimis* of the need to give some satisfaction to a public opinion in ferment, assuring them that these partial reforms would be placed under their authority. But he came up against not only their hostility, but also the indifference of the Provisional Government's representatives, who paralysed his efforts by constantly delaying the dispatch to Bukhara of the Russian advisers needed to put into effect the manifesto's promises.[88] This strengthened the position of the *qadimis*, who in addition found an important moral support in the approach made to Bukhara in June 1917 by a Tashkent *'alim*, Mulla Hamurad, who arrived with a *rivayat* accusing all the Jadids of Bukhara and Turkistan of being 'declared enemies of the Islamic faith' and, therefore, summoning the faithful to oppose them. Vvedenskii wrote that the effect of the *rivayat* was very great, upon both urban and rural population.[89] Such a condemnation, pronounced by an *'ulama* foreign to the emirate's internal disputes, was highly significant for a people attached so strongly to the Islamic faith. For their own ends the *qadimis* adopted Fitrat's call to holy war and turned it against Fitrat and his friends, whose crime was to have allied themselves with the emirate's foes.

Not content with having affected public opinion in this way, the *qadimis* also attacked the ruler, who had to confront specific threats. In this connection Vvedenskii wrote as follows:[90] 'For the first time, the reactionary party demanded that the emir be deposed, for his concessions in the matter of the reforms, and replaced by his uncle the Beg of Gusar.' But these threats were vain. The emir, weary of the Provisional Government's intrigues, weary too of its weakness in the face of the soviets, reckoned from this moment on that the agreements which bound him to Russia were outdated.[91] Above all he saw that for the first time since 1868 Russia, wracked by violent convulsions, was close to falling apart. The time seemed to have come to separate the emirate's destiny from that of the old protecting power. The problem of Bukhara's independence had been posed at the Lausanne Conference. Despite his not very representative character, the orator who had spoken in the name of Bukhara had been defending an aspiration common to all trends of opinion, conservative and reformist. For the emir, the moment to realize the Lausanne programme was approaching.

He began by drawing closer to the *qadimis*: he reshuffled the government in accordance with their wishes and replaced the prime minister Nasrallah by Nizam al-Din Khvaja, who pursued all the Jadids and their sympathizers mercilessly. He also brought other no less zealous conservatives to power, such as Tura Khvaja Sudur.[92] Then the emir turned towards the masses: at the beginning of summer 1917 he informed his people that — because of the drought, the inadequate harvests, and the increase in the cost of living, which had been continuous from March to June — half of the *kharaj* and of all taxes levied in the emirate would not be collected, but would be made up by the royal exchequer. This decision achieved the anticipated effect and had major consequences. By relieving all his subjects of part of their fiscal obligations, the emir had done much more for them than if he had granted them reforms whose precise import they, for the most part, had some difficulty in grasping. What is more, it seemed — and the officials of the emirate helped to spread this idea — that such a measure was possible only because the disintegration of Russian power was at last allowing the emir to act freely. The peasants had been crushed by taxes well before 1868, but for half a century all taxes had been justified by Russian demands. It is not surprising that they should have associated the reduction of taxes with the weakening of Russia.

While the emir was hastily restoring a kind of national unanimity around him, the Jadids, excluded from this unanimity, were forced into exile. They had a choice between Turkistan and the Russian towns of the emirate, but they preferred to stay in the emirate because they had more specific concerns than their Turkistani friends. Bukhara and its future interested them, in the first instance. They had already engaged in political activity, so the discussions of the Muslim congresses of Russia about federalism or autonomy struck them as too theoretical and well short of reality; hence, they eventually chose Kagan as their land of exile because there they sought to endow the party with the means for the struggle they envisaged.

The situation of the Young Bukharan Party was, at this juncture, unfavourable: it had been hit hard, its members scattered, and its ideas overturned; some stock-taking was in order. The moderate right took the initiative in the discussion, arguing that the extremists were responsible, by their very excesses, for the situation in which the party found itself. In May 1917 Burkhanov, Fazil al-Din Makhdum, and Muhyi al-Din Rafat convened a meeting of the survivors, whose aim was to 'reorganize the hierarchy'. This meeting was all the more opportune, from their point of view, inasmuch as most of the extremist members of the Central Committee (like Fitrat or 'Usman Khodzhaev) were absent. The session, opened by Burkhanov, led to the creation of a new Central Committee presided over by Muhitdin Mansurov, of whom Burkhanov said in his speech that he had the great merit of being level-headed and of being in close contact with the Russian commercial bourgeoisie.[93] Around Muhitdin Mansurov, the Central Committee grouped a large number of moderates and only a few extremists.[94] Thus, the leadership of the party passed, in this period, into the hands of the 'Old Jadid' temporizers.

The theoretical problems to be resolved by the party were of two kinds. It was first of all necessary to define what reforms the party intended to urge upon the emirate: reform or revolution; political revolution, or political and social revolution? It was necessary also to determine the ways of getting there and, primarily, the limits of the alliance with the Russians: how far could this alliance go; and with whom should they ally themselves, the Russian liberal bourgeoisie or the soviets? Finally, how were they to achieve power: by preparing the hostile masses of the emirate through a slow work of persuasion or by imposing a new order from outside, with Russian help?

For the moderates who formed the majority on the leading body, the reply to all these problems was clear: the programme should be directed towards legal activity. What they wanted was to appeal to the emir's clemency, ask him for an amnesty, return to Bukhara, and in legality prepare with him a reform limited to the institutions, a reform acceptable to everyone because it would not overturn the social order and because it would be not of Russian origin, but a purely internal affair.

The left wing — for which Fayzallah Khodzhaev, who had returned in haste, spoke — replied that though this was an ideal which it too would like to achieve, it was necessary even while pursuing it to make provision for a more realistic alternative policy. Khodzhaev suggested that the party should simultaneously start negotiations with the emir and develop a clandestine activity designed, in the event of the former proposal failing, to prepare — with such allies as could be found — an armed insurrection against him.[95] The majority contented itself with the right's position and accepted — as a minimal concession to the extremists — the creation of little groups of agitators who would prepare the Bukharan population for the idea of a reform, by explaining its necessity and scope. Such reformist preaching was a far cry from the preparation of an armed uprising; yet even this decision remained a dead letter: the only group of agitators ever formed was that of Fayzallah Khodzhaev and Yusufzada, which did not go beyond the bounds of Charju'i. The programme of the Young Bukharan party was resumed in this way by 'Ubaydallah Khvaja, the party's envoy to the Muslim congress in Moscow:[96] 'implementation of the Manifesto's promises and propaganda in favour of reform among the masses'. The party's extremist wing thus seemed condemned to inactivity, its ideas having been rejected and the emir showing no intention of amnestying the Young Bukharans.

Soon convinced that the moderate position was ruining all the party's chances of playing a role in the events now taking shape, the extremists decided to move to act. At a meeting from which the moderates were absent, Fayzallah Khodzhaev proposed that they should move immediately to prepare an armed uprising. This required money — 100,000 roubles, which he thought could be obtained either from the resident, whom he reminded of the emir's now declared hostility, or from the soviets — and weapons, to be obtained from the Turkmen tribes. The financial difficulties encountered, and the Residency's systematic opposition to these revolutionary plans,[97] led the party towards the soviets and towards new allies capable of helping it, the Russian soldiers. At Kerki, where the Russian garrison was large and the troops already won over to the soviets, the Jadids found a warm reception. With the Kerki reformists they organized a 'club', which Russian officers and soldiers used to attend. Strengthened by the Russian troops' support, the Young Bukharans obliged the Beg of

Kerki to have the manifesto proclaimed in the great mosque after prayers. Thus, in the late summer of 1917 when the Provisional Government was still master of Russia, Russian troops in a state of quasi-rebellion who obeyed only the Kerki Soviet had helped the Jadids to stir up one region of Bukhara against the emir's authority. This collusion and the circumstances surrounding it — the manifesto was read at the mosque after the *salat* — oddly prefigured the revolution in Bukhara and the mullas who would write up Bolshevik slogans on streamers in the mosques.

Lessons of February

Study of the evolution of the Jadid movement in Bukhara from February to October 1917, and of the policy that the Provisional Government then conducted in the emirate, raises several questions. First, what precisely was the Provisional Government's policy in Bukhara? It seems that in Turkistan and the two 'protected' khanates, the Provisional Government was from the outset far from liberal; what emerges is its absolute refusal to take account of the national demands of the indigenous population. When, in August 1917, a delegation from Turkistan composed of Bukharan Jadids exiled in Samarqand and Jadids from the former guberniya came to plead the cause of its national ideal to Kerenskii, the latter replied,[98] 'I know Turkistan and its population well. I believe in your loyalty and reject the rumours about disturbances supposedly being prepared among you against Russia. But I warn you that if such an eventuality were to occur, I should take the most far-reaching measures of coercion'.

These far-reaching measures included, among others, the annexation of Bukhara whenever the opportunity should present itself. Consulted on this subject by the minister of foreign affairs, Tereshchenko, on 13 May 1917, Kuropatkin replied to the minister, who favoured integrating all Turkistan including the khanates into Russia, as follows:[99] 'It is preferable to preserve the autonomy of the khanates, an autonomy tightly controlled by Russia, which would — in appearance — leave power to a higher Muslim Council wherein Young Bukharans and reactionaries, closely intermingled, would obviously be unable to adopt any common political line, thus leaving the door open to all Russia's interventions and directives.'

In any case, Kuropatkin reckoned that integration of the khanates into Turkistan would merely aggravate the problems posed by the region for Russia, by adding a mass of individuals fanatically attached to their faith and their religious authorities. The autonomy of Bukhara presented the advantage of showing to the Turkistani's brethren, whose condition was tragic and who were torn apart by internal schisms, the advantages of being attached to Russia — a particularly opportune policy, according to Kuropatkin, at a time when the Turkistani élite was preparing a whole programme aimed at eliminating the Russians. Bukhara, eternally unsettled and wretched, should provide the Turkistanis with an image of what would happen in the event of their gaining autonomy. So that Bukhara might better play this exemplary role, it was of course necessary to avoid all progress. So the Provisional Government, in a last fit of energy, strove above all to prevent the emir from implementing the manifesto.

It seems also that in the emirate, as throughout Turkistan, the Provisional Government was from the outset constrained also by the reactions of the Russian elements. From Petrograd to Bukhara the distance was immense, and problems were viewed differently. For the Russians, Turkistan was a colony and Bukhara a future colony. A real 'poor-white' reflex operated here; after the February Revolution the first need the Russians perceived was to maintain Russian positions in the region. The continuity of Russian political personnel from one régime to the next was justified precisely by the need to have Turkistan 'specialists' directly on the spot, all of whom had demonstrated their severity and repressive authority to the Turkistanis in the time of the empire. Nowhere in Russia did the March declaration have so little meaning as in Turkistan, where weapons were distributed to the Russian colonists alone, 'in case it became necessary to defend the revolution'.

But this leads on to a second question: what exactly did the Provisional Government represent in Bukhara? It seems that neither in Bukhara nor in Turkistan was the Provisional Government at any time really present. Even in February it was already superseded and annihilated, on the one hand by officials of the former régime, on the other, by the soviets.

The officials of the former régime — as was the case with the Russian resident in Bukhara, who played a considerable personal role in that period, and with Kuropatkin in Turkistan, who was the intermediary between Bukhara and Petrograd — implemented the policy of the Turkistan Russians and perhaps also that of the former régime more than they did Petrograd's general directives.

As for the soviets, they called into question the very existence of the government. Brojdo summed up the situation thus:[100] 'All power was in the hands of the soviets from the first days of the February Revolution. October, in this region, preceded the Russian October'.

Thus, if the Provisional Government really had any representatives in Bukhara, it had scarcely any possibility of action. From the start, it was a fractured régime, at best capable of receiving criticisms and crystallizing bitternesses.

The third question relates to the image of the Provisional Government that prevailed in Bukhara. What ultimately characterized the reactions of the various political forces in Bukhara towards the Provisional Government was that, from the summer of 1917 onwards, without this implying any alliance, they nevertheless found themselves all equally hostile to the Russian leaders. How had this come about? For the emir, the answer seems simple. He had hoped initially to be able to preserve the status quo of pre-February 1917. He had retained this hope so long as he saw in the Provisional Government a real force, capable of keeping its commitments. Thinking initially that the power of the Petrograd government was real, he had yielded to Miller's reformist promptings, believing him genuinely to be the agent of the new rulers' will and capable of providing him with support in the internal crisis that the reforms would precipitate. If he had accepted the reforms, it was because he had judged the situation clearly.

The innovative ideas that had troubled the emirate for years were suddenly transformed into an ideology reflecting all the needs of the masses and thereby capable of mobilizing them. To resist this current would have been suicidal, especially since at the frontiers of the emirate the revolution was triumphing and even had a certain number of forward posts — the soviets — against which the emir intended to struggle. By accepting a few reforms, he could save not only the emirate's independence, but also its juridical and political foundations, the essential components of its social structures, and the régime itself. As soon as he felt the popular tension slackening, however, the emir thought that the idea which sustained the tension was itself on the retreat. At the same time, he saw the degeneration of the Russian power in which he had believed; so he decided to follow the path outlined by the emirate's traditional authorities: the path of coercion and rejection of reforms. Now he had also to separate himself from that lacerated Russia and look for his salvation outside the country and then against it. The Russian situation seemed to permit the hope of recovering total independence.

The position of the Jadids is more complicated to define. There was an astonishing continuity in their political dream before and after February 1917. The revolution that had occurred in Russia and the ideological and political transformation that it implied did not deflect them from their determination to restore their country's greatness around the emir. They simply thought that the national reconquest — against Russia — could be achieved with the aid of the Russian revolutionaries: initially confident in the egalitarian ideals of the February Revolution, for a time they rallied to it; but when they were disappointed by it, in the same manner they opted for the Bolsheviks.

Of all the Russian political parties, however, the Bolshevik Party was the one which least corresponded to their aspirations, whether in social and political matters or in the national domain. The Jadids dreamed of a parliamentary monarchy or a régime inspired by the Young Turks, in which social justice would be preserved and which would make Bukhara a rallying-point for the Muslim lands of Central Asia. They did not dream at all of a state springing from the class struggle and the victory of the proletariat. They eventually went over to the Bolsheviks not through a deliberate choice, but because in the total political void and power vacuum to which the Provisional Government's rule in fact amounted, all that stood out was the authority of the soviets, which were supporting them in Bukhara — basically, the authority of the Bolsheviks. Disappointed by the Provisional Government upon which they had based great hopes, the Young Bukharans were irretrievably drawn towards the Bolsheviks, whom they joined — as they had initially joined the February revolutionaries — with their support limited just to the realization of their own aspirations. In fact, the Young Bukharans had managed to pass through the first revolution of 1917 without their horizon having been altered in the slightest. They were pursuing, untroubled, their dream of national and Islamic reconquest.

8

The October Revolution: Alliance between the Jadids and the Bolsheviks

According to some historians, the October Revolution in Turkistan was a victory by 'Russians and Muslims united in a single struggle'.[1] If this view were accurate and the Jadids had been true Bolsheviks, the alliance between those two very different groups would pose few problems. If, on the other hand, historical truth is otherwise, two questions are raised: what was the course of the October Revolution in Turkistan; and how did the Jadids understand that revolution and by what means were they won over to it?

Numerous historians have told us that the Bolshevik revolution in Turkistan was a Russian revolution.[2] Safarov wrote:

> It was inevitable that the Russian revolution in Turkistan should have been colonialist. The Turkistani working class was numerically small and had no leader, programme, party or revolutionary tradition. It thus could not rise up against colonial exploitation. Under Tsarist colonialism, it was a privilege of the Russians to belong to the industrial proletariat. Because of this, the dictatorship of the proletariat here took on a typically colonialist character.[3]

The Bolshevik Revolution began in Turkistan on 12 September 1917. It did not achieve victory until two months later. In the interim, the organs of the Provisional Government remained in place; but even at this time the soviets had definitively liquidated their power. On 12 September a coalition of Left Socialist-Revolutionaries (SRs), Left Mensheviks, and Bolsheviks seized power in Tashkent and entrusted authority to a new soviet of worker and soldier deputies that was made up of eighteen Left SRs, ten Left Mensheviks, and seven Bolsheviks. The new committee governed in the name of the revolution and according to principles laid down in the main resolution of the meeting of railway workers and soldiers, held on the same day, which had brought it to power.

This resolution was basically concerned with social reforms: nationalization, agrarian reform, and workers' control over production.

Nalivkin, president of the executive committee of the Provisional Government, had to recognize the new committee even as he called on Petrograd for assistance. On 16 September the rebellion was quelled, thanks to moderate Russian elements — troops who had remained loyal or swiftly changed sides again — that soon afterwards received additional support from Kerenskii's special envoy, General Korovnichenko. The general, however, succeeded only in preserving a fictive power; in reality, the soviets remained masters of the situation.

On 26 October, after Lenin had taken power in Russia, the Turkistani soviets met and passed a motion refusing to obey the authority of the Provisional Government and rallying to the Bolsheviks. General Korovnichenko tried to halt this new movement. On the night of 27 and 28 October he arrested the ringleaders, including Kazakov, future president of the Turkistan central executive committee, and Uspenskii, who had rallied to the Bolsheviks after having been a member of the Union of the Archangel Saint Michael and who later joined the Socialist-Revolutionary party. General Korovnichenko's troops at first disarmed certain elements of the Second Siberia Regiment, but then came up against the opposition of the majority of troops present in Turkistan. After a four-day struggle, they were defeated on 1 November; General Korovnichenko surrendered and soviet power was proclaimed at Tashkent.

On 2 November the Socialist-Revolutionaries and Mensheviks of the Tashkent executive committee tried to limit the Bolsheviks' place in the régime that was being organized, by advocating the formation of a nine-member coalition committee that would include two locals. This project did not succeed in its initial form and the revolutionary coalition committee included no Muslim: it was made up of four Russians (Kolesov, Kazakov, Pershin, and Tomilin), four Jews (including Tobalin and Weinstein), a German, a Moldavian, and a Pole.

The locals were firmly excluded from this revolution, in which they had been present only as powerless 'witnesses'. This corresponded perfectly to the deeply contrasting aspirations that separated the two communities cohabiting in Central Asia. For the Russians, the revolution meant bread and individual freedom; for the locals, it implied bread, but above all independence.[4] This difference of viewpoint, which appeared clearly from the summer of 1917 on, merely grew sharper thereafter. In the Bolshevik Revolution the indigenous population placed their sole hope in the revolution keeping its promises to the oppressed nations when the party was in opposition.

Before April 1917 only Lenin had supported the idea of national self-determination;[5] but the resolution passed on this question in April by the Seventh All-Russia Conference of the Bolshevik Party stated clearly: 'The right of all the nations forming part of Russia freely to secede and form independent states must be recognized. To deny them this right, or to fail to take measures guaranteeing its practical realization, is equivalent to supporting a policy of seizure or annexation. Only the recognition by the proletariat of the right of nations to secede can ensure complete solidarity among the workers of the various nations and help to bring the nations closer together on truly democratic lines.'[6]

The Bolsheviks' adoption of such positions won the Muslims of Turkistan to their side. The Bolsheviks' promises represented an important milestone on the road to national reconquest along which the Jadids had been advancing since Danish and opened up new possibilities for them. The Jadids accordingly made an alliance with the victors of October, despite all their mistakes in Turkistan. They considered that the power of the Bolsheviks was sufficiently strong to triumph also over those who represented it so badly in Tashkent.

Muslim Reformism and Russian Chauvinism

From the inception of the revolution, Bolshevik power in Turkistan was a Russian power. The first Turkistan Sovnarkom was made up of eight Left Socialist-Revolutionaries and six Bolsheviks, all of Russian or European origin.[7] Nevertheless, the Muslim professional unions and liberal groups were favourable to the new leaders and their conviction extended even to the conservative group of 'ulama. On 15 November 1917 the Third Conference of Muslims of Central Asia held its sessions in Tashkent, presided over by Shir 'Ali Lapin. A few representatives of Muslim socialist groups had been invited, but no Jadid nor even any member of the Shawra-yi Islam. The conference, totally dominated by the 'ulama, decided to propose to the victors of 1 November a coalition government made up of six representatives of the 'ulama, three of the municipalities, and three from the Tashkent Soviet and

Revkom.[8] However, this offer was rejected by the Congress of Soviets, which declared that:[9] 'Entry of the Muslims into the supreme territorial organ of revolutionary power is impossible at the present juncture, both because of the doubtful attitude of the local population towards the authority of the soviets of worker and peasant deputies, and because no proletarian organization exists among the indigenous peoples.'

The 'ulama were swift to react. They at once turned to the Shawra-yi Islam, with whom they founded a coalition Muslim organization, Ittifaq al-Muslimin, which united all tendencies from conservatives to liberals. Thus, barely a few days after the revolution that had raised such great hopes among the Muslims of Turkistan, a split had emerged between them and a régime dominated by the Russians, which had turned a deaf ear to their proposals for cooperation. This refusal, however, produced a unity among Muslims that they had never previously been able to achieve.

At the end of November 1917 the 'ulama and the Shawra-yi Islam convened the Fourth Conference of Muslims of Central Asia at Khoqand.[10] This sought to define the relations between Muslims and the Soviet régime. On 27 November 1917 the conference proclaimed the autonomy of Turkistan,[11] and relied on the declarations the Bolsheviks made on 24 November concerning the right of peoples to dispose of themselves.[12] In relation to the Soviet régime it adopted an open position by systematically refusing all offers of support from the counter-revolutionary movements then making their appearance in Turkistan.

The Tashkent authorities could not immediately break the Khoqand government, since they were at the time seriously threatened by the Dutov movement: on 17 October 1917, the cossack Colonel Dutov had managed to capture Orenburg and, after arresting the revolutionary committee of the town, had replaced it with a 'Committee for Defence of the Fatherland and the Revolution' of counter-revolutionary complexion. The troops deployed along the railroad had entirely cut off Turkistan from Russia and were moving southwards to join up with the counter-revolutionary elements posted on the frontier with Iran. The Turkistan authorities, caught in a tightening circle, could not obtain assistance from Russia and their positions collapsed one after another before the cossacks. At the beginning of 1918 Katta Qurghan, Charju'i and Samarqand fell in this way into the hands of the counter-revolutionary troops. Having to confront so many enemies, the Soviet authorities attached particular importance to preventing Bukhara from becoming a base for intervention against them: a base all the more to be feared since reinforcements and arms could easily come in from Afghanistan and British troops were stationed in northern Iran.

One of the first acts of the Tashkent Sovnarkom was to establish contact with the government of Bukhara, with the aim of securing its neutrality. On 29 November the Sovnarkom declared the following in a message to the emir: 'The Sovnarkom of Turkistan, born of the will of the revolutionary people, confirms to Your Highness that the Soviet will adhere strictly to the principles adopted by the Russian government for relations with smaller States. For its part, the Sovnarkom counts upon your loyalty and begs you to take all necessary measures for the maintenance of order and peace. Under these conditions Your Highness can count upon a benevolent attitude on Russia's part towards Bukhara.'[13]

This telegram represented a recognition of the emirate's sovereignty, but it had little effect upon the emir. A few days later, the Tashkent authorities dispatched to the ruler a three-member mission,[14] designed to re-establish normal diplomatic links with Bukhara, since the residency had been suppressed.[15] The emir, however, refused to receive it, as he was to refuse henceforth to receive any representative of the Soviet régime.[16] In the eyes of the ruler of Bukhara, the newly established régime merged with the soviets he had seen operating in the emirate at the time of the Provisional Government and whose intention it had been, in his opinion, to provoke an armed uprising against his authority. Since October he had seen the pressure of the soviets increasing and was not unaware that they constituted an advanced detachment of the revolution upon his own soil.

Emir 'Alim Khan, in the memorandum he presented to the League of Nations,[17] wrote that until 1917 he had scrupulously respected his obligations to Russia, but that subsequently he felt such a threat weighing upon him that he had to provide for his country's defence and military organization, because of the assault that the Bolsheviks would launch upon it as soon as they had the chance. The winter of 1917–18 was propitious for such a policy. The Bolsheviks of Turkistan were isolated from Russia, and had simultaneously to face Dutov's threats, the Khoqand government and British encroachment.[18] Witnessing these difficulties, the ruler sought to guarantee the emirate's independence by providing it with internal cohesion and external backing. Domestic peace he viewed as indispensable, so despite the previous spring's virtual rupture with the Jadids he sought, by promises of eventual reforms with which they would be associated, to draw them closer to him.[19]

This little known circumstance, which historians rarely mention, judging as they do that the spring rupture had been definitive,[20] nevertheless played a certain role in relations between the Jadids and the Bolsheviks. The Russian mission to Novaya Bukhara, aware of the dangers of a *rapprochement* between the Young Bukharans and the emir, moved to 'clarify the situation' by affirming that it would struggle to obtain firm guarantees for the Jadids.[21] The Jadids accepted the Bolsheviks' backing and, calculating that this alliance would be enough to guarantee their security in the emirate, organized a demonstration in the streets of Bukhara to demand an immediate reform plan. The demonstration, which was brutally repressed, deprived the emir of all hope that he could ever cooperate with them.[22] The Bolsheviks' support for the Jadids contrasted with their general attitude in Turkistan, where they refused the Muslims any participation in their action. Bukhara posed a specific problem: it was indispensable to preserve a link there with the indigenous population through the vehicle of the reformist party.

During this time the emir was pursuing his 'measures necessary for defence of the State'. Between October 1917 and January 1918, he decreed three mobilizations, fortified the entire region by surrounding the Russian towns, and sought arms everywhere. It seems that General Dunsterville, commander of the British troops in Iran, sent him advisers and that volunteers arrived from Afghanistan.[23] Purchases of arms were made from all quarters: Afghanistan supplied them openly[24] and the emir even managed to have some bought from the Russian troops stationed in Bukhara.

As the resistance of Dutov's troops crumbled, followed by that of Khoqand, the emirate opened its doors to fugitives from these movements. The Russian mission to Novaya Bukhara, which the emir refused to recognize, could only warn Tashkent that Bukhara was becoming the counter-revolutionaries' rallying-ground.[25] While, in this manner, an army was being formed in the emirate out of the most heterogeneous elements, the emir's entourage and the *qadimi* clergy were maintaining a climate of tension and religious fervour in the population that was entirely directed against the Bolsheviks.

Exiled in the Russian towns, the Young Bukharans saw the emir increasingly abandon the promises he had made. In the fevered atmosphere then reigning in Bukhara, it was hardly difficult to channel popular discontent outwards. In December 1917 a Young Bukharan delegation led by Fayzallah Khodzhaev travelled to Tashkent and proposed to the Sovnarkom that they should pool their efforts to provoke an armed uprising in Bukhara that would destroy the emir's military preparations.[26] However, Tashkent was not only busy at the time with preparations for the attack on Dutov and Khoqand, but also it was still poorly informed about the scale of the military efforts that had been made by 'Alim Khan. The idea of an attack on the emirate was rejected; the Young Bukharans, however, did not renounce action. They wanted to prevent the ruler from embarking on a course that would cut him off irretrievably from them and from Russia. They also wanted reforms, but within the framework of the emirate, rather than that of the Turkistan revolution. By calling upon the Bolsheviks to act, they believed they could save the emir from an irreversible choice that would condemn Bukhara to outright reaction, to the ossification from which they were striving to extract it, or to outright annexation.

By February 1918, Dutov and Khoqand were defeated and the Bolshevik authorities in Turkistan were free to carry the fight elsewhere. Their representatives in Bukhara multiplied their warnings about the regroupment of counter-revolutionary forces in the emirate. Fayzallah Khodzhaev and his friends returned to the attack, assuring the Bolsheviks that in the emirate there were 80,000 rebels ready to rise up,[27] provided they were supported by the Russians. This support was necessary, they added, to prevent reprisals against Russians in the (anyway unlikely) event of failure.[28]

Pressed by the Young Bukharans and Bolsheviks from the Russian areas of the emirate,[29] the president of the Turkistan Sovnarkom, Kolesov[30] finally accepted the principle of an intervention. He attended the plenum of the Young Bukharan party's central committee, which met in Novaya Bukhara to discuss the insurrection and work out a programme. There was general agreement about delivering an ultimatum to the emir, demanding the immediate inauguration of a reform plan. But the debate revolved around the question, what should be done with the emir? Kolesov wanted to eliminate him in favour of a revolutionary committee. The Young Bukharans were against this, however, arguing that their country's hopes lay in a constitutional monarchy, and that the population would not be able to accept the installation of a more advanced order; the emir was the only guarantee of popular backing for the uprising and for reforms. Kolesov eventually rallied to this position; but he obtained the establishment of a revolutionary committee,[31] which would be ready to take power if the emir did not accept the ultimatum.

In the last days of February, Kolesov moved on Bukhara at the head of 600 or 700 armed men, supplemented by 200 of the emirate's Russian railwaymen. He was bearing an ultimatum drawn up jointly with the Jadids, which stipulated implementation of the reforms projected in the April manifesto, elimination of the emirate's high officials, and establishment of an executive committee that would supervise all the régime's actions. The emir began by refusing then pretended to accept, to initiate a discussion — on condition that Kolesov's troops leave the soil of the emirate. Kolesov withdrew to Kagan, where he awaited the emir. In his place the emir sent his *qush-begi*, who he said would be ready for whatever was expected of him. The *qush-begi,* however, apologized for the absence of the emir — 'prevented from coming by the circumcision of his son' — and asserted that, for his part, he had no power to sign anything whatsoever.

Much annoyed, Kolesov decided to take the initiative in the operations, so he threw his troops into an attack on the capital. When the Soviet troops arrived before the walls of Bukhara, they saw a mob emerge led by mullas; armed only with sticks, the mob was powerless to defend itself. The Russian troops had to be forced to fire.[32] The result was a bloodbath. It seemed Kolesov's troops would have no trouble in entering Bukhara; as they were advancing towards the city, however, a delegation arrived from the emir, headed by the *qush-begi* bearing the manifesto, finally signed,[33] and the emir's offer to abdicate in favour of the revolutionary committee (*Revkom*).

Proclaiming a truce, Kolesov agreed with the emir's negotiators upon the immediate dispatch under escort of a delegation charged with officially obtaining the emir's surrender and supervising the disarming of his troops. In a second phase, the Revkom would be established the next day and take over control of the state, while the emir would leave Bukhara for ever.[34] Kolesov wished to hold the negotiators as hostages until the Revkom had been installed; but the Young Bukharans were violently opposed to this idea,[35] so the Bolshevik delegation — which had five members, including Utkin and Abdurrahmanov, and a twenty-five-strong escort —

took them back with it.

On its arrival, the delegation found a very different welcome from that which it was expecting. All its members except two were massacred; the two survivors fled during the next day's battle and took the story of what had occurred back to the Soviet troops. The emir had made good use of the respite that his ruse gave him: during the night he had the railway-line linking Charju'i and Qarshi to Samarqand and Marv cut,[36] had the electricity poles torn down, had the water mains and tanks destroyed, and collected a sizeable military force.[37] At dawn, while Kolesov was preparing to send off the revolutionary committee to the capital, the city gates opened to let through not only the army but, as on the previous day, the mob led by its mullas, which on this occasion flung itself not at the Russian troops, but at the Russian inhabitants of Kagan.

Kolesov tried to resist, but the destruction of the railroad prevented the arrival of reinforcements or, more important, of munitions, of which he was very short. Since the telegraph was no longer functioning, he could not communicate with Tashkent. The most alarming reports began to circulate: people were saying that the Turkistan soviet had been overthrown by counter-revolutionary forces and that it was necessary to rush to its assistance and not carry on with a lost struggle. Kolesov withdrew to Samarqand under dreadful conditions, towing in his wake the Russians of the emirate who feared they would all be massacred. Kolesov's column had to cross a desert, where all water reserves had been destroyed. Exhausted, suffering from hunger and thirst, and harassed by the emir's troops, the Russians (soldiers and civilians alike) urged the expedition's leader to hand over the revolutionary committee to the emir, in order to placate him. At last troops from Tashkent came to Kolesov's assistance; but the Sovnarkom reckoned it was preferable to halt the conflict.

Peace was signed on 25 March 1918 at Qizil Teppe. The emirate's independence was recognized by the Sovnarkom of Turkistan. The emir, for his part, pledged himself to disarm his troops and not support movements hostile to the Soviet régime. 'Alim Khan was the great victor of this conflict. He had succeeded in forcing the Bolshevik troops to retreat and in having the independence of the emirate recognized anew. After the treaty was signed, he set about purging the state of all reformists and all who sympathized with them, while asking neighbouring countries for help and seeking to ally himself with them.

Thus ended the first joint attempt by the Bolsheviks and the

Young Bukharans to transform the emirate's régime. Many aspects of this attempt remain ambiguous, so it is understandable why historians' explanations of it have differed so widely. It is astonishing to see with how little concern the Turkistan Sovnarkom launched Kolesov upon his venture: without munitions; almost without troops; lightmindedly risking all Russian lives in the emirate; and blindly relying on the Young Bukharans's assertions, even though it was highly suspicious of them. It is also astonishing to realize how unconcernedly Kolesov viewed the venture: putting his trust in the emir; sending him men virtually without an escort, although a few days earlier at Kagan the emir had shown his bad faith; and for twenty-four hours allowing the emir full latitude to sabotage means of communication indispensable to himself. Lastly, what can explain the fact that at Qizil Teppe the emir was the great victor when, after it came to Kolesov's assistance, the Red Army had inflicted serious defeats upon him in his turn? From 19 March on, the emir's situation had become difficult: the Red Guards occupied the fortresses of Hatyrchi and Karaman; the beg of Charju'i, Muhammad 'Anis Beg, negotiated with them, but was recalled to Bukhara and hung and his post entrusted to the former *qush-begi* Nizam al-Din, who could not prevent the Russians from taking the city, which was pillaged and burned.

Kolesov, one of the main protagonists of this affair, has provided his version of it in a collection devoted to the Bukharan revolution.[38] He argues that there was indeed mistaken assessment on the part of the Young Bukharans, too sure of their sympathizers in the emirate and their ability to bring about a popular uprising.[39] Nevertheless, according to Kolesov, the real problem lay elsewhere. Whatever the true strength of the Jadids, their proposal was accepted because it was necessary to act immediately to prevent the emirate from becoming a haven for all forces hostile to the revolution — and a haven infinitely more to be feared, because of its geographical position, than Khoqand or the Dutov group.[40] So it was not the intervention of the Jadids that determined the campaign of March 1918, but the situation in Central Asia and the emir's policy.

For the Jadids, of course, the truth was somewhat different.[41] If they agreed with Kolesov in saying that the emirate was embarking upon a course opposed to that of the Bolsheviks, their criterion was not the same. What they denounced was a reactionary option on the domestic front, rather than the emir's external alliances.

They saw the cause of the debacle in the attitude of the Russian troops, which had outraged the population of Bukhara.

The Emir of Bukhara, in his memorandum to the League of Nations,[42] admitted that after the October Revolution he had opted for an anti-Soviet line, which implied a policy of military preparation at home and foreign alliances. But he laid the responsibility for this choice at the door of the Soviets and recalled how after the threats already made by Kerenskii against the sovereignty of the emirate,[43] Kolesov himself had told him that: 'The emir knows better than we do that it is not possible for him to live in peace and good relations with us. One day or another it will be necessary to speak and the language of the debate will be that of cannon and machine-guns.'[44]

For a few years Kolesov's view seemed to prevail in Soviet historiography. But post-war historians modified it in two particulars: entire responsibility for the affair was ascribed to the Young Bukharans, who in this case had played a provocative role;[45] and the Qizil Teppe agreement was seen not as a setback, but as the result of a clear-sighted realization that any revolutionary attempt in the emirate would be premature. Subsequently, a more nuanced thesis emerged:[46] the Jadids had been prevented by their social origins from understanding popular reactions, so had been unable to draw the masses behind them; the Sovnarkom's mistake had been to misjudge this reality, whereas its wisdom had been to appreciate, in time, the premature character of the revolution, so that its retreat had essentially been based on revolutionary strategy.

What can be accepted of these various arguments? It is certain not only that the Emirate of Bukhara represented, in the short term, a threat to Turkistan, but, more important, that in March 1918 the emir was still far from capable of implementing that threat. We may concede that as a general rule an offensive position is a favourable one — that seems to have been the Turkistan Sovnarkom's idea — but Kolesov's offensive lacked the necessary means. One other point seems undeniable: the Jadids really believed they could rally a great part of the population to their cause. But here an ambiguity arises: the Jadids envisaged this occurring solely in response to their call for reform and a constitution, whereas the Russians' aim was to destroy the anti-Soviet bastion of Bukhara. The brutal treatment of the population by Russian troops demonstrates accurately the extent of the misunderstanding.

Finally, the Russian withdrawal seems to have been brought about by the explosion of popular rage and fanaticism which, beneath the banner of holy war, threatened to spread throughout Turkistan. This explosion came from an accumulation of wretchedness and disappointed hopes, channelled into hostility towards the dominant infidels. It was not an unexpected reaction. Almost everywhere in the colonial world since the nineteenth century, society's ills have been expressed through religious and national demands. So what the Turkistan Sovnarkom registered was the threat of a general explosion, which threatened to sweep away the entirety of Soviet power. Lenin drew the theoretical lesson of this event when he wrote that it was necessary to move cautiously in the matter of revolution: 'Can we approach these peoples [such peoples as the Kirghiz, the Uzbeks, the Tajiks, the Turkmen] and tell them that we shall overthrow their exploiters? We cannot do this, because they are entirely subordinated to their mullahs.'[47]

The Kolesov expedition, and the development of Muslim fanaticism that it provoked, had the effect of drawing Moscow's attention to Turkistan. In April 1918, Moscow sent a commissar-general, Kobozev, to Tashkent to implement a total revision of the Bolsheviks' relations with the local population. Kobozev convened the Fifth Congress of Soviets of Central Asia, which proclaimed the federation of the Autonomous Republic of Turkistan with the Russian Soviet Socialist Republic,[48] and elected a central executive committee for Turkistan which contained ten Muslims, several of them Jadids, among its twenty-six members.[49] Kobozev's mission was to put an end to the 'chauvinist' attitude of the Russian authorities in Turkistan, who had just endangered the whole Soviet order in the region. He was to offer the indigenous population a chance to cooperate with that order. The Young Bukharans, forced to flee even the Russian towns of the emirate, found new scope for their activity in this new orientation imposed by Moscow.

The Bolsheviks' Difficulties in Turkistan

Barely two years after the failure of the Kolesov operation, Bukhara was to collapse beneath the combined blows of the Bolsheviks and the Jadids, joined in a fresh alliance. This coalition was to bring the reformists to power, as masters of the People's Republic of Bukhara. How did the Bolsheviks come to associate themselves anew with these unreliable allies, indeed give them power, despite their extremely critical attitude towards the revolutionaries of Turkistan?[50] Circumstances themselves seem to have determined the Soviet choice, rather than any change in their view of the problem.

After the peace treaty of Qizil Teppe, for a while the Bolsheviks attempted to coexist smoothly with Bukhara's ruler. They were hostile to repeated demands for intervention from the Jadids, whose only chance lay in a fresh assault on the emirate. From the summer of 1918 on, however, the civil war spread to Central Asia, after which it became essential to avoid unrest in Bukhara. On 1 July 1918 the recapture of Orenburg by the Whites opened the Aktubinsk front,[51] which stabilized along the Orenburg-Tashkent railway: Turkistan was once again isolated. Shortly afterwards, a second front was opened in the Trans-Caspian region, where British troops were occupying Ashkhabad.[52] Meanwhile, the Semirechye region too was becoming a combat zone, where the Reds were confronting cossacks led by the atamans Anenkov and Dutov and by General Shcherbakov.[53]

Bukhara now figured largely in Soviet concerns. On 8 July 1917 Stalin, then People's Commissar for Nationalities, cabled from Tsaritsyn to Shaumian, president of the Council of People's Commissars at Baku:[54] 'We urgently request you to aid Turkistan, where the English are getting ready to act via Bukhara and Afghanistan.'

The emir, who was in a position to cut off Soviet troops on the Trans-Caspian front entirely from the rest of Turkistan, held this perpetual threat over the Bolsheviks' heads. The Soviet army's base on the trans-Caspian front was Charju'i, and communications between the troops on this front and the Turkistan authorities necessarily passed through the territory of the emirate, as did the Red Army's supply lines.[55] He was at the time negotiating openly with Britain[56] and subsequently made no secret of his intention to take advantage of the Soviets' difficulties by joining forces with their enemies:[57] 'My intention was initially to declare war on the Bolsheviks; and I added that, according to accurate information, their situation was quite precarious at that moment and it was necessary to take advantage of this.'

The consequences of any such action were highlighted by a member of the Turkistan regional soviet, in a cable addressed to the People's Commissariat for Foreign Affairs:[58] 'The army isolated in Bukhara will not be able to hold out for long and will be utterly destroyed.'

The Soviet difficulties were not only military, but also political; when the civil war died out in 1919–20, these political problems were to come to the fore. The crucial problem — more serious than the fighting — that confronted the authorities in Central Asia from 1918 on was that posed by the indigenous population's own aspirations.

The central government's envoy, Kobozev, who had come to put the situation in Turkistan to rights, once he had organized the state laid the foundations for a genuinely Turkistani Communist organization.[59] However, the interest the Russian authorities in Turkistan showed in his endeavours was minimal, and soon all the Russians, including Kobozev himself, stopped thinking about the national question. The Turkistani Jadids, on the other hand, were extremely interested in the possibilities for action opened up for them. Accordingly, in January 1919 they took advantage of the fact that the ranks of the Russian leaders in Turkistan had been decimated by Ossipov's putsch to enter the Communist organizations. Ossipov seized power for a time in Tashkent and had a large number of Soviet leaders executed, but he was defeated by an alliance between the Bolsheviks and the Left SRs.[60] When in February 1919 the second regional party conference established a Regional Bureau of Muslim Organizations of the RCP (b) (the Russian Communist Party (Bolsheviks)),[61] this bureau incorporated old Jadid leaders such as Tursun Khodzhaev, Turar Ryskulov, and Nizam al-Din Khvaja.[62] The first conference of Muslim Communists of Central Asia took place from 24 to 30 May 1919.

Under the influence of those Jadids who had embraced Communism, whose role in the party was growing continuously, this assembly drew up an indictment of the revolution as carried out by the Russians: 'We were still forced to support an attitude of contempt on the part of representatives of the old privileged classes towards the native masses. That attitude is shared by the Communists, who retaining the mentality of rulers view the Muslims as their subjects.'[63] And again, 'the delegates to this congress concluded by calling upon all the peoples of the East to support the revolutions of the oppressed workers of India, Afghanistan, Persia, China, Bukhara . . .'[64]

Thus, barely were the Jadids of Turkistan incorporated into the ranks of the Communist party than — like such other Muslim Communists of Russia as Vahidov or Sultan Galiev, about whose activities and views they knew little, so great was their isolation — they worked out a theory in which the proletarian revolution was first interpreted in the sense of a liberation of the oppressed peoples of the East; and in which a *de facto* separation was quite naturally established between proletarians of the old colonizing power and eternally oppressed native workers. The idea of a qualitative difference between the Western proletariat and Eastern proletariat — the idea of a continuation of the colonial tradition among the Russian Communists, seen as spiritual heirs of the old ruling classes — emerged in Tashkent through the voice of Turar Ryskulov, who in 1920 took these ideas to the Baku Congress.

From this moment on, the role of the Turkistan Jadids in the local Communist organizations grew steadily. By the time of the fifth regional conference of the party, the Muslims held a majority in the bureau, and its secretary was Tursun Khodzhaev.[65] The stronger the Jadids' position became, the further away they moved from the Bolsheviks. The third conference of Muslim Communists, which took place in January 1920, decided to transform Turkistan into an 'Autonomous Turkish Republic' and the Turkistani organization of the RCP (b) into a Turkish Communist Party.[66] Not content with presiding over the destinies of Turkistan, the Jadids of the Tashkent Communist organization adopted as their own the old pan-Turanian dream and proposed that all the Turks of Russia should renounce their particularisms and join the Turkish Soviet Republic — that is, Turkistan.[67] Ryskulov asserted that, for the Turkic peoples, the revolution was to be identified not with the class struggle, but with the common struggle of all oppressed peoples for a transformation of their destiny.[68]

When communications were re-established with Turkistan, a special Turkish commission (the *Turkkommission*[69]) was dispatched to Tashkent. Frunze, who commanded the Russian troops in the region, multiplied his warnings to Lenin: 'The Muslims are on the way to achieving full power . . . their wish is to obtain the most total independence possible.'[70] At the same time, Lenin had to confront the demands of the Turkistanis themselves. They gave Validov, in Moscow pleading the cause of Bashkir autonomy, the job of asking Lenin to have the Turkish commission modified, in order to include as many Muslims as there were Russians. The

After dilatory replies from Lenin and Stalin, the definitive response arrived when, in June 1920, Russia's military situation was restored thanks to the cessation of Polish operations in the Ukraine. The calm more or less re-established in Turkistan and on the Ukrainian front allowed new arrangements to be made. The central committee of the RCP (b) opposed the entry of Muslims into the Turkish commission; instead, they sent in new members expressly charged with purging the Turkish Communist Party.[71] Peters, a member of the commission, drew up the act of indictment against the native Communists: he accused them of having attempted to seize power; of having wanted to replace communism by a national and pan-Islamic propaganda; and finally, of having created a clandestine organization *Ittihad va Taraqqi* (Union and Progress) uniting all Russia's Muslims. The hour of cooperation had passed.[72]

End of the Emirate

The Jadids from the emirate exiled in Turkistan saw the evolution of their brethren as an example to be followed in every aspect. After the congress convened by Kobozev at Tashkent in April 1918, which decided upon the creation of Muslim Communist organizations, the Russian Communist organizations of Novaya Bukhara organized a joint meeting with all the 'émigrés' — the proscribed Jadids from the emirate — at Tashkent on 20 April.[73]

The participants in the meeting adopted a whole variety of positions, but three broad tendencies can be distinguished. The 'Old Jadids' on the right affirmed their attachment to the *Shawra-yi Islam*; their hostility to the idea of creating a new party; and the impossibility of joining forces with the Bolsheviks. In the centre a faction demanded espousal of the programme of the Left Socialist-Revolutionaries on the grounds that it was favourable to an essentially agrarian country. Finally, on the left the extremists, who were most numerous, maintained that only a close alliance with the Bolsheviks, which meant joining the party, would allow the revolution to be successfully carried through in the emirate. At the end of the congress, the Bukharan Communist Party (BCP) was founded.

The Soviet historian Ishanov asserts that by the beginning of 1920 the BCP had 5,000 native members, grouped into forty-three cells.[74] This figure, however, seems highly exaggerated. The main centres of the BCP indicated by Ishanov, apart from the capital, were Novaya Bukhara and Charju'i, in other words Russian towns. Or at least it should be admitted that the members were mostly Russian Communists from the emirate, since the Jadids played virtually no part in the life of the Bukharan Communist Party,[75] until 1920.[76]

In February 1920 the leaders of the Young Bukharan party created a 'Bureau of Bukharan Revolutionaries' at Tashkent, with the task of preparing an insurrection in the emirate. The Young Bukharans' action was severely criticized by the Bukharan Communist Party, whose central committee published a resolution asserting that it represented 'a brake on the revolution'.[77] Eventually, however, in the summer of 1920 the Bureau of Revolutionaries drew closer to the BCP[78] and decided upon a joint action in which the Young Bukharans would retain their autonomy, but would commit themselves to joining the communist party once a revolutionary régime had been installed in the emirate.[79]

This *rapprochement* on the eve of military conflict was unavoidable. From July 1920 on it became clear that the Soviet government would soon have to tackle the emirate, last stronghold of 'reaction'. Moreover, since the beginning of the Basmachi rebellion,[80] the threat hanging over the Soviets had grown even greater, since the emirate was not only a zone of British influence, but also a sanctuary for the rebels.[81]

Until the outbreak of hostilities, the Young Bukharans were mostly hostile to a Russian intervention in the emirate and relied upon a popular uprising. On 23 August 1920 an uprising had broken out at Shakar-Bazr, in the Charju'i region, where the fourth *quriltay* (congress) of the BCP had just been taking place; the emir's troops had been unable to control the disturbance, and on 20 August the rebels seized Old Charju'i. The unrest immediately spread throughout the emirate and the BCP's underground organizations called on the Red troops in Turkistan for assistance. On 1 September 1920, forty-eight hours after Frunze's troops had received the order to attack the emirate, the reformists were still meeting in Charju'i to decide on the advisability of an armed assault.[82] The majority lined up behind Fayzallah Khodzhaev — and in opposition to the tendency led by Mirza 'Abd al-Qadir Muhitdinov — in condemnation of an intervention that would reopen the crisis of March and April 1918.[83] The discussion was in full swing when Frunze's cable arrived announcing the start of military operations.[84] The Jadids then joined the Russian troops and entered Bukhara on 2 September with the Red Army.[85]

The emir had already left his capital under shellfire forty-eight hours earlier. He had gone to Gijuvan, then to eastern Bukhara, thinking he would easily be able to regroup his troops there.[86] On 2 September, Frunze was able to report to Lenin: 'The fortress of old Bukhara was taken today following a powerful attack by Red and Bukharan units. Tyranny and coercion have been vanquished, the red flag of revolution is floating over the Rigistan.'[87]

In the space of a few days, the secular power of the emirs had crumbled. *Izvestiya* announced the event thus:[88] 'The revolution in Bukhara has triumphed. The two capitals, centres at once strategic and commercial, are in the hands of Bukharan red troops and Muslim regiments of the Red Army. Because of Bukhara's religious character, this revolution will have a considerable importance for the whole of Central Asia.'

Why did the Soviet government enhance the part played by the Jadids in the conquest of Bukhara, when their role in the event had essentially been quite limited? It appears to have been motivated by the desire to avoid any degeneration of the uprising and the intervention into an explosion of fanatical masses, who would have found support among the rebels in Turkistan and even in the Jadid group of the Musburo. By associating the Jadids with the attack on the emirate, the Soviets gave the movement a national coloration and could hope the Jadids would win public opinion over to their ideas. At the same time, it was hoped that the role allotted to the Jadids would satisfy them and that they would really become integrated into the party. Forced by circumstances to act in this way, the Soviet leaders strove to avoid in Bukhara the mistakes they had made in Tashkent.[89]

The Baku Congress revealed the difficulties of Soviet policy in this respect. The leaders of the Communist International, by announcing the fall of the emirate at Baku,[90] attempted to counterbalance in delegates' minds the deplorable effect of the Turkistani Narbutabekov's words, describing the reality of the revolution in Turkistan: 'Comrades, I shall tell you that the toiling masses of Turkistan have to struggle on two fronts: on the one hand, against the reactionary mullas and, on the other, against the narrowly nationalistic tendencies of the Europeans.'[91]

Narbutabekov, after recalling Lenin's appeal to the Muslims of Russia and the East in November 1917, went on to say, 'Well, here we have Muslims coming to us and saying that their beliefs are being trampled underfoot, that they are forbidden to pray, that they are prevented from burying their dead according to the rites of their religion. What does this mean? This is called sowing counter-revolution among the toiling masses.'[92]

It is worth recalling here the conditions outlined by Narbutabekov, for maintaining Muslim faith in the revolution: 'Nobody is unaware that the East is very different from the West and that its interests are quite other. Hence, direct application of the principles of Communism would encounter resistance there. If, therefore, we wish the 4 million Muslims to initiate themselves into the Soviet order, this must be achieved by adapting it . . . '[93] At the conclusion of the congress the leaders of the International condemned Narbutabekov's position. Nevertheless, for four years the People's Republic of Bukhara was to be the prime illustration of Communism adapted to the specific conditions of a backward country, under the leadership of the national bourgeoisie.

9

The People's Republic of Bukhara

Born in defeat, as the last ruler of the ancient Uzbek state was leaving his capital, the new state of Bukhara seemed to bear witness to the triumph of the Jadids and to the success of their alliance with the Bolsheviks. Revolutionary Bukhara, like Khiva, was established as an independent People's Republic. Notably, however, *Pravda* put its coverage of these two states under the heading of provincial rather than foreign news.

Why did the Soviet government grant the defeated emirate this privileged status? Why did it tolerate in Bukhara the Jadids, whose nationalist excesses it condemned in Tashkent? What political and social reality was the destination of that revolution, whose success had been saluted at the Baku Congress as an important milestone for the colonial revolutions?[1]

The New State

At the Charju'i Congress on 1 September the two extreme tendencies of the Young Bukharan Party[2] had merged into an Independence Committee (*Istiqlal Qomitasi*) that had planned to organize a provisional government,[3] grouping in a more or less balanced manner those Young Bukharans who had joined the party after an activity in favour of reformism with the more left-wing elements linked to the Bukharan Communist Party. Mirza 'Abd al-Qadir Muhitdinov became head of state; Fayzallah Khodzhaev, president of the council of ministers and minister of foreign affairs; 'Abd al-Hamid Arifov, minister of war; 'Usman Khodzhaev, minister of finance; Qari Yuldash Pulatov, public education and worship; Mukammil al-Din Makhdum, justice; Ata Khodzhaev, interior; Hasan Bay, public health; and Mukhtar Khan, economy and finance.[4]

On their return to Bukhara on 3 September, pending the installation of the government, the main leaders of the *Istiqlal Qomitasi* set themselves up as a 'revolutionary committee' (Revkom) — members included Fayzallah Khodzhaev, 'Usman Khodzhaev, and

Arifov — in which BCP influence was greater than in the future administration projected at Charju'i. This difference was to have major consequences in the ensuing history of the people's republic.

The Revkom spelled out its promises. It would nationalize not only the land of the former rulers, but also all vacant land, underground resources, water, and means of production. Henceforth anyone who dealt in or rented out land, or imposed forced labour on the poor, would be indicted for a crime against the state. Nationalized land and tools would be distributed to the poor peasants, who would also have financial facilities to begin new cultivation or improve the land allotted to them.[5]

These declarations had the merit of responding very precisely to the most ancient and pressing aspirations of the Bukharan masses: their need for land. Thus, by promising in the first days of its existence a radical agrarian reform, the Revkom of Bukhara at once obtained the support of the masses, who until then had stood somewhat apart from events.[6] When it proclaimed in October 1920 that it was 'supported by the people of Bukhara',[7] the Revkom was genuinely expressing popular feelings.

Unfortunately, however, the Revkom's promises were just that — only promises. Although ratified by the First Congress of the Toilers of Bukhara, they were never in fact applied and were even invalidated by the constitution. This, the fundamental text of the Bukhara People's Republic, adopted at the Second Congress (*quriltay*)[8] of the Bukhara soviets on 25 September 1921, attempted to reconcile certain democratic aspirations of the Bukharan intelligentsia with traditional principles: it stipulated that central power in the people's republic was an expression of popular sovereignty organized into soviets; but in no way did it seek to connect that power with any idea of dictatorship of the proletariat — a term in any case entirely absent from the constitution.[9]

This definition of power was the most advanced part of the 1921 text. The articles that followed presented the image of a state and society that the revolution had not yet transformed. The state itself remained basically Muslim, since under the terms of Article 26 'no law of the Republic can be in contradiction with the fundamental principles of Islam'.[10] The central power, legislative and executive, at first sight seemed quite close to soviet power. Legislative power belonged to the Congress of Soviets,[11] but its scope for action was considerable inasmuch as it was not limited by the constitution, which it alone could modify. The only limit upon the power of the legislative branch — as formerly of the emir — were the fundamental rules of Islam. The extent of the compromise with tradition was plain to see. Executive power belonged to the Central Executive Committee, a body emanating from the Congress of Soviets that functioned in the intervals between congresses. During these intervals, the committee possessed almost all the attributes of the congress itself (Article 25).[12] This left little initiative to the Council of People's Commissars, whose powers of decision were strictly limited by the laws which the Congress of Soviets laid down.[13]

But the influence of traditional administrative rules was most evident at the level of local institutions, for which no soviet-type body (even of a modified kind) was provided. The system was based on the village assembly, which would delegate executive power to an *aqsaqal* (elder) elected for a year.[14] The villages of Bukhara had been electing representatives for centuries, and this system truly reflected the interests and will of the peasants. Here, even the individuals would not have to be changed.

The real innovation of the constitution was its extension of the suffrage: it was no longer to be just adult men who would participate in these choices, but (under Article 58) 'any citizen of either sex having completed eighteen years'.[15] This widening of the electorate was highly significant, since it ran counter to the entire traditional way of life that excluded women and young people from public life. It was, however, in line with the ideas expressed by the Jadids since 1910.

The articles dealing with citizens' rights likewise convey the idea of a society that had little to do with the Revkom's promised changes of September 1920. Article 5 of the constitution guaranteed 'the right to property' in all circumstances, and assured citizens of 'the unfettered right to use and dispose of their own movable and immovable goods'.[16] The text involved no limitation of that right, at no moment did it conjure up the possibility of a nationalization of large estates or industry; and it even protected the people as a whole against any arbitrary act directed at it by the government. Articles 7, 8, and 9 defined individual freedoms (conscience, expression, writing, assembly, and association) and absolute respect for the person and abode.[17]

The image thus emerged of a state still characterized by the traditional concept of the primacy of Islam; by organs of authority which, under various names, were directly or indirectly linked to the former system; and, above all, by a conception of society that did not modify the former structures. And yet, so far as popular participation through elections was concerned, different perspectives did appear. It was not only voting rights for women, which overturned some ancient traditions, but something more important still, a class criterion; for Article 59 provided for withholding civic rights not merely from individuals who had served the former régime, but also from 'big landowners and capitalists'.[18]

These dispositions revealed the first beginnings of the class struggle. Like Article 58, Article 59 showed clearly that for a section however small of the Jadids, the hope of transforming the structures of Bukhara radically was a real one. What emerged from these texts was the impossibility for the government installed by the Revkom of keeping the promises of reform made on the morrow of the revolution. (The government had undergone a few minor modifications: Mirza 'Abd al-Rahim (Abdurrahimov) took the portfolio of justice, and a ministry of agriculture was set up and entrusted to 'Alim 'Ashur-ughli.) Although the congress could have introduced these reform projects into the constitution, it had done just the opposite. It is enough to consider the make-up of the Executive Committee (*Khalq Vakillari Shawrasi*) to understand that soon after the revolution the non-Communist forces had made their full weight felt within the alliance. Out of the eighty-five members of the Executive Committee, organized during the second session of the *quriltay*,[19] there were five representatives of what might be called the right, eight from the left, with all the remainder forming the centre. In the same way, the seven members of the presidium included two conservatives and one 'progressive'.[20] So even though the Young Bukharans occupied an important place in the organization as a whole, it is clear that conservative elements exercised considerable weight and prevented the implementation of fundamental reforms.

This situation was really just a consequence of the fundamental difficulties besetting the infant state. The revolution had been carried out in an extremely backward country — a country permanently threatened by the demands of the various national groups that made it up. The Jadids who came to power in September 1920 had been obliged to take account of these problems. The institutions established and solutions adopted reflected this situation.

Bukhara's first problem was political. To reform its structures and carry through the Revkom's promises, clearly it was necessary to draw a line through the past and turn to new people in order to run the new institutions. But this was impossible, since Bukhara possessed neither the people nor the material means for such a change.

So, not surprisingly, whatever the deeper aspirations of the more advanced Jadids may have been, the activity of the government of the people's republic was not basically revolutionary in the domestic sphere, especially so far as agrarian problems were concerned. In its first statements, the Revkom had committed itself to providing the peasants with financial help in the form of credits. But the State Bank had remained in the hands of its former directors, no competent replacements being available. Since most of these were scions of the commercial bourgeoisie — a Mansurov figured among them — they were conceivably more concerned with granting credits to big business than to peasant cooperatives, which according to Pozdnyshev received a mere fifth of the credits allocated.[21] It was the same story with the livestock confiscated from the emir (2,000 head), which went almost entirely to big landowners.[22]

The failure of the Bukhara government's agrarian policy was matched by another no less significant, since it related to the place of religion in the state:[23] the failure of the judicial reform. When the republic was established, a new judicial system made its appearance, inspired by the Russian model. Popular tribunals, an assembly, and a supreme court were to coexist with the Muslim system, control it, and progressively supplant it.[24] In reality, these tribunals were never able to play such a role and for several years the traditional judicial organization was barely shaken. In 1924 the government, which the year before had been called to order by the party, tried to introduce at least a few changes into the religious courts to bring them more into line with the new régime.[25] The *qazis* were in principle supposed to submit themselves for election and to be flanked by popular assessors. Furthermore, in criminal cases, Muslim procedure and law were supposed to give way to a procedure and law likewise strongly inspired by Soviet legislation. These provisions were never applied, since soon after their adoption the people's republic ceased to exist.

Any attempt to draw up a balance-sheet of what, out of the promises made in the régime's first moments, was actually realized must concern itself with what seemed most positive in the constitution: the role in public life allotted to women, that allotted to young people, and that to be taken away from the wealthy.

No source indicates whether women really took part in elections as they had the right to do, but it is reasonable to doubt it. At the beginning of 1924 a congress of the 'progressive clergy of Bukhara'[26] asked for women finally to be acknowledged as equal to men. Among the proofs of continuing inequality, the progressive clergy quoted the fact that in trials 'two women are needed to constitute a witness'.[27] They further protested against forced marriages and marriages of girls below the age of puberty, which nothing forbade.[28] It is hard to imagine these women — their word accorded only half-value, their destiny ruled by the family — having either the time to take part in a vote or the least notion of doing so.

In the case of young people it is also difficult to say how far they in practice took part in public life, even though it was possible for them to do so in the electoral domain. Here again, we come up against the fact that elections were organized by officials who had not changed: there is no evidence that they sought to bring the new generations into political life. What is certain, on the other hand, is that the limitations imposed by the constitution upon former officials of the toppled régime and the wealthy were never in fact applied, for both continued to exercise real power under the new régime.

Does this mean that the government of the people's republic, paralysed by difficulties that were quite beyond it — touching as they did the social condition of the country itself — and that it could not resolve in the short term, was prepared to abandon the hopes for a renewal of society that had been such an essential ingredient in the thinking of Fitrat and, with him, all the Jadids? In actual fact, Bukhara's rulers (that is, the national bourgeoisie) were keenly aware of at least one of their problems: that of giving some concrete basis to the popular support they sought, by extending culture to the people. This aspect of their activity was certainly the most productive and interesting. The new government's cultural policy was the work of 'Abd al-Ra'uf Fitrat, the minister of public education, who at last had the means to put his reform programme into effect.

The government's most revolutionary measure was to proclaim Uzbek as the state language.[29] By eliminating Persian — which was not only the official language of the emirate, but above all the language of the élite — and replacing it by Uzbek, the language of the people, the government was signalling clearly its intention of being a people's government and no longer that of a few privileged groups; it was also facilitating social mobility. This reform had a further significance: under its impact the old pan-Turanian dream sprang to life again, which had the merit of making the theoretically independent state of Bukhara once more into an important centre of spiritual renewal for all Muslims in Russia who had not forgotten their reformist aspirations.

There arrived in Bukhara such Turkistani reformers as Munavvar Qari, 'Abd al-Qadir Qushbegi-ughli, and Sa'dallah Khodzhaev,[30] who could not apply their ideas in Soviet Turkistan. In Russia, Muslim Communists were discussing methods of anti-religious propaganda,[31] and Bukhara once again seemed to be the only Turkish territory in Russia that was independent.

In his work as an educator, Fitrat remained faithful to the idea that it was necessary to form modern élites able to stand comparison with the élites of Europe and that it was necessary to produce a conscious population, capable of being educated, which in the first place meant literate. As early as in 1917 he had furnished the Young Bukharan party with a twenty-six-point programme, proposing a set of reforms. This programme was the basis for the Jadids' programme which appears in Appendix 4. The political climate in the emirate, and the hostility that enveloped all the liberals' proposals, prevented this programme from being even discussed. After the revolution, however, the Jadids adopted the core of Fitrat's proposals, laying particular stress on those concerned with culture.

The first problem for Fitrat was to train teachers capable in their turn of educating the people as a whole. Where were they to be trained? He first had recourse to the already existing institutions: the ancient and prestigious *madrasas*. After the revolution their situation was difficult: those that survived on subsidies from the emir had to close their doors; the others, which had *vaqf* property, were transformed. The ideas of the reformists were finally triumphing. Secular knowledge was introduced, which caused numerous problems. Muslim scholars were for the most part scarcely equipped to teach mathematics or chemistry (this was one of the great obstacles to an extension of modern education, as the 'progressive mullas' were still lamenting in 1924).[32] Where were the teachers to be found? Fitrat decided to send young students to European universities, so that they would subsequently be able to teach in Bukhara the knowledge and techniques that gave the West its strength. Thus, in 1922 seventy students set off for German universities.[33] But Fitrat also wanted to create new universities along European lines;[34] in 1922, he laid the first stone of a modern university in the capital. Since he had scarcely any resources with which to take the project further, he organized a fête to collect the money needed to begin work.[35] Such were the difficulties by which the government of the young republic was constantly beset.

The material problems Fitrat encountered in implementing his programme often took him back to Russia. One of Bukhara's riches was its cultural patrimony, especially the books of incalculable value that crammed her libraries. Frunze's Soviet troops had behaved with great heedlessness towards the libraries of the emirate. Barthold has indicated that the libraries of twenty-seven *madrasas* were totally destroyed, among them the famous library founded by Emir Nasrallah. In Bukhara's destitute condition, such destruction was particularly tragic and Fitrat never ceased to remind people that it was the handiwork of the Russians. This grievance helped to reinforce the state of tension that had simultaneously been developing uninterruptedly between Bukhara and the Soviet state.

The government of the Jadids had taken power under particularly disastrous conditions. The interruption of economic exchanges between Russia and the emirate had engendered famine and considerable social unrest. The share of the harvest that was traditionally hoarded in case of possible calamity no longer existed and the population of Bukhara thus has neither immediate resources nor seed for the following year.[36] The two Soviet military invasions had caused immense destruction (Bukhara itself was bombarded in September 1920 by Frunze's troops). Despite all its efforts, the government could not right the economic situation of the Bukharan state. Exchanges had in 1921 reached such a low level, production was so reduced, that only total support from the Soviet government could have altered things (see Tables 9.1 amd 9.2). But the Soviet government had too much to do elsewhere. It refused to deliver goods, arguing that the exchange-rate of Bukhara's currency was so high that any trade had become impossible.[37] At the beginning of 1922, Fayzallah Khodzhaev acknowledged: 'The misery of the population is much worse under our government than it was in the emir's day.' A terrible confession for a Jadid, who in the period of the clandestine struggle had accused the emir and his entourage of being solely responsible for popular misery. The Jadids were all the more bitter about seeing Soviet aid limited, since it had been one of the conditions for their alliance with Russia and the concessions they believed they had made to Moscow.

Table 9.1
Bukhara's Foreign Trade

	Until 1917	*In 1921*
Imports:		
Manufactured products	550,000 puds	3,850 puds
Tea	500,000 kg.	1,000 kg.
Sugar	150,000 puds	—
Metalware	200,000 items	8,240 items
Chinaware	15,000 items	—
Exports		
Cotton	2,000,000 puds	142,000 puds
Astrakhan	2,000,000 items	100,000 items
Silk	350,000 puds	14,000 puds
Fruit	990,000 puds	—

Sources: Soloveichik, 'Revolyutsionnaya Bukhara', p. 20; M. N., 'Pod znakom Islama', p. 82.

Table 9.2
Annual Production

	Until 1917	*In 1921*
Cotton	2,000,000 puds	100,000 puds
Astrakhan	1,700,000 items	200,000 items
Silk	280,000 puds	50,000 puds

Source: See Table 9.1.

Having recognized the sovereignty of the people's republic — announced at the first *quriltay* of the soviets by Lyubimov, representative of the RSFSR[38] — the Soviet government regulated its relations with the republic on the basis of a treaty of alliance.[39] By virtue of this, Russia gave up all the rights it had formerly enjoyed in the emirate; all its concessions; and all its holdings in land, together with those of Russian citizens settled there (articles 1, 7, and 9 of the treaty). On the other hand, and this was important, Russians 'from the working class or from the peasantry' who chose to reside in Bukhara were to enjoy the same rights as Bukharan citizens (articles 11 and 12). Russia pledged herself to assist the new state's cultural development (article 14). Defence was to be organized around a common programme, with structures common to the signatory powers (article 2).

One of the first subjects of disagreement concerned military cooperation.[40] The Soviet government wished to place Bukharan troops on the Afghan frontier under the authority of its Turkistan high command. The Bukharan government opposed this, and a state of considerable tension ensued between Bukhara and Moscow, which lasted until the signature of an economic agreement on 4 March 1921.[41] However, this agreement regulated only customs problems; the military demands remained in suspense. The convention of 31 May 1923 terminated the debate for good;[42] it made the RSFSR responsible for ensuring the security of the frontier with Afghanistan, and placed the frontier troops under the authority of the Turkistan military command. Although until 1923 no document spelled out under what conditions Russian troops could be in Bukhara, part of Frunze's army did stay there, moving as it pleased over the republic's territory and requisitioning supplies from an already impoverished populace. Furthermore, the Soviet government demanded that maintenance of the Russian troops stationed in Bukhara should be the responsibility of the local government.[43]

The presence of Russian troops in Bukhara provoked considerable popular feeling. The masses tended to think that replacing the emir by the revolutionaries had changed nothing, since the Russian soldiers were still there. The Bukharan government began to discuss this after the second *quriltay,* which had signalled a turning-point in Bukhara's political life: the moment when the leaders became aware of the state's real situation and problems and of the true extent of the sovereignty granted on 10 December 1921. Unable to obtain from Russia's representative any promise that the troops would be withdrawn, 'Usman Khodzhaev then appealed to Bukharan public opinion in a declaration to which wide publicity was given; this was facilitated by the fact that the 'talking newspaper' system had been introduced in public places with great success shortly beforehand.[41] He appealed also to neighbouring Afghanistan,[45] then bound by a friendship treaty with Russia, asking that it intervene on that basis against the continual violations of Bukhara's sovereignty. However, there was some reason for keeping Soviet troops on Bukharan territory, given that a revolt by the Basmachis was developing there, which was shortly going to assume the guise of a movement of national resistance to the Bolsheviks.

Basmachi Resistance

When Frunze launched a massive attack upon Bukhara in September 1920, the emir decided that resistance in the capital was impossible and it was preferable to regroup his forces in the mountains of the eastern part of the state.[46] Among the population of the Qarategin region, the Turkmens of the plain and the Tajiks of the mountains, the emir had a wide following; so his two main lieutenants, Ibrahim Beg[47] and Dawlatmand Beg Divan-begi[48] had no difficulty in mustering real forces. These were Bukhara's first Basmachi troops: tribes drawn to revolt for reasons that had to do with their traditions or their own disputes; peasants and citizens who no longer had any other hope of survival.

When the uprising broke out, two Jadids, who had always fought against the authoritarian power of the emir, judged that the resistance he was leading and the Basmachi movement to which it adhered were in strict continuity with their own national struggle. These Jadids, Mirza 'Abd al-Qadir Muhyi al-Din[49] and Muhyi al-Din Makhdum,[50] joined the ranks of the rebels taking a number of men with them. The impression caused by their decision was considerable and gave the movement a powerful impetus. The population, irked by the Russian presence, had since 1918 been following attentively the movement's vicissitudes in Bukhara. The backing the two rebel Jadids now gave it confused people and sowed division within the government.

Certain Communist Young Bukharans, who together with BCP members dominated the Revkom, came out violently against the insurrectionary movement and urged support for the military struggle being waged against it by the Soviets. But for most Jadids in the government, the choice was far more difficult. Should they break with the Soviets and support the insurrectionary movement? Should they prefer Soviet power and the gains of revolution to support for the emir and a return to the old order? It seems certain that the emir's presence at the head of the insurrection initially restrained Bukhara's leaders from taking the plunge.

In the autumn of 1921 Soviet troops managed to recapture the Baysun region. However, they carried out such harsh reprisals against the populace that the revolt, temporarily subdued, flared up again and assumed considerable dimensions, such was the increase in the number of peasants joining it. This gave the movement a new character. At the beginning, the movement had clearly been an opposition to Soviet power led by the emir. After the reprisals of autumn 1921, however, the situation had changed. The emir had left the territory of Bukhara for Afghanistan, perhaps feeling that his presence was preventing the movement from drawing to it the country's liberal élite. Jadids were now fighting among the rebels. The rebellion was becoming a refuge for all who had been victims of Soviet repression. Moreover, the rebels took care to clarify their attitude towards the national government of Bukhara: 'We are struggling against the Russians and not against the national government. If the Russians leave, we are ready to rally to the national government.'[51]

However, the insurrectionary movement in Bukhara suffered from the same trouble as in the province of Ferghana. Though for the Soviets there may have been only one Basmachi movement, in reality there was a multitude of disconnected and sometimes warring rebel bands.[52]

But the arrival in Bukhara of Enver Pasha was for a time to achieve unity among the rebels.[53] The Turco-Soviet treaty of March 1921 had temporarily put an end to Enver Pasha's hopes of returning to his homeland in triumph, with Soviet assistance. At the request of Mustafa Kemal, the Soviet authorities had stopped supporting the Turkish government which Enver had established in Batum; they had insisted that he should cease his activities and leave the Caucasus. Determined in spite of everything to pursue his plan, Enver Pasha now saw another possibility of achieving it: Turkistan, cradle of the Turkish race, was troubled by innumerable movements and bands of unorganized rebels who lacked only a leader and a definite orientation. Enver Pasha appropriated the old dream of a pan-Turanian empire, which from the springboard of Turkistan would reproduce the conquests of Chingiz Khan and Taymur. He would be the new conqueror, and Turkey would rid itself of Kemal and join his empire. The situation of Bukhara in 1921 struck him as perfectly suited to his plans: the revolt had considerable strength there and external backing; the Caliph's son-in-law could speak of a holy war and rally the faithful around him more easily there than anywhere else.

He suggested to the Soviet leaders to dispatch him to Turkistan as a mediator, and on 8 November 1921 he arrived in Bukhara. After a few interviews with the authorities he used the pretext of a hunting-trip to the mountains to reach the rebels' camp. From there he sent a message to the Bukhara government, inviting it to join him; he also sent an ultimatum to the Soviet government, bidding it withdraw its troops from the entire region and promising it in return the friendship of the great Turkistani empire that he was going to found.[54] Though the Soviet government's only response to his appeal was to send troops against him, the Bukhara government fell to pieces.

Enver Pasha took command of the movement and sought to extend his authority over all Turkistan's Basmachis,[55] stressing that they all shared the project of 'driving the Europeans out and creating the great Central-Asian Muslim state'.[56] But his dream was an impossible one, since the Basmachis were incapable of uniting and their great weakness was the constant rivalry among their chieftains.[57] Enver was initially able to impose his authority; but his personal ambition and lack of tact soon alienated many of his associates and the coalition he had assembled fell apart. He used to sign his orders with the pompous title 'Commander in chief of all the Muslim troops, son-in-law of the Caliph and representative of the Prophet';[58] he also entitled himself 'Emir of Turkistan',[59] which won him the enmity of the Emir of Bukhara, who still maintained contact with the movement. He was abandoned by Ibrahim Beg and his Loqays, who had at first placed themselves under his command.[60]

Defeated at Baysun, Enver attributed his defeat to the desertion of Ibrahim Beg's Basmachis. Henceforth, he fought also against those tribes that rebelled against his authority.[61] The end of the movement was drawing near. The Red Army, swollen by Muslim recruits,[62] embarked upon an intensive propaganda campaign among the population, presenting the Basmachis as brigands — brigands who were weak and doomed to imminent defeat. During the summer of 1922, Fayzallah Khodzhaev barely escaped an assassination attempt, which was ascribed to Enver Pasha.[63] Increasingly isolated, Enver eventually had to confront the final assault, which took place on 4 August 1922 at Baljuan, where he was killed.[64] Taking advantage of the shock caused by his death, the Soviet troops attacked a series of Basmachi groups in quick succession. By the autumn of 1922, it was once again possible to consider the movement quelled.[65]

The Soviet government realized that its policy in Central Asia must be revised, since displays of military might were not enough to prevent the population from joining the rebels. At the same time that a general offensive was launched against the Basmachis with the aim of definitively annihilating them, the 'Turkburo' of the Bolshevik central committee and the Turkish commission took a series of measures reversing the 1920 reforms: the *vaqf* lands whose confiscation had so shocked the Muslims of Central Asia were returned to the religious authorities; the *madrasas* and *maktabs* reopened their doors; and religious courts began to sit again.[66] In economic terms, the New Economic Policy (NEP) made it possible to relax the situation of the Muslims; private business was re-established; and the requisitions of cotton and foodstuffs that had enraged the Muslims were ended.[67]

These conciliatory measures quickly bore fruit. The population of Turkistan was tired of struggle; the return to an order in conformity with its traditions was seen by it as a sufficient guarantee to abandon the Basmachi movement. Deprived of its popular support, the movement gradually weakened and disappeared. But in Bukhara itself the revolt continued, expanded anew and lasted for several years more (since rebel groups were still being captured at the end of 1929). As late as 1931, the movement was to draw new strength from the resistance to collectivization.[68]

While Enver Pasha was fighting in the mountains of eastern Bukhara, in the capital a government was being slowly reconstructed. After Enver's appeal, the Jadids had found themselves facing an old dilemma: whether to defend the national cause by offering armed resistance or by remaining in power and trying from there to safeguard what was essential. This second option was adopted by the most eminent of the Jadids, perhaps because they had not had the chance of leaving Bukhara in time, perhaps also because they did not want to abandon the state to the Communists.

The 1923 Crisis and the End of Bukhara

Until 1923 the Soviet authorities scarcely intervened in the republic's internal policies. The government in Bukhara carried out an essentially national policy, wavered in its relations with the Basmachis and drew increasingly further away from Russia.[69] The Bukharan Communist Party, attached since 2 February 1922 to the RCP (b), had in two years become a relatively large party (around 10,000 members[70]); but it did not seem to wield any influence over the government in the direction of a greater social openness.

In the spring of 1923 this situation changed quite radically, as a result of open intervention by the RCP (b) within both the local party and the local government. This change in the Soviet leaders' attitude towards a theoretically sovereign republic was related not only to Bukhara, but also to a revision of Russia's Muslim policies.

This revision began at the Bolshevik party's tenth congress, which attacked the native Communists: 'They neglect the class interests of the workers and confuse them with so-called national interests. They are unable to distinguish the former from the latter, or to orient the party's work towards the toiling masses alone. This situation explains the appearance of bourgeois-democratic nationalism, which in the East often takes the form of pan-Islamism and pan-Turkism.'[71]

The first party to be hit by measures implementing the new line was the Turkistan Communist Party:[72] a purge was initiated in early 1922 and the Bolshevik party's eleventh congress was to draw its balance-sheet.[73] But the indictment of the national Communist movements culminated in 1923 at the fourth conference of the Bolshevik party central committee, 'enlarged to include leading party workers from the national republics and regions' (Moscow, 9–12 June 1923), during which Stalin[74] condemned the activities of Sultan Galiev and denounced his plans for the creation of a clandestine organization of Muslims in Russia.[75] At the same time, Stalin insisted that national deviations had reached such a serious level that a strict purge of all the Muslim parties was essential.

Though Stalin's accusations seem excessive in many respects, Russia's Muslims were nevertheless fired by projects that, however vague they may have been, were dangerous in the difficult conditions Russia was having to contend with in 1920; and that Bukhara's rulers did indeed figure somehow in these projects. The first of them was advanced by an illegal underground organization named *Ittihad va Taraqqi*, which aimed to found a pan-Turk state of Russia's Muslims with the assistance of counter-revolutionary movement like the Basmachis.[76] There is also some evidence concerning another project, which this time aimed to give the Muslims not a state of their own, but a political force within Socialism, through the establishment of an autonomous pan-Turk Socialist party. Here again, socialists from Bukhara and from Tashkent, Kirghizis and Bashkirs, all began to come together around this idea. The promotors of the project at first considered affiliating to the Third International as fully-fledged members. Subsequently, however, realizing the vanity of any such hope, they decided to establish their association of Muslim Socialists without worrying about its official fate. The programme of this organization, named the *Turkistan Sosyalistlar Tudasi* or Tuda (Turkistan League of Socialists), was worked out at Bukhara in January 1921.[77]

On 23 April 1923 the first secretary of the Bukharan Communist Party's central committee, Pozdnyshev, tackled the political problem of Bukhara in a letter addressed to the Central Asia bureau (*Sredazbyuro*) of the Bolshevik party's central committee: 'From the point of view of organization, the Bukharan CP is of all parties to be placed on the bottom-most rung. Figures do not exist. The party claims to have 16,000 members but this cannot be verified. Base organizations and cells do not exist anywhere, not even in the city of Bukhara.'[78]

In a similar vein Pozdnyshev denounced the invasion of the party by individuals utterly alien to the working class; he pointed out that the party, far from controlling the government, could easily be likened to it. But also, in what was perhaps the first step towards controlling the party, he drew up an indictment of the republic's leaders, almost all of them in any case Communists.[79] He judged that 'F. Khodzhaev's group had turned its back entirely on the tasks it had to fulfil' and accused it of various acts of treason or deviations.

Stalin repeated these accusations at the June 1923 conference at which Sultan Galiev was condemned, and the Bukharan government of having in three years done nothing that 'was popular, or Soviet'. He explained this by the class nature of that government, which was made up of eight merchants, two intellectuals, and a mulla; but contained not a single peasant.[80] 'This group had seized hold of state power . . . used it for its own ends and in the interests of the wealthy alone.'[81] After such attacks, it was clear that the wave of purges was going to sweep through Bukhara. The Communist party was so thoroughly purged that of the 16,000 members it had boasted a few weeks before, barely 1,000 remained.[82] Among those expelled who had occupied senior posts in the party there were twenty-five mullas, eighty-three merchants, forty-seven landowners, and twenty-one former officials of the emir;[83] and in the government the purge was no less radical. Reduced to its simplest terms, the BCP stripped of their functions the ministers of foreign affairs, education, and finance: a majority of central committee members; and numerous local officials, some of whom were arrested. The new government was made up of 'representatives of the workers and peasants'. It took various measures aimed at placing Bukhara on the road to socialism. First, the right to vote was taken away from all those who had links with the bourgeoisie, whether former officials, ecclesiastics, landowners or merchants. The new government decided that the peasantry would be awarded large credits to repair its situation. It embarked on an active struggle against religion, both by initiating a programme of legal reform[84] and by trying to replace certain Muslim ceremonies by civil ceremonies of a spectacular nature.[85] But the main activity of the new government was exerted in two directions — towards the party and towards the national groups.

First, the reconstitution of the BCP on new, proletarian foundations was pursued so actively that towards the end of 1924 the party already had 2,226 members, who for the most part had no link with the Jadid movement or the Bukharan bourgeoisie. The second important fact was the beginning of a certain division among the national groups. Even in 1921 the members of the second *quriltay* of the soviets had proclaimed the equality of all Bukhara's ethnic groups, notably guaranteeing them the use of their languages in schools and courts.[86] In fact, however, there had been no change at all in the status of non-Uzbek groups following this declaration. At the twelfth congress of the RCP (b) in 1923 — at the moment when the attack was being launched on the 'bourgeois nationalists of Bukhara' — the 'bourgeois chauvinism' of the Uzbeks towards other national groups in the state was violently denounced as a manoeuvre by the bourgeoisie to obstruct change in its country.[87] So the new government took great pains to initiate some resolution of the problem. The regions populated by Turkmens were made into autonomous regions.[88]

In 1923, when he was attacking 'the group of Fayzallah Khodzhaev', Pozdnyshev raised the question of integrating Bukhara into the Soviet Union. This integration was first achieved through an economic reorganization of Central Asia. In March 1923, the first conference was convened of the republics of Central Asia (Turkistan, Bukhara, and Khvarazm). It laid down the principle of a common economic policy for the participating states and to this end established an 'Economic Council of Central Asia'. The currencies, transport systems, and telecommunications of the two people's republics of Bukhara and Khvarazm were to be integrated into the Russian system. Irrigation, commerce, agriculture, and planning became a common domain for the whole of Central Asia. While preserving the juridical character of independent states, Bukhara and Khvarazm were already irreversibly committed to the process of unification, which was completed the following year by an internal reorganization of the states involved.

On 19 September 1924 the fifth *quriltay* met to examine this question. Its representatives voted unanimously to suppress the people's republic and establish a Socialist republic.[89] Furthermore, they recognized the need for all Bukhara's national groups to regroup into national states of their own and join the USSR.[90] At the beginning of 1925 the whole of Turkistan was remodelled in accordance with this intention.[91] The Republic of Turkistan and the two people's republics disappeared, giving way to Uzbek,[92] Tajik, Kirghiz, Kazakh, and Turkmen national states. The ancient state of Bukhara was thus erased from the map: its name henceforth designated only a region of the Tajik Republic. (Tadjikistan, formed out of eastern Bukhara, was initially an autonomous republic attached to the Uzbek SSR, until 1929 when it became an SSR itself.)

This radical transformation was effected without fuss and without opposition. The few Jadids who had escaped the purges, such as Fayzallah Khodzhaev, accepted the new situation without demur and often even became its defenders. Khodzhaev explained his attitude in the course of his trial in 1938.[93] Despite the extraordinary circumstances of his admissions, what he said seems of authentic assistance in understanding his attitude and that of his companions. He explained that he had realized as early as 1922 that the economic union of the Central Asian states was leading to a political merger, implying the end of Bukhara as an independent and multinational state; but that he had also realized the impossibility of opposing that reorganization and the need, if he was to continue to take part in the public life of Bukhara, to support changes that were in any case inevitable.

With its reorganization of Central Asia the Soviet government delivered a terrible blow to the pan-Turk dreams of the Jadids. The fragmentation of Turkistan into national republics endowed with national languages and, worse still, the creation of a non-Turkish republic of Tajikistan, in which a Persian dialect was spoken, put an end to any hope of a regroupment and unification of all the Turks of Central Asia. As early as 1923, moreover, Kaganovich had stressed that the existence of a region called 'Turkistan' was impossible, since it was the most blatant demonstration of a 'Great-Turkish aspiration which should be erased from Soviet terminology as soon as possible'.[94]

Conclusion

The history of reformism in Bukhara is a local aspect of the great crisis of the Muslim world face-to-face with the modern world. But it is a particularly important aspect of it, since in Russia socialist revolution gave a new dimension to the reformists' fight. The choice of Bukhara is interesting because in many respects it is the most specific case of them all, the one that best allows us to hold both ends of the chain: to analyse reformist ideas with precision from starting-point to final outcome.

In dwelling on events of the nineteenth and early twentieth centuries, I have striven to bring out the most original aspects of the Emirate of Bukhara, which was simultaneously one of the highest summits of the Muslim mind and the most backward region of the entire Russian empire. Precisely because of this, reaction was particularly strong to the new situation created by the arrival of the Europeans and the penetration of a different economic system. All the values upon which the social order and social relations were organized suddenly found themselves called into question. The holy protectors of Bukhara, as presented to popular piety by official religion — the ruler with his unchallenged power, the social hierarchy, the tribal or village order — what did they mean henceforth? In all spheres new needs made their appearance. Some kind of reordering of social relations and moral values within a new perspective came to be seen as indispensable. Limited at first to a little group of intellectuals, this realization became very powerful and widespread because it corresponded to the needs — however confusedly felt — of the masses. In this way reformism was born in Bukhara.

Until 1917 a combination of external events helped to speed up the process whereby these problems came to be identified and consequently the process whereby a reformist movement was formed in Bukhara. So far as events within the Russian empire were concerned, the geographical continuity that linked Russia organically to the peoples it had conquered contributed in no small

185

measure to ensuring that those events would cause particular stir, hence have considerable influence, in the emirate. Already at the time of the conquest of Central Asia, the Russian empire, still seemingly all-powerful, was in fact riven by revolutionary currents which filled with excitement a spirit as free and curious as that of Ahmad Danish. But with the twentieth century external upheavals gave the emerging reformist movement a more concrete impetus and direction: first the Russo-Japanese War, which for the entire colonial East was to signal the dawn of an immense hope for external liberation and internal regeneration; and thereafter, the 1905 Revolution, which was to have limitless consequences, since the liberal ideas and the hopes for change that it brought were to carry to the farthest confines of the empire. In Bukhara that revolution heightened awareness of the régime's despotic character and the need for both political and also economic transformation. Outside Bukhara, in neighbouring Turkey and Iran, under the influence at least in part of that revolution, constitutional régimes were installed; spirits eager for change in Bukhara thus found in them models of evolution in which the reconciliation of reformist aspirations with the liberal spirit of the West appeared to be achieved. Reaction might unfurl over the Russian empire; the echo of 1905 would still be heard on the emirate's frontiers.

What characterized Bukhara's reformism was that, though originally a reaction against the stagnation of Islam and against the spirit of the traditional *madrasas*, it really took shape within Islam and within the *madrasas*. There, students from India or Afghanistan brought in the forbidden newspapers and the echo of changes accomplished elsewhere, and there, after 1905, the cry of 'Asia for the Asians' was most frequently heard.

The First World War helped to clarify the main lines of the reformist appeal. National independence was to be a propaganda theme that the European adversaries utilized against one another. Should we be surprised if, in the emirate, this theme had particular resonance? In spite of its multinational composition, Bukharan society was that of an old nation. The Russian presence — the economic and social difficulties connected with that presence — helped to create a certain national cohesion. The attachment of the masses to the ancient Muslim state grew, both through opposition to the Russians and because it underlay the struggle of traditional authorities and reformists alike. The work of unification embarked upon by the Uzbek rulers in the eighteenth century found its culmination in the conquest and the reactions the conquest provoked.

The Russian Revolution utterly transformed the terms of the problem posed by the reformists, driving the movement onto the path of action. With the revolution, two essential facts came to dominate history: the collapse of the Russian empire and the extension of a world ideology of revolution to the Muslim periphery. Until then, revolution had concerned only the industrialized peoples of the colonizing West; suddenly, it extended to the backward East. What did these changes mean for Bukhara? They meant independence, thanks to the disintegration of the empire; yet that independence, which for the reformists represented an opportunity at last to implement a programme of political and social reform, for the emir meant an opportunity to avoid the revolutionary process that had just engulfed the Russian empire and to maintain the established order. This totally different vision of independence meant that the Jadids, eager for change, were obliged to opt for an orientation towards the Bolsheviks. Having for the first time an immediate hope of being able to reform society, they did not want to allow the opportunity to escape them — which explains their astonishing alliance with a party whose ideology could not hold any attractions for them.

But if, from 1900 to 1917, the reformist movement was propelled forward and sustained by ideas that came from throughout the Muslim world, after the revolution its fate was to be quite different. Cut off from the Bukharan régime and the traditional authorities and lacking any solid popular foundations, the movement became dependent upon the Bolsheviks and participated in the general imperatives of the new Russian régime's policy. The revolution thus marked a radical break in the life of the Jadid movement. Until then it had been one of the links in the great movement of reform and protest of the peoples of the Muslim East. After the revolution its existence became entirely tied to the Bolsheviks and to their options, and within that purely Russian context it had to evolve.

The history of Bukhara in the years 1917–24 is easy to understand if the essential lines of Bolshevik policy in this period are borne in mind. When the October Revolution broke out, it was in principle supposed to be the first in a long series of European revolutions. In this perspective, the disintegration of the empire and the centrifugal tendencies of the subject peoples were of only relative importance. After 1920 the Bolshevik leaders' optic changed radically. The long awaited European revolutions had failed or had never broken out. The European proletariat had shown itself none too anxious to defend the revolution, when it had occurred. Lenin was able to verify how correct his earlier analyses had been on the ebb of the revolutionary spirit in Europe. So it was necessary to consolidate and organize the existing Socialist state and attempt to strike at Europe by running her to ground in her 'colonial preserves'. By the same token, the value of the old Russian colonies changed in the Bolsheviks' calculations. If the first Socialist state was to survive, it would have to be reconstituted: that is, the fragments of the empire shattered by revolution would have to be reassembled. But this imperative of reunification had to be reconciled with the theme of national independence, dear to the countries of the East. So it was a question not of recreating the old empire, but of making it join Soviet Russia of its own accord. In this perspective, Turkistan and Bukhara played a key role, precisely because the revolution there had taken a profoundly Russian turn and was coming up against self-proclaimed national opposition.

At the end of 1921, Lenin wrote to Joffe:

> I personally *very much* suspect 'Tomskii's line' (perhaps it would be more correct to say Peters's line? or Pravdin's line? etc.) of engaging in Great-Russian chauvinism, or, to put it more correctly, in *deviating* in that direction. It is terribly important for all our Weltpolitik to win the confidence of the natives; to win it over again and again; to *prove* that we are *not* imperialists, that we shall *not* tolerate any *deviation* in that direction. This is a worldwide question, and that is no exaggeration. There you must be especially strict. It will have an effect on India and the East; it is no joke, it calls for exceptional caution.[1]

Lenin's thought is quite clear here: it was necessary to win over the Muslims at all costs, but to ensure that doing so did not appear as an imperialist action. The People's Republic of Bukhara, an independent state that was making its revolution alone under the leadership of its national élite, provided a perfect illustration of this doctrine. It is thus easy to understand why for four years the Soviet government tolerated that state, despite the fact that it was growing increasingly hostile. Bukhara proved that the Russian Revolution respected national aspirations and even allowed them to be expressed, since the Bolsheviks had brought to power those who for years had represented hopes for reform and a transformation of traditional society. The People's Republic of Bukhara led by the Jadids was infinitely more reassuring for the East than it would have been had it been led by the Communists. The fact that for four years the same national and religious themes were defended there as before 1917 was clear evidence of the Bolsheviks' tolerance.

In 1924 the Bolsheviks were at last able to begin to organize, and give some juridical form to, the first Socialist state. Since the Soviet state existed and had become quite solid, it was necessary to put an end to the national movements and reintegrate all the countries that had formerly made up the empire. Here again, the example of Bukhara was very important. The integration of Bukhara into the Soviet federation did not, like that of Georgia, require armed intervention, nor did it provoke disputes within the party. A *quriltay* bringing together Bukhara's national élite decided that independence no longer had any meaning and socialist brotherhood alone was essential. It was not the Soviet state that annexed Bukhara, but Bukhara's leaders who themselves suppressed their national state. And among those leaders, there were still Jadids. Perhaps they really believed it would be possible to pursue the national struggle within the Turkistani context into which it was about to be integrated, whereas in the people's republic the native and Russian Communists had gradually destroyed the reality of the national state.

Why did Bukhara's national bourgeoisie fail in its attempt at government? Its failure cannot be credited entirely to the Red Army, since even if the army did make its weight felt, it is nevertheless clear that one at least of the essential reasons for the collapse of the people's republic was of an internal nature.

For half a century, everything seemed to have paved the way for the Jadids to assume power. They had succeeded in thinking through in fresh terms the problems and needs of the society that was emerging from the conquest, and that was no longer the traditional society. Out of ill-expressed aspirations, regrets, and resentments and out of explosive demands, they had gradually fashioned an ideology that linked their own experience to the great movement of thought that was then upturning the Muslim world. But it was from their own experience that they drew their originality: a keen awareness of social problems. The revolution was first of all a response to the problems which Bukhara's national bourgeoisie had clearly posed: the revolution gave that bourgeoisie independence, then power, with the opportunity and even the task of realizing the social reforms of which it had dreamed. So from 1917 to 1924 history seemed to be moving in the direction in which Bukhara, and especially its most lucid minds, had been evolving for half a century. Yet this was where they failed.

Von Mende has written that, for Russia's Muslims, the revolution had come ten years too early; this was certainly one of the great problems for the Jadids: they had come too early themselves; in so backward and wretched a society, they found themselves isolated. Even if the Jadids succeeded in expressing the problems of the masses, the masses were incapable of following them; tradition kept them tied to their religious leaders. The conquest, by aggravating their economic difficulties, did not help to hasten their political maturity; on the contrary, it drove those wretched masses, obsessed with the sole problem of survival, back towards the traditional order, towards stability.

Not surprisingly, the regions where the reformists found a popular base (where the reformed *maktabs* were attended by poor children) were the Shi'i regions of eastern Bukhara, and the Basmachi rebellion survived in those same regions: the Shi'a were oppressed people ready to revolt. But most of Bukhara's population, who in 1924 submitted to the suppression of the national state without protesting or defending their national leaders, were Sunni; and Sunni Islam did not predispose its followers to conflicts with authority or to violent rebellion. The Jadids, though claiming to represent those Sunni masses, were in fact cut off from them — and even found themselves in conflict with them.

Whereas for the masses the fundamental problem was poverty, for the Jadids it was first necessary to resolve the question of independence. They thought no solution could be applied to internal problems that in the slightest way questioned the independence which had been won and which had always to be defended. This is why they could not accept that the young national state, under the watchful eye of Russia, should launch itself prematurely into class conflicts which would weaken it, deprive it of the only cadres it could find, and perhaps provoke intervention from outside. Without popular support, without cadres other than those inherited from the previous régime, could the rule of the Jadids really survive for long?

The Jadids were not even a coherent social class, but a group of well-intentioned individuals, without common social roots. From which classes could they draw support to retain power? The old ruling strata could accept neither their own dispossession nor the Jadids' programme of social reforms. The mass of peasants and nomads had contradictory demands, all of which were also in opposition to the ideology and policies the Jadids pursued. Social reforms were subordinated to national demands. But at the same time that they wanted an absolute change in their material situation, the masses remained attached to the conservative Islam of their ancestors. Therefore, to gain an audience among them, it was necessary to move in the direction of religious orthodoxy, which ultimately put a brake on social transformations. It was that isolated position within Bukharan society that constituted the tragedy of the local reformism and the basic reason for its collapse.

The case of Bukhara presents another interest for the historian. This was in effect the only experience the International had, at the time, of Socialism in a backward country: Bukhara alone illustrated that adaptation of socialism to the specific conditions of the East which Russia's Muslims were demanding at the Baku Congress. And when the Comintern subsequently condemned premature revolutions in backward countries, when it opposed the leadership of revolutionary movements by national bourgeoisies, it was able to refer to the example of the people's republics of Turkistan and especially Bukhara, where such an experience had resulted in the greatest difficulties. The brief adventure of reformism in a small and faraway Central Asian state was in the last resort to have global significance, since it weighed long upon the Comintern's vision of revolution in a colonial context.[2]

But there is another lesson to be drawn from a study of the Jadid movement in Bukhara. That movement developed out of the encounter of two very different currents of thought. One of these, common to all the Muslim world and even to all the colonial world in search of regeneration, was in reality founded upon an ideology of European origin: the national and liberal ideology of the nineteenth century. To this ideology Bukhara's élite had recourse to define and resolve its own specific problems: despotic rule and external dependence. The other current, which made its appearance in 1905 and triumphed with the October Revolution, was a Socialism whose function was to resolve the internal problems of Western society and which had barely — with only a few exceptions — given a moment's thought to backward societies.

After the revolution, local consciousness had to make a synthesis of those two currents, and their synthesis gave one idea victory over the other. What emerges clearly from the example of the Bukharan Jadids is that all their efforts were turned towards the realization of their national aspirations, to the detriment of the

social battle. The struggle of the Jadids within the people's republic genuinely expressed a national opposition to Russia. It was
never a struggle by Communists inside the party around differing
interpretations of Marxism. When, at the Baku Congress, the
leaders of the Comintern declared that the revolution in backward
countries had necessarily to carry social and national demands
forward in tandem, they did not yet know something that the
Jadids of Bukhara were going to demonstrate and that was subsequently seen in most countries of the East: that for as long as there
exists a problem of national liberation, social problems cannot be
posed clearly but merge with those of independence.

Appendix 1

Dynasties and Rulers of the Khanate of Bukhara

	Dynasty Ruler	Date of accession to throne A.H.	A.D.
Shaybanids	Mir Muhammad I	963	1556
	Iskandar	968	1560
	'Abdallah II	991	1583
	'Abd al-Mu'min	1006	1598
	Mir Muhammad II	1007	1598–9
Janids or Ashtarkhanids	Baqir Muhammad	1007	1599
	Vali Muhammad	1014	1605
	Imam Quli	1020	1611
	Nadir Muhammad	1051	1642
	'Abd al-'Aziz	1055	1645
	Subhan Quli	1091	1680
	'Ubaydallah I	1114	1702
	Abu'l Fayz	1123	1711
	'Abd al-Mu'min	1160	1747
	'Ubaydallah II	1164	1751
	Muhammad Rahim (Manghit)	1167	1753
	Abu'l Ghazi	1171	1758
Manghits	Mir Masum Shah Murad	1200	1785
	Haydar	1215	1800
	Husayn	1242	1826
	'Umar	1242	1826
	Nasrallah	1242	1827
	Muzaffar	1277	1860
	'Abd al-Ahad	1303	1885
	'Alim	1330	1910

Appendix 2

Statutes of the Benevolent Society of Bukhara for the Dissemination of Knowledge among the Masses

Founded: 11 Shavval 1327 (end of 1909)
Headquarters: Istanbul, Vazir Building (Vazir Khan)
Printed on its own press (morning)

Fundamental principles of the statutes of the Benevolent Society of Bukhara for the Dissemination of Knowledge among the Masses

1. Members of the Society comprise two categories: active members, corresponding members. From among the active members fourteen individuals will be chosen to make up the deliberative council (consultative body). From within the deliberative council members of the administrative council will be chosen.

2. For the first year, exceptionally, the deliberative council will be elected by the founders themselves. Subsequently election of active members and members of the deliberative council, to replace those who resign or for any reason give up their functions, will be carried out by members of the deliberative council. The election of corresponding members will be left to the discretion of active members.

3. Individuals wishing to become active members of the Society will be admitted or refused by the council. New members (when admitted) commit themselves to paying a once-off fee of half a lira and monthly dues of 10 piastres.

5. Any individual who commits himself to paying yearly dues of 120 piastres is admitted as a corresponding member.

6. The money paid in by members — if they resign or if they are expelled for any reason whatsoever — will not be returned to them.

8. For students checked by the Society and who merit it, dues are reduced by 3 per cent; in other cases, the yearly dues of 120 piastres remain obligatory.

9. The administrative council, which is made up of the president, secretary-general, treasurer and secretary, will be elected by secret ballot at the

194

extraordinary assembly that will take place once a year, in conformity with paragraphs 1 and 2. The extraordinary assembly is general and private.

13.   The accredited delegate will be in permanent correspondence with the Society, but will be able to address only the president. This is why the president is responsible for correspondence between corresponding members and the accredited delegate.

14.   The accredited delegate will recruit students (supporters), in accordance with the regulations which will be published by the Society. For the election of students, a meeting must be held in which ten corresponding members take part; the election arrived at in such a meeting must be ratified by a minimum of 7 members.

16.   When the accredited delegate is invited to come to Constantinople, at the suggestion of the Society, his travel expenses (both ways) will be reimbursed by the Society.

17.   The functions of the accredited delegate will last for one year; on expiry of this term the deliberative council will decide upon his replacement.

Regulations concerning students to be admitted by the Society

1.   Students will be recruited at Bukhara and in Turkistan. Provided they do not go beyond the limited number fixed by the deliberative council, corresponding members will be chosen in accordance with paragraph 2 in their towns and villages of origin.

2.   In each town 30 corresponding members have the right to recruit a student. If the number of corresponding members goes beyond 30 individuals, the remaining members have the right to choose a single student who will be sent to Turkey.

3.   Money bequeathed to the Society will be used in conformity with the testator's wishes.

4.   Future students cannot be admitted by the accredited delegate if they do not have the following qualities: (a) ability to write; (b) possession of a strong, robust constitution; (c) age between 10 and 15 years (children of rich parents are excluded).

5.   The contract imposing upon the Society the obligation to cover expenses cannot be signed if it turns out that children of the same family are admitted, or that their qualities have not been submitted to examination, or that having been examined the candidate commits an act contrary to the Society's regulations.

Note (report) on the activity of the Benevolent Society of Bukhara for the Dissemination of Knowledge among the Masses

1.   The Bukhara Society for the Dissemination of Knowledge among the Masses has been established in Turkistan, especially at Bukhara with the sole aim of spreading knowledge and building schools. Given that the Society is a benevolent body, it pursues no other aim and bears no resemblance or relation to other societies existing in the state.

2.   Its sole aim is to send every year from Turkistan and Bukhara a certain number of students to continue their studies in the schools of Constantinople, to the extent of the means at its disposal.

3.   The students who are under the Society's patronage must act in accordance with its customs (its practice) and are charged with fulfilling all its missions and all its orders.

4.   The Society will take care of the future of students who have completed their studies and none shall have the right to oppose the decision of the majority; if he does so, he will be obliged to reimburse all his educational expenses.

5.   For the establishment of new schools at Bukhara and for other more sizeable expenses in connection with the students sent to Turkey, gifts from wealthy Bukharan benefactors will be accepted and will be reimbursable in the future.

6.   The newly created schools will admit, as administrators and members of the teaching staff, only individuals named by the Society, provided that they observe its rules strictly.

7.   Children of wealthy parents may be admitted under the supervision and patronage of the Society, provided the parents cover all expenses and pay in addition a sum of 50 roubles per year.

11.   If the conduct of the accredited delegates is found to be in contradiction with the Society as a result of the decision taken by the corresponding members and made public, they will be relieved of their functions.

12.   A library established by the Society will be equipped with books and treatises offered by devoted members.

Source: Arsharuni and Gabidullin, *Ocherki,* pp. 135–8.

Appendix 3

The Emir of Bukhara's Manifesto of 30 March 1917

In the name of the All-powerful, who displays his mercy to our subjects, We, whose sole concern is the welfare and happiness of our people, have decided in accordance with their wishes to carry out extensive reforms in all spheres of our administration, suppressing all defects and injustices through the principles of election.

We remind our subjects that all the necessary reforms and changes can be based only upon one single principle, one single basis: that of the Holy *shari'at*. For this reason, We appeal to all to help us realize our decision to illumine Bukhara with the light of progress and culture, to the benefit of our people.

Above all, We shall be striving to achieve the establishment of an equitable justice and the suppression of unjust taxes, and We shall be devoting our particular attention to the development of commerce and industry in our Emirate.

A strict supervision will be exercised over officials and civil servants of all categories, who will receive fixed salaries and be forbidden to accept any kind of gratuity for their services. We shall take all measures to disseminate education and the sciences in our country, in strict accordance with the *shari'at*.

Concerned for the health and well-being of our subjects living in the capital, We have decided to grant the population the right to elect a council made up of our most respected fellow-citizens, which should take charge of public sanitation and the health of our Emirate's capital city.

Furthermore, We judge it necessary to create a State exchequer and to establish a budget governing the Emirate's precise income and expenditure.

We have studied the need for our citizens to be informed concerning all our undertakings and ordinances which will be implemented for the welfare and happiness of the State of Bukhara. For this reason, We have ordered the establishment of a printing press in our capital Bukhara, whose first task will be to print, so far as possible, texts of general interest in order that the inhabitants of Bukhara may become acquainted with them.

With an eye to the well-being of our people, We have taken measures for the development of autonomy in the Emirate of Bukhara, which will be implemented as soon as a suitable occasion presents itself.

Following in this the events that have taken place in the land of our great protectress Russia, We shall, in accordance with the wishes of the people, grant freedom to all those presently held in prison.

Sources: Vojna v Peskah, pp. 236–7; 'Ayni, *Vospominaniya,* pp. 158–9.

Appendix 4
Reform Programme for Bukhara, drawn up by the Young Bukharan Party

Land and Water Problems

The cultivated land of Bukhara can be divided into three categories:

1. Clerical holdings belonging to the religious institutions (*vaqf*).
2. Holdings exempt from taxation (*milk-i hurr*).
3. *Milk-i kharaj.*

Amlak and *milk-i kharaj* holdings are subject to taxation (*kharaj*).

Bukhara's *milk-i hurr* holdings, however many they may be, will retain their old status.

A special office will be established with the task of administering lands which formerly belonged to the clergy (*vaqf*). *Milk-i kharaj* holdings must be registered in special books. Each *tanab* will be taxable at a rate of two or three roubles. Each *vilayat* will be divided into between five and one hundred districts (*aqsaqal'stvo*); an honest and intelligent *aqsaqal* will be appointed for each of these units. Each *aqsaqal* maintains a register of the land coming under his authority. At the beginning of the year, he hands over the sums collected in the form of taxation to the beg, in accordance with the register. The begs in turn hand over the sums collected by them to the State Exchequer, in accordance with the entries registered in their books.

When tax rates are being fixed, there are no grounds for making any difference between sown and unsown land. For example, someone who owns four *tanabs* must pay a yearly tax of between two and eight roubles, or between three and twelve roubles, irrespective of whether he does or does not cultivate his land. At present, uncultivated land is not taxable. This involves disadvantages, since many people refrain from sowing their land in order to avoid paying taxes. So there is a great deal of uncultivated land. If the tax were to be fixed on the basis of total area, as we indicate, the taxpayer would be obliged to sow his land.

This system does not apply to non-irrigated land. In this case, the tax is levied on cultivated land alone, the remainder not being taxable; it is not fixed in relation to the quantity of *tanabs* and the sum levied is minimal. This tax is not very large and less heavy than that imposed on the third category of holding. Taxes on buildings and pens should be suppressed.

Producers should be freed from the duties on horse-fodder and from various other similar obligations.

Water installations must be improved and correctly sited, so that the *mirabs* cannot sell the water to just anyone. Everybody should know the quantity of water to which they are entitled. Everybody should receive their due share. During the *hashar* (compulsory work to clear the irrigation canals, carried out collectively), the practice of paying the *mirab* for the water should be abolished. The *hashar* cannot be ordered on state lands or orchards, nor for construction work. It must be reserved for water service alone. The *hashar* supervisers should be paid by the state. It is forbidden to ask money from those working on the *hashar* on the pretext that funds are needed to cover the cost of it; similarly it is forbidden to pay a special tax to the *mirab*. Those who absent themselves from the work should pay a fine.

On the other hand, there is a real problem of water in Bukhara, especially because there is not enough of it. Certain measures must be taken in this respect. As is well known, the Khanate of Bukhara draws water supplies from Samarqand, which in the past used to give Bukhara two thirds of its water. After the *vilayat* of Samarqand was incorporated into Russia it began to progress and grow wealthy. The area of sown land increased. But since one third of the water could no longer satisfy Samarqand's needs, it began to give Bukhara only half. Even this share was obtained only after big arguments. Today, the half of the water retained by Samarqand is not enough for it. This is why the share formerly channelled to our country has been taken away from us. After a stubborn fight and losing a great deal of money, the government of Bukhara has managed to receive only 20 per cent of the total quantity of water. This is the reason for the shortage of water in Bukhara. But that will not be the end of the story. Samarqand is expanding daily; the area of its cultivated land is increasing. So it is likely that its inhabitants once again do not have enough water. So we may be deprived even of that 20 per cent presently granted us. In such circumstances, agricultural work will become more difficult and it will no longer be possible to irrigate our land.

The government is obliged to seek a way out of this dilemma. The following measures should be taken: seek to obtain water from any river whatsoever apart from the Zarafshan; devote funds from the public exchequer to digging a canal from the Amu Darya to Bukhara; save Bukhara from water shortage.

There are many things to be done in order to improve and develop the rural economy. Everyone knows how the peasants (*dihqan*) have been ruined as a result of the practice of usury. They must be rid of this evil. But there is no way of freeing them from their enslavement to usurers except by prohibiting usurious lending. It is necessary to find credit for farmers. Only on this condition could usury be suppressed. In order to do this, an agricultural bank should be established in Bukhara, with branches in every *vilayat*. This bank would each year guarantee to the peasants the necessary means that would allow them to work their land; it would advance loans at a minimal rate of interest, of two or three roubles per year. Having thus placed the necessary facilities within reach of the peasants, it would be possible to ban Hindu and Muslim usury.

That done, there will still be many things to be accomplished. We know that at present all kinds of machines are produced: to prepare cattle food, to carry heavy loads and so on. Thanks to such machines, great savings of labour and time can be made. There are also machines that process agricultural produce. It is necessary to acquire these for Bukhara, to fix their price and to supply them to the peasants. Farmers unfamiliar with them should be shown how to operate and maintain them.

There are many peasants in our country who, as a result of the oppression and injustice of the authorities (*amlakdar*) and usurers, have lost their lands and dwellings and been thrown onto the street. There are also many available uncultivated lands, abandoned by their owners as a consequence of various exactions. As soon as the canal to the Amu Darya has been dug, the irrigation of cultivable land will be organized on both sides of it.

The government will distribute the land to peasants who do not own any. They must also get interest-free loans, vital if they are to start cultivation. In return they will give the public authorities a share of the harvest, with a view to acquiring the land they occupy. The land they have paid for in this way will become their property. They will be obliged to pay taxes in accordance with the generally established norms.

Agricultural schools will be set up throughout the country, to instil some notion of agronomy into the population.

This is the path that will enable us to save our country from ruin.

A single *qush-begi* (prime minister) cannot do all this work. To direct these undertakings, the government of Bukhara will have to establish a ministry of agriculture, at whose head a competent man will be placed as minister of agriculture.

Clerical holdings (*vaqf*)

As we indicated above, it will be necessary to create a special body to administer the lands that formerly belonged to the clergy, which will first and foremost take account of those destined for Bukhara's national education. If the revenues deriving from these were straightened out and if the expenditure were used properly, Bukhara could in the domain of education surpass the most developed city in Europe. At present, the least ordered and most chaotic state of affairs in our country involves the clerical lands, which are in the hands of managers and tenants. As everybody knows, in Bukhara there is no occupation as advantageous and lucrative as tenant-farming. To put it bluntly, on average half of our *vaqf* endowments go into the pockets of managers and tenants. It is the duty of every good Muslim to think of reform in this domain. A ministry of clerical lands must be set up in Bukhara. The post of minister will be given to an intelligent, educated man aware of these issues. All problems related to clerical property will be under his jurisdiction. The sums hitherto levied by the public exchequer — on reading-rooms, libraries, refectories — must be reimbursed. The minister for former clerical lands must put their revenues in order and use them in conformity with the law (*shari'at*). There are good grounds for setting up a special exchequer for these domains. All sums deriving from the *vaqfs* will obligatorily be handed over to it. This money will be put into circulation in commerce and will help to finance important works. The profits obtained will serve to repair the confessional or secular schools and the mosques. New schools (*maktabs, madrasas*), libraries, orphanages, hospices for the poor and refectories will be built. Each year the minister will present the people with an account of his expenditure.

Cash *vaqf* endowments too should come under the jurisdiction of this minister. The ministry for clerical domains is charged with preventing abuses by tenants and managers. It will grant land tenancies to the peasants themselves on equitable conditions. The profits from cash *vaqfs* must be used in conformity with the law. Apart from the domains themselves, warehouses, dwellings etc. belonging to the *vaqfs* will likewise be placed under the ministry in question.

Military affairs

Under the terms of a convention concluded with Russia, the government of Bukhara has the right to maintain an army of twelve thousand men under the colours. But at present that army numbers no more than 4,000 or 5,000. The Bukharan government could have used the convention to increase the draft. However, those in power have not understood this. The government should now take advantage of the convention and raise the number of men under the colours to twelve thousand. However, the soldiers must not be recruited as has happened hitherto in a chaotic manner and as volunteers. Military service must be compulsory. Apart from individuals belonging to the emir's own family and students, all males in the Khanate of Bukhara will have to undergo military service at the age of twenty-two. A large number of young men will be collected in this way. It will be necessary to subject them to a preliminary medical examination and exempt those with illnesses or disabilities from service. Service should last for two years. During that period recruits will be given a military training and learn to stand guard. Those who have carried out military service for two years will be released and replaced by others, called up under the conditions indicated above. In Bukhara and other towns it will be necessary to build large barracks, each of which will be furnished with a mosque and a school for which *imams* and teachers will be appointed. In the course of those years, illiterate soldiers could thus learn to read and write, and to assimilate religious prescriptions and the rules of prayer. Twice a year, the soldiers will be properly equipped. Men with military training will be appointed as troop commanders.

It is true that we lack such commanders. So we shall have to seek Muslim officers in Russia and give the posts to them. It is necessary to establish a military school in Bukhara, with Muslim officers as administrators and instructors. After a time, our Bukharans trained in this school will form an officer corps for the army. The latter needs doctors, hospitals and pharmacies. Cavalrymen must receive fodder for their horses from the state. It is the state which must supply the army. In addition, the soldiers will receive a modest monthly payment.

All these matters will be administered by the ministry of war. The person appointed to the post of minister will be intelligent and experienced in such questions.

Financial affairs

In the entire world there does not exist a public exchequer as disorderly as in Bukhara. Where does the exchequer's money come from and how does it arrive there? How is it spent? Who is it handed over to? For what services do people receive it? Nobody knows. The public exchequer, particularly in recent times, finds itself in a very confused situation. Order must be restored to it. It is necessary to establish a ministry of finance and put someone in charge of it.

We spoke earlier of taxes levied on cultivated land. The sums due in this respect should go into the departments of the finance ministry. Customs transactions too should be concentrated there. Offices collecting customs duties in the towns will be closed down, apart from the customs house which will be set up at the frontier.

The tax on livestock requires reform. It would be a good idea to fix a special tax for merchants operating within the country, once their yearly turnover has been established, and to give receipts to those who pay what is due from them. In addition, a special court treasurer will be appointed, in charge of expenditure incurred by the emir. The latter will receive money on the basis of accounts presented to the minister of finance.

The minister of finance will record all sums entering the country, regulate all state expenditure and present the people with an account.

Internal affairs

A minister of the interior will be appointed to administer the state's internal affairs. It will be up to him to maintain order in the country and to divide the latter into a number of regions. In this way the Khanate of Bukhara might comprise ten provinces (*kurgans*), each of which would be headed by a governor or *kurgan-begi*. A governorship (*kurgan-begstvo*) might be subdivided into ten regions, each headed by an *il-begi*. Each region (*il-begstvo*) would be divided into ten districts (*tumans*), each headed by a *tuman-begi*.

Matters concerning the people and falling within the jurisdiction of the *tuman-begis* are examined by officials with the title of *aqsaqal* (*starshina* in Russian) and by mullas. The *kurgan-begis, il-begis* and *tuman-begis* are appointed by the minister of the interior, once the emir has approved the nominations. The same goes for the police chiefs and district *mirshabs*. The *aqsaqals*, popularly elected, are confirmed in office by the *tuman-begis*. Neither the minister of the interior, nor the *kurgan-begis*, the *il-begis* or the *tuman-begis*, are entitled to meddle in judicial business. They simply apply and implement decisions by the judicial instances of the *shari'at*. The minister of the interior brings government decrees to the notice of the *kurgan-begis*, who do the same for the *il-begis*. The latter in turn communicate them to the *tuman-begis*, who transmit them to the *aqsaqals*, who finally make them known to the populace.

Judicial institutions

The man who knows the religious commentaries and *shari'at* laws thoroughly is in Bukhara called the high judge (*qazi-kalan*). He fulfils the function of a justice minister. The minister cannot direct judicial business himself. Bukhara will be broken up into two or three judicial divisions.

The minister of justice nominates judges (*qazis*) at the level of the province (*kurgan*), region (*il-begstvo*) and district (*tuman*). And a judge together with the two muftis who assist him constitute a court, which judges such disputes and conflicts as may arise in the populace. A higher judicial instance, the *istinaf*, is also established.

Individuals not satisfied by the judgement of the first court may appeal to this higher instance, which examines the matter afresh.

The minister and judges (*qazis*) receive their salaries from the public exchequer. Those staffing the judicial system are likewise paid by the exchequer. Each *qazi* can employ no more than twenty examining magistrates. A citizen can be called before the lower court only by a formal notification. A modest sum will be collected for release from any testamentary or other deed, on behalf of the public exchequer.

Protection of the State

The chief of police of the city of Bukhara will hold the rank of minister. His deputy will have the task of supervising public order and protecting the city's security.

Communications and Mines

A minister of transport and mines will be appointed, whose job will be to see to the upkeep of the communications network, the construction of railways and modern roads, and the exploitation of such natural resources as coal, gold, ferrous minerals or oil.

Foreign affairs

The minister of foreign affairs will be responsible for relations with the Russian and other governments. At the same time, he will perform the function of president of the council.

Public education

The minister of public education will have the task of overseeing the scholastic establishments set up in Bukhara by the state. It will be up to him to appoint teachers, establish training colleges, formulate curricula and so on. In addition to the public schools and those maintained by the clergy (vaqfs), educational establishments may be founded by individuals. Nobody is entitled to prevent this.

The minister of public education, with the help of the higher pedagogic council, awards students who have completed their studies the appropriate diplomas as mullas, teachers, muftis, judges or qazis.

Council of ministers

There will be ten ministries in our country: agriculture, clerical lands, war, finance, interior, justice, police, transport and mines, public education, foreign affairs. The minister for foreign affairs will also perform the function of president of the council.

Each minister will be able to call upon advisers from outside, who will all have to be Muslims, competent in the matters of their department, who will have to remain in position until we have formed our own specialists.

These ten ministers form the council. All decisions concerning public matters are taken by common agreement in the council of ministers. Outside it, no minister can decide on any matter. The minister who is not in agreement with the council's decisions must resign. He is replaced by an individual appointed, with the emir's approval, by the president of the council.

Communal councils

Councils will be established in the communes, made up of elected representatives of the people. Each council will have the task of overseeing public order, maintaining streets and roads, fixing the price of goods, controlling markets, etc.

Control bodies

It is essential to exercise control over the activity of ministers, in order to avoid mistakes or abuses. For this purpose, two bodies will be established, one special and the other general. The former will comprise twenty individuals charged with forming a control commission. Out of that number, ten will be Muslim jurists from Russia and the Caucasus, invited on the recommendation of the associations existing in those countries. The ten others, chosen from the indigenous population, will all be educated people who command authority and are distinguished by their intelligence.

Each minister will be obliged to draw up an estimate covering all spending projected by his ministry and to present it to the council. When it has been examined, the president of the council and the minister responsible sign this estimate and transmit it to the control commission. Once the latter has studied and approved it, it is submitted to the emir for his signature. It is only upon the basis of such an estimate that the minister of finance can release funds.

The second control body is constituted by the people, expressing themselves via the press. Every individual is free, in Bukhara, to publish newspapers and books without hindrance and to distribute them. Citizens have the right to express their opinions, in the press, on the government's activity, to criticize the various ministers, to point out the good sides of their actions as well as injustices, abuses and mistakes, so that the whole people and the control commission may be aware of ministerial practice.

Year 1338 A.H. (1917)

Source: Revoljucija i nacional'noj vopros, pp. 353–60.

Notes

Notes to the Introduction

1. On the name Turkistan and the use of the name Bukhara for certain regions of Turkistan, see M. A. Terent'ev, *Istoriya zavoevaniya Srednei Azii*, St Petersburg, 1906, vols. 1–3; V. V. Barthold, 'Turkestan', *Encyclopaedia of Islam*, 1st edn, Leiden, 1913– ; *The Encyclopaedia Britannica*, 1910–11 edn, pp. 619–20; and Z. V. Togan (Validov), *Turkili haritasi ve ona ait izahlar*, Istanbul, 1943, p. 1.

2. A. Vambéry, *Voyages d'un faux derviche dans l'Asie centrale de Téhéran à Khiva, Bukhara et Samarkand par le grand désert turcoman*, Paris, 1863, pp. 148 and 149. The desert of Qizil Kum extends over some 250,000 sq. km between the Sir Darya and the Amu Darya. The sands of the Qara Kum cover a more or less comparable area in the Trans-Caspian region.

3. The Zarafshan flows from east to west for over 600 km. It was formerly a tributary of the Amu Darya, from which it gradually became diverted. It is on the banks of the Zarafshan (the Datya of the Avesta), where the house of Porushaspa, father of Zoroaster, is said to have stood.

4. The Amu Darya is far longer than the Zarafshan; it is a powerful river, and its yellowish waters flow in a bed so broad that it is often hard to see from one bank to the other. Like the Zarafshan, the Amu Darya is so potent a symbol of life in Bukhara that natives have manifested a devotion to it that often surprises travellers.

5. Magidovich, *Materialy po raionirovaniyu Srednei Azii*, Tashkent, 1926, vol. 1, p. 164.

6. A first Arab incursion seemingly took place in 674, led by 'Ubaydallah b. Ziyad: M. Narshahi, *Istoriya Bukhary*, Tashkent, 1897, p. 7.

7. Shaybani Khan, 1451–1510, was the grandson of Abu'l-Khayr, whose constant attacks ruined the Taymurid empire. The story of his exploits was recorded by Muhammad Salih of Khvarazm in an epic Chagatay poem, the *Shaybani-nama*.

Notes to Chapter One

1. Vambéry, *Voyages*, p. 332.

2. A. Olufsen, *The Emir of Bokhara and his Country*, Copenhagen, 1911, pp. 1–2.

3. Zel'kina, 'Zemel'naya reforma v Srednei Azii', *Revolyutsionnyi Vostok*, no. 3 (1928), p. 138.

4. B. Gafurov, *Istoriya tadzhikskogo naroda*, Moscow, 1952, p. 422.

5. A. Semenov (*Ocherk pozemel'no podatnogo i nalogovo ustroistva Bukharskogo khanstva*, Stalinabad, 1954, p. 25) says mistakenly that confiscated land remained the property of the emir, whereas in fact it went to swell the state lands.

6. Gifts of state land are a very ancient institution in the Orient. Trace can be found of them in Persia before the Arab conquest, in the eleventh century among the Qarakhanids, and then among the Seljuqs. In Central Asia, after the Mongol invasion, the institution was known by the Arabic term *iqta*, later as *suyurghal*, and finally as *tankhvah*. (See K. Mirzaev, 'Tankho, kak raznovidnost' feodal'nogo zemlevladeniya v Bukharskom khanstve', *Trudy Instituta Ekonomiki*, no. 3 [1952], p. 7.)

7. A. Fedchenko, *Zapiski o mangianskom bekstve, materialy dlja statistiki turkestanskogo kraya*, item 2, St Petersburg, 1873, p. 53.

8. Semenov (*Ocherk pozemel'no podatnogo*, p. 28) gives particular emphasis to this temporary character.

9. Especially in the eastern part of the emirate. See Semenov, *Ocherk pozemel'no podatnogo*, p. 12; Gafurov, *Istoriya*, p. 422; D. Logofet, *Bukharskoe khanstvo pod russkim protektoratom*, St Petersburg, 1911, p. 58; and V. V. Bartol'd, *Istoriya kul'turnoi zhizni Turkestana*, Leningrad, 1927, p. 247.

10. Logofet (*Bukharskoe khanstvo*, vol. 1, p. 244) indicates that there was a strict hierarchy for *tankhvah* lands given to the army: a soldier received a plot with one family living on it; a *qaravul-begi* received a plot inhabited by six families; a *mirakhur* received a plot with thirteen families; and so on.

11. See O. A. Suhareva, *K istorii gorodov Bukharskogo khanstva: Istoriko-etnograficheskie ocherki*, Tashkent, 1959, p. 118.

12. See *Istoriya Uzbekskoi SSR*, Tashkent, 1957, book 1, vol. 2, p. 76; and *Dokumenty k istorii agrarnykh otnoshenii*.

13. Bartol'd, *Istoriya*, p. 245.

14. Ivanov, *Vostanie kitai-kipchakov v bukharskom khanstve, 1821–1825 godov*, Moscow, 1937, p. 33.

15. Semenov, *Ocherk pozemel'no podatnogo*, p. 28.

16. Zel'kina, 'Zemel'naia reforma', pp. 138–68.

17. N. A. Kislyakov, *Patriarkhal'no–feodal'nye otnohseniya sredi osedlogo sel'skogo naseleniya Bukharskogo khanstva v kontse XIX-go i nachale XX-go veka*, Moscow/Leningrad, 1962, p. 99.

18. Narshahi, *Istoriya*, p. 41.

19. N. V. Khanykov, *Opisanie Bukharskogo khanstva*, St Petersburg, 1843, pp. 114–19.

20. Ibid.

21. J. Schacht, 'Mirath', *Encyclopaedia of Islam*, 1st edn (Leiden, 1913), vol. 3, pp. 577–84.

22. The process is described in B. Iskandarov, *O nekotorykh izmeneniyakh v ekonomike vostochnoi Bukhary na rubezhe XIX–XX vek*, Stalinabad, 1958, p. 9.

23. D. Logofet, *Strana bezpraviya*, St Petersburg, 1909, pp. 32–90.

24. Ibid., p. 87.

25. Logofet, *Strana bezpraviya*, p. 87; P. P. de Semenov, *La Russie extra-européenne et polaire*, Paris, 1900, p. 145; Olufsen, *Emir*, pp. 486–501; and A. I. Shahnazarov, *Sel'skoe khoziaistvo v Turkestanskom krae*, St. Petersburg, 1908, pp. 52–6.

26. Iskandarov, *O nekotorykh izmeneniyakh*, p. 17.

27. In Bukhara the term *qishlaq* (normally the winter quarters of a nomadic tribe) was used for villages in general.

28. Iskandarov, *O nekotorykh izmeneniyakh*, p. 20.

29. Khanykov, *Opisanie*, pp. 75–6.

30. V. I. Masal'skii, *Turkestanskii krai*, St Petersburg, 1913, p. 649.

31. Logofet, *Bukharskoe khanstvo*, vol. 1, p. 187.

32. Vambéry, *Voyages*, p. 331.

33. Olufsen, *Emir*, p. 282.

34. Magidovich, *Materialy*, p. 149.

35. Kislyakov, *Patriarkhal'no-feodal'nye otnosheniya*, p. 19.

36. Lt Col. Sneysareff (*Eastern Bokhara: A Military and Geographical Description*, Simla, 1909, p. 23) writes of them: 'they are keenly interested in foreign affairs

and very well informed.'

37. Abramzon, 'Tyan-Shanskaya Etnograficheskaya ekspeditsiya', *Kratkie soob-shcheniya instituta etnografii*, no. 4 (1948), pp. 68–73.

38. The Tajiks constituted the second ethnic group of the emirate, with 476,000 inhabitants in 1920. Originally the Tajiks occupied the fertile plain of the Zaraf-shan, but under Uzbek domination they were pushed back into the inhospitable Darvaz and Qarategin mountains. Others inhabited the Kulab and Baljuan valleys; they engaged in agriculture and, again, were among the poorest. Most of the Tajiks were Sunnis, but a minority were either twelver Shi'a or Isma'ilis. See further V. V. Bartol'd, *Tadzhiki, istoricheskii ocherk: Tadzhikistan*, Tashkent, 1925, pp. 93–112; and M. Andreev, *Po etnografii Tazhikov: Nekotorye svedeniya — Tadzhikistan*, Tashkent, 1925, pp. 151–78.

39. Questions of genealogy had considerable importance for ensuring the uncon-tested pre-eminence of the tribal chiefs. In the Pamir regions, most claimed descent from Alexander the Great. (B. Iskandarov, *Social'no ekonomicheskii i politicheskii stroi vostochnoi Bukhary i Pamira nakanune prisoedineniya Srednei Azii k Rossii*, Stalinabad, 1960, p. 96.)

40. Ivanov, *Vostanie*, p. 33.

41. Khanykov, *Opisanie*, p. 182.

42. Ibid., pp. 182–3.

43. Ivanov, *Vostanie*, p. 26.

44. The Arabs established in the emirate all claimed descent from the warriors of Qutayba. In the middle of the nineteenth century, there were some 60,000 of them, all proud of their ancestry but very well integrated into the mass of the population. Vambéry (*Voyages*, p. 313) asserts that they no longer knew their language; whereas Kun ('Izucheniya etnicheskogo sostava Turkestana', *Novyi Vostok*, no. 6 [1924], p. 356) referring to the testimony of the Arabs of Samarqand, writes that 'the language of the Arabs of Bukhara is Arabic'. According to Kislyakov (*Patriakhal'no-feodal'nye otnosheniya*, p. 32), there were 47,000 of them.

45. A. Semenov, *Ocherk ustroistva tsentral'nogo administrativnogo upravleniya v Bukharskom khanstve pozdneishego vremeni*, Stalinabad, 1954, pp. 14, 66, and 67.

46. Ibid., p. 21.

47. Ibid.

48. Alim Khan, *La voix de la Boukharie opprimée*, Paris, 1929, p. 52.

49. Muhammad Rahim eliminated the last two Ashtarkhanids, Abu'l-Fayz (1747) and 'Abd al-Mu'min (1748), and replaced them by first 'Ubaydallah (son of Shah Taymur, Sultan of Khvarazm) and then Abu'l-Ghazi, before he married the daugh-ter of Abu'l-Fayz Khan and was proposed for the throne by the Bukharan clergy, as a (very indirect) descendant of Chingiz Khan. His successor and uncle, Danial, Bay placed Abu'l-Ghozi back on the throne; but subsequently Shah Murad — who took the title of Amir al-Mu'minin (but not that of Khan) — married the widow of Rahim Bay, so that through his son and successor Haydar the descent from Chingiz Khan (by the female line) was re-established. (Bartol'd, *Istoriya*, p. 106.)

50. Semenov, *Ocherk ustroistva*, pp. 21–3; and Olufsen, *Emir*, pp. 574–6.

51. Vambéry, *Voyages*, p. 175.

52. Masal'skii, *Turkestanskii krai*, p. 420.

53. Bartol'd, *Istoriya*, p. 247.

54. A. Semenov, 'Bukharskii traktat o chinakh i zvaniyakh i ob obyazannostyakh ikh nositelei i Srednevekovoi Bukhare', *Sovetskoe Vostokovedenie*, no. 5 (1948), pp. 137–53.

55. Khanykov, *Opisanie*, pp. 183–5.

56. Semenov, *Ocherk ustroistva*, p. 64.

57. The post of *qush-begi* took on great importance in the nineteenth century (Semenov, 'Bukharskii traktat', pp. 137–53; and G. Safarov, *Kolonial'naya revolyutsiya: 'Opyt Turkestana*, Moscow, 1921, p. 45.

58. Vambéry, *Voyages*, p. 336.

59. Kislyakov, *Patriarkhal'no-feodal'nye otnosheniya*, p. 37; and Khanykov, *Opisanie*, pp. 183–5.

60. *Sayyids* are descendants of Muhammad through his daughter Fatima. See Narshahi, *Istoriya*, p. 16. *Khvajas* claim descent from the Arab conquerors.

61. Khanykov, *Opisanie*, pp. 189–93; and V. Krestovskii, *V gostyakh u emira Bukharskogo*, St Petersburg, 1887, p. 108.

62. Vambéry, *Voyages*, p. 328; and Olufsen, *Emir*, p. 386.

63. Zel'kina, 'Zemelnaya reforma', p. 156.

64. Vambéry, *Voyages*, p. 335; and Semenov, *Ocherk ustroistva*, p. 13.

65. S. 'Ayni, *Vospominaniya*, Moscow/Leningrad, 1960, pp. 426–9.

66. Olufsen, *Emir*, p. 297.

67. Vambéry, *Voyages*, p. 179. On the Jews of Bukhara, see also 'Antisemitizm v Turkestane', article by I. Grubjak appended to the book by L. Kantor, *Tuzemnye evrei v Uzbekistane: Samarkand*, Tashkent, 1929, pp. 38–44.

68. Ivanov, *Vostanie*, pp. 18–19; and Logofet, *Bukharskoe khanstvo*, vol. 1, p. 187.

69. Ivanov, *Vostanie*, p. 19.

70. *Istoriya Uzbekskoi SSR*, book 2, vol. 1, p. 138.

71. Russian travellers estimated that this salary amounted to about ten roubles (Khanykov, *Opisanie*, p. 332).

72. M. N., 'Pod znakom Islama', *Novyi Vostok* (1924), p. 76.

73. Ibid.

74. Ibid.

75. M. N. (ibid.) in these statistics considers smallholders and landless peasants together, estimating that landless peasants represent almost half of this group of peasants, which he evaluates at 67 per cent of the population of Bukhara.

76. L. Klimovich, *Islam v Tsarskoi Rossii*, Moscow, 1936, p. 193.

77. Sukhareva, *K istorii*, pp. 12–48. See also, on urban life and the artisanate, O. Sukhareva, *Pozdne-feodal'nyi gorod Bukhara, kontsa XIX nachalo XX veka (remeslennaya promyshlennost')*, Tashkent, 1962; and *idem*, 'Byt zhilogo kvartala goroda Bukhary v kontse XIX nachale XX veka', Akademiya Nauk SSSR, Institut Etnografii, *Kratkie soobshcheniya*, no. 28 (1957), pp. 35–8.

78. F. Khodzhaev, 'O mlado–Bukhartsakh', *Istorik marksist*, no. 1 (1926), p. 128.

79. Vambéry, *Voyages*, pp. 153–79.

80. Semenov, *Ocherk ustroistva*, p. 13.

81. Vambéry (*Voyages*, p. 179) describes the slave market.

82. S. Zhukovskii, *Snosheniya, Rossi s Bukharoi i Khivoi za poslednie trëkhsotletie*, Petrograd, 1915, pp. 36–67; and Vambéry, *Voyages*, p. 76.

83. Vambéry, *Voyages*, p. 233.

84. Ibid.

85. Ibid., p. 153.

86. These were mainly Persian slaves, whose prestige, according to Vambéry, was due to the fact that they were considered more adept than others at negotiating with *farangis* (Europeans), because they possessed a smattering of the 'devilish arts' through which the *farangis* had won an illegitimate superiority.

87. Since these last two domains are indissociable, juridical and religious organization have been postponed to the section (pp. 31–5) dealing with Islam.

88. As late as the eighteenth century the *qush-begi* was merely an official of second rank, responsible for organizing the Khan's hunting and particularly his fowling: the right arm of the Emir was then the *shaykh al-islam*. See Semenov, 'Bukharskii traktat', pp. 137–53, and *Ocherk ustroistva*, p. 54.

89. Under the last emirs, *mirs* or begs were theoretically elected (Alim Khan, *La voix*, p. 54) but in practice appointed by the emir (Sneysareff, *Eastern Bukhara*, p. 39). One exception was the *vilayat* of Bukhara, which belonged by right to the *qush-begi;* another was that of Qarshi, which was administered by the heir to the throne (Semenov, *Ocherk ustroistva*, p. 24).

90. Logofet, *Strana bezpraviya*, p. 12; and Magidovich, *Materialy*, p. 64.

91. Bartol'd, *Istoriya;* and I. Gajer, *Turkestan*, Tashkent, 1909, p. 192.

92. Logofet, *Strana bezpraviya*, p. 34; and Sneysareff, *Eastern Bokhara*, p. 39.

93. Semenov, *Ocherk ustroistva*, p. 33; and Alim Khan, *La voix*, p. 54.

94. Ibid. In practice, the army was mainly made up of common prisoners, guilty of more or less real crimes. A. R. Fitrat, *Bayanat-i sayyah-i hindi*, Istanbul, n. d.), p. 35.

95. Semenov, *Ocherk ustroistva*, p. 59; Ivanov, *Vostanie*, p. 163; and V. L. Vyatkin, 'Karshinskii okrug, organizatsiya v nem voiska i sobytiya v period 1215–1217 (1800–1803) godov', *Izvestiya sredneaziatskogo otdela Russkogo geograficheskogo obshchestva*, no. 28, Tashkent, 1928, pp. 15–19. According to Vyatkin, the *nawkars* constituted a regular army; because of this apparently contradictory information, it seems that Semenov was describing the army of Bukhara as it became organized in the second half of the nineteenth century.

96. *Istoriya Uzbekskoi SSR*, book 2, vol. 1, p. 136.

97. Mirzaev, *Tankho*, p. 8.

98. *Istoriya Uzbekskoi SSR*, book 2, vol. 1, p. 136; and Semenov, *Ocherk ustroistva*, p. 48.

99. In the capital a geographical division along a line from north-west to southeast separated the town into two sectors or *sahms*, themselves subdivided into six *jaribs*. The *sahms* were administered by *babas*, who held authority over the *dahbashis* or *jarib* leaders, each of whom had ten policemen under his orders. (See Semenov, *Ocherk ustroistva*.)

100. Vambéry, *Voyages*, p. 331.

101. Semenov (*Ocherk ustroistva*, p. 66) writes that 'Centralization killed all the vital forces of the nation, displaying unbelievable despotism and scandalous excesses.'

102. M. N., 'Pod znakom Islama', p. 79.

103. Logofet, *Strana bezpraviya*, p. 36.

104. M. N., 'Pod znakom Islama', p. 74.

105. Such was, notably, the case with Emir Muzaffar's *qush-begi*, Muhammad Bay, who was still a slave under Emir Nasrallah.

106. The *khvajas* of Ju'ibar constituted a real caste, whose religious power was also considerable.

107. Safarov, *Kolonial'naya revolyutsiya*, p. 45.

108. Semenov, 'Bukharskii traktat', pp. 137–53.

109. Safarov, *Kolonial'naya revolyutsiya*, p. 54.

110. On this point, see Semenov, *Ocherk ustroistva*, pp. 48–51; Masal'skii, *Turkestanskii krai*, pp. 556–7; Logofet, *Bukharskoe khanstvo*, p. 39; and A. Gubarevich-Radobylskii, *Ekonomicheskii ocherk Bukhary i Tunisa*, St Petersburg, 1905, p. 140.

111. Bartol'd, *Istoriya*, p. 108.

112. Koran XIII [22], XXXV [26], LXX [24], etc.

113. Originally the *kharaj*, like the *jizya*, was a tribute to which unbelievers had to submit; later, at the time of the conquests, it was decided that the conquered population would pay the *kharaj* even if it converted to Islam.

114. Logofet, *Strana bezpraviya*, p. 48. Sneysareff (Eastern Bokhara, p. 102) indicates the following conditions for stock: a sheep for five camels, a sheep or cow for between 40 and 100 sheep or goats, plus an extra one per hundred. Beyond that, the most eccentric increases came into play. There might easily be an extra half-animal levied between 500 and 900 sheep, then an additional animal between 900 and 1,000, and so on.

115. See Masal'skii, *Turkestanskii krai*, pp. 556–7; Sneysareff, *Eastern Bokhara*, pp. 101–4; A. M. *Taxation in Bokhara* (n. p., n. d.), based on the same author's article 'Nalogi v Bukhare', *Turkestanskie vedemosti*, 10, 11, and 13 January 1906; and Logofet, *Strana bezpraviya*, pp. 48–9.

116. M. N., 'Pod znakom Islama', p. 79.

117. Contemporary authors perhaps tend to give an exaggerated description of it (see Kislyakov, *Patriarkhal'no-feodal'nye otnosheniya*, p. 101); nevertheless, it is important to appreciate the seriousness of the masses' situation.

118. See Khanykov, *Opisanie*, pp. 189–93.

119. In the last decades of the emirate, the title of *shaykh al-islam* was accorded by the emir to clerics whom he wished to honour; their role was confined in practice to serving as experts on genealogies claimed to go back to the Prophet.

120. Semenov, *Ocherk ustroistva*, p. 45; Khodzhaev, 'O mlado-Bukhartsakh', p. 133*n* 1; Logofet, *Strana bezpraviya*, p. 32; and Alim Khan, *La voix*, p. 54. There is a close relationship between the figure of the *ra'is* and that of the classical oriental *muhtasib* (see Bernhauer, *Mémoires sur les institutions de police chez les Arabes, les Persans et les Turcs*, Paris, 1861, pp. 74–5; and P. I. Petrov, 'Bukharskii muhtasib v nachale XX veka', *Problemy Vostokovedeniya*, no. 1 [1959], pp. 139–44.)

121. Khodzhaev, 'O mlado-Bukhartsakh', p. 125.

122. Vambéry, *Voyages*, pp. 327 ff.

123. Barthold, *Histoire*, p. 184.

124. Logofet, *Strana bezpraviya*, p. 33; Safarov, *Kolonial'naja revolyutsiya*, p. 46.

125. The number of mosques in the emirate is not known, but in Bukhara itself Vambéry says that the population boasted of 365 mosques, of which he located only half (Vambéry, *Voyages*, p. 328).

126. The inhabitants of Bukhara put the number of *madrasas* in the capital at 365; Vambéry (ibid.) counted 80 of them.

127. *Aziatskaya Rossiya*, no. 1 (1910), p. 213.

128. For discussions of the origin of the *madrasa* in Bukhara see Barthold, *Turkestan*, part 2, p. 105; Bartol'd *Istoriya*, p. 42 and N. Pigulevskaya, *Goroda Irana v rannem srednevekove*, Moscow, 1956, p. 32.

129. 'Shkol'noi vopros v Russkom Musul'manstve', *Mir Islama*, vol. 2, no. 6 (1913), pp. 378–80.

130. Olufsen, *Emir*, p. 387.

131. Semenov, *Ocherk ustroistva*, p. 68.

132. The order of *khvajagan* was a branch of the Yassawiyya specific to Bukhara.

133. K. Bendrikov, *Ocherki po istorii narodnogo obrazovaniya v Turkestane*, Moscow, 1960, pp. 31–2.

134. Vambéry, *Voyages*, pp. 157 ff.; and Olufsen, *Emir*, pp. 397–8 and 544.

135. Logofet, *Strana bezpraviya*, p. 94.

136. Ivanov, *Vostanie*.

137. Khodzhaev, 'O mlado–Bukhartsakh', p. 128; and K. Z. Muhsinova, 'K istorii vystuplenii Bukharskikh krestyan protiv nalogovogo gneta v kontse XIX veka', *Problemy Vostokovedeniya*, no. 1 (1959), pp. 94–100.
138. M. N., 'Pod znakom Islama', p. 79.

Notes to Chapter Two

1. Zhukovskii, *Snosheniya;* V. V. Grigoriev, *Russkaya politika v otnoshenii k Srednei Azii*, St Petersburg, 1874; A. N. Popov, *Snoshenie Rossii s Khivoyu i Bukharoyu pri Petre Velikom*, St Petersburg, 1853; and E. Kaidalov, *Karavan zapiski*, Moscow, 1928, 3 vols.
2. D. Boulger, *England and Russia in Central Asia*, London, 1879, 2 vols.
3. Ibid., vol. 2, p. 72.
4. Logofet, *Strana bezpraviya*, p. 13.
5. M. G. Chernaev was military governor of the region (*oblast'*) of Turkistan from 1865 to 1866 and governor general of Turkistan from 1882 to 1884.
6. Logofet, *Strana bezpraviya*, p. 11.
7. Zhukovskii, *Snosheniya*, p. 192.
8. This implied that Russia could instal a postal and telegraphic service in the emirate and had the right of navigation on the Amu Darya, with crews furnished by the emirate.
9. Bartol'd, *Istoriya*, p. 229.
10. Semenov, *Ocherk ustroistva*, p. 22.
11. Gafurov, *Istoriya*, vol. 1, p. 431.
12. F. I. Lobuishevich, *Opisanie Khivinskogo Pokhoda 1873 goda*, St Petersburg, 1898), p. 280.
13. Zhukovskii, *Snosheniya*, p. 192.
14. Bartol'd, *Istoriya*, p. 117.
15. Ibid., p. 118.
16. Logofet (*Strana bezpraviya*, p. 25) states that this was also the result of a 'whim' of the minister of foreign affairs, enraged by the fact that he had seen the war minister's domain grow by virtue of the authority he was granted over Turkistan.
17. The Asiatic section of the general staff won a partial authority over relations with Bukhara, but the absence of precise definitions limited its role and contributed to the emirate's considerable independence. In practice, throughout the period of the protectorate there were constantly two Russian policies towards the emirate — that of the political agent and that of the governor-general of Turkistan — and the rulers took advantage of this duality. (A. Woeikof, *Le Turkestan russe*, Paris, 1914, pp. 189–90.)
18. Ibid., pp. 278–82; and *Istoriya Uzbekskoi SSR*, book 2, vol. 1, p. 130.
19. Russia refrained from defining the frontier between Bukhara and Afghanistan in the 1868 and 1873 accords, which led the Afghans to claim the Pamirian and pre-Pamirian regions of Shugnan and Vakhan and compelled Russia to fortify the frontier, which was settled only in 1895 (see Logofet, *Strana bezpraviya*, pp. 25 and 144).
20. A. Ryabinskii, 'Tsarskaya Rossiya i Bukhara v epokhu imperializma', *Istorik Marksist*, no. 4 (1941), p. 18.
21. A. P. Fomchenko, *Russkie poseleniya v Bukharskom emirate* (Tashkent, 1958), p. 8.

22. Ibid., p. 12.

23. Ibid., p. 58.

24. Protocol of agreement with the Bukhara government regarding the establishment of settlements near railways and river stations, dated 23 June 1888.

25. Fomchenko, *Russkie poseleniya*, p. 51.

26. Ibid. p. 53.

27. D. Soloveichik, 'Revolyutsionnaya Bukhara', *Novyi Vostok*, no. 2 (1922), p. 215.

28. Ibid., p. 225.

29. Semenov, *La Russie*, pp. 151–2.

30. Soloveichik, 'Revolyutsionnaya Bukhara', p. 237.

31. *Istoriya Uzbekskoi SSR*, book 2, vol. 1, p. 311.

32. Semenov, *Ocherk ustroistva*, p. 81.

33. *Istoriya Uzbekskoi SSR*, book 2, vol. 1, p. 312.

34. P. G. Galuzo, *Turkestan Koloniya*, Tashkent, 1928, p. 12; and A. Pyaskovskii, *Revolyutsiya 1905–1907 godov v Turkestane*, Moscow, 1958, p. 13.

35. Logofet, *Strana bezpraviya*, p. 145.

36. On the eve of the war, Bukhara possessed some fifty factories almost all belonging to Russians (Fomchenko, *Russkie poseleniya*, p. 23).

37. Logofet, *Strana bezpraviya*, p. 145.

38. Ibid., p. 78. At the end of the nineteenth century, the Russian engineer Zhuravsko-Pukorskii, associated with an English firm, tried to take over all prospecting.

39. Since the gold belonged to the emir, prospectors had to hand it over to the *zakatchi* at the official rate; the emir, acting through the *zakatchi*, would then resell it at a rate bearing no relation to the purchase price.

40. Sukhareva, *K istorii*, pp. 50–87.

41. Soloveichik, 'Revolyutsionnaya Bukhara', p. 278.

42. A. Khamraev, 'K voprosu o zemel'no-vodnykh otnosheniyakh v Bukharskom Khanstve v XIX veke', *Trudy SAGU*, no. 9 (1948), pp. 29–30.

43. *Istoriya Uzbekskoi SSR*, book 2, vol. 1, p. 316; and A. F. Demidov, *Ekonomicheskii ocherk khlopkovodstva i khlopkovoi torgovli i promyshlennosti*, Moscow, 1926, p. 124.

44. Vambéry, *Voyages*, p. 325.

45. Vambéry (ibid.) nevertheless asserts that the *qazi* was often in cahoots with the usurer, but since this was forbidden it remained limited.

46. If the creditor was Russian, conflicts between creditor and debtor were outside the jurisdiction of local courts, which was also astonishing to the Muslims.

47. Soloveichik, 'Revolyutsionnaya Bukhara', p. 275.

48. Khodzhaev, 'O mlado-Bukhartsakh', p. 126.

49. Ibid., p. 127.

50. Ibid., p. 126.

51. R. Pierce, *Soviet Central Asia*, Berkeley, 1960, p. 58; and Logofet, *Strana bezpraviya*, p. 5.

52. The legend about the total ignorance of the emirs as to how much treasure they had lying buried in the cellars of the Arg was widely believed among the Russians (Semenov, *Ocherk ustroistva*, p. 58).

53. Logofet, *Strana bezpraviya*, p. 158.

54. Ibid.

55. M. N., 'Pod znakom Islama', p. 80.

56. Iskandarov, *O nekotorykh izmeneniyakh*, p. 19.

57. M. N., 'Pod znakom Islama', p. 80.

58. Logofet, *Strana bezpraviya*, p. 11.

59. On the occasion of the Vakhan troubles of 1903, a delegation of peasants from Shugnan, Rushan, and Vakhan visited the commander of the Pamir garrison with a petition requesting that these territories be attached to Russia; such examples are numerous (*Istoriya Uzbekskoi SSR*, book 2, vol. 1, p. 319).

60. R. Rozhevitsa, *Poezdka v yuzhnuyu i srednyuyu Bukharu v 1906 g.*, St Petersburg, 1908), p. 70.

61. Ibid., pp. 71–2.

62. Ibid., p. 73.

63. Semenov, *Ocherk ustroistva*, p. 15.

64. All of Logofet's investigations tend to demonstrate this necessity: *Strana bezpraviya; V gorakh i na ravninakh Bukhary*, St Petersburg, 1913; and *Bukharskoe khanstvo*.

65. Semenov, *Ocherk ustroistva*, p. 16.

66. Logofet, *V gorakh*, p. 220.

67. Ibid., p. 270.

68. Iskandarov, *O nekotorykh izmeneniyakh*, p. 22.

69. Ibid., p. 23.

70. Report by Dr Grekov of the European medical mission to Kerki in 1898 (ibid.).

71. Logofet, *Strana bezpraviya*, p. 32.

72. Iskandarov, *O nekotorykh izmeneniyakh*, p. 27.

73. Masal'skii, *Turkestanskii krai*, pp. 532–6.

Notes to Chapter Three

1. Ann K. S. Lambton, 'The theory of kingship in the *Nasihat-ul-Muluk* of Ghazali', *The Islamic Quarterly*, no. 1 (1954), pp. 47–55; and Leonard Binder, 'Al-Ghazali's theory of Islamic government', *The Muslim World*, no. 45 (1953), pp. 229–41.

2. For this entire current, see H. A. R. Gibb, *Modern Trends in Islam*, Chicago, 1947, p. 141; G. E. von Grunebaum, *Islam: Essays in the Nature and Growth of a Cultural Tradition*, London, 1955, pp. 185–236; and Wilfred C. Smith, *Islam in Modern History*, Princeton, 1957.

3. Its founder, Ibn 'Abd al-Wahhab (1703–87), to reinforce his reform, relied upon a ruling monarch, Ibn Sa'ud (d. 1765).

4. Jamal al-Din al-Afghani (1837–97) was counsellor at the English embassy in Constantinople when Lord Dufferin was ambassador. Both advocated a union among the Muslim states bordering Russia (Turkey, Iran, and Afghanistan); but when Jamal al-Din lost his post, he ended his cooperation with the English and went to St Petersburg. His role as an agitator was important in a series of anti-Western movements in the Middle East at the end of the nineteenth century, such as the struggle in Iran against the monopoly over trade in tobacco granted in 1891 and the assassination of the Shah in 1898.

5. Smith, *Islam*, p. 50; see also 'Panislamizm i pantyurkizm', *Mir Islama*, vol. 2, no. 3 (1913), pp. 559–62.

6. The order was founded in 1862 by Muhammad al-Sanusi, who travelled in about 1830 from Mostaganem to Mecca, and then to Alexandria, where he founded a religious community. Driven from Egypt by the Shaykh al-Islam, he took refuge at

Jebel al-Akbar near Benghazi, then at Jerabuh, where he founded the Sanusi order, which immediately recruited 1,000 disciples and by the end of the century had 3 million.

7. A. Toynbee 'Islam, the West and the future', in A. Toynbee (ed.), *Civilization on Trial*, London, 1948.

8. A. Arsharuni and H. Gabidullin, *Ocherki panislamizma i pantyurkizma v Rossii*, Moscow, 1931, p. 9.

9. Kursavi was sentenced to death by Emir Haydar as 'infidel and impious', but he managed to escape, helped by Shaykh Niyaz Quli; his conviction caused a short-lived reformist upsurge in Bukhara.

10. A Tatar mulla and theologian of Kazan who was also a historian of the Volga Tatars.

11. Arsharuni and Gabidullin, *Ocherki*, p. 10; and G. Gubaydullin, 'Iz istorii torgovogo klassa u privolzhakikh tatar', *Vostokovedenie*, Baku, Faculty of Orientalism, 1926, vol. 1, pp. 49–74.

12. Ibid., p. 11.

13. Ibid.

14. Gasprinski was a Crimean Tatar. On his ideology, see A. Gubaydullin, 'K voprosu ob ideologii Gasprinskogo', *Izvestiya Vostochnogo Fakulteta*, no. 4 (Baku, 1919), pp. 179–203.

15. 'K voprosu o panislamizme', *Mir Islama*, pp. 10–11.

16. Galuzo, *Turkestan*, p. 114.

17. Arsharuni and Gabidullin, *Ocherki*, p. 76.

18. Khodzhaev, 'O mlado-Bukhartsakh', p. 118.

19. Known as *kala* (the head), Danish was born and died in Bukhara. He used to say of himself that he was a doctor, poet, musician, painter, astronomer, scientist, and calligrapher all at once. (Gafurov, *Istoriya*, vol. 1, p. 145.) S. 'Ayni says of him that he was 'the most brilliant star in the dark sky of Bukhara' (*Buhara inqilabi tarihi ichim materiyallar*, Moscow, 1926, p. 25). Despite the mistrust the clerics felt towards him, he was secretary to three Bukharan missions to St Petersburg (1856, 1868, and 1870) and in Bukhara, as *yasavul-i'ulama*, was responsible for liaison between the emir and the *'ulama*. See I. M. Muminov, *Uzbekistanda ijtima'i falsafi tafakkurning tarihidan (XIX asrning ahirlari va XX asrning bashlari)*, Tashkent, 1960, pp. 116–43; E. Bertels, *Rukopisne proizvedeniya Akhmada Donisha*, Trudy tadzhikskoi Bazy Akademii Nauk SSSR, vol. 3, Moscow/Leningrad, 1936; Z. Ragabov, *Razvitie obshchestvennoi mysli tadzhikskogo naroda vo vtoroi polovine XIX i v nachale XX veka*, Stalinabad, 1951; I. S. Braginskii, *S. Aini — ocherk zhizni i tvorchestva*, Stalinabad, 1954, pp. 15–19; R. Hodi Zade, *Istochniki k izucheniyu tadzhikskoi literatury vtoroi polovinu XIX veka*, Moscow, 1954, pp. 17–18; 'Ayni, *Vospominaniya*, pp. 252–78; B. Hayit, *Turkestan im XX Jahrhundert*, Darmstadt, 1956, p. 5; and *Istoriya Uzbekskoi SSR*, book 1, vol. 2, p. 171.

20. Muminov, *Özbekistonda*, p. 129. Danish was in Russia at the time of the Chernshevskii trial; he then became intensely interested in the ideas highlighted by the trial, just as in 1881 the assassination of Tsar Alexander II filled him with curiosity (Kamol Ayni, 'Vstrechi Akhmada Donisha s P. I. Pasino', *Narody Azii i Afriki*, no. 6 [1963], pp. 144–7).

21. S. 'Ayni, *Namunaha-yi adabiyat-i Tajik*, Moscow, 1926, pp. 287–301, 318, and 350–1.

22. Danish was himself officially termed a *kafir* by the religious authorities when he advocated the teaching of science in the *madrasas* (Hayit, *Turkestan*, p. 6).

23. Ahmad Danish, *Navodirul vakoe* (unpublished): see Muminov, *Özbekistanda*,

p. 123.
24. Ibid., p. 101.
25. S. 'Ayni, *Esdaliklar*, Tashkent, 1953, book 2, pp. 61–3.
26. Zakirjan Furqat was the son of a small shopkeeper in Khoqand. A disrespect-ful poem about a Russian general made it necessary for him to travel; he went to Turkey and to Arabia and finally ended up at Yarkend, where he remained until his death.
27. Muqimiy was born in 1850 at Khoqand and died there in 1903.
28. [Russian Muslimism: Thoughts and notes on a Muslim's observations], 1st edn, Simferopol, 1881.
29. [Muhammad as the Prophet], St Petersburg, 1881.
30. [The Attitude of Islam towards science and the infidels], St Petersburg, 1887.
31. Pyaskovskii, *Revolyutsiya*, p. 102.
32. *Turkestanskie vedomosti*, no. 48 (1898).
33. Terent'ev, *Istoriya*, vol. 3, p. 42.
34. In Bukhara, up to the beginning of the twentieth century, the religious author-ities and even the emir thought of the Russians established there as belonging to the same category as the *kafir* merchants who had always circulated in the Muslim Orient.
35. M. N., 'Pod znakom Islama', p. 89.
36. Arsharuni and Gabidullin, *Ocherki*, p. 17.
37. A. Z. V. Togan, *Bugünkü Türkili (Türkistan) ve yakin tarihi*, Istanbul, 1942–7, p. 220.

Notes to Chapter Four

1. See B. Vernier, *Kédar, Carnets d'un méhariste syrien*, Paris, 1938, p. 202.
2. During the years 1903–10 the Turkistan Guberniya organized a series of trips to Russia for native schoolchildren and students to show them the greatness and power of the Russian empire (Bendrikov, *Ocherki*, p. 221).
3. Sneysareff, *Eastern Bokhara*, p. 32.
4. Archives of the Uzbekistan RSS quoted by V. V. Ershov, 'Revolyutsiya 1905–1907 v Uzbekistane', in *Revolyutsiya 1905–1907 v Uzbekistane*, Tashkent, 1955, p. 31.
5. A. Kuropatkin, 'Dnevnik', *Krasnyi Arkhiv*, 1922–7, vol. 2, p. 73.
6. N. Ostrumov, 'Musul'manskie maktaby i russko-tuzemnye shkoly v Turkestans-kom krae', *Zhurnal ministerstva narodnogo prosveshcheniya*, no. 2 (1906), p. 311.
7. On Namaz, see D. Sharipov, S. Babaev, and S. Khudaibergenov, 'O Namaze premkulove', in *Revolyutsiya 1905–1907 v Uzbekistane*, pp. 137–9.
8. Ibid.; see also Galuzo, *Turkestan*, p. 136.
9. Ibid., p. 134.
10. Ibid., p. 136.
11. The commission of enquiry presided over by Count Palen in 1908 had been very conscious of this danger (*Otchët o revizii Turkestanskogo Kraya proizvedennoi po Vysochaishemu Poveleniyu Senatorom, gofmeisterom Grafom K. K. Palenom*, St Petersburg, 1909–10, vols. 5 and 11).
12. Turkistan was not a region where plundering raids were a normal practice or feature of the local economy.
13. These figures only record the most serious cases (Galuzo, *Turkestan*, p. 95).
14. *Otchët*, p. 139.

15. See Galuzo, *Turkestan*, p. 138.
16. Ibid., p. 140.
17. Logofet, *Strana bezpraviya*, pp. 70–1.
18. Iskandarov, *O nekotorykh izmeneniyakh*, pp. 113 ff.
19. Logofet, *Strana bezpraviya*, p. 72.
20. Iskandarov, *O nekotorykh izmeneniyakh*, p. 116.
21. The First Duma contained twenty-five Muslims, all members of the *Ittifaq al-Muslimin*, some of them sitting with the Constitutional Democrats.
22. These representatives were Tashpulat 'Abd al-Jalil-ughli, Salihjan Muhammadjan-ughli, Nurberdi Khan Makhdum Qulikhan, Valiallah Allahbergen-ughli and Mulla 'Abd al-Qari (Kariev) (Togan, *Bugünkü*, p. 347).
23. *Programma musul'manskoi parlamenskoi fraktsii v gosudarstvennoi Dume*, St Petersburg, 1909.
24. E. Fedorov, *1905 god i korennoe naselenie Srednei Azii*, Moscow, 1926, p. 16.
25. Togan, *Bugünkü*, p. 347.
26. Khodzhaev, 'O mlado-Bukhartsakh', p. 81.

Notes to Chapter Five

1. Khodzhaev, 'O mlado-Bukhartsakh', p. 123.
2. Togan, *Bugünkü*, p. 353; Z. Saidov, '*Uzbek vaqitli matbu'ati tarihiga materiyallar*, Tashkent/Samarqand, 1927, p. 43.
3. Pyaskovskii, *Revolyutsiya*, p. 546. On the paper's ideology, Togan (*Bugünkü*, p. 353) asserts that *Taraqqi* was under social-democratic influence; see also Vakhabov, *Tashkent v period trëkh revolyutsii*, Tashkent, 1957, pp. 95 ff.
4. On Munavvar Qari Abdurrashidov, see Jarçek, 'Türkistan cadidçiliginin atasi', *Milli Türkistan*, no. 77A (1952), pp. 1–6.
5. On Sayyid 'Azimbay, see Bendrikov, *Ocherki*, pp. 68–9.
6. Vakhabov, *Tashkent*, p. 95.
7. Bartol'd, *Istoriya*, p. 138.
8. Vakhabov, *Tashkent*, pp. 95–8.
9. Pyaskovskii, *Revolyutsiya*, p. 552.
10. Bendrikov, *Ocherki*, p. 423.
11. Ibid., p. 87.
12. Ibid., p. 84.
13. Ibid.; see also Jarçek, 'Türkistan', pp. 1–6.
14. I. Umnyakov, 'K istorii novometodnoi shkoly v Bukhare', *Byulleten' SAGU*, no. 16 (1927), p. 85.
15. A. Pashickii, 'Materialy po istorii Bukharskoi revolyutsii', *Vestnik NKID* (April–May 1922), p. 122.
16. Ibid., pp. 122–3; see also Umnyakov, 'K istorii', p. 85.
17. Ibid., pp. 85–6.
18. Ibid., p. 86.
19. The development of reformist education in Turkistan passed almost unnoticed until 1908. The commission of inquiry headed by Senator Palen wrote: 'The administration and the educational authorities of Turkistan have not been informed in any way about the development of reformist tendencies in the native schools. This merits the closest attention.' (See *Otchët*, book 6, p. 134.)
20. Umnyakov, 'K istorii', p. 87.
21. Damulla Ikram caught the attention of the religious authorities in Bukhara by

publishing, during the reign of Emir Muzaffar, a leaflet directed against the emirate's religious hierarchy. He was sent to the distant *vilayat* of Zlandan and returned to Bukhara only at the time of Emir 'Abd al-Ahad. In 1917 he was exiled once again to the Hisar.

22. Ibid., p. 82.
23. Ibid., p. 85.
24. Illustrated satirical weekly, appearing at Tiflis in the Azari language from 1906.
25. Ibid., p. 87.
26. P. Savel'ev, *Bukhara v 1835 godu,* St Petersburg, 1836, pp. 8–11.
27. S. Gramenickii was inspector of schools for the Sir Darya region in the first years of the twentieth century; he strove to devise educational methods for the natives that could result in a cultural Russification.
28. Bendrikov, *Ocherki,* p. 270.
29. Umnyakov, 'K istorii', p. 85.
30. Muminov, *Özbekistanda,* pp. 259–61.
31. M. N., 'Pod znakom Islama', p. 89; see also Jarçek, 'Türkistan', p. 2.

Notes to Chapter Six

1. The *shahsay-vahsay* is the Shi'i passion play commemorating the martyrdom of the Imam Husayn see Lewis Peluy, *The Miracle Play of Hasan and Husain,* London, 1879, 2 vols; C. Virolleaud, *La passion de l'émir Hossein,* Paris, 1927; and M. de Gobineau, *Les religions et les philosophies dans l'Asie centrale,* Paris, 1886.
2. Sukhareva, *K istorii,* p. 85.
3. Umnyakov, 'K istorii', p. 85; see also the article by Khamraev in *Pravda Vostoka,* 2 March 1951.
4. Sukhareva, *K istorii,* pp. 84–5.
5. Ibid., p. 85; and M. N., 'Pod znakom Islama', p. 80.
6. Ibid., p. 79.
7. Ibid., p. 80.
8. E. Schuyler, *Turkistan: Notes of a Journey,* London, 1876, vol. 2, pp. 100–9.
9. E. Fedorov, *Ocherki natsional'no-osvoboditel'nogo dvizheniya v Srednei Azii,* Tashkent, 1925, p. 27.
10. Logofet, *Strana bezpraviya,* p. 12.
11. Stolypin, moreover, was a convinced advocate of this solution, and Logofet's mission corresponded to his wish to base his position on concrete information.
12. Umnyakov, 'K istorii', p. 89.
13. 'Ayni, *Vospominaniya,* p. 88.
14. Umnyakov, 'K istorii', p. 90.
15. 'Ayni, *Vospominaniya,* p. 90.
16. Umnyakov, 'K istorii', p. 90.
17. Khamraev ('K voprosu', p. 14) says that the emir personally owned 1,700 *desiatins* of irrigated land. Gafurov (*Istoriya,* p. 456) indicates that the emir owned a considerable fortune, deposited in various Russian banks.
18. M. N., 'Pod znakom Islama', p. 86; and Umnyakov, 'K istorii', p. 87.
19. Khodzhaev, 'O mlado-Bukhartsakh', p. 122.
20 Between 1910 and 1914, cotton exports to Russia tripled (see H. Tursunov, *Obrazovanie Uzbekskoi SSR,* Tashkent, 1957, p. 19).
21. Khodzhaev, 'O mlado-Bukhartsakh', p. 123.
22. Togan, *Bugünkü,* p. 354.
23. Arsharuni and Gabidullin, *Ocherki,* pp. 135–8.

24. Togan, *Bugünkü*, p. 354.

25. 'Ayni, *Vospominaniya*, p. 87; Umnyakov, 'K istorii', p. 88; and M. N., 'Pod znakom Islama', p. 87.

26. Khodzhaev, 'O mlado-Bukhartsakh', p. 128.

27. At Khiva there existed a similar organization, but it was infinitely less important and less effective (see A. Samoilovich, 'Pervoe tainoe obshchestvo mlado-bukhartsev', *Novyi Vostok*, no. 1 [1922], p. 98).

28. Above all, fear of homosexuality provoked such investigations, since scandals of this kind were very frequent in Bukhara, where it was generally the best way of compromising a political or religious personality (S. 'Ayni, *Bukhara*, Stalinabad, 1949, vol. 2, pp. 148–51).

29. Samoilovich, 'Pervoe tainoe obshchestvo', p. 98. In spite of the Koranic prescriptions, the use of alcoholic drinks seems to have been very widespread in the emirate.

30. On this procedure, see ibid., p. 98; and 'Ayni, *Vospominaniya*, pp. 86–7.

31. 'Ayni, *Vospominaniya*, pp. 86–7.

32. Samoilovich, 'Pervoe tainoe obshchestvo', p. 98.

33. 'Ayni, *Vospominaniya*, p. 87.

34. The son of a rich Bukhara merchant, Khodzhaev put his fortune at the disposal of the reformist movement, of which he was one of the most active and advanced elements. From 1920 to 1924 he was president of the Council of Ministers of the People's Republic of Bukhara, then from 1925 to 1937 president of the Council of People's Commissars. Tried in 1938 with the 'Bloc of Rightists and Trotskyites', he was sentenced to death and executed. (J. Castagné, 'Le bolchevisme et l'Islam: les organisations soviétiques de la Russie musulmane', *Revue du monde musulman*, no. 51 [October 1922].)

35. Khodzhaev, 'O mlado-Bukhartsakh', p. 129.

36. Arsharuni and Gabidullin, *Ocherki*, pp. 135–8.

37. Samoilovich, 'Pervoe tainoe obshchestvo', p. 98.

38. *Yaş Türkistan* (review edited by Mustafa Choqay and published in Paris and Berlin), no. 22 (1931), pp. 92 ff.

39. Khodzhaev, 'O mlado-Bukhartsakh', p. 128.

40. 'Ayni, *Vospominaniya*.

41. See the 26 April 1960 issue of *Kommunist Tadzhikistana*, celebrating the seventy-fifth birthday of the writer Sadr al-Din 'Ayni.

42. M. N., 'Pod znakom Islama', p. 89; and A. Zavqi and I. Tolqun, 'Shair Colpan', *Milli Türkistan*, no. 76, p. 17.

43. Khodzhaev, 'O mlado-Bukhartsakh', p. 128.

44. Samoilovich, 'Pervoe tainoe obshchestvo', p. 97.

45. 'Ayni, *Vospominaniya;* and Khodzhaev, 'O mlado-Bukhartsakh'.

46. Samoilovich, 'Pervoe tainoe obshchestvo', pp. 97–9.

47. Gafurov, *Istoriya*, pp. 439–40.

48. S. A. Zenkovsky, *Pan-turkism and Islam in Russia*, Cambridge, Mass., 1960, p. 90.

49. M. N., 'Pod znakom Islama', p. 85; and Gafurov, *Istoriya*, p. 440.

50. Pashitskii, 'Materialy', p. 123.

51. Umnyakov, 'K istorii', p. 90.

52. In 1904 the emir of Bukhara had been appointed an imperial aide, which meant that he was of higher rank than the governor-general, who thus lost his remaining authority over him (Logofet, *Strana bezpraviya*, p. 14).

53. Umnyakov, 'K istorii', p. 87.

54. 'Ayni, *Vospominaniya*, p. 40.
55. Umnyakov, 'K istorii', p. 91.
56. Ibid., pp. 91–2.
57. Ibid., p. 92.
58. Ibid.
59. Ibid.; see also Khodzhaev, 'O mlado-Bukhartsakh', p. 129.
60. Umnyakov, 'K istorii', p. 92; and 'Ayni, *Vospominaniya*, p. 37.
61. Khodzhaev, 'O mlado-Bukhartsakh', p. 129.
62. Umnyakov, 'K istorii', p. 91.
63. Ibid., p. 92.
64. Khodzhaev, 'O mlado-Bukhartsakh', p. 130.
65. Umnyakov, 'K istorii', p. 93.
66. F. Khodzhaev, *Dzhadidy, ocherki revolyutsionnogo dvizheniya v Srednei Azii*, Moscow, 1937, p. 11.
67. Gafurov, *Istoriya*, p. 445; and O. Gloratskii, *Revolyutsiya pobezhdaet*, Tashkent, 1920, p. 4.
68. 'Ayni, *Vospominaniya*, pp. 161–70.
69. Arsharuni and Gabidullin, *Ocherki*, p. 139.
70. Samoilovich, 'Pervoe tainoe obshchestvo', p. 99.
71. Klimovich, *Islam*, p. 188.
72. Samoilovich, 'Pervoe tainoe obshchestvo', p. 99.
73. Umnyakov, 'K istorii', p. 90.
74. Ibid., p. 91.
75. *Bukhara-yi Sharif* sometimes published articles in Uzbek; *Turan* sometimes contained Persian texts.
76. Umnyakov, 'K istorii', pp. 91–2.
77. I. Braginskii, *Ocherki iz istorii tadzhikskoi literatury*, Stalinabad, 1956.
78. Khodzhaev, 'O mlado-Bukhartsakh', p. 129.
79. Umnyakov, 'K istorii', p. 91.
80. M. N., 'Pod znakom Islama', p. 90.
81. Galuzo, *Turkestan*, p. 142.
82. Khodzhaev, 'O mlado-Bukhartsakh', p. 124.
83. This newspaper was subsequently renamed *Sebil al-Reshad* (*Mir Islama*, vol. 2, no. 8 [1913], pp. 566–7; and M. N., 'Pod znakom Islama', p. 90).
84. M. N., 'Pod znakom Islama', p. 87.
85. Ibid., p. 91.
86. Umnyakov, 'K istorii', p. 83.
87. The first volume of this immensely influential book was published *circa* 1895 in Cairo; the second was printed in Tehran in 1905. The third volume was published in a complete edition in 1909 at Calcutta.
88. E. Bertels, *Ocherk istorii persidskoi literatury*, Leningrad, 1928, p. 140.
89. *Munazara* was first published in Istanbul. It was then translated into Russian and published at Tashkent in 1911, as Fitrat Bukharets, *Spor Bukharskogo mudarrisa s evropeitsem v Indii o novometodnykh shkolakh: Istinyi rezultat obmena myslei*. The translation was the work of Colonel Jagello, one of the moving spirits of the Tashkent group of Orientalists; it was published in a very limited edition. Circulation was confined largely to the Russian administration, which saw it as an important source of information concerning the ideology of the empire's Muslims.
90. Published in Russian at Samarqand in 1913, under the title *Rasskazy indiiskogo puteshestvennika*, by one of Turkistan's most prominent Jadids, Mufti Bihbudi. This version was signed 'Abd al-Ra'uf to circumvent the police bans.

91. At Istanbul.

92. Umnyakov, 'K istorii', p. 92.

93. Pyaskovskii, *Revolyutsiya*, p. 548; and Arsharuni and Gabidullin, *Ocherki*, pp. 15–6.

94. 'Ayni, *Vospominaniya*, p. 133.

95. M. N., 'Pod znakom Islama', p. 80.

96. Mufti Bihbudi, *Pidarkush*, Samarqand, 1913.

97. Klimovich, *Islam*, p. 196.

98. *Voina v peskakh — materialy k istorii grazhdanskoi voiny: Grazhdanskaya voina v Srednei Azii*, Leningrad, 1935, p. 238.

99. Fitrat the reformist must not be confused with his compatriot Fitrat Mulla Qurbankhan (d. 1888), a well known poet, but whose work does not anticipate the reform spirit.

100. *Istoriya Uzbekskoi SSR*, which devotes many pages to the Jadid movement of Bukhara, does not mention Fitrat. However, Pyaskovskii (*Revolyutsiya*) quotes him on a number of occasions (pp. 546, 563, and 564) and writes thus of him in the index (p. 588): 'one of the master figures of the Jadid movement in Turkistan and Bukhara.'

101. Khodzhaev, 'O mlado-Bukhartsakh', p. 126; Zavqi and Tolqun, 'Shair Colpan', p. 17; and Erturk, 'Abdur Rauf Fitrat', *Milli Türkistan*, no. 5, 80–81 (1952), p. 9. See also the first issue of the journal *Milli Edebiyat* in 1943, devoted to a presentation of the journal by Gayyum Khan (pp. 4–5).

102. Zavqi and Tolqun, 'Shair Colpan', p. 17; and Khodzhaev, 'O mlado-Bukhartsakh', p. 126.

103. Khodzhaev, 'O mlado-Bukhartsakh', p. 129.

104. Fitrat, *Munazara*, p. 12. All quotations from this book are taken from Colonel Jagello's Russian translation.

105. Ibid., p. 23.

106. Ibid., pp. 40–41; and Fitrat, *Rasskazy*, pp. 64–6.

107. Ibid., p. 58.

108. Smith, *Islam*, p. 227.

109. Fitrat, *Munazara*, p. 51.

110. Ibid., p. 14.

111. Ibid., p. 18; and Fitrat, *Rasskazy*, pp. 36–8.

112. Ibid., pp. 24–6.

113. Ibid., p. 22.

114. Ibid., p. 16.

115. Ibid., p. 27.

116. Fitrat, *Munazara*, pp. 4–5.

117. Fitrat, *Rasskazy*, p. 21.

118. In *Munazara* (p. 4) the *mudarris* replies as follows to his interlocutor, who asks him if he knows geography: 'In the evening I prepare my lessons, during the day I deliver them, when should I read such balderdash? In any case, such books do not exist here.'

119. Fitrat, *Munazara*, p. 46.

120. Ibid.

121. Ibid., pp. 21–4.

122. Ibid., p. 25.

123. See J. Jomier, *Le commentaire coranique du Manar*, Paris, 1954, p. 25.

124. Fitrat, *Rasskazy*, pp. 12–16.

125. Vambéry, *Voyages*, p. 237.

126. A. R. Fitrat, *Qiyamat*, Tashkent, 1961, pp. 29–48.

127. Ibid., p. 47. The same attitude is to be found in 'Ayni, *Vospominaniya*, pp. 464–71.

128. Fitrat, *Rasskazy*, p. 46.

129. Ibid., pp. 77–8.

130. Ibid., p. 78.

131. Ibid.

132. In *Munazara*, pp. 19 and 28. The same pragmatic estimate of scientific knowledge can be found in the work of Muhammad 'Abduh, who wrote in *al-Manar*: 'The knowledge worthy of its name is that which is gained in the swiftest and easiest manner and which is useful . . . let us rather call aberration a knowledge that one seeks to gain for a [given] purpose and that absolutely does not allow that particular purpose to be achieved, after much time has been expended for its acquisition. To call it knowledge is thus a mistake.' (See A. Merad, 'L'enseignement politique de Muhammad Abduh aux Algériens [1903]', *Orient*, no. 28 [1963], p. 104.)

133. Fitrat, *Rasskazy*, pp. 32–3.

134. Ibid., p. 33.

135. Ibid.

136. Fitrat's descriptions in *Qiyamat* (p. 29) of the rich man and his relations with his servant are particularly revealing about his positions.

137. Fitrat, *Munazara*, pp. 52–3.

138. Fitrat, *Rasskazy*, p. 35.

139. Fitrat, *Munazara*, p. 16.

140. Ibid., p. 32.

141. Ibid., p. 56.

142. Fitrat does not seem to have considered the problem, which H. A. R. Gibb raises in connection with all the modernizers, of the authority upon which individuals or groups who claimed to reform Islam were basing themselves (see Gibb, *Modern Trends*, p. 104).

143. 'If only Tashkent and Petersburg wished it, one might make Bukhara into a better organized and cultivated country with a better adapted administration' (*Tarjuman*, 21 June 1910).

144. Khodzhaev, 'O mlado-Bukhartsakh', p. 129; and 'Ayni, *Vospominaniya*, p. 92.

145. Khodzhaev, 'O mlado-Bukhartsakh', p. 130.

146. *Rigaer Tageblatt* (25 December 1912).

147. See H. M. Tsavikyan, 'Vliyanie russkoi revolyutsii 1905 goda na revolyutsionnoe dvizhenie v Turtsii', *Sovetskoe Vostokovedenie*, no. 3 (1945), pp. 15–35; E. E. Ramsaur, *The Young Turks: Prelude to the Revolution of 1908*, Princeton, 1957; and P. P. Ivanov, *Iranskaya revolyutsiya 1905 goda*, Moscow, 1957.

Notes to Chapter Seven

1. *Byloe*, nos. 27/28 (1924), pp. 243–5; and U. Gehbke, *Persien in der Deutschen Orientpolitik*, Stuttgart, n. d., vol. 1, pp. 136 ff.

2. Z. A. B. Zeman, *Germany and the Revolution in Russia, 1915–1918*, London, 1958, p. 145; and Arsharuni and Gabidullin, *Ocherki*, pp. 49–50.

3. Among the committee members were Yusuf Akchurin, R. Ibragimov and Husaynzada (Togan, *Bugünkü*, p. 561; and *Die Welt des Islams*, no. 4 [1916], p. 35).

4. Set up by liberal notables in 1913, it published the journal *Annale des nationalités*.

5. A. Kuropatkin, 'Dnevnik', *Krasnyi Arkhiv*, no. 34 (1929) (supplement to the 1922–7 series); T. Ryskulov, 'Vostanie tuzemtsev Turkestana v 1916 godu', in *Ocherki revolyutsionnogo dvizheniya v Srednei Azii*, Moscow, 1926; G. Brojdo, 'Materialy k istorii vostaniya Kirgiz', *Novyi Vostok*, no. 6 (1924), pp. 407–35; *Vostanie 1916 goda v Srednei Azii i Kazahstane*, Moscow, 1960; and E. D. Sokol, *The Revolt of 1916 in Russian Central Asia*, Baltimore, 1954.

6. *Istoriya narodov Uzbekistana*, Tashkent, 1946–51, vol. 2.

7. One of the founders of the Khvarazm People's Republic in 1919, he served as its president from 1921 to 1923.

8. A member of the Khoqand government in 1917.

9. A few weeks later, he was to head the insurrection in the Samarqand region.

10. B. Hayit, *Die nationalen Regierungen von Kokand und Alash Orda*, Münster, 1950, p. 18; and A. Baysun, *Türkistan milli hareketleri*, Istanbul, 1943, pp. 18–19.

11. Text in J. Benzing, 'Das Turkestanische Volk im Kampf um seine Selbständigkeit', *Die Welt des Islams*, no. 20, pp. 117–18.

12. Kuropatkin, 'Dnevnik', p. 46.

13. See M. Ferro, 'La politique des nationalités du gouvernement provisoire', *Cahiers du monde russe et soviétique*, no. 2 (April/June 1961), pp. 131–66.

14. Safarov, *Kolonial'naya revolyutsiya*, pp. 64–7.

15. T. Ryskulov, 'Iz istorii bor'by za osvobozhdenie Vostoka', *Novyi Vostok*, no. 6 (1924), pp. 267–71; and Vakhabov, *Tashkent* p. 147.

16. Nalivkin had been a regional deputy in the Second Duma, where he had sat on the benches of the far left, and vice-governor of the Ferghana. Before that he had lived in a Namangan village like a true 'Sart'. After the dissolution of the Duma, he retired to the neighbourhood of Tashkent and refused to see anyone until the February Revolution, when his fellow-citizens came to fetch him. In September 1917 he was driven from power, held in suspicion and, following threats, eventually committed suicide. (See *Voina v peskakh*, p. 49.)

17. The Provisional Government had kept with Kuropatkin in Turkistan some particularly unpopular men, various 'pacifiers' from summer 1916, like Generals Ivanov and Papengut. See Kastel'skaya, 'Natsional'naya politika vremennogo pravitel'stva Uzbekistane', *Istoricheskii Zhurnal*, vol. 2 (1937), p. 31; and Kuropatkin, 'Dnevnik', pp. 65 and 75.

18. G. I. Brojdo was later to be a member of the Narkomnats and Director of the University of Workers of the East.

19. Safarov, *Kolonial'naya revolyutsiya*, p. 122.

20. Castagné, 'Le bolchevisme', pp. 30 ff.

21. Safarov, *Kolonial'naya revolyutsiya*, p. 126.

22. P. Alekseenkov, 'Natsional'naya politika vremennogo pravitel'stva v Turkestane v 1917 godu', *Proletarskaya revolyutsiya*, no. 89 (1928), p. 120. See also *Revolyutsiya v Srednei Azii: Sbornik*, Tashkent, 1928, vol. 1, pp. 30 ff.

23. M. N., 'Pod znakom Islama', pp. 80–81; see also Shestakov, 'Vostanie 1916 goda v Srednei Azii', *Istorik marksist*, no. 2 (1926), p. 94.

24. M. N., 'Pod znakom Islama', pp. 79–80.

25. Fomchenko, *Russkie poseleniya*, p. 42; Kh. Inoyatov, *Ozbekistonda oktyabr'revolyucyasi*, Tashkent, 1957.

26. This figure does not take into account Russian military personnel (ibid. p. 12).

27. E. I. Iskandarov, 'Bukhara v 1918–1920 godu: Likvidatsiya Bukharskogo Emirata', *Trudy Akademii Nauk Tadzhikskoi SSR*, no. 29 (1954), pp. 7–8.

28. Poltoracky (Pavel Gerassimovich), a Russian printer, was a very active revolutionary in Baku during the First World War. In 1916 he arrived at Novaya Bukhara; and, while working at the Levin printing-works, he organized and politically educated the Russian workers. Under the Provisional Government, he established a Bolshevik group among the railwaymen of Novaya Bukhara. In 1918 he was appointed commissar of the Working People of the Republic of Turkistan (*Turkrespublika*) and in February of the same year was put in charge of a Red Guard unit that went to the aid of the Samarqand garrison, under threat from the cossacks of Colonel Zaichev falling back from the Caucasus front. President of the Workers' Commission at Kagan, organizer of the first soviet in Bukhara and then of the first congress of soviets from the Russian enclaves of the Emirate, Poltoracky was truly the founder of the Bukharan Communist Party. On 22 July 1918 he was captured at Marv by British and White troops, and shot. (See Iskandarov, 'Bukhara', p. 9; *Istoriya Uzbekskoi SSR,* vol. 2, p. 36, 55, 56, 58, 60, 72, and 87; and Fomchenko, *Russkie poseleniya,* p. 42.

29. 'Bukhara v 1917 godu', *Krasnyi Arkhiv,* no. 20, p. 80.

30. Fomchenko, *Russkie poseleniya,* p. 43.

31. Cable no. 128 of 18 March 1917 (see 'Bukhara v 1917 godu') p. 81.

32. *Voina v peskakh,* p. 235.

33. Khodzhaev, 'O mlado-Bukhartsakh', p. 131.

34. A minor official in the local administration, Burkhanov belonged to the 'minimalist' and temporizing faction of the party, which he was subsequently to reorganize (ibid., pp. 128, 133, and 138).

35. Ata Khodzhaev had since 1914 devoted himself to organizing the demands of Bukhara's artisans. He was arrested during the riots of March 1917. A member of the government of the people's republic, he was to 'disappear' in about 1930. (Ibid., p. 128.)

36. Ibid., p. 131.

37. Kerenskii subsequently had such a plan (Kuropatkin, 'Dnevnik', p. 71; and Alekseenkov, 'Natsional'naya politika', p. 120).

38. Decision of the Provisional Government of 17 March 1917.

39. Kastel'skaya, 'Natsional'naya politika', p. 30, quoting *Vestnik vremennogo pravitel'stva,* no. 15 (20 March 1917), which published provisions suppressing all statutory distinctions between the various peoples of Russia.

40. Kuropatkin ('Dnevnik', p. 65) provides an account of an interview with Kerenskii on 29 April 1917.

41. *Istoriya Uzbekskoi SSR,* vol. 2, p. 163.

42. Miller's dispatches never mentioned the Jadids before this approach (see 'Bukhara v 1917 godu', pp. 78–123).

43. Kuropatkin, 'Dnevnik', p. 76. Kerenskii owed this reputation as an expert in 'Asian problems' to the sole fact that he had been brought up in Turkistan, where his father was inspector-general of education.

44. Khodzhaev, 'O mlado-Bukhartsakh', pp. 131–2.

45. Telegram from Kuropatkin to the minister of foreign affairs of the Provisional Government, no. 360, 24 March 1917 (see 'Bukhara v 1917 godu', p. 84).

46. Telegram from Miller to the minister of foreign affairs, no. 4476, 30 March 1917; ibid. p. 88.

47. This explains the contradiction to be found in various documents regarding the resident's attitude in this business.

48. Khodzhaev ('O mlado-Bukhartsakh', p. 132) says that Miller accepted the idea of reforms only under compulsion from his government; in total contrast, B. Hayit

(*Turkestan im XX Jahrhundert,* Darmstadt, 1956, p. 121) writes thus: 'The Political Agency, under the guidance of Miller, Shulga and Vvedenskii, likewise took up the cudgels for reform.'

49. L. Shek, 'Iz istorii Bukhary v period fevral'skoi burzhuazno-demokraticheskoi revolyutsii 1917 goda', *Trudy SAGU,* no. 90 (1957), pp. 57–62.

50. Cable from Miller to the minister of foreign affairs, no. 39-39, 17 March 1917 (see 'Bukhara v 1917 godu', p. 80). In a secret telegram to the minister of foreign affairs (no. 129, 20 March 1917 [ibid., p. 81]) Miller returned to his religious concern: 'The reforms must be made bearing the *shari'at* in mind, otherwise they would be taken as an anti-Muslim act on Russia's part.'

51. Khodzhaev, 'O mlado-Bukhartsakh', pp. 132–3.

52. Cable from Miller, no. 132, 20 March 1917: 'Bukhara v 1917 godu', p. 82.

53. Cable no. 151, 30 March 1917: ibid., pp. 87–8. Cables in identical terms: no. 154, 31 March 1917 (p. 90); no. 156, 5 April 1917 (p. 90).

54. Ibid.

55. Shek, 'Iz istorii', p. 58.

56. Ibid., p. 59, drawing on the archives of the Uzbek Republic.

57. Khodzhaev, 'O mlado-Bukhartsakh', p. 133; and 'Ayni, *Vospominaniya,* pp. 158–60.

58. See text in Appendix 3.

59. *Turkestanskie vedomosti* (25 June 1917); Shek, 'Iz istorii', p. 59; L. K. Shek, *Pobeda narodnoi sovetskoi revolyutsii v Bukhare,* Tashkent, 1956, pp. 9–11; A. I. Ishanov, *Pobeda narodnoi sovetskoi revolyutsii v Bukhare,* Tashkent, 1957, p. 6; and A. Aliev, *Velikii oktjabr' i revolyutsionnizirovanie narodov Bukhary,* Tashkent, 1958, p. 14.

60. Hayit, *Turkestan,* p. 122; and Shek, *Pobeda,* p. 10.

61. Khodzhaev, 'O mlado-Bukhartsakh', p. 133; F. Khodzhaev, *K istorii revolyutsii v Bukhare,* Tashkent, 1926, p. 77; and 'Ayni, *Vospominaniya,* p. 170.

62. Hayit, *Turkestan,* p. 123.

63. Khodzhaev, 'O mlado-Bukhartsakh', p. 135.

64. Ibid.

65. The Rigistan is the main square in Bukhara. The emir's palace, the Arg, stood on the Rigistan, as did the city's largest mosque, Masjid-i Kalan, built by 'Abdallah Khan Shaybani.

66. Khodzhaev, 'O mlado-Bukhartsakh', p. 135.

67. Vyat'kin, Vassili Lavrentievich (1869–1932), was a Russian archaeologist educated at the Tashkent Seminary, where he learned Uzbek; he discovered the observatory of Ulug Beg in 1907 and was a passionate preserver of the monuments of Samarqand.

68. Cable to Milyukov, no. 6647, 10 April 1917, in 'Bukhara v 1917 godu', p. 92.

69. Secret cable no. 161, 11 April 1917, in ibid., p. 93.

70. Cable from 'the members of the Samarqand Executive Committee attached to the Regiment sent to Bukhara, the Young Bukharans, the soviet of worker and soldier deputies of Samarqand', addressed to Milyukov, 14 April 1917, in ibid., pp. 93–4.

71. The delegation of twelve members led by Mukhitdin Mansurov and including notably 'Abd al-Qadir Muhyi al-Din-ughli (Mukhitdinov), Mirza Isham Mukhitdinov, Musa Saizhanov, 'Abd al-Vahid Burkhanov, Ata Khodzhaev and Fayzallah Khodzhaev (see Khodzhaev, 'O mlado-Bukhartsakh', p. 139).

72. 'Ayni, *Vospominaniya,* pp. 170–72.

73. Cable from Miller, no. 4624, 10 April 1917, in 'Bukhara v 1917 godu', p. 91.

74. Khodzhaev, 'O mlado-Bukhartsakh', p. 140. Hayit (*Turkestan*, p. 123) gives a different version; the emir supposedly said the following, in relation to the *qadimis*: 'they want people to act in conformity with the *shari'at* and they are also my subjects.'

75. The two attempted to make them sign a declaration by which they renounced reforms (Hayit, *Turkestan*, p. 124).

76. Klimovich, *Islam*, p. 195.

77. Klimovich denounces the mistake of historians such as Amir Sagirzon or I. Kramkov, who held the Young Bukharans to be anti-imperialists and Bolsheviks from the outset.

78. Fomchenko, *Russkie poseleniya*, p. 46; and I. K. Dodonov, *Pobeda oktyabr'skoi revolyutsii v Turkestane*, Tashkent, 1958, p. 44.

79. Cable from Shulga, no. 4753, 17 April 1917, in 'Bukhara v 1917 godu', p. 99.

80. Cable of 17 April 1917 from Chertov, Chernevskii and Berezni, delegates to the Samarqand regiment, who claimed to represent Miller in his absence (ibid, p. 97); cable from Shulga, no. 4753, 17 April 1917 (ibid.); cables from the representatives of Russian financial, commercial and industrial firms in Bukhara to the president of the Council of Ministers, the minister of foreign affairs, the minister of war and the minister of justice (17 April 1917) that protested against the arrest of Miller and the 'would-be representation of Russia' by Chertov and Chernevskii and that requested the Provisional Government to intervene and re-establish order.

81. Already, out of nine members, only six had been appointed by the Provisional Government.

82. On 31 March 1917 the Turkistan soviets had demanded the departure of Kuropatkin, 'the legacy of tsarism', who had been replaced by the Constitutional Democrat Shchepkin (see Kastel'skaya, 'Natsional'naya politika', p. 31).

83. See 'Bukhara v 1917 godu', p. 101.

84. Shek, 'Iz istorii', p. 60; and *Voina v peskakh*, p. 237.

85. 'Bukhara v 1917 godu', p. 102.

86. Fomchenko, *Russkie poseleniya*, p. 49.

87. To Chirkin's question about what attitude should be adopted towards this event and the Committee for Bukharan Affairs that was about to be established, the Turkistan committee replied, 'we must wait and see'.

88. Shek, 'Iz istorii', p. 61.

89. Cable no. 5118, 8 May 1917, in 'Bukhara v 1917 godu', p. 110.

90. Cable no. 5141, 11 May 1917, in ibid., p. 11.

91. Alim Khan, *La voix*, p. 33.

92. Cable of protest from the Young Bukharan party to the minister of foreign affairs of Russia, 25 June 1917, in 'Bukhara v 1917 godu', p. 105.

93. Mirza Muhitdin Mansurov was a large merchant of Bukhara who had to flee the city because his business rivalry with another merchant — a reactionary and a friend of the emir's, Karavanbashi Azizov — had degenerated into a political conflict. After March 1917 he settled with his sons, who like him were members of the Young Bukharan Party, at Kagan and became president of the Central Committee. (See Khodzhaev, 'O mlado-Bukhartsakh', p. 137.)

94. The members of the Central Committee were 'Abd al-Qadir Muhitdinov (Mukhitdin Mansurov's eldest son), Muhyi al-Din Rafat, 'Abd al-Vahid Burkhanov, Usman Khodzhaev, 'Arif Karimov, Mirza Isham Mukhitdinov, Musa Saizhanov and Fayzallah Khodzhaev. Later Fitrat and Ata Khodzhaev were to be included. (Ibid., p. 109.)

95. Ibid.; see also *Voina v peskah*, p. 237.

228   ISLAM AND THE RUSSIAN EMPIRE

96. The pan-Russian congress of Muslims, convened by the Russians (*Vremennoe Tsentral'noe byuro rossiiskikh musul'man*) and made up essentially of Muslim deputies to the Fourth Duma, was held in Moscow from 1 to 11 May 1917. The resolutions of the congress were published in Russian in a collection of documents edited by Dimanstein (*Revolyutsiya i natsional'nyi vopros,* vol. 3 [the only volume published], February/October 1917 [Moscow, 1930]).
97. 'Bukhara v 1917 godu', p. 106.
98. Kastel'skaya, 'Natsional'naya politika', p. 34.
99. Kuropatkin, 'Dnevnik', pp. 70–1.
100. Shek, 'Iz istorii', p. 61; see also Vakhabov, *Tashkent,* pp. 168–72.

Notes to Chapter Eight

1. K. E. Zitov, *Pobeda velikoi oktyabr'skoi revolyutsii v Uzbekistane,* Tashkent, 1957, p. 2. See also Inoyatov, *Özbekistonda,* p. 96; and *idem,* 'Rol' narodnykh mass v svershenii oktyabr'skoi revolyutsii v Turkestane', *Izvestiya Akademii Nauk Uzbekskoi SSR (Seriya obshch. nauk),* no. 2 (1959), pp. 49–53.
2. E. Stemberg, *Ocherki po istorii Turkmenii,* Moscow, 1934, p. 154.
3. Safarov, *Kolonial'naya revolyutsiya,* p. 10.
4. *Voina v peskakh,* p. 45; Dodonov, *Pobeda,* pp. 40 ff.; Vakhabov, *Tashkent,* p. 240 ff.; Muraveiskii, *Ocherki po istorii revolyutsionnogo dvizheniya v Srednei Azii,* Tashkent, 1926; Muraveiskii, 'Sentyabr'skie sobytie v Tashkente', *Proletarskaya revolyutsiya,* no. 10 (1924), pp. 138–61; and I. Fedorov, *Oktyabr'skaya revolyutsiya v Turkestane,* Tashkent, 1924, p. 32.
5. See D. Boersner, *The Bolsheviks and the National and Colonial Questions 1917–1918,* Paris/Geneva, 1957; and R. Pipes, *The Formation of the Soviet Union,* Harvard, 1954.
6. V. I. Lenin, *Collected Works,* 4th edn, vol. 24, Moscow, 1964, pp. 302–3.
7. Safarov, *Kolonial'naya revolyutsiya,* p. 70.
8. Ibid., p. 68.
9. Ibid., p. 70; and M. Chokai, *Turkestan pod vlastiyu sovetov,* Paris, 1935, p. 14.
10. On the conference programme, see Castagné, 'Le bolchevisme', p. 46; M. Alekseenkov, 'Kokandskaya avtonomiya', in *Revolyutsiya v Srednei Azii',* p. 31; and B. Hayit, *Die nationalen Regierungen von Kokand und Alash Orda,* Münster, 1950, p. 67 (mimeographed thesis).
11. Castagné, 'Le bolchevisme', p. 49; and Safarov, *Kolonial'naya revolyutsiya.*
12. Pipes, *Formation,* pp. 86–92.
13. Iskandarov, 'Bukhara', p. 10; and Shek, 'Iz istorii', p. 106.
14. Poltoracky, Utkin, and Preobrazhenskii (see *Voina v peskakh,* p. 238; and Ishanov, *Pobeda,* p. 7).
15. Iskandarov, 'Bukhara', p. 9.
16. L. Shek, 'Iz istorii sovetsko-Bukharskikh otnoshenii', *Trudy SAGU,* no. 78 (1956), p. 108.
17. Alim Khan, *La voix,* p. 6.
18. For an account of British military operations against Bukhara see E. Etherton, *In the Heart of Asia,* London, 1925.
19. Samoilovich, 'Pervoe tainoe obshchestvo', p. 95.
20. Aliev, *Velikii oktyabr',* p. 18; and Iskander, 'Podgotovka angliei bukharskogo pladtsdarma dlya interventsii v Sovetskii Turkestan 1918–1920 gg.', *Istoricheskie zapiski,* no. 36 (1951), pp. 17–18.
21. *Voina v peskakh,* pp. 237–8.

22. Iskander, 'Podgotovka', p. 11; *Istoriya Uzbekskoi SSR*, vol. 2, p. 113; and Etherton, *In the Heart*, p. 158.

23. The emir sent a mission to Afghanistan at the end of 1917, proposing to the Afghans a 'pan-Muslim' union that would struggle against the Soviets (Iskander, 'Podgotovka', p. 13; and Ishanov, *Pobeda*, p. 7).

24. *Ashkhabad* (7 March 1918).

25. *Voina v peskakh*, p. 238.

26. *Istoriya Uzbekskoi SSR*, vol. 2, p. 164; and Shek, *Pobeda*, pp. 16–17.

27. *Voina v peskakh*, p. 250; and Khodzhaev, *K istorii*, p. 45.

28. *Voina v peskakh*, p. 242.

29. Poltoracky was then writing to Tashkent: 'Our forces are growing daily and units have been formed which could be termed an army' (*Nasha gazeta* [1 May 1918]).

30. On Kolesov, Tobalin delivered this judgement: 'He was a good revolutionary, but a bad politician. If he had been listened to, the whole commissariat would have been made up of workers.' (Hayit, *Turkestan*, p. 73.) *Nasha gazeta* (2 April 1918) quotes Tobalin as saying, 'The central government does not understand the problems of Turkistan.'

31. The revolutionary committee was made up of Fayzallah Khodzhaev, Ata Khodzhaev, Fitrat, Burkhanov, Azharov, Pulatov and Makhdum (see *Voina v peskakh*, p. 242).

32. Ibid., p. 250.

33. The manifesto began in the following way: 'There exists no greater happiness for a nation than equality and liberty' (see 'Ayni, *Vospominaniya*, p. 232).

34. *Voina v peskakh*, p. 255; and Khodzhaev, 'O mlado-Bukhartsakh', p. 133.

35. *Voina v peskakh*, p. 256; and Khodzhaev, *K istorii*, p. 46.

36. *Voina v peskakh*, p. 249; and Shek, *Pobeda*, p. 19.

37. An emergency tribunal was set up in Bukhara under the chairmanship of Mufti 'Abdullah Makhdum, to try 'Jadid crimes'. All those who had not managed to escape — and they were sympathizers rather than active Jadids — were convicted. (See Hayit, *Turkestan*, pp. 129–30.)

38. *Voina v peskakh*, pp. 274–5.

39. Ibid., pp. 238–40.

40. Ibid., p. 240.

41. Khodzhaev, 'O mlado-Bukhartsakh', p. 58; 'Ayni, *Vospominaniya*, p. 233; and Khodzhaev, Fedorov, Ryskulov, and Ginzburg, *Ocherki revolyutsionnogo dvizheniya v Srednei Azii*, Moscow, 1926.

42. Alim Khan, *La voix*, p. 9.

43. Gafurov, *Istoriya*, p. 463.

44. *Voina v peskakh*, p. 234.

45. Iskandarov, 'Bukhara', pp. 19–20; Shek, 'Iz istorii sovetsko-Bukharskikh otnoshenii', p. 105; and Zitov, *Pobeda*.

46. *Istoriya Uzbekskoi SSR*, pp. 165–6; Ishanov, Zitov, *Pobeda*, p. 55; and Aliev, *Velikii oktyabr'*, p. 19.

47. Eighth Congress of the RCP (b), 19 March 1919, in Lenin, *Works*, vol. 29, p. 172.

48. *Istoriya Sovetskoi konstitutsii*, Moscow, 1957, p. 126.

49. Muraveiskii, *Ocherki*, p. 20.

50. S. Dimanstein ('Ocherednye zadachi natsional'noi raboty', *Revolyutsiya i Natsional'nosti* [10 November 1931], pp. 27–41, p. 36) writes the following to illustrate the attitude of the Russian Bolsheviks in Turkistan: 'Who made the

revolution for the Uzbeks? We, the Russian workers, while the Uzbeks were sleeping on their stoves at home; and now, just imagine, these Uzbeks cannot be touched.'

51. V. Salikov, 'Bor'ba za Orenburg' and K. Vlasov, 'Petrovskii Otryad', in *Voina v peskakh,* pp. 504–19 and 525–8.

52. S. T. Filipov, *Boevoe deistviya na zakaspiiskom fronte,* Ashkhabad, 1928; L. V. Blacker, *On Secret Patrols in High Asia,* London, 1922; and M. Malleson, 'The British Military Mission to Turkestan, 1918–1920', *Journal of the Royal Central Asian Society,* no. 9 (1922), pp. 96–110.

53. Mel'kumov, *Turkestantsy,* Moscow, 1960, p. 9.

54. S. Shaumian, *Statii i rechi,* Baku, 1924, p. 225.

55. See Gurko-Kryazhin, 'Angliiskaya interventsiya v 1918–19 g. v Zakaspii i Zakavkaz'e', *Istorik marksist,* no. 2 (1929), p. 135.

56. Ibid., p. 134; Shek, 'Iz istorii sovetsko-Bukharskikh otnoshenii', p. 114; and Zitov, *Pobeda,* p. 58; *M. V. Frunze na frontakh grazhdanskoi voinu: Sbornik dokumentov,* Moscow, 1941, p. 320.

57. Alim Khan, *La voix,* pp. 17–18.

58. Iskandarov, *'Bukhara',* p. 23.

59. Lenin had since March and April 1918 repeatedly sent instructions to the Turkistan authorities urging them to draw the Muslim masses over to their side (*Muzhestvennye bortsy za delo kommunizma: Sbornik statei,* Tashkent, 1957, pp. 96–7). From 17 to 22 June 1918 the First National Congress of the RCP (b) convened in Tashkent and lay the foundations for a native Communist organization (Safarov, *Kolonial'naya revolyutsiya,* p. 86; and Muraveiskii, *Ocherki,* p. 21). Out of fifty delegates there were only five natives; and according to Safarov, only ten real Communists and 125 sympathizers were to be found among the native population in Tashkent, a city with half a million inhabitants (P. Antropov, *Materialy i dokumenty 1-go s"ezda kompartii Turkestana,* Tashkent, 1934, pp. 67–8).

60. S. Bolotov, 'Iz istorii Osipovskogo myatezha', *Proletarskaya revolyutsiya,* no. 153 (1926), pp. 114–37; *Voina v peskakh,* pp. 393–9; and F. Bailey, *Mission to Tashkent,* London, 1946, p. 121.

61. Muraveiskii, *Ocherki,* p. 26.

62. Togan, *Bugünkü,* p. 393.

63. Muraveiskii, *Ocherki,* p. 27.

64. Ibid., p. 28.

65. Safarov, *Kolonial'naya revolyutsiya,* p. 110.

66. R. Abdushukurov, *Oktyabr'skaya revolyutsiya ractsvet uzbekskoi socialisticheskoi natsii i sblizhenie eë s natsiami SSSR,* Tashkent, 1962, pp. 144–5.

67. 'For the Turks, Communism is not an ideal, but a means. The ideal of the Turks is the unification of the Turkish nation.' G. Safarov, *Problemy vostoka,* Petrograd, 1922, p. 177.

68. Safarov, *Kolonial'naya revolyutsiya,* p. 109: 'The Turkish nationalists must rectify a historic error that the Communists commit with respect to Turkistan. The Turkish Communists are struggling not just for the interests of the industrial proletariat and for the railwaymen, but for all the people who live in the deserts and *qishlaqs,* moving towards them.'

69. The first Turkish commission was formed by S. Z. Eliava, Y. Z. Rudzutak, M. V. Frunze, F. Goloshchokov, and V. V. Kuybishev. On its orientation, see Abdushukurov, *Oktyabr'skaya revolyutsiya,* pp. 146–7.

70. M. V. Frunze, *Izbrannye proizvedeniya,* Moscow, 1934, pp. 119–20.

71. L. Kaganovic, G. Safarov, G. Sokolnikov-Brilliant, and Y. Peters. See T.

Ryskulov, *Revolyutsiya i korennoe naselenie Turkestane*, Tashkent, 1922, pp. 76 ff.

72. Y. Peters, 'Stranitsa predatel'stva', *Pravda vostoka* (16 and 18 December 1934).

73. Aliev, *Velikii oktyabr'*, p. 20.

74. Ishanov, *Pobeda*, p. 19.

75. Mel'kumov, *Turkestantsy*, p. 11.

76. The BCP had an information organ in the Uzbek language, *Qutulush* (Liberation), which appeared irregularly in Tashkent between July and September 1920, with a print run of 3,000 copies.

77. *Vooruzhennye sily Bukharskogo Khanstva*, Tashkent, 1920, p. 17.

78. Soloveichik, 'Revolyutsionnaya Bukhara', p. 279.

79. See the interrogation of Fayzallah Khodzhaev in *Trial of the Bloc of Rightists and Trotskyites*, Moscow, 1938, p. 230.

80. The revolt of the Basmachis had begun in the province of Ferghana as early as 1918. Irgash, the most famous Basmachi chieftain, addressed a declaration of war to the Tashkent government.

81. M. V. Frunze, *Izbrannye proizvedeniya*, 2nd edn, Moscow, 1950, p. 101; and *M. V. Frunze na frontakh*, p. 320.

82. M. V. Frunze, *Sobranie sochinenii*, vol. 1, Moscow/Leningrad, 1929, p. 131; and N. E. Kakurin, 'Boevoe operatsii v Bukhare', in *Grazhdanskaya voina*, vol. 3, Tashkent, 1922, p. 4.

83. Soloveichik, 'Revolyutsionnaya Bukhara', pp. 272–88.

84. Frunze, *Izbrannye proizvedeniya*, 2nd edn, pp. 103–4; and *M. V. Frunze na frontakh*, pp. 323–5.

85. Kakurin, 'Boevoe operatsii', pp. 3–17; Dervish, 'Bukharskaya sovetskaya narodnaya respublika', *Zizhn' natsional'nostei*, no. 1 (1923), pp. 195–201; and *Yaş Türkistan*, no. 55 (Paris/Berlin, 1934), p. 7.

86. Alim Khan, *La voix*, p. 22.

87. *Krasnyi Arkhiv*, no. 3 (1949), p. 77.

88. *Izvestiya* (4 September 1920).

89. Chokai, *Turkestan*, p. 21. 'Relations between the immigrant European population and the native peoples of Turkistan, during the two years and a half of the Soviet régime dominated by a layer of Russian workers all imbued with colonialist psychology, scarcely improved — on the contrary they became worse.' A similar judgement is made by Peters, who presided over the purge of the Communist party in the years 1933–4 and who said the following of the régime in the Turkistan Soviet Republic: 'Who did not belong to the government of the Turkish republic? Even a horse-thief found his way into it. And everybody knew that. When we began to look for honest people in order to remedy this ill, in order to have people of local origin, workers and labourers, dedicated to the cause of the proletariat, we were obliged to persuade these comrades at length because they were troubled by the colonialist spirit that was then prevalent among certain of our Russian comrades. They did not believe in their own strength and were afraid of entering the government.' (*Pravda Vostoka* [24 May 1934], quoted by Hayit, *Turkestan*, p. 108.)

90. *Le 1er Congrès des peuples de l'Orient, 1–8 septembre 1920*, Petrograd, 1921, p. 204.

91. Ibid., p. 85.

92. Ibid., p. 83.

93. Ibid., pp. 179–97; see also Bela Kun's theses on pp. 168–79.

Notes to Chapter Nine

1. *Le 1er Congrès,* p. 204.
2. Baysun, *Türkistan,* p. 41.
3. Togan, *Bugünkü,* p. 406.
4. Different authors give their own variants of the government's composition. The list above is taken from Baysun (*Türkistan,* p. 42). It is confirmed in certain details by Castagné ('Le bolchevisme', p. 225) and adopted by Hayit (*Türkestan,* p. 236); but Togan (*Bugünkü,* p. 406) puts Hashim Shaykh at foreign affairs, Nasr Hakim at finance, Qari 'Abd al-Vahid at public health and gives no incumbent for the war portfolio.
5. Pashitskii, 'Materialy', pp. 127–8.
6. Soloveichik, 'Revolyutsionnaya Bukhara', p. 273.
7. 'Proclamation of Revkom to the Peoples of the East', in *Izvestiya,* 9 October 1920.
8. The first *quriltay,* which had begun on 6 November 1920 in the presence of 2,000 delegates, had not settled the problems of the new state (see *Pravda,* 27 November 1920).
9. N. Arkhipov, 'Buharskaya narodnaya sovetskaya respublika', *Sovetskoe pravo,* vol. 1, no. 4 (1923), p. 134.
10. Ibid., p. 136.
11. Ibid., p. 137.
12. Ibid., pp. 135–6.
13. Ibid., p. 137.
14. Ibid.
15. Ibid., p. 134.
16. Ibid., p. 135.
17. Ibid.
18. Ibid., p. 134.
19. Castagné, 'Le bolchevisme', p. 225.
20. Ibid.
21. Abdushukurov, *Oktyabr'skaya revolyutsiya,* p. 178.
22. Ibid., p. 179. See also R. H. Aminova, *Agrarnye preobrazovaniya v Uzbekistane,* Tashkent, 1965, pp. 120–23.
23. The place accorded to Islam in the people's republic was denounced not only by the Russians, but also by Muslims, notably by Sultan Galiev ('Metody anti-religioznoi propagandy sredi musul'man', *Zhizn'natsional'nostei* [14 and 23 December 1921]).
24. N. Fioletov, 'Sudy Kaziev v sredne aziatskih respublikah', *Sovetskoe pravo,* vol. 1, no. 25 (1927), p. 144.
25. *Pravda,* 20 March 1924.
26. Ibid., 5 January 1924.
27. Ibid., 5 February 1924.
28. Ibid.
29. Ibid., 20 March 1921.
30. Togan, *Bügunkü,* p. 406.
31. Sultan Galiev, 'Metody'.
32. *Pravda,* 5 February 1924.
33. Hayit, *Turkestan,* p. 136.
34. *Pravda,* 24 February 1921, notes the opening of a printing course and a military school, and the graduation of the first speeded up batch of teachers.

35. Hayit (*Turkestan,* p. 136) quoting the unpublished journal of Qayyum Khan, who in 1943 founded *Milli Edebiyat* in Berlin.

36. Soloveichik, 'Revolyutsionnaya Bukhara', p. 17.

37. T. P. Avetisov, 'Nashi ekonomicheskie vzaimno-otnosheniya s Bukharoi — v proshlom i nastoyashchem', *Voennaya mysl'*, no. 2 (May/June 1921), p. 235.

38. *Izvestiya,* 27 November 1920.

39. A. Sabanin, ed., *Sbornik deistvuyushchikh dogovorov i Konventsii zaklyuchennikh s inostrannami gosudarstvami,* Moscow, 1924–8, vol. 1, pp. 42–6.

40. Article 2 of the Treaty of Alliance.

41. Sabanin, *Sbornik,* vol. 2, pp. 12–14; and vol. 4, pp. 9 and 10.

42. *Sobranie uzakonenii i rasporyazhenii rabochego i krest'yanskogo pravitel'stva RSFSR,* Moscow, 1923, pp. 961–4.

43. Castagné, 'Le bolchevisme', p. 224.

44. *Pravda,* 9 February 1921.

45. Memorandum of 29 April 1922 addressed to the Afghan government by Usman Khodzhaev.

46. Alim Khan, *La voix,* p. 27; and A. R. Rahimbaev, *Tadzhikistan,* Moscow, 1936, p. 16.

47. Ibrahim Beg (Mulla Muhammad) was an Uzbek from eastern Bukhara, whom 'Alim Khan on his departure for Afghanistan appointed commander-in-chief of the rebels. After several defeats, he managed to wrest Kulab and the Baljuan region from the Russian troops; after allying himself with Enver Pasha he established his rule over the province of Hisar. He managed to leave Bukhara when the resistance movement was vanquished, and to rejoin 'Alim Khan in Afghanistan, where he settled. In 1931 he returned to Tajikistan and organized a peasant uprising there; he was captured in 1933 and shot. (Alim Khan, *La voix,* pp. 30–43, *passim.*)

48. Dawlatmand Beg Divan-begi was, like Ibrahim Beg, appointed by 'Alim Khan to lead the resistance. He was killed in 1922 with Enver Pasha at the battle of Baljuan; he had the title of minister of war in the government-in-exile. (Ibid., pp. 30 and 40.)

49. Mirza 'Abd al-Qadir Muhyi al-Din had played an important role at the Charju'i congress and in setting up the revolutionary committee (Hayit, *Turkestan,* p. 182). In 1937, he was accused of bourgeois nationalism and condemned to death (see Castagné's notes).

50. Muhyi al-Din Makhdum, a member of the Young Bukhara party, was chief of police in Bukhara at the time he went over to the rebellion. He joined the Emir with 300 policemen. (Hayit, *Turkestan;* see also Castagné's notes.)

51. Baysun, *Türkistan,* p. 45.

52. M. Chokaev, 'The Basmaji Movement', *The Asiatic Review* (London, April 1928), pp. 284–5.

53. Enver Pasha, a Turkish general born at Constantinople in 1882, was killed at the battle of Baljuan on 4 August 1922. After entering the army, he soon became a leader of the Young Turk party and helped to topple Sultan Abdul Hamid in 1909. During the Turkish–Italian war of 1911 he led the resistance in Cyrenaica. Sent in 1913 to Berlin as a military attaché, he contributed towards his country's alliance with the Central Powers. In June 1913, he took advantage of the war between the Balkan states to attack Bulgaria's rear and reoccupy Adrianople. Becoming minister of war in 1914, he committed Turkey against the Entente powers in the First World War. Both a pasha and the Sultan's son-in-law, he was at the time the real master of the Ottoman Empire. Taking command of Turkish forces in the Caucasus at the outset of the war, he was forced by the Russians to evacuate part of Armenia.

Returning to Constantinople, he threw himself into the defence of the Dardanelles. After the Mudros armistice in October 1918, Enver Pasha was obliged to leave Turkey and took refuge in Germany. His constant rival Mustafa Kemal made the revolution that Enver had dreamed of making himself. When Kemal took power, Enver Pasha came out against the Kemalism that had dispossessed him. Turkey was henceforth closed to him. In Germany he had known Karl Radek, during Radek's imprisonment in Berlin; he was subsequently to be consigned by Radek to Moscow, where he was received by Lenin, to whom he proposed a great plan for a Soviet–Muslim alliance. Working for the Bolsheviks in the Caucasus, he established a Soviet administration in Adzharia; thereafter, he rallied the Muslims of Turkistan and turned against the Soviets. After defeating the Soviets at Baysun in June 1922, he was driven by the Red Army towards the Pamirs. His last battle took place at Baljuan. (See Castagné's notes.)

54. Ultimatum addressed to Narimanov on 19 May 1922 (Castagné, 'Le bolchevisme', p. 226).

55. Ibid.

56. Soloveichik, 'Revolyutsionnaya Bukhara', p. 283.

57. Vasilevskii, 'Fazy basmacheskogo dvizheniya v Srednei Azii', *Novyi Vostok*, no. 29 (1929), p. 134.

58. Soloveichik, 'Revolyutsionnaya Bukhara', p. 284.

59. F. Maclean, *Another Traveller in Turkestan*, London, 1957, p. 343.

60. Ilyutko, *Basmachestvo v Lokae*, Moscow, 1929, p. 132.

61. D. Manzhara, *Revolyutsionnoe dvizhenie v Srednei Azii, 1905–1923*, Tashkent, 1934, pp. 79 ff.; D. Zuev, 'Krasnaya gvardiya Turkestana', *Novyi Mir*, nos. 6/7 (1929), p. 116; and E. Kozlovskii, *Krasnaya armiya v Srednei Azii*, Tashkent, 1928, pp. 65 ff.

62. Soloveichik, 'Revolyutsionnaya Bukhara', p. 283.

63. Ibid., p. 286.

64. Maclean, *Another Traveller*, pp. 347–59.

65. Castagné, 'Le bolchevisme', p. 232.

66. Vasilevskii, 'Fazy', p. 135; and J. Castagné, *Les Basmatchis*, Paris, 1925, p. 34.

67. Vasilevskii, 'Fazy', p. 135; see also Aminova, *Agrarnye preobrazovaniya*, pp. 38 ff.

68. T. Ryskulov, *Kirghizstan*, Moscow, 1935, pp. 66–7; and 'Observer' [Jeyun Bay Khajibayli], 'Soviet Press Comments on the Capture of Ibrahim Bey', *The Asiatic Review*, vol. 27, no. 92 (London, 1931), pp. 682–92.

69. Hayit (*Turkestan*, p. 140), basing himself on Qayyum Khan's memories, records that Fitrat, who used to avoid all contact with the Russians, whenever he had to receive one always took pains to make him wait endlessly, saying, 'We have waited for a very long time, it is the turn of the Russians now to learn how to wait.' Fitrat was minister of foreign affairs at the time.

70. Stalin, *Works*, Moscow, 1946–51, vol. 5, p. 330.

71. *Revolyutsiya i natsional'nosti*, no. 11 (1933), pp. 98–102.

72. *Zhizn' natsional'nostei*, vol. 3, no. 132 (26 January 1922).

73. *Protokoly s"ezdov i konferentsii vsesoyuznoi Kommunisticheskoi partii (b): odinnatsatyi s"ezd RKP (b)*, Moscow, 1936, p. 396.

74. Stalin, *Works*, vol. 5, pp. 301–3.

75. On Sultan Galiev's plans, see E. H. Carr, *The History of Soviet Russia*, London, 1954, vol. 4, pp. 285–6. On the real scope of these plans, see A. Bennigsen and C. Quelquejay, *Les mouvements nationaux chez les Musulmans de Russie: Le sultangaliévisme au Tatarstan*, Paris, 1960, pp. 167–8.

76. See Peters, 'Stranitsa'.

77. The 'party council' held at the beginning of 1926 changed the name *Tuda* into *Socialist Erk Firkasi* (Erk Socialist Party of Turkistan). It also adopted on 8 and 9 January 1926 the nine-point programme worked out in 1921. On these various plans, see V. Nepomnin, *Istoricheskii opyt stroitel'stva sotsializma v Uzbekistane*, Tashkent, 1960, pp. 131 ff.

78. Abdushukurov, *Oktyabr'skaya revolyutsiya*, pp. 176–7.

79. Ibid., pp. 177–80.

80. Stalin, *Works*, vol. 5, p. 332.

81. Ibid.

82. Abdushukurov, *Oktyabr'skaya revolyutsiya*, p.191.

83. Ibid.

84. *Pravda*, 20 March 1924.

85. Ibid., 14 February 1924, reported that for the first time some Bukhara workers, instead of 'baptizing' their children in accordance with Islamic tradition, had given them a communist baptism at the House of the People. In relation to this, it is odd to note that in *Pravda* circumcision became 'baptism' — and that the story was in any case about a child with a Tatar father and a Russian mother!

86. Dervish, 'Bukharskaya respublika', pp. 197–8.

87. Abdushukurov, *Oktyabr'skaya revolyutsiya*, pp. 183–4.

88. O. Galucian, 'Smena pravitel'stva v Bukhare', *Izvestiya* (11 July 1923).

89. Text in Ksenofontov, *Uzbekistan i Turkmenistan: K voprosa ob ikh vhozhdenii v SSSR*, Moscow/Leningrad, 1925, pp. 31–3.

90. Zel'kina ('Zemel'naja reforma', p. 134) notes that Bukharan peasants in 1926 were often unable to say whether they were Uzbeks or Kirghiz.

91. Lenin himself had in 1920 studied very closely the territorial reorganization of Central Asia; see *Leninskii sbornik*, 2nd edn, Moscow, 1925, vol. 45, p. 326.

92. Uzbekistan was established on 10 February 1924 and immediately set up as an SSR. The proclamation can be found in Ksenofontov, *Uzbekistan*, pp. 32–3.

93. Khodzhaev, 'O mlado-Bukhartsakh', p. 230.

94. *Yaş Türkistan* (13 May 1943).

Notes to Conclusion

1. 13 September 1921. See Lenin, *Collected Works*, vol. 45 (Moscow, 1970), pp. 297–8 (author's stress). This letter was in reply to a cable from Adolph Joffe, sent to Turkistan by the Communist party's central committee; he was reporting the differences that had arisen between Tomskii and Safarov in the sphere of nationality policy and saying that the result was the prevailing state of hostility between Russians and natives. Safarov attacked Russian policy in Turkistan equally violently at the tenth congress of the RCP (b), where he led the Turkistan delegation. (*Desyatyi s"ezd RKP (b): Stenograficheskii otchët*, Moscow, 1963, pp. 189 ff.)

2. To this day Soviet analyses of the Third World refer to the experience of Bukhara as an example of the transition to socialism of a non-capitalist country (V. Tyagunenko, 'Aktual'nye voprosy nekapitalisticheskogo puti razvitiya', *Mirovaya ekonomika i mezhdunarodnye otnosheniya*, no. 10 [1964], p. 19).

Select Bibliography

Abdushukurov, R. *Oktyabr'skaya revolyutsiyac rastsvet uzbekskoi socialisticheskoi natsii i sblizhenie eë s natsiami SSSR* [The October Revolution, development of the Uzbek socialist nation and its *rapprochement* with the peoples of the USSR], 728 pp., Tashkent, 1962.

Abramzon, S. 'Tyan-Shanskaya etnograficheskaya ekspeditsiya' [The Tian-shan ethnographical expedition], *Kratkie Soobshcheniya Instituta Etnografii*, no. 4 (1948).

Afganskoe razgranichenie: Peregovory mezhdu Rossiei i Velikobritaniei 1872–1885 [Demarcation of the Afghan Frontier: Negotiations between Russia and Great Britain 1872–1885], 142 pp., St Petersburg, Ministry of Foreign Affairs, 1886.

Albrecht, M. *Russische Centralasien* [Russian Central Asia], 249 pp., Hamburg, 1896.

Alekseenkov, P. *Chto takoe basmachestvo* [What are the Basmachis?], 162 pp., Tashkent, 1931.

————— 'Natsional'naya politika vremennogo pravitel'stva v Turkestane v 1917 g.' [The national policy of the Provisional Government in Turkistan], *Proletarskaya revolyutsiya*, no. 8 (1928), pp. 104–132.

Alektorov, A. 'Novoe techenie v zhizni musul'manskikh shkol' [New tendencies in the life of Muslim schools], *Zhurnal Ministerstva Narodnogo Prosvyashcheniya* (April 1909), p. 195.

Aliev, A. *Velikii oktyabr' i revolyutsionizirovanie narodov Bukhary* [The great October and bringing revolution to the peoples of Bukhara], 46 pp., Tashkent, 1958.

Alim Khan, Emir Said. *La voix de la Boukharie opprimée* [The voice of oppressed Bukhara], 71 pp., Paris, 1929.

Allworth, E. *Central Asia. A century of Russian rule*, New York/London, 1967.

A. M. 'Nalogi v Bukhare' [Taxes in Bukhara], *Turkestanskie vedemosti* (10, 11 and 13 January 1906).

————— *Taxation in Bukhara* (based on foregoing), no place or date of publication.

Aminova, R. H. *Agrarnye preobrazovaniya v Uzbekistane* [Agrarian reforms in Uzbekistan], Tashkent, 1965.

Andreev, M. *Po etnografii Tadzhikov. Nekotorye svedeniya. Tadzhikistan* [On the ethnography of the Tajiks. Some indications. Tajikistan], Tashkent, 1925.

Antropov, P. *Chto i kak chitat' po istorii revolyutsionnogo dvizheniya v Srednei Azii* [What and how to read about the history of the revolutionary movement in Central Asia]. Bibliographical guide. 118 pp., Samarqand, 1929.

————— *Materialy i dokumenty 1-go s"ezda kompartii Turkestana* [Materials and documents of the first session of the Communist Party of Turkistan], Tashkent, 1934.

Arkhipov, N. 'Bukharskaya Narodnaya Sovetskaya Respublika' [The People's Soviet Republic of Bukhara], *Sovetskoe pravo*, no. 1/4 (1923).

————— *Sredne-aziatskie respubliki* [The Central Asian republics], 139 pp., Moscow, 1927.

237

Arsharuni, A. and Gabidullin, K. *Ocherki panislamizma i pantyurkizma v Rossii* [Studies on pan-Islamism and pan-Turkism in Russia], 138 pp., Moscow, 1931.

Ashurov, J., Gelah, T. and Kamalov, U. *Bukhara, kratkii spravochnik putevoditel'* [Bukhara, a short handbook and guide], 84 pp., Tashkent, 1956.

Avetisov, T. P. 'Nashi ekonomicheskie vzaimno-otnosheniya s Bukharoi — v proshlom i nastoyashchem' [Our economic interrelations with Bukhara — past and present], *Voennaya mysl'*, no. 2 (May/June 1921).

Ayni, K. 'Vstrechi Ahmada Donisha s P. I. Pashino' [Ahmad Danish's encounters with P. I. Pashino], *Narody Azii i Afriki*, no. 6 (1963).

'Ayni (Aini), S. *Bukhara*, Russian translation by S. Borodin, 2 vols, 207 and 184 pp., Stalinabad, 1949.

——————— *Buhara inqilabi tarihi ichim materiyallar* [History of the revolution in Bukhara], in Uzbek, 147 pp., Moscow, 1926.

——————— *Bukhara: Reminiscences*, Moscow, 1986.

——————— 'Korotko o moei zhizni' [My life in brief], reminiscences written in 1940 and translated into Russian from Tajik, *Druzhba Narodov* (April 1957), pp. 83–135.

——————— *Namunaha-yi adabiyat-i tajik* [Examples of Tajik literature], Moscow, 1926.

——————— *Skhola* [School], 188 pp., Moscow, 1949.

——————— *Vospominaniya* [Reminiscences], translated by A. Rozenfel'd, 1088 pp., Moscow, 1960.

Babakhodzhaev, A. *Proval agressivnoi politiki angliiskogo imperializma v Srednei Azii v 1917–20 gg.* [The failure of English imperialism's policy of aggression in Central Asia in 1917–20], 160 pp., Tashkent, 1955.

——————— and Kel'diev, T. *Razgrom kontr revolyutsii v Ferganskoi i Samarkandskoi oblastyakh v 1918–23 gg.* [The defeat of the counter-revolution in the regions of Ferghana and Samarqand in 1918–23], 237 pp., Tashkent, 1959.

Bailey, F. *Mission to Tashkent*, 312 pp., London, 1946.

Bajazitov. *Otnoshenie Islama k nauke i k inovertsam* [Islam's attitude to science and unbelievers], St Petersburg, 1881.

Barthold [Bartol'd], V. V. *Four studies on the history of Central Asia*, vol. 1, 183 pp., Leyden, 1956.

——————— *Histoire des Turcs d'Asie Centrale* [History of the Turks of Central Asia], 203 pp., Paris, 1945.

——————— *Istoriya kul'turnoi zhizni Turkestana* [History of civilized life in Turkistan], 254 pp., Leningrad, 1927.

——————— *Tadzhiki, istoricheskii ocherk. Tadzhikistan* [The Tajiks, a historical sketch. Tajikistan], Tashkent, 1925.

——————— *Teokraticheskaya ideya i svetskaya vlast' v musul'manskom gosudarstve* [The theocratic idea and secular power in the Muslim state], 25 pp., St Petersburg, 1905.

——————— 'Turkestan', *Encyclopaedia of Islam, 1st edn, Leiden, 1913– .*

——————— *Turkestan down to the Mongol Invasion*, London, 1977.

Baysun, A. *Türkistan milli hareketleri* [The national movements of Turkistan], Istanbul, 1945.

Bendrikov, K. *Ocherki po istorii narodnogo obrazovaniya v Turkestane* [Studies on the history of public education in Turkistan], 510 pp., Moscow, 1960.

Bennigsen, A. and Quelquejay, C. *Les mouvements nationaux chez les musulmans de Russie: le sultangaliévisme au Tatarstan* [National movements among the Muslims of Russia. Sultangalievism in Tataristan], Paris, 1960.

Benzing, J. 'Das Turkistanische Volk im Kampf um seine Selbständigkeit: 1. Von der russischen Eroberung bis zum sturz des Zarentums' [The Turkistani nation in struggle for its independence: 1. From the Russian conquest to the fall of Tsarism], *Die Welt des Islams*, no. 19 (December 1937), pp. 94–137.

——————— *Turkestan*, Berlin, 1943.

Bernhauer, *Mémoires sur les institutions de police chez les Arabes, les Persans et les Turcs* [Memoranda on police institutions among the Arabs, Persians and Turks], Paris, 1861.

Bertels, E. *Ocherk istorii persidskoi literatury* [Outline of the history of Persian literature], Leningrad, 1928.

——————— *Rukopisnye proizvedeniya Akhmada Donisha* [Manuscript works of Ahmad Danish], *Trudy tadzhikskoi bazy Akademii Nauk SSSR* [Transactions of the Tajik centre of the USSR Academy of Sciences], vol. 3, Moscow/Leningrad, 1936.

Bibliografiya Tadzhikistana [Bibliography of Tajikistan], 28 pp., Tashkent, 1926.

Binder, L. 'Al-Ghazali's theory of Islamic government', *The Muslim World*, no. 45 (1953).

Bisnek, A. G. and Safranovskij, K. I. *Bibliografiya bibliografii Srednei Azii* [Bibliography of bibliographies of Central Asia], 98 pp., Moscow, Izdatel'stvo Akademii Nauk, 1936.

Blacker, L. V. *On Secret Patrols in High Asia*, London, 1922.

Blue Books: Central Asia, London, 1864–88, one vol. per year.

Boersner, D. *The Bolsheviks and the National and Colonial Questions 1917–1918*, Paris/Geneva, 1957.

Bolotov, S. 'Iz istorii Osipovskogo myatezha' [From the history of Ossipov's revolt], *Proletarskaya revolyutsiya*, no. 153 (1926).

Boulger, D. *Central Asian Portraits: The celebrities of the Khanates and the neighbouring states*, viii/310 pp, London, 1880.

——————— *Central Asian Questions*, 475 pp., London, 1885.

——————— *England and Russia in Central Asia*, 2 vols., London, 1879.

Braginskii, I. S. *Ocherki iz istorii tadzhikskoi literatury* [Sketches from the history of Tajik literature], Stalinabad, 1956.

——————— *Sadriddin Aini: Ocherk zhizni i tvorchestva* [Sadriddin 'Ayni: Sketch of his life and creative work], Stalinabad, 1954.

Brojdo, G. 'Materialy k istorii vostaniya Kirgiz' [Documents on the history of the Kirghiz rising], *Novyi Vostok*, no. 6 (1924).

'Bukhara v 1917 godu' [Bukhara in 1917], *Krasnyi Arkhiv*, no. 20 (1927).

Buhari, M. A. *Histoire de l'Asie centrale* [History of Central Asia], published, translated and annotated by C.Schefer, 2 vols, Paris, 1876.

——————— *'Ubaydallah nama* [The story of 'Ubaydallah], (translated into Russian and annotated by A.Semenov), 326 pp., Tashkent, 1957.

——————— *O nekotorykh sobytiyakh v Bukhare, Kokande i Kashgare* [On certain events in Bukhara, Khoqand and Kashgar], (Memoirs of M.S.Buhari, published in the original with translation and notes by V. B. Grigorieva), 125/38 pp., Kazan, 1861.

Burnes, A. *Travels into Bukhara: Being an account of a journey from India to Kaboul, Tartary and Persia, etc.*, 3 vols, London, 1834. (Russian translation: A. Borns, *Puteshestvie v Buharu — leitenanta Ost-Indskoi Kompaneiskoi sluzhby*, 3 vols, Moscow, 1848.) See vol. 3, x/628 pp. with illustrations, for Bukhara.

Carr, E. H. *The History of Soviet Russia*, vol. 4, London, 1954.

Castagné, J. *Les Basmatchis: Le mouvement national des indigènes d'Asie centrale*

[The Basmachis. The national movement of the natives of Central Asia], 88 pp., Paris, 1925.

——————— 'Le bolchevisme et l'Islam: les organisation soviétiques de la Russie musulmane' [Bolshevism and Islam: the soviet organizations of Muslim Russia], *Revue du monde musulman,* no. 51 (October 1922).

——————— 'Le Turkestan depuis la revolution russe (1917–1921)' [Turkestan since the Russian Revolution], *Revue du monde musulman,* no. 50 (1922), 48 pp.

Chokaev, M. 'The Basmaji movement in Turkestan', *The Asiatic Review,* no. 24 (1928), London.

Chokai (Cokajoglu), M. *Turkestan pod vlast'ju Sovetov* [Turkistan under the rule of the Soviets], 127 pp., Paris, 1935.

Cholet. *Excursions en Turkestan et sur la frontière russo-afghane* [Excursions into Turkistan and on the Russo-Afghan frontier], 280 pp., Paris, 1889.

Clarke, T. *Encyclopaedia of Religion,* Edinburgh, 1908–28.

Cochard, L. *Paris-Boukhara-Samarkande,* 147 pp., Paris, 1891.

Croizier, Marquis de *Le Bazar de Boukhara* [The Bazaar at Bukhara], 28 pp., Marseille, 1892 (offprint from *Bulletin de la Société de géographie de Marseille*).

——————— *Le dernier Emir de Boukhara: Souvenirs de voyage en Turcomanie* [The last Emir of Bukhara. Memories of a journey among the Turcomans], 13 pp., Rouen, 1893 (offprint from the *Bulletin de la Societe normande de géographie*).

Curzon, C. *Russia in Central Asia in 1889 and the Anglo-Russian Question,* 477 pp. with map, London, 1889.

Demidov, A. F. Ekonomicheskii ocherk khlopkovodstva i khlopkovoi torgovli i promyslennosti [Economic outline of cotton-growing and the cotton trade and industry], Moscow, 1926.

Dervish 'Bukharskaya Sovetskaya Narodnaya Respublika' [The Bukhara Soviet People's Republic], *Zhizn'Natsional'nostei,* no. 1 (1923), pp. 195–201.

Desyatyi s"ezd RKP (b): Stenograficheskii otchët [Tenth Congress of the RCP (b): stenographic record], Moscow, 1963.

Dimanshtein, S. 'Otserednye zadachi natsional'noi raboty' [Next tasks of national work], *Revolyutsiya i Natsional'nosti* (10 November 1931).

——————— (ed.) *Revolyutsiya i natsional'nyi vopros* [Revolution and the national question], vol. 3 (February–October 1917), Moscow, 1930.

Dodonov, I. K. *Pobeda oktyabr'skoi revolyutsii v Turkestane* [The victory of the October Revolution in Turkistan], Tashkent, 1958.

Dokumenty k istorii agrarnykh otnoshenii v bukharskom khanstve: Acty feodal'noi sobstvenosti na zemlyu [Documents on the history of agrarian relations in the Khanate of Bukhara. Deeds of feudal land ownership], 268 pp., Tashkent, 1954.

Donish, A. *Kratkaya istoriya mangytskikh emirov v Bukhare* [Short history of the Manghit emirs in Bukhara], viii/185 pp., Stalinabad, 1960.

Efremov, F. S. *Stranstvovanie (Efremova) v Kirgizskoi stepi, Buharii, Khive, Persii i Tibete i Indii is vozvrashchenie ego ottuda cherez Anglii i Rossiyu* [Efremov's journey to the Kirghiz steppe, Bukhara, Khiva, Persia and to Tibet and India and his return therefrom through England and Russia], third edn, 159 pp., Kazan, 1811.

Ershov, V. V. 'Revolyutsiya 1905–1907 v Uzbekistane' [The 1905–7 revolution in Uzbekistan', in *Revolyutsiya 1905–1907 v Uzbekistane: Sbornik statei i vospominanii,* Tashkent, 1955.

Erturk, 'Abdur Rauf Fitrat', *Milli Turkestan,* nos. 80/81 (1952), pp. 9–16.

Etat présent de la Boukharie, contenant une description exacte de la situation des moeurs, de la forme du gouvernement et du commerce, avec relation de la dernière révolution dans ce pays, de la fin tragique du prince Bosto-Cham: Tiré du manuscrit d'un voyageur [Present condition of Bukhara, containing an exact description of the situation regarding its mores, form of government and commerce, with an account of the latest revolution in that country and of the tragic end of Prince Bosto-Cham: Drawn from a traveller's manuscript], 47 pp. with street-plan and map, Cologne.

Etherton, P. *In the Heart of Asia,* London, 1925.

Eversmann, E. *Reise von Orenburg nach Buhara* [Journey from Orenburg to Bukhara], viii/150/40/4 pp., Berlin, 1823.

Fedchenko, A. *Zapiski o mangianskom bekstve, materialy dlya statistiki turkestanskogo kraya* [Notes on the Manghit begs: materials for statistics on the region of Turkistan], St Petersburg, 1873.

Federov, E. *Ocherki natsional'no-osvobobitel'nogo dvizheniya v Srednei Azii* [Studies on the national liberation movement in Central Asia], 325 pp., Tashkent, 1925.

———— *1905 god i korennoe naselenie Srednei Azii* [1905 and the native population of Central Asia], 233 pp., Moscow, 1926.

Fedorov, I. *Oktyabr'skaya revolyutsiya v Turkestane* [The October Revolution in Turkistan], Tashkent, 1924.

Ferro, M. 'La politique des nationalités du gouvernement provisoire' [The nationality policy of the Provisional Government], *Cahiers du monde russe et soviétique,* no. 2 (April/June 1961).

Filipov, S. T. *Boevoe deistviya na zakaspiiskom fronte* [Military activities on the Trans-Caspian front], Ashkhabad, 1928.

Fioletov, N. 'Sudy Kaziev v sredne aziatskikh respublikakh' [*Qazi*'s (*shar'i*) courts in the Central Asian republics], *Sovetskoe Pravo,* no. 1/25 (1927).

Fitrat, A. R. *Munazara* [The discussion], in Persian, 60 pp., Istanbul, 1909. (Russian translation: Fitrat Bukharets, *Spor bukharskogo mudarrisa s evropeitsem v Indii o novometodnykh shkolakh,* translated by Colonel Jagello, 98 pp., Tashkent, 1911.)

———— *Qiyamat* (The resurrection), Tashkent, 1961.

———— *Raskazy indiiskogo puteshestvennika* [Tales of an Indian traveller], 111 pp., Samarqand, 1913.

Fomchenko, A. *Russkie poseleniya v Bukharskom Emirate* [Russian settlements in the Emirate of Bukhara], 77 pp., Tashkent, 1958.

Friedrih, N. L. *Bukhara, etnograficheskii ocherk* [Bukhara, an ethnographical sketch], 79 pp. with illustrations, St Petersburg, 1910.

Frunze, M. *Izbrannye proizvedeniya* [Selected works], 600 pp., Moscow, 1934. (Second edn, 584 pp., Moscow, 1950.)

———— *Sobranie sochinenii* [Selected works], vol. 1, Moscow/Leningrad, 1929.

Frunze, M. V., *na frontakh grazhdanskoi voiny* [M. V. Frunze on the fronts of the civil war], 202 pp., Moscow, 1941.

Gafurov, B. *Istoriya tadzhikskogo naroda* [History of the Tajik nation], vol. 1, 503 pp., Moscow, 1952.

Galucian, O. 'Smena pravitel'stva v Bukhare' [A change of government in Bukhara], *Izvestiya,* 11 July 1923.

Galuzo, G. P. *Turkestan, koloniya* [Turkistan, a colony], 139 pp., Tashkent, 1935.

———— *Vooruzhenie russkikh pereselentsev v Srednei Azii: Istoricheskii ocherk* [The arming of the Russian settlers in Central Asia. A historical outline], 90 pp., Tashkent, 1926.

Gasprinski, I. B. *Russkoe Musul'manstvo: Mysli, zametki, o nabljudeniyah Musul'manina* [Russian Islam: Thoughts and notes on a Muslim's observations], 1st edn, Simferopol, 1881.

Gavazzi, M. *Alcune notizie raccolte in un viaggio a Bucara* [Some information gathered on a journey to Bukhara], 172 pp. with maps, Milan, 1865.

Gehrke, U. *Persien in der Deutschen Orientpolitik* [Persia in Germany's Eastern policy], Stuttgart, n.d., 2 vols.

Geier, I. *Turkestan*, 346/34 pp., in Russian, Tashkent, 1909.

Gibb, H. A. R. *Modern Trends in Islam*, Chicago, 1947.

Gloratskii, O. *Revolyutsiya pobezhdaet* [The revolution triumphs], Tashkent, 1930.

Gloukhovsky, A. 'Captivité en Boukharie: données géographiques' [Captivity in Bukhara: geographical information], translated from Russian by M.Woelkel with notes by M. de Khanikof, *Bulletin de la Société de Géographie*, Paris, 1868, pp. 265–96.

Gobineau, M. de *Les religions et les philosophies dans l'Asie centrale* [Religions and philosophies in Central Asia], Paris, 1886.

Gordienko, A. *Sozdanie narodno-sovetskogo gosudarstva i prava i ikh revolutsion-nopreobrazuyushchaya rol' v Khorezme i Bukhare 1920–1924 gg.* [Establishment of a people's and soviet economy and law and their revolutionizing role in Khvarazm and Bukhara 1920–24], 199 pp., Tashkent, 1959.

Gorodetskii, V. and Gorodetskaya, M. *Bibliografiya turkestana* [Bibliography of Turkestan], vol. 1, 150 pp., Tashkent, 1913.

Grigoriev, V. V. *Karakhanidy Mavara-al-Nahra* [The Qarakhanids of Transoxania], 70 pp., St Petersburg, 1874.

———— *Russkaya politika v otnoshenii k Srednei Azii* [Russian policy in relation to Central Asia], 30 pp., St Petersburg, 1874.

Grousset, R. *L'empire des steppes: Attila, Gengis Khan, Tamerlan* [The empire of the steppes. Attila, Genghis Khan, Tamerlane], 651 pp., Paris, 1939.

Grubjak, I. 'Antisemitizm v Turkestane' [Antisemitism in Turkistan], appended to L. Kantor, *Tuzemnye evrei v Uzbekistane: Samarkand* [Indigenous Jews in Uzbekistan. Samarqand], Tashkent, 1929.

Grulev, M. *Sopernichestvo Rossii s Angliei v Srednei Azii* [The rivalry between Russia and England in Central Asia], 380 pp., St Petersburg, 1909.

Grunebaum, G. E. von. *Islam: essays in the nature and growth of a cultural tradition*, London, 1955.

Gubarevich-Radobylski, A. *Ekonomicheskii ocherk Bukhary i Tunisa: Opyt sravnitel'nogo issledovaniya dvukh sistem protektorata* [Economic sketch of Bukhara and Tunis. An experiment in comparative research into two systems of protectorate], 201 pp., St Petersburg, 1905.

Gubaydullin, A. 'K voprosu ob ideologii Gasprinskogo' [On the question of Gasprinski's ideology], *Izvestiya Vostochnogo Fakulteta* (Baku), no. 4 (1919).

Gubaydullin, G. 'Iz istorii torgovogo klassa u privolzhakikh tatar' [From the history of the merchant class among the Volga Tatars], *Vostokovedenie*, no. 1 (1926).

Gurko-Kryazhin, V. 'Angliiskaya interventsiya v 1918–19 g. v Zakaspii i Zakavkaz'e' [English intervention in 1918–19 in Trans-Caspia and Trans-Caucasia], *Istorik marksist*, no. 2 (1929).

Hambis, L. *La Haute Asie. Histoire de l'Asie centrale* [High Asia. History of Central Asia], 136 pp., Paris, 1953.

Hayit, B. *Die nationalen Regierungen von Kokand und Alash Orda* [The national governments of Khoqand and Alash Orda], 111 roneo pp. (thesis), Münster,

1950.

————— *Turkestan im XX Jahrhundert* [Turkistan in the 20th century], 406 pp., Darmstadt, 1956.

Helmersen, G. *Nachrichten uber Buchara, Chiva, Chokand und den Merw: Teil des chinesischen Staates* [Reports on Bukhara, Khiva, Khoqand and Merv: Part of the Chinese state], viii/124 pp., St Petersburg, 1839.

Heumann, C. *Les Russes et les Anglais dans l'Asie centrale* [Russians and English in Central Asia], 95 pp., Paris, 1885.

Hodi Zade, R. *Istochniki k izucheniyu tadzhikskoi literatury vtoroi polovinu XIX veka* [Sources for the study of Tajik literature in the second half of the 19th century], Moscow, 1954.

Holdsworth, M. *Turkestan in the 19th Century: Brief history of Bukhara, Kokand and Khiva*, 81 pp., London/Oxford, 1959.

Ibragimov, J. 'Yanvar'skie sobytiya v Tashkente' [The January events in Tashkent], *Zhizn' natsional'nostei*, no. 10/19 (30 March 1919).

————— 'Krasnyi Turkestan' [Red Turkistan], *Zhizn'natsional'nosteii*, no. 12/20 (4 April 1919).

————— 'Krasnyi Turkestan — Bukhara' [Red Turkistan — Bukhara], *Zhizn'natsional'nosteii*, no. 13/21 (13 April 1919), p. 1.

Ilyutko. *Basmachestvo v Lokae* [The Basmachi movement in Lokai], Moscow, 1929.

Inoyatov, Kh. *Ozbekistonda oktyabr'revolyucyasi* [The October Revolution in Uzbekistan], Tashkent, 1957.

————— 'Rol' narodnykh mass v svershenii oktyabr'skoi revolyutsii v Turkestane' [The role of the popular masses in the accomplishment of the October Revolution in Turkistan], *Izvestiya Akademii Nauk Uzbekskoi SSR: Seriya obshch. nauk* [Transactions of the Academy of Sciences of the Uzbek SSR. Social science series], no. 2 (1959).

Ishanov, A. 'Pobeda narodnoi Sovetskoi revolyutsii v Bukhare [The victory of the people's soviet revolution in Bukhara], in *Materialy obedinennoi nauchnoi sessii po istorii narodov Srednei Azii i kazakhstana v ephoku sotsializma*, 56 pp., Tashkent, 1957.

————— *Sozdanie Bukharskoi Narodnoi Respubliki 1920–24 gg.* [The creation of the People's Republic of Bukhara], 155 pp., Tashkent, 1955.

Iskandarov, B. I. 'Bukhara v 1918–1920 godu: Likvidatsiya bukharskogo emirata' [Bukhara in 1918–20. The liquidation of the Bukharan Emirate], *Trudy Akademij Nauk Tadzhikskoi SSR,* no. 29 (1954).

————— *Iz istorii Bukharskogo emirata* [From the history of the Emirate of Bukhara], 132 pp., Moscow, 1958.

————— *O nekotorykh izmeneniyakh v ekonomiki vostochnoi Bukhary na rubezhe XIX–XX vv.* [On certain changes in the economy of eastern Bukhara in the late 19th and early 20th centuries], 143 pp., Stalinabad, 1958.

————— 'Podgotovka angliei bukharskogo pladtsdarma dlya interventsii v Sovietskii Turkestan 1918–1920 gg.' [The preparation of an Anglo-Bukharan bridgehead for intervention in Soviet Turkistan in 1918–20], *Istoricheskie zapiski,* no. 36 (1951).

————— *Sotsial'no ekonomicheskii i politicheskii stroi vostochnoii Bukhary i Pamira nakanune prisoedineniya Srednei Azii k Rossii* [The socio-economic and political order in eastern Bukhara and the Pamir region on the eve of Central Asia's union with Russia], Stalinabad, 1960.

————— *Vostochnaya Bukhara i Pamir v period prisoedineniya Srednei Azii k*

Rossii [Eastern Bukhara and the Pamir region in the period of Central Asia's attachment to Russia], 215 pp., Stalinabad, 1960.

Islamov, N. *Tadzhikskaya SSR: Istoriko-ekonomicheskii ocherk* [The Tadjikistan SSR: A historical and economic sketch], 196 pp. with fig. and maps, Moscow, 1958.

Ismailova, R. 'Iz istorii formirovaniya pervykh kadrov rabochego klassa v Turkestane na rubezhe XIX–XX vv' [From the history of the formation of the first cadres of the working class in Turkistan in the late 19th and early 20th centuries], *Vestnik Leningradskogo Universiteta,* no. 20/4 (1957), pp. 135–47.

Istoriya narodov Uzbekistana [History of the peoples of Uzbekistan], 2 vols, Tashkent, 1946–51.

Istoriya Sovetskoi konstitutsii [History of the Soviet constitution], Moscow, 1957.

Istoriya Uzbekskoi SSR [History of the Uzbek SSR], with maps, Tashkent, 1957.

Ivanov, P. *Iranskaya revolyutsiya 1905 goda* [The 1905 Iranian revolution], Moscow, 1957.

———— *Khozyaistvo dzhuibarskikh sheikhov* [The domain of the Juyibar sheikhs], 328 pp., Moscow/Leningrad, 1954.

———— *Ocherki po istorii Srednei Azii (XVI–XIX v.)* [Studies on the history of Central Asia], 248 pp., Moscow, 1958.

———— *Vosstanie Kitai-kipchakov v bukharskom khanstve, 1821–1825 godov; istochniki i ikh issledovaniya* [The uprising of the Khitay-Qipchaqs in the Khanate of Bukhara, 1821–5; sources and their investigation], 131 pp., Moscow, 1937.

Jarcek 'Türkistan cadidçiliginin atasi. (Munavvar Qarinin bolşeviklar tamanindan öldüruluvini' [Father of the Turkistani Jadid movement: Munavvar Qari's murder by the Bolsheviks], *Milli Turkestan,* no. 77/A (March 1952), pp.1–6.

Jaschke, G. 'Ankara und Buchara', *Die Welt des Islams,* 1923.

Javorskii, I. *Puteshestvie Russkogo posol'stva po Avganistanu i Bukharskomu khanstvu v 1878–1879 gg.* [Travels of a Russian embassy in Afghanistan and the Khanate of Bukhara in 1878–9], 2 vols, St Petersburg, 1882–3.

Jomier, J. *Le commentaire coranique du Manar* [The Koranic commentary of al-Manar], Paris, 1954.

Kaidalov, E. *Karavan-zapiski: Pokhod v bukhariyu rossiiskogo karavana v 1824–45 gg.* [Caravan notes. Journey of a Russian caravan into Bukhara in 1824–5], 3 vols, Moscow, 1828.

Kajum Khan, V. 'Milli edebiyat', *Milli Edebiyat,* no. 1 (1943), pp. 3–11.

Kakurin, N. E. 'Boevoe operatsii v Bukhare' [Military operations in Bukhara], in *Grazhdanskaya voina* [The Civil War], vol. 3, Tashkent, 1922.

Kastel'skaja 'Natsional'naya politika vremennogo pravitel'stva v Uzbekistane' [The Provisional Government's national policy in Uzbekistan], *Istoricheskii Zhurnal,* no. 2 (1937).

Khamraev, A. 'K voprosu o zemel'no-vodnykh otnosheniyakh v bukharskom khanstve v XIX veke' [On the problem of land and water relations in the Khanate of Bukhara during the nineteenth century], *Trudy SAGU,* no. 9 (1948), 31 pp.

Khanykov, N. V. *Opisanie Bukharskogo Khanstva* [Description of the Khanate of Bukhara], vi/279/iv pp., St Petersburg, 1843.

Khodzhaev, F. 'Dzhadidy' [The Jadids] *Ocherki revolyutsionnogo dvizheniya v Srednei Azii,* Moscow, 1937.

———— *K istorii revolyutsii v Bukhare* [Contribution to the history of the revolution in Bukhara], 77 pp., Tashkent, 1926.

———— *Natsional'noe razmezhevanie Srednei Azii* [The national demarcation of Central Asia], 32 pp., Bukhara, 1924.

————— 'O mlado-Bukhartsakh' [On the Young Bukharans], *Istorik marksist,* no. 1 (1956), pp. 123–41.

—————, Fedorov, S., Ryskulov, T. and Ginzburg, E. *Ocherki revolyutsionno-go dvizheniya v Srednei Azii* [Studies on the revolutionary movement in Central Asia], 152 pp., Moscow, 1926.

Kil'deev, D. *Mahomet kak prorok* [Muhammad as a prophet], St Petersburg, 1881.

Kislyakov, N. *Patriarkhal'no-feodal'nye otnosheniya sredi osedlogo sel'skogo naseleniya Bukharskogo khanstva v kontse XIX-go i nachale XX-go veka* [Patriarchal feudal relations among the settled peasant population of the Khanate of Bukhara in the late 19th and early 20th centuries], 568 pp., Moscow/Leningrad, 1962.

Klimovich, L. *Islam v Tsarskoi Rossii* [Islam in Tsarist Russia], State Anti-religious Press, Moscow, 1936.

Komitet Mlado-Bukharcev 'Vozvanie k Narodam Vostoka' [Call to the peoples of the East], *Zhizn'natsional'nostei,* no. 7/15 (2 March 1919), p. 1.

Korzhenevskii, N. *Tadzhikistan: Sbornik statei* [Tajikistan. Anthology of articles], 290 pp. with map, Tashkent, 1925.

Kostenko, A. 'Gorod Bukhara v 1870 godu' [The city of Bukhara in 1870], *Voennyi Sbornik,* no. 76 (1870), pp. 411–25.

Kostenko, L. *Puteshestvie Russkoi missii v Bukharu v 1870 godu* [Journey of the Russian mission to Bukhara in 1870], 100 pp. with map, St Petersburg, 1871.

Kozlovskii, E. *Krasnaya armiya v Srednei Azii* [The Red Army in Central Asia], Tashkent, 1928.

Krestovkii, V. *V gostyakh u emira bukharskogo (1883)* [Visiting the Emir of Bukhara], 431 pp., St Petersburg, 1887.

Ksenofontov. *Uzbekistan i Turkmenistan. K voprosu ob ikh vkhozhdenii v SSSR* [Uzbekistan and Turkmenistan. On the question of their entry into the USSR], Moscow/Leningrad, 1925.

Kuibyshev, V. 'Basmacheskii front' [The Basmachi front], *Zhizn' natsional'nostei,* no. 16/73 (1920).

Kuropatkin, A. 'Dnevnik', *Krasnyi Arkhiv,* nos. 2, 5, 7, 8 and 9 (1922–7).

'K voprosu o panislamizme', *Mir Islama.*

Lambton, A. K. S. 'The theory of kingship in the Nasihat-ul-Muluk of Ghazali', *The Islamic Quarterly,* no. 1 (1954).

Lenin, V. I. *Collected Works,* 4th edn, vol. 24, Moscow, 1964; vol. 29, Moscow, 1965; vol. 45, Moscow, 1970.

Leninskii sbornik [A Lenin anthology], 2nd edn, vol. 45, Moscow, 1925.

Lobuishevich, F. I. *Opisanie Khivinskogo Pokhoda 1873 goda* [Description of the 1873 Khiva campaign], St Petersburg, 1928.

Logofet, D. *Bukharskoe khanstvo pod russkim protektoratom* [The Khanate of Bukhara under the Russian protectorate], 2 vols, St Petersburg, 1911.

————— *Na granitsakh Srednei Azii* [On the frontiers of Central Asia], 3 vols, 245, 208 and 208 pp. with maps, St Petersburg, 1909.

————— *Strana bezpraviya: Bukharskoe khanstvo i ego sovremennoe sostoyanie* [Country without law: the Khanate of Bukhara and its present condition], vii/240 pp., St Petersburg, 1909.

————— *V gorakh i na ravninakh Bukhary* [In the mountains and on the plains of Bukhara], 619 pp., St Petersburg, 1913.

M. A. 'Nalogi v Bukhare' [Taxes in Bukhara], *Turkestanskie Vedemosti* (10, 11, and 13 January 1906).

MacGovern, V. M. *The Early Empire of Central Asia,* xiii/329 pp., Durham (N.C.), 1939.

Maclean, F. *A Person from England and Other Travellers to Turkestan,* 384 pp., London, 1957.

Maer, A. *Boevye epizody Basmachestva v Bukhare* [Episodes from the Basmachi conflict in Bukhara], 139 pp., Moscow/Tashkent, 1944.

Magidovich *Materialy po raionirovaniyu Srednei Azii* [Materials on the internal demarcation of Central Asia], Tashkent, 1926.

Maillart, E. *Des monts célestes aux sables rouges* [From celestial mountains to red sands], 300 pp., Paris, 1934.

————— *Turkestan Solo,* 335 pp., London, 1938.

Malleson, W. 'The British military mission to Turkistan 1918–1920', *Journal of the Royal Central Asian Society,* 9(1922), pp. 96–110.

Manzhara, D. *Revolyutsionnoe dvizhenie v Srednei Azii, 1905–1920. Vospominaniya* [The revolutionary movement in Central Asia, 1905–1920. Memories], 147 pp., Tashkent, 1934.

Masal'skii, V. I. *Turkestanskii Krai* [The Region of Turkistan], in V. P. Semenov-Tian-Shanskii (ed.) *Rossiya: Polnoe geograficheskoe opisanie nashego ofechestva,* St Petersburg, 1913.

Mel'kumov. *Turkestantsy* [The Turkistanis], Moscow, 1960.

Merad, A. 'L'enseignement politique de Muhammad Abduh aux Algériens (1903)' [Muhammad Abduh's political education of the Algerians], *Orient,* no. 28 (1963).

Middendorf, A. *Ocherki ferganskoi doliny* [Sketches of the Ferghana basin], St Petersburg, 1825.

Mirzaev, K. *Amlyakovaya forma feodal'noi zemel'noi sobstvennosti v bukharskom khanstve* [The *amlak* form of feudal land ownership in the Khanate of Bukhara], 105 pp., Tashkent, 1954.

————— 'Tankho, kak raznovidnost' feodal'nogo zemlevladeniya v bukharskom khanstve' [The *tankhvah* as a specific form of feudal land ownership in the Khanate of Bukhara], *Trudy Instituta Ekonomiki,* no. 3 (1952), pp. 5–22.

M. N. 'Pod znakom Islama' [Under the banner of Islam], 87 pp., *Novyi Vostok,* 1924.

Mukhsinova, K. Z. 'K istorii vystuplenii Bukharskikh krestyan protiv nalogovogo gneta v kontse XIX veka' [Contribution to the history of Bukharan peasant reactions against the burden of taxation at the end of the 19th century], *Problemy Vostokovedeniya,* no. 1 (1959).

Muminov, I. *Uzbekistanda ijtima'i falsafi tafakkurning tarihidan, XIX asrning akhirlari va XX asrning bashlari* [On the history of the development of socio-philosophical thought in Uzbekistan in the late 19th and early 20th centuries], in Uzbek, 290 pp., Tashkent, 1960.

Muraveiskii, S. *Ocherki po istorii revolyutsionnogo dvizheniya v Srednei Azii* [Studies on the history of the revolutionary movement in Central Asia], Tashkent, 1926.

————— 'Sentyabr'skie sobytie v Tashkente' [The September events in Tashkent], *Proletarskaya revolyutsiya,* no. 10 (1924).

Muzhestvennye bortsy za delo kommunizma: Sbornik statei [Manly warriors for the cause of communism. Selection of essays], Tashkent, 1957.

Narshahi, M. *Istoriya Bukhary* [History of Bukhara], translated by Likosyn, 123/11/2 pp., Tashkent, 1897.

Narzikulova and Rjazancev. *Tadzhikskaya SSR* [Tajikistan SSR], 223 pp., Moscow, 1956.

Nazmi. *Kafkasya ve Asiasi vusta ve Turkistan vilayetleri Buhara ve Hive Hanliklari Hakkunda čografi siyasi, tarihi ve istatistiki mücere malumat* [General information on geography, politics, history and statistics in the vilayets of Caucasus, Central Asia and Turkistan, in the khanates of Bukhara and Khiva and in Khoqand], in Turkish, 63 pp., Istanbul, 1934.

Nechaev, A. *Po gornoi Bukhare: Putevye ocherki* [Through the mountains of Bukhara. Travel sketches], iv/107 pp., St Petersburg, 1914.

Nepomnin, V. *Istoricheskii opyt stroitel'stva socializma v Uzbekistane* [Historical experience of the construction of socialism in Uzbekistan], Tashkent, 1960.

'Observer' (Jeyun Bay Khajibayli) 'Soviet press comments on the capture of Ibrahim Bey', *The Asiatic Review*, no. 27/92 (1931).

Ocherki revolyutsionnogo dvizheniya v Srednei Azii [Studies on the revolutionary movement in Central Asia], Moscow, 1926.

Olufsen, A. *The Emir of Bokhara and his Country*, 599 pp., Copenhagen, 1911.

Ostroumov, N. 'Musul'manskie maktaby i russko-tuzemnye shkoly v Turkestanskom kraie' [Muslim *maktabs* and native-Russian schools in the province of Turkistan], *Zhurnal Ministerstva Narodnogo Prosveshchenija*, no. 2 (1906).

Otchët o revizii Turkestanskogo Kraia proizvedennoii po vysochaishemu poveleniyu senatorom, gofmeisterom Grafom K. K. Palenom [Report on the census of the province of Turkistan carried out at the imperial command of Senator Hofmeister, Count K. K. Pahlen], St Petersburg, 1909–10.

Palyukaitis. 'Turkestan i revolyutsii Vostoka' [Turkistan and the revolutions of the East], *Zhizn' natsional' nostei*, no. 19/27 (25 May 1919).

'Panislamizm i pantyurkizm' [Pan-Islamism and pan-Turkism], *Mir Islama*, vol. 2/8 (1913).

Parks, A. *Bolshevism in Turkestan*, 428 pp., New York, 1957.

Pashitskii, A. 'Materialy po istorii Bukharskoi revolyutsii' [Materials on the history of the Bukharan revolution], *Vestnik NKID* (April–May 1922), pp. 122–36.

Pavlovskii, A. *Istoriya Bukhary ili Transoksanii s drevneishikh vremën do nastoyashchego* [History of Bukhara or Transoxania from the earliest times to the present], 2 vols, 274 and 228 pp., St Petersburg, 1873.

Peluy, L. *The Miracle Play of Hasan and Husain*, 2 vols, London, 1879.

Peters, Y. 'Stranitsa predatel'stva' [A page of treachery], *Pravda vostoka*, 16 and 18 December 1934.

Petrov, P. I. 'Bukharskii mukhtasib v nachale XX veka' [The *muhtasib* of Bukhara in the early 20th century], *Problemy Vostokovedeniya*, no. 1 (1959).

Pierce, R. *Soviet Central Asia*, Berkeley/Los Angeles, 1960.

Pigulevskaya, N. *Goroda Irana v rannem srednevekove* [The towns of Iran in the early middle ages], Moscow, 1956.

Pipes, R. *The Formation of the Soviet Union*, Cambridge, Mass., 1954.

Polovtzov, A. *The Land of Timour*, 206 pp., London, 1932.

Popov, A. N. *Snoshenie Rossii s Khivoyu i Bukharoyu pri Petre Velikom* [Russia's relations with Khiva and Bukhara at the time of Peter the Great], St Petersburg, 1853.

Poslavskii, P. *Bukhara*, 102 pp., St Petersburg, 1891.

Premier congrès des peuples de l'Orient: 1–8 septembre 1920 [First congress of the peoples of the East], Petrograd, 1921.

Programma musul'manskoi parlamentskoi fraktsii v gosudarstvennoi Dume [Programme of the Muslim parliamentary fraction in the state Duma], St Petersburg, 1909.

Protokoly s"ezdov i konferentsii vsesoyuznoi Kommunisticheskoi partii (b): Odin-natsatyi s"ezd RKP (b) [Protocols of the congresses and conferences of the All-Union Communist Party (b): eleventh congress of the RKP (b)], Moscow, 1936.

Pyaskovskii, A. *Revolyutsiya 1905–7 gg. v Turkestane* [The 1905–7 revolution in Turkistan], 616 pp., Moscow, 1958.

Radzhabov, Z. *Razvitie obshchestvennoi mysli tadzhikskogo naroda vo vtoroi polovine XIX i v nachale XX veka* [Development of social thought in the Tajik nation in the second half of the 19th and early 20th centuries], Stalinabad, 1951.

Rakhimbaev, A. R. *Tadzhikistan* [Tajikistan], Moscow, 1936.

Ramsaur, E. E. *The Young Turks: Prelude to the revolution of 1908*, Princeton, 1957.

Revolyutsiya v Srednei Azii: Sbornik [Revolution in Central Asia. An anthology], Tashkent, 1928.

Revolyutsiya 1905–1907 v Uzbekistane [The 1905–7 Revolution in Uzbekistan], Tashkent, 1955.

Rizenkampf, G. *Problemy orosheniya Turkestana* [Problems of irrigation in Turkistan], 428 pp., Moscow, 1921.

Rozhevitsa, R. 'Poezdka v yuzhnuyu i srednyuyu Bukharu v 1906 g.' [Journey in southern and central Bukhara in 1906], *Izvestiya Imperatorskago Russkago geograficheskogo obshchestva, XIX, 1908.*

Ryabinskii, A. 'Tsarskaya Rossiya i Bukhara v epokhu imperializma' [Tsarist Russia and Bukhara in the epoch of imperialism], *Istorik Marksist*, no. 4 (1941).

Ryskulov, T. 'Iz istorii bor'by za osvobozhdenie Vostoka' [From the history of the struggle for liberation of the East], *Novyi Vostok*, no. 6 (1924).

———— *Kirghizstan*, Moscow, 1935.

———— *Revolyutsiya i korennoe naselenie Turkestane* [Revolution and the native population of Turkistan], Tashkent, 1922.

Sabanin, A. (ed.) *Sbornik deistvuyushchih dogovorov i konventsii zaklyuchennikh s inostrannami gosudarstvami* [Collection of operative treaties and conventions concluded with foreign states], Moscow, 1924–8.

Safarov, G. *Kolonial'naya revolyutsiya: Opyt Turkestana* [Colonial revolution. The experience of Turkistan], 148 pp., Moscow, 1921.

———— *Problemy vostoka* [Problems of the East], Petrograd, 1922.

Saidov, Z. *Uzbek vaqitli matbu'ati tarihiga materiyallar 1870–1927* [Materials on the history of the Uzbek periodical press 1870–1927], Tashkent/Samarkand, 1927.

Samoilovich, A. 'Pervoe tainoe obshchestvo mlado-bukhartsev' [The first secret society of the Young Bukharans], *Novyi Vostok*, no. 1 (1922), pp. 97–9.

Sarty: Etnograficheskie materialy [The Sarts: Ethnographical materials]: I. *Obshchii ocherk* [General outline]; II. *Narodnye skazki sartov* [Popular tales of the Sarts]; III. *Poslovitsy i zagadki* [Proverbs and riddles]. 4 vols, 137, 272, 288 and 175 pp., Tashkent, 1890, 1896, 1908 and 1892.

Savel'ev, M. *Bukhara v 1835 godu: S prisoedineniem izvestii obo vsekh evropeiskikh puteshestvennikakh, poseshchavshikh etot gorod do 1835 goda vklyuchitel'no* [Bukhara in 1835. With additional information concerning all European travellers to have visited that city, up to and including 1835], 26 pp., St Petersburg, 1836.

Schacht, J. 'Mirath' *Encyclopaedia of Islam,* Leiden, 1913.

Schuyler, E. *Turkistan. Notes of a Journey in Russian Turkistan, Khokand, Bukhara and Kuldja,* 2 vols, 411 and 463 pp., New York, 1876.

Semenov, A. 'Bukharskii traktat o chinakh i zvaniyakh i ob obyazannostyakh ikh nositelei v Srednevekovoi Bukhare' [The Bukharan treaty on ranks and titles and on the obligations of those who hold them in mediaeval Bukhara], *Sovetskoe Vostokovedenie*, no. 5 (1948), pp. 137–50.

────── *Ocherk ustroistva central'nogo administrativnogo upravleniya bukharskogo khanstva pozdneishego vremeni* [Outline of the organization of central administrative power in the Khanate of Bukhara], 75 pp., Stalinabad, 1954.

────── *Ocherk pozemel'no podatnogo i nalogovogo ustroistva bukharskogo khanstva* [Sketch of the organization of taxes and duties on land in the Khanate of Bukhara], 54 pp., Tashkent, 1929.

Semenov, P. P. de *La Russie extra-européenne et polaire* [Extra-European and polar Russia], Paris, 1900.

Shakhnazarov, A. I. *Sel'skoe khozyaistvo v Turkestanskom krae* [Peasant economy in the region of Turkistan], St Petersburg, 1908.

Shaumian, S. *Stat'i i rechi* [Essays and speeches], Baku, 1924.

Shek, L. 'Iz istorii Bukhary v period fevral'skoi burzhuazno-demokraticheskoi revolyutsii 1917 g.' [From the history of Bukhara in the period of the February 1917 bourgeois-democratic revolution], *Trudy SAGU* (1957), pp. 57–62.

────── 'Iz istorii sovetsko-bukharskikh otnoshenii' [From the history of Soviet-Bukharan relations], *Trudy SAGU* (1956), pp. 105–28.

────── *Pobeda narodnoi sovetskoi revolyutsii v Bukhare* [Victory of the people's soviet revolution in Bukhara], 78 pp., Tashkent, 1956.

Shestakov 'Vostanie 1916 goda v Srednei Azii' [The 1916 insurrection in Central Asia], *Istorik marksist*, no. 2 (1926).

Sitnyakovskii, N. F. 'Popytki k ischisleniyu narodonaseleniya v gornoi Bukhare' [Attempts to estimate the population of upper Bukhara], *Izvestiya Turkestanskogo otdela imperatorskogo russkogo geograficheskogo obshchestva* [Proceedings of the Turkistani section of the Imperial Russian Geographical Society], no. 1 (1898), pp. 77–85.

Skopin, V. *Srednyaya Aziya i Indiya* [Central Asia and India], 266 pp., Moscow, 1904.

Skrine, F. and Ross, E. *The Heart of Asia: History of Russian Turkestan*, 449 pp., London, 1899.

Smith, W. C. *Islam in Modern History*, Princeton, 1957.

Sneysareff, Lt.-Col. *India, the Chief Factor in the Central Asian Question*, 103 pp., London, 1906.

────── *Eastern Bokhara: A military and geographical description*. Secret collection of geographical, topographical and statistical material concerning Asia, vol. 79, 135 pp., Simla, 1906–9.

Sobranie uzakonenii i rasporyazhenii rabochego i krest'yanskogo pravitel'stva RSFSR [Code of statutes and decrees of the workers' and peasants' government of the RSFSR], Moscow, 1923.

Sokol, E. D. *The Revolt of 1916 in Russian Central Asia*, Baltimore, 1954.

Soloveichik, D. 'Revolutsionnaya Bukhara' [Revolutionary Bukhara], *Novyi Vostok*, no. 2 (1922), pp. 272–89.

Stalin, J. *Works*, Moscow, 1946–51, vol. 5.

Stemberg, E. *Ocherki po istorii Turkmenii* [Studies on the history of the Turkmens], Moscow, 1934.

Suhareva, O. 'Byt' zhilogo kvartala goroda Bukhary v kontse XIX nachale XX veka' [Life in the residential areas of the city of Bukhara in the late 19th and early 20th centuries], *Akademiya Nauk SSSR, Institut Etnografii, Kratkie Soobshcheniya* [Academy of Sciences of the USSR, Institute of Ethnography, Short

Reports], 28 (1957).

————— *Islam v Uzbekistane* [Islam in Uzbekistan], 88 pp., Tashkent, 1960.

————— *K istorii gorodov bukharskogo khanstva (Buhoro khonlidzh shaharlar-ining tarikhitsa gup): Istoriko-etnograficheskie ocherki* [Contribution to the history of towns in the Khanate of Bukhara: Historico-ethnographical studies], 148 pp., Tashkent, 1959.

————— *Pozdne-feodal'nyi gorod Bukhara, kontsa XIX veka, nachala XX veka* [The late-feudal town of Bukhara in the late 19th and early 20th centuries], 194 pp., Tashkent, 1962.

Sultan Galiev, M. S. 'Metody anti-religioznoi propagandy sredi Musul'man' [Methods of anti-religious propaganda among the Muslims], *Zhizn' natsional'nostei* (14 and 23 December 1921).

Tadzhikistan: Sbornik statei s kartoi [Tajikistan. Anthology of articles with map], 290 pp., *Obshchestvo dlya izucheniya Tadzhikistana i iranskikh narodnostei za ego predelami* [Society for the study of Tajikistan and the Iranian nationalities outside its borders], Tashkent, 1925.

Terent'ev, M. A. *Istoriya zavoevaniya Srednei Azii* [History of the conquest of Central Asia], 3 vols, St Petersburg, 1906.

Togan, A. Z. V. *Bugünkü Türkili (Türkistan) ve yakin tarihi* [Contemporary Turkistan and its recent history], 696 pp., Istanbul, 1942–7.

————— *Türkili haritasi ve ona ait izahlar,* Istanbul, 1943.

Toynbee, A. 'Islam, the West and the future', in A. Toynbee (ed.), *Civilization on Trial,* London, 1948.

Trial of the Bloc of Rightists and Trotskyites, Moscow, 1938.

Tsavikyan, H. M. 'Vliyanie russkoi revolyutsii 1905 goda na revolyutsionnoie dvizyenie v Turtsii' [The influence of the 1905 Russian Revolution on the revolutionary movement in Turkey], *Sovetskoe Vostokovedenie,* no. 3 (1945).

Tursunov, H. 'Natsional'noe razmezhevanie Srednei Azii i obrazovanie Uzbekskoi SSR' [The national demarcation of Central Asia and the formation of the Uzbek SSR], *Voprosy Istorii,* no. 10 (1954), pp. 38–49.

Tyagunenko, V. *Obrazovanie Uzbekskoi SSR* [The formation of the Uzbek SSR], 243 pp., Tashkent, 1957.

————— 'Aktual'nye voprosy nekapitalisticheskogo puti razvitiya' [Current problems of the non-capitalist path of development], *Mirovaya ekonomika i mezhdunarodnye otnosheniya,* no. 10 (1964).

Umnyakov, I. 'K istorii novometodnoi shkoly v Bukhare' [Contribution to the history of the reformed schools in Bukhara], *Byulleten' SAGU,* no. 16 (1927), pp. 81–99.

Uzbekskaya SSR, vol. 15, part D: *narodnost', yazyk, vozrast, gramotnost'* [The Uzbek SSR: nationality, language, age, literacy], 200 pp., Moscow, 1928.

Vakhabov, M. G. *Tashkent v period trëkh revolyutsii* [Tashkent in the period of three revolutions], Tashkent, 1957.

Vambéry, A. *Central Asia and the Anglo-Russian Frontier Question,* 385 pp., London, 1874. German translation, 351 pp., Leipzig, 1873.

————— *Istoriya Bukhary ili Transoksanii s drevneishikh vremën do nastoyash-chego* [History of Bukhara or Transoxania, from the earliest times to the present], 247 pp., St Petersburg, 1873. German translation, 248 pp., Stüttgart, 1872. English translation, *History of Bokhara,* New York, 1973.

————— *La lutte future pour la possession de l'Inde* [The coming struggle for the possession of India], 296 pp., Paris, 1885.

————— *Voyages d'un faux derviche dans l'Asie centrale de Téhéran à Khiva,*

Bukhara et Samarkand par le grand désert turcoman, 402 pp., Paris, 1863. Russian text, ii/ii/221 pp., published St Petersburg, 1865. English translation, *Travels in Central Asia*, London, 1864.

Vasilevskii, K. 'Fazy basmacheskogo dvizheniya v Srednei Azii' [The stages of the Basmachi movement in Central Asia], *Novyi Vostok*, no. 29 (1929), pp. 121–41.

Vernier, B. *Kédar. Carnets d'un mehariste syrien* [Qadar. Notebooks of a member of the Syrian Camel Corps], Paris, 1938.

Virolleaud, C. *La passion de l'émir Hossein* [The miracle play of Emir Husayn], Paris, 1927.

Voina v peskakh. Materialy k istorii grazhdanskoi voiny. Grazhdanskaya voina v Srednei Azii [War in the sands. Materials for the history of the civil war. The civil war in Central Asia], 541 pp., Leningrad, 1935.

Vooruzhennye sily bukharskogo khanstva [The armed forces of the Khanate of Bukhara], Tashkent, 1920.

Vostanie 1916 goda v Srednei Azii i Kazakhstane [The 1916 insurrection in Central Asia and Kazakhstan], Moscow, 1960.

Vyatkin, V. L. 'Karshinskii okrug, organizatsiya v něm voiska i sobytiya v period 1215–1217 (1800–1803) godov' [The Karshinski district, internal organization, army and events in the period 1215–17/1800–03], *Izvestiya sredneaziatskogo otdela Russkogo geograficheskogo obshchestvo* [Proceedings of the Central Asian section of the Russian Geographical Society], no. 28, Tashkent, 1928.

Wessels. *Early Jesuit Travellers in Central Asia, 1603–1721*, xvi/344 pp., The Hague, 1924.

Woeikof, A. *Le Turkestan russe* [Russian Turkistan], Paris, 1914.

Wolff, J. *Mission to Bukhara*, 515 pp., London, 1845.

Zarubin, L. *Spisok narodnostei Turkestanskogo kraya* [List of nationalities of the Turkistan region], 24 pp., Leningrad, 1925.

Zavqi, A. and Tolqun, I. 'Shair Colpan', *Milli Türkestan*, 76, 51/52, pp. 17–23.

Zel'kina 'Zemel'naya reforma v Srednei Azii' [Land reform in Central Asia], *Revolyutsionnoi Vostok*, no. 3 (1928).

Zeman, Z. A. B. *Germany and the Revolution in Russia 1915–1918*, London, 1958.

Zenkovsky, S. 'Kulturkampf in pre-revolutionary Central Asia', *American Slavic and East European Review*, no. 14 (1954), pp. 15–42.

———— *Pan-Turkism and Islam in Russia*, 345 pp., Cambridge Mass., 1960.

Zhitov, K. *Pobeda velikoi oktyabr'skoi revolyutsii v Uzbekistane* [Victory of the Great October Revolution in Uzbekistan], 232 pp., Tashkent, 1927.

Zhukovskii, S. *Snosheniya Rossii s Bukharoi i Khivoi za poslednee trëkhsotletie* [Russia's relations with Bukhara and Khiva during the last three centuries], 214 pp., Petrograd, 1915.

Zuev, D. 'Krasnaya gvardiya Turkestana' [The Turkistan Red Guard], *Novyi Mir*, nos. 6/7 (1929).

Supplementary Select Bibliography

Akiner, S. *The Islamic Peoples of the Soviet Union*, 1984.

Allworth, E. (ed.) *Ethnic Russia in the USSR: the dilemma of dominance*, New York/Oxford, 1980.

———————— (ed.) *The Nationality Question in Soviet Central Asia*, New York, 1973.

———————— *Uzbek Literary Politics*, The Hague, 1964.

Ashirov, N. *Evoliutsiya Islama v SSSR* [The evolution of Islam in the USSR], Moscow, 1972.

Becker, S. *Russia's Protectorates in Central Asia: Bukhara and Khiva, 1865–1924*, Cambridge, Mass., 1968.

Bennigsen, A. 'The Crisis of the Turkic national epics: 1951–1952: local nationalism or internationalism?', *Canadian Slavic Papers*, no. 19 (1975), pp. 463–75.

———————— and Lemercier-Quelquejay, C. *Islam in the Soviet Union*, New York/ London, 1967.

———————— and Lemercier-Quelquejay, C. *La Presse et le mouvement national chez les Musulmans de Russie avent 1920*, The Hague, 1964.

———————— and Winbush, S. E. *Muslim National Communism in the Soviet Union: a revolutionary strategy for the colonial world*, Chicago/London, 1979.

———————— and Winbush, S. E. *Muslims of the Soviet Empire: a guide*, London, 1985.

Carrère d'Encausse, H. *L'empire éclaté*: [The shattered empire], Paris, 1978.

Critchlow, J. 'Signs of emerging nationalism in the Moslem Soviet Republics', in T. D. Norton (ed.), *The Soviets in Asia*, Mechamicsville, Md., 1972, pp. 18–29.

———————— 'Uzbeks and Russians', *Canadian Slavonic Papers*, no. 17 (1975), pp. 366–74.

Demko, G. J. *The Russian Colonization of Kazakhstan 1896–1916*. Bloomington, 1969.

Fierman, W. 'Two young Uzbek writers: perspectives on assimilation', *Central Asian Survey*, vol. 2, no. 3 (Nov 1983), pp. 63–79.

Hambly, G. et al. *Central Asia*, London, 1969.

Hayit, B. 'Demographic and economic situation of the Muslims of Turkestan', *ABN Correspondence*, vol. 23, nos 1–2, (Jan–April 1982).

———————— 'Some reflections on the subject of the Annexation of Turkestan and Kazakhstan by Russia', *Central Asian Survey*, vol. 3, no. 4, (Nov 1984), pp. 61–77.

Inojatov, H. *Central Asia and Kazakhstan Before and After the October Revolution (Reply to Falsifiers of History)*, Moscow, 1967.

———————— *Towards Freedom and Progress (the Triumph of Soviet Power in Central Asia)*, Moscow, 1970.

Istoriya Uzbekskoi SSR [The history of the Uzbek SSR], 4 vols, Tashkent, 1967–68.

Istoriya Bukharskoi i Khorezmskoi Narodnykh Sovetskikh Respublik [History of the peoples of the Soviet Republic of Bukhara and Khvarazm], Moscow, 1971.

Junger, H. (ed.) *The Literatures of the Soviet Peoples: a historical and biographical survey*, New York, 1970.

Karklins, R. *Ethnic Relations in the USSR: the view from below*, London, 1985.

Katz, Z. (ed.) *Handbook of Major Soviet Nationalities*, London/New York, 1975.

Lane, D. *Politics and Society in the USSR* (revised and updated edn), London, 1978.

Lemercier-Quelquejay, Ch. et al. (eds) *Turco-Tatar Past, Soviet Present: studies presented to Alexandre Bennigsen*, 564 pp., Paris, 1986.

McCagg, W. A. and Silver, B. D. (eds) *Soviet-Asian Ethnic Frontiers*, New York/ Oxford, 1979.

Medlin, W. K. et al. *Education and Development in Central Asia: a case study of social change in Uzbekistan*, Leiden, 1971.

Nove, A. and Newth, J. A. *The Soviet Middle East: A Model for Development?* London, 1967.

Pierce, R. A. *Soviet Central Asia: A Bibliography*, Berkley, 1966.

Rahman, F. 'Evolution of Soviet policy towards Muslims in Russia, 1917–1965', *Journal of the Institute of Muslim Minority Affairs*, King Abdulaziz University, Jeddah, vol. 1, no. 2, (1980), pp. 28–46.

Rakowska-Harmstone, T. *Russia and Nationalism in Central Asia: The Case of Tadzhikistan*, Baltimore, 1970.

—————— 'Islam and nationalism: Central Asia and Kazakhstan under Soviet rule', *Central Asian Survey*, vol. 2, no. 2 (Sept. 1983), pp. 7–89.

Ro'i, Y. (ed.) *The USSR and the Muslim World*, London, 1984.

Rywkin, M. *Russia in Central Asia*, New York, 1973.

—————— 'First Muslims or first Soviet', *Journal of Muslim Minority Affairs*, vol. 3, no. 2, (Winter 1981), pp. 277–79.

Saray, M. 'The Russian conquest of Central Asia', *Central Asian Survey*, vol. 2, no. 2, (Sept. 1983), pp. 7–89.

Soper, J. 'Shakeup in the Uzbek literary elite', *Central Asian Survey*, vol. 1, no. 4, (April 1983), pp. 59–83.

Tillett, L. *The Great Friendship: Soviet Historians on the Non-Russian Nationalities*, Chapel Hill, 1969.

Vaidyanath, R. *The Formation of the Soviet Central Asian Republics: a study in Soviet nationalities policy, 1917–1936*, New Delhi, 1976.

Wheeler, G. *The Peoples of Soviet Central Asia*, London, 1966.

—————— *The Modern History of Soviet Central Asia.* London, 1974.

Winbush, S. E. 'The politics of identity change in Soviet Central Asia', *Central Asian Survey*, vol. 3, no. 3, (July 1984), pp. 69–79.

—————— *The Peoples of the USSR: an ethnographic handbook*, New York, 1984.

Glossary of Arabic, Persian and Turkish Terms

'adat, custom.

akhund, a member of the religious class.

'alaf-puli, a tax on vegetable plots, orchards and fields.

'alim (pl. *'ulama'*), a learned man, one learned in religious law.

amaj, a wooden plough.

'amal, an official task or function.

'amaldar, a functionary of the state.

aminana, a bazaar tax.

amir (emir), a prince, chief, commander.

amlak (sing. *milk*), state lands. The usage is specific to Central Asia.

amlakana, tax paid by cultivators of *amlak* land.

amlakdar, an official in charge of state lands.

aqsaqal, elder, village headman.

araba, a cart.

'askar, army.

'askariyya, pertaining to the army.

ataliq, state functionary attached to the office of the *qush-begi,* major-domo.

bahadur, title of a lower-ranking member of the state hierarchy.

baj, a toll; customs duty.

bay, title given to the lowest ranking officials of the Manghit court. Also a rich man or a man of high status.

bunak, credit extended to peasants or craftsmen by landlords and merchants.

charakar, contraction of *chahar va yak kar*; an agricultural labourer who receives one-quarter of the produce.

chigin, sledge.

chihra-aghasi-bashi, a civil or military rank; literally one in charge of 20–30 persons.

dadkhvah, a rank in the military-bureaucratic hierarchy; literally a plaintiff or petitioner.

dahbashi, head of a unit of ten; functionary in charge of nine men.

dar al-harb, 'the abode of war'; lands in which Islamic law is not in force.

dar al-islam, 'the abode of Islam'; lands in which Islamic law is in force.

darugha, a tax collector. In the nineteenth century this usage appears to have been confined to Central Asia; in Persia at this time the *darugha,* an urban official, performed functions resembling those of a modern police officer.

das, billhook, scythe.

255

dihqan, villager, peasant.

divanbegi, head of the civil bureaucracy.

du'akhvan, a lesser member of the religious class, a prayer-reader.

falbin, fortune-teller.

fatva, a ruling on a point of religious law.

fuqara (sing. *faqir*), the poor, the lower classes.

hashar, corvee.

ijtihad, independent interpretation by a properly qualified *'alim* (known as a *mujtahid*) on matters relating to religious law or doctrine.

ilat (sing. *il*), nomadic tribes.

imarat-panah, a category of military and court ranks; literally, 'refuge of power'.

inaq, a rank in the military-bureaucratic hierarchy of the Manghit state.

ishan, sufi master; title given to an older member of a sufi order. The usage is confined to Central Asia.

ishan-ra'is, chief of Bukhara's police forces.

ishik-aghasi-bashi (ishaq bashi), a rank in the military-bureaucratic hierarchy of the Manghit state.

istinaf, court of appeal.

jadid, a modernist.

jarib, a measure of land equivalent to approximately 144 yards.

jibachi (sometimes *jabbachi*), a rank in the military-bureaucratic hierarchy of the Manghit state; literally, keeper of the armoury or arsenal.

jizya, poll tax paid by non-Muslim minorities.

jul, a tax levied for the maintenance of troops.

kafir, unbeliever, non-Muslim.

kafshan, a tax in kind levied on cultivators of state (*amlak*) lands by *amalakdars*.

ketmen, ploughshare.

kharaj, land tax.

khish-puli, a tax on draught animals.

khvaja, a gentleman. The *khvajas* of Bukhara claimed descent from the Arab conquerors.

kupruk-puli, bridge toll, customs duty.

kushachi, an agricultural labourer; one who collects fallen remains after the harvest.

lashkar, army.

madrasa, a college of religious learning.

majlis, assembly; in modern usage a parliament.

maktab, an elementary Koranic school.

milk, landed property; privately owned as opposed to state land.

milk-i hurr va khalis, free land; land from which *kharaj* has been remitted.

milk-i kharaji, privately-owned land subject to the *kharaj* or land tax.

milk-i kharaj-i sulhi, land surrendered at the time of the Arab conquest by treaty rather than by force.

milk-i nim-kharaji, privately-owned land partially exempted from tax.

milk-i 'ushri, privately-owned land subject to the tithe.

min-bashi, official in charge of a group of villages; literally, 'leader of a thousand'.

mir, provincial governor. Also one claiming descent from any of the first three caliphs.

mirab, official responsible for distributing water.

mirabana, a tax levied to support the *mirab.*

mirakhur, a rank in the military-bureaucratic hierarchy of the Manghit state; literally, master of the horse.

mirshab, head of the night police.

mirza, a scribe.

mirzabashi, a rank in the civil bureaucracy; an official in charge of the registration and keeping of documents.

mubarizat-panah, 'refuge of war', the lowest category of military and court ranks in the Manghit state.

mudarris, teacher; one who has charge of a *madrasa.*

mufti, a high-ranking religious official qualified to issue a *fatva.*

muhtasib, official charged with the supervision of moral behaviour and the supervision of markets (known in Bukhara as the *ra'is*).

mulla, a lesser member of the religious class.

multani, Hindus originating from the province of Multan; sometimes applied in Central Asia to all Hindus.

murid, disciple.

mushtibar, a tax in kind amounting to one-fifth of the harvest.

musta 'jir, tax collector, tax farmer.

mutavalli, administrator of a *vaqf.*

namaz, prayers.

nawkar, temporary troops.

pakhtakash, a petty intermediary in the cotton trade.

panjah, pitchfork.

parvanachi, title given to high-ranking officials in the Manghit state.

qadimi, a traditionalist, a conservative.

qalandar, a wandering ascetic.

qara-chirik, troops.

qaravul-begi, a rank in the military-bureaucratic hierarchy of the Manghit state; an officer in command of between 100 and 200 troops.

qazi, judge applying *shar'* law.

qazi-kalan, chief *qazi* of Bukhara.

qhazavat (syn. *jihad*), holy war.

qishlaq, in Bukhara a village; the term usually means the winter quarters of a nomadic tribe.

qul-i qush-begi, official attached to the office of the *qush-begi.*

quriltay, an assembly.

qush-begi, chief official of the Bukharan state.

ra'is, chief local official of a town.

rivayat, a religious opinion formed on the basis of the traditions or *hadith.*

sadr, a high-ranking cleric.

salat, the ritual prayer of Islam.

sarbaz, soldier, infantryman.

sayyid, a descendant of the prophet through his daughter Fatima.

shahsay-vahsay, colloquial term used in Turkish-speaking areas of northern Iran and Central Asia for the *taqziya* or Shi'i passion play performed in memory of the martyrdom of the Imam Husayn. Contraction of *Shah Husayn va Shah Hasan.*

shaman, a seer; in Shamanism one who mediates between man and the world of spirits.

shari'at, the law of Islam.

shaykh al-islam, religious official presiding over *shar'i* courts.

sipah, army.

sudur, a high-ranking cleric.

supar, a ploughshare.

tajik, term applied in the Saljuq period to non-Turks and in the Ilkhanid period to non-Mongols. It was later used in Central Asia to denote a Persian as opposed to an Arab or Turk.

tullab (sing. *talaba*), religious students.

tanab, a measure of land equivalent to 60 by 60 *zar,* or a little over one acre.

tanaf-puli, a tax on vegetable crops.

tankhvah, an assignment of state land. The usage is confined to Central Asia.

taqlid, acceptance of religious doctrine as laid down by a school or earlier authority, or of the pronouncements and practices of a religious scholar.

tarazudar, intermediary dealing in cotton; literally, 'one who owns scales'.

tupchi-bashi, commander of the artillery.

tuqsaba, a rank in the military-bureaucratic hierarchy; an official in charge of a section of the civil bureaucracy.

tura, honoured member of a Sufi order; literally, a prince or beloved child.

uraq, a title granted to members of the religious classes by the Emir; also a sickle.

'ushr, tithe.

vakil, deputy, representative.

vaqf, religious endowment.

vaqf-i mutlaq, a religious endowment made in perpetuity.

vilayat, province.

vizarat-panah, highest category of ranks in the civil bureaucracy; office of the *qush-begi.*

yakshira, tax on animals.

yarmichi, sharecropper; one who takes half the produce.

zakat, obligatory alms paid by Muslims on various forms of property for

purposes outlined in the Koran IX, 60. In Bukhara the term was
generalized to all kinds of tax.

zakatchi, collector of the *zakat.* In Bukhara the term was applied to all tax
collectors.

zakatshakan, taxes levied locally for the payment of officials.

zarkharid, a slave; literally, 'purchased with gold'.

zikr, a Sufi ceremony at which, following the commandment 'Remind
thyself of thy Lord when thou forgettest' (Koran XVII, 24), litanies are
recited to the name of God.

Index of Subjects

Administration, 25-31, 90-1
Afghanistan, 37, 39, 40, 41, 46, 61, 102, 131, 152, 153, 160, 161, 176, 178, 186
Afghans, 15, 24, 104
'A'ila (Fitrat), 111
Aktubinsk, 160
Alexandria, 80
America, 104
Amu Darya, 1, 24, 37, 38, 39, 40, 41
Andalusia, 105, 108
Andijan, 39, 66, 67, 68, 82
Arabic language, 85, 87, 106-7
Arabs, 1, 17, 28
Armenians, 40
Ashkhabad, 39, 160
Ashtarkhanids, 2
Aulie-Ata, 66
Ayvaje, 40
Azarbayjan, 72
Azaris, 104

Babism, 79, 93
Baghchesaray, 82, 88
Bahsu, 43
Baku, 101, 160
Baku Congress, 162, 165-6, 167, 191-2
Baljuan, 27, 35, 179
Balkh, 37, 39
banking, 42-3; Azov and Don Commercial Bank, 42-3; Russian Foreign Trade Bank, 42-3; Russo-Asiatic Bank, 41-2; Siberian Commercial Bank, 42-3; State Bank, 42, 171; Volga and Kama Commercial Bank, 42
Barakat, 92, 103-4
Bashkirs, 181
Basmachi movement, 73, 75, 164, 176-80, 181, 190
Batum, 178
Bayanat-i Sayyah-i Hindi (Fitrat), 103, 107, 108-9
Baysun, 177, 179
Bogaran, 40
Bolsheviks, xvi-xviii, 125, 126, 138-40, 148-66; and national self-

determination, 150-2; revision of Muslim policies, 180-4
bourgeoisie, 19-20, 45-6, 53, 77, 83, 85, 91-2, 95, 99-100, 102-4, 126, 171, 172, 182-3, 189-91
Britain, 37, 39, 152, 160, 164
Bukhara: end of emirate, 163-5; establishment of protectorate, 37-9; population of, 1, 16; travellers' descriptions, xii, xix, 2, 7
Bukhara, People's Republic of, 159, 166, 167-84, 188-9; treaty of alliance with RSFSR, 175-6; integration into Soviet Union, 183-4;
Bukharan Communist Party (BCP), 163, 164, 167-8, 177, 180, 182-3

Cairo, 80, 108
capitalism, 39-46
Caucasus, 178
Charju'i, 23, 27, 39, 40-1, 43, 125, 138, 143, 151, 156, 157, 160, 163, 164, 167, 168
China, 109, 127, 161
Chorzoy, 41
Christians, 20, 47
Chubak, 40
clan organization, 16-17
Committee for Defence of the Fatherland and the Revolution, 151
Committee for Defence of the Rights of the Muslim Peoples of Russia, 119
Conference of Muslim Communists of Central Asia, 161, 162
Conference of Muslims of Central Asia, 150, 151
Congress of Muslims, 143
Congress of the Toilers of Bukhara, 168
Constantinople, 88, 92, 97, 100, 101, 104, 119
Constitutional-Democrats, 76, 80, 122-3
Corvee, 12, 15, 23, 31, 41, 49-50, 53
Council of Political Organizations, 123

261

Council of Soldier Deputies, 123
Council of Worker Deputies of
    Tashkent, 123
Crimea, 86
customs system, 40

Darvas, 17
Duma, 76-7, 80-1, 99

Economic Council of Central Asia, 183
Egypt, 108

Ferghana, 33, 66, 73, 74, 75, 124, 178
Finland, 120
First World War, 94, 103, 104, 105,
    115, 116, 119-21, 124, 186
France, 104

Germany, 173
Gijuvan, 98, 164
Gurkhans, 2
gypsies, 20

Hatyrchi, 157
Herat, 39
Hindus, 1, 20
Hisar, 27, 38, 52

India, 34, 37, 41, 56, 61, 64, 102, 108,
    161, 186, 188
Indians, 104
industrialization, 433
inheritance laws, 13
Iran, 61, 88, 92, 116, 151, 152, 153, 161,
    186
Islam, 1, 31-5, 44-5, 48-9; crisis of, 55-
    68, 78-82, 105-16, 185-92; and
    reformed schools, 82-8; Shi'a, 31, 56,
    97, 100, 108, 126, 133, 190;
    Sunni, 16, 31-3, 97, 99-100, 108, 190;
    Sunni–Shi'a relations, 85, 89-90, 97,
    112
Istanbul, 80
Istiqlal Qomitasi, 167
Ittifaq al-Muslimin (Muslim
    Union), 76, 80, 151
Ittihad va Taraqqi (Union and
    Progress), 163, 181

Jadid movement, xiv-xv, xvi, xviii, 78-
    81, 88, 91-116, 120, 123, 124, 126-66,
    180, 188-91
Jam'iyat-i Tarbiyat-i Atfal (Society for

the Education of Youth), 92-6
Jews, 1, 20-1, 40, 126, 133, 134
Jizakh, 37, 38, 120, 123
Ju'ibar, 29, 33

Kabul, 39
Kafiristan, 24
Kafirnigan, 51
Kagan, 40, 41, 89, 131, 134, 138, 142,
    155, 156, 157
Kalmyks, 24, 115
Karaman, 157
Katta Qurghan, 23, 38, 151
Kazakh SSR, 184
Kazan, 86
Kelif, 40
Kenegesh, 16, 98
Kerki, 35, 40, 41, 43, 52, 98, 125, 143
Kermine, 23
Khiva, 8, 17, 25, 38, 47, 48, 129, 167
Khoqand, 13, 25, 35, 37, 38, 47, 48, 67,
    151, 152, 153, 154, 157
Khurasan, 23
Khvajagan brotherhood, 33-4
Khvarazm, 33, 183
Kirghiz SSR, 184
Kirghizis, 1, 120-1, 181
Komitet po Bukharskim voprosam
    (Committee for Bukharan
    Affairs), 140
Krasnovodsk, 39
Kubrawiyya brotherhood, 33
Kushki, 39

land tenure, 9-15, 21-2, 24
Lausanne Conference, 119-20
League of Nations, 152, 158
Lezghins, 133
Loqays, 179

Manghits, 3, 16, 17, 25, 28, 98
Margelan, 66
Ma'rifat, 92, 103-4
Marv, 31, 35, 39, 156
Mashhad, 39
Mensheviks, 123, 124, 148
Mikhailovsky gulf, 39
Mongols, 2
Moscow, 143, 159, 174, 176
Munazara (Fitrat), 103, 106, 108, 111,
    112
Muslim Socialist Movement, 123-4
Musulman Dini Idarasi, 77

Namangan, 66
Naqshbandi brotherhood, 33-4, 108-9
New Economic Policy (NEP), 180
Nizhny-Novgorod, 40
nomads, 16-17, 21-2, 25-6, 33, 120-1
Novaya Bukhara, 40, 41, 82, 101, 125, 127, 134, 135, 137, 138, 139, 153, 154, 163
Novy Margelan, 39
Nubi, 43

Orenburg, 39, 40, 86, 88, 128, 151, 160
Osh, 66
Ottomanism, 58, 60

Palen Commission, 75
pan-Islamism, 58-68, 102, 112-14, 163, 181
pan-Turkism, 58-68, 101, 104, 162, 173, 178-9, 181, 184
Panj, 17, 40, 43
Pata-Hisar, 40, 41
peasantry, 44-6, 49-53, 124-6, 136-7, 171. *See also* corvee; land tenure; revolts; taxation
People's Commisariat for Foreign Affairs, 160
Persian language, 86, 87, 88, 97, 101, 103, 172, 184
Persians, 1, 17, 23, 29, 40, 89, 133
Pidarkush, 104
Poland, 162
press, 78-82, 100-2; *al-Manar*, 108; *Asiya*, 79; *Bukhara-yi Sharif*, 101-2; *Chardzhuiskii Listok*, 138; *Habl al-Matin*, 102; *Irshad*, 79; *Izvestiya*, 165; *Khurshid*, 79, 80; *Mulla Nasr al-Din*, 85; *Pravda*, 167; *Qanun*, 66, 102; *Shuhrat*, 79, 80; *Siraj al-Akhbar*, 102; *Sirat-i Mustaqim*, 102; *Taraqqi*, 79, 80; *Tarjuman*, 60, 65, 79, 85; *Tujjar, 79, 81; Turan*, 97, 101-2; *Turkestanskie Vedemosti*, 120; *Ulfat*, 79; *Vaqit*, 88; *Yulduz*, 79
Provisional Government, 121-47, 148
public health campaigns, 52
Pustinduzan, 82

Qadiriyya brotherhood, 33
Qandahar, 39
Qarakul, 98
Qara Kum, 1, 39

Qarategin, 17, 177
Qarshi, 23, 156
Qislaq Ayvaj, 76
Qiyamat (Fitrat), 109
Qizil Arvat, 39
Qizil Kum, 1
Qizil Teppe peace treaty, 156-7, 158, 160
Qizilsu, 40, 43
Qulab, 27
Qulab-Darya, 43

Rahbar-i Nijat (Fitrat), 103, 111
revolts, 2, 35-6, 49-51, 72-6, 90, 120-1
Revkom, 151, 155, 167-71, 177
Rushan, 17, 76
Russian Communist Party (Bolsheviks) — RCP (b), 161-3, 180, 183
Russian Imperial Political Agency, 46-7
Russian language, 97
Russian revolution (1905), 71, 72, 77, 79, 116, 186; (February 1917), 121-6, 127, 134, 145, 146, 147; (October 1917), 148-65, 187
Russians: political deportees, 72; relations with indigenous population, xvii-xviii, 47-53, 150-9, 161-2, 188; workers in Turkistan, 40-1, 43, 125-6, 148-53
Russo-Japanese War, 64, 71, 77, 186

St Petersburg (Petrograd), 46, 47, 48, 122, 128, 130, 135, 140, 145, 146, 149
Samarqand, 23, 33, 35, 38, 39, 41, 50, 65, 73, 74, 82, 88, 98, 101, 120, 121, 124, 128, 131, 135, 137, 144, 151, 156
Sanusis, 57-8
Saray, 40, 43
Sayha (Fitrat), 103, 111
schools, 82-8, 96-100
Semirechye, 74, 160
Shahrisabz, 27, 35, 38, 98
Shakar-Bazr, 164
Shamanism, 34, 52
Shawra-yi Islam (Muslim Council), 123, 150-1, 163
Shirabad, 22, 76
Shirbudun, 27
Shirkat-i Bukhara-yi Sharif (Union of Bukhara the Noble), 87-8, 92
Siberia, 67
Sir Darya, 65, 74
Siyahatnama-i Ibrahim Beg

(Maragha'i), 103
slavery, 17, 23-4, 29, 89-90
Social-Democrats, 123, 125, 138-9
social structure, 16-24, 44-6
Socialist-Revolutionaries, 79, 123-4,
    148, 149, 150, 161, 163
Society for Disseminating Knowledge
    Among the Masses,   92
soviets, 122, 123, 131, 135, 138-40, 144,
    145-6, 148-9, 150-1, 159, 168-9
Sovnarkom, 150, 152, 154-9
Sredazbyuro (Central Asian
    Bureau), 182
Sufism, 33-4, 55, 108-9
Sujnan, 76

Tajik SSR, 184
Tajiks, 1, 17, 28, 177
Tashkent, 39, 46, 48, 65, 77, 79, 82, 98,
    121, 122, 123, 140, 148, 149, 150, 151,
    152, 153, 154, 156, 159, 160, 161, 162,
    163, 165, 167, 181
Tatars, 40, 58-61, 64-5, 78-9, 82-8, 104
taxation, 9-13, 19, 20, 22-3, 28, 29-31,
    35, 49
Termez, 40, 41, 43, 125
theatre, 104-5
Tokmak, 82
trade, 40, 42-3, 44, 174-5
Trans-Caspia, 74, 160
Trans-Caspian railway, 39, 42
Tsaritsyn, 160
Turco-Soviet Treaty, 178
*Turkestanskii Kraevoi Sovet rabochikh i
    soldatskikh deputatov*, 140
Turkey, 58, 60, 61, 65, 67, 78, 82, 85,
    88, 92, 100, 102, 104, 106, 115, 116,
    178, 186
Turkish Communist Party, 163
Turkistan, Autonomous Republic, 159

Turkistan Communist Party, 181
*Turkistan Musulman Markazi
    Shawrasi*, 123
Turkistan Sosyalistar Tudasi (Turkistan
    League of Socialists), 181
Turkkommission (Turkish
    Commission), 162-3, 179-80
Turkmen SSR, 184
Turkmens, 1, 23, 28, 35, 177

Ufa, 86
Ukraine, 162
Jam'iyat-i 'Ulma, 123
Union of the Archangel Saint
    Michael, 149
Union of Muslim Workers (MSM), 124
Union of Nations, 119, 120
Uratube, 37, 38
Uzbek language, 86, 101, 172
Uzbek SSR, 184
Uzbeks, xvi-xvii, 1, 3, 16, 17, 21, 28,
    71, 79, 81, 82, 83, 85

Vahsh, 51
Vakhan, 76

Wahhabis, 56, 57, 60, 68, 108
women, 34, 104, 113, 169-72

Yaksu, 43
Yassawiyya brotherhood, 33
Young Bukharans, 78, 88, 127-30, 132-
    8, 140, 142-4, 153-7, 167, 170, 177
Young Turks, 85, 88, 93, 96-7, 100,
    126, 147

Zarafshan, 1, 14, 21, 39, 50
Ziandan, 98
Zaydis, 108

Index of Names

'Abdallah Khvaja Tura, 138
'Abd al-Ahad, Emir, 48, 51, 68, 83, 84, 89, 106, 114
'Abd al-Malik Khan, 38
'Abd al Qadir Qushbegi-ughli, 173
'Abd al-Qasim, Shaykh, 97-8
'Abd al-Rafiq, Damulla, 86
'Abd al-Vasi, 35
'Abduh, Muhammad, 108, 113
Abdurrahimov, Mirza 'Abd al-Rahim, 170
Abdurrahmanov, 155
Abdurrashidov, Munavvar Qari 'Abd al-Rashid Khan-ughli, 79, 80, 82, 86-7, 88, 120, 173
Abijan Mahmud, 120
Abramov, A.K., General, 38
Abu Hanifa, 32
Ahmadjan Makhdum, 87, 92
al-Afghani, Jamal al-Din, 56-7, 60, 64, 66, 112-13
'Alim 'Ashgur-ughli, 170
'Alim Khan, Emir, 17, 90-1, 97, 114-15, 140-1, 146-7, 152, 154, 155, 156, 157, 158, 160, 177
Amanallah, King of Afghanistan, 102
Anenkov, 160
Arapov, 45
Arifov, 'Abd al-Hamid, 167, 168
Arsharuni, A., 59
Astanqul Bay, 85
Aviccena (Abu 'Ali Sina al-'Arabi), 105
'Ayni, Sadr al-Din, 31, 88, 94, 95, 96, 98, 100, 105, 113, 134
Azimbaev, Mir Sayyid 'Azimbay, 79, 80, 81

Baba Beg, 38
Bajazitov, 65
Barelawi, Ahmad, 61
Barthold, V.V., 11, 17, 39, 80, 174
Belinskii, 63
Bihbudi, Mufti, 80, 88, 104, 120, 123, 133
Brojdo, G.I., 123, 146

Bukeykhanov, Alikhan, 123
Burhan al-Din, 98
Burkhanov, 'Abd al-Rashid Burhan, 95, 127, 130, 133, 134, 142
Burnashev, Burnash-ughli, 82-3

Chernaev, M.G., General, 37
Chernyshevskii, N.G., 63
Chingiz Khan, 17, 178
Chirkin, 139
Chokay-ughli, Mustafa, 123

Danish, Ahmad Makhdum, 62-4, 68, 96, 150, 186
Darvish Khan Tura, 66
Davlechin, 123, 139
Devlet Kil'deev, 65
Divan-begi, Dawlatmand Beg, 177
Dobrolyubov, 63
Dunsterville, L.C., General, 153
Dust Muhammad, King of Afghanistan, 37
Dutov, A., Colonel, 151-4, 157, 160

Elpatiev, 122
Enver Pasha, 178, 80

Fazl al-Din Makhdum, 88, 142
Fitrat, 'Abd al-Ra'uf, 92, 95, 96, 99, 103, 105-13, 114, 127, 128, 133, 140, 142, 172-4
Frunze, M.V., General, 162, 164, 174, 176, 177
Furqat, Zakirjan, 64

Gabidullin, K., 59
Gafur, Nurallah, 136
Gafurov, B., 9
Galuzo, G.P., 102
Gasprinski, Isma'il Bay Gaspirali, 60, 63, 65-6, 79, 82-3, 84, 85, 88, 96, 113, 114
Ghulam Qadiri, 98
Gramenickii, S.M., 87, 97

Hajji Rafiq, 88

265

Hakim Bay, 24
Hamurad Mulla, 140
Hasan Bay, 167
Haydar, Emir, 11, 24
Herzen, 63
Husni, Isham al-Din Makhdum, 101

Ibn Balkhi, xix
Ibragimov, Husayn, 101
Ibrahim Beg, 177, 179
Ikram, Damulla, 84, 85, 86, 95, 98, 114
Iskharov, 131, 135
Ishanov, A., 163
Islamqul Tuqsaba, 98
Isma'il 'Abidi, 79
Isma'il Khan Tura, 66
Ivanov, P., 11, 17, 21

Jaqubov, 92
Joffe, A., 188
Jora Bay, Mulla, 82
Jora Beg, 38

Kamalov, Galiaskar, 104
Kariev, Mulla 'Abd al-Qari, 76
Kaufman, K.P., General, 38, 48
Kazakov, 149
Kaypov, 82
Kemal, Mustafa, 178
Kemal, Namiq, 58
Kerenskii, A.F., 128, 144, 149, 158
Khanykov, N.V., 16, 17
Khodzhaev, Ata Khvaja-ughli, 99, 127, 134, 167
Khodzhaev, Fayzallah Khvaja-ughli, 78, 94, 95, 96, 99, 113, 114, 128, 130, 133, 134, 143, 154, 164, 167, 174, 179, 182, 183, 184
Khodzhaev Mihri, Ishan Hamid, 88, 92, 97
Khodzhaev, Sa'dallah, 173
Khodzhaev, Tursun, 161, 162
Khodzhaev, Ubaydallah, 123, 143
Khodzhaev, Usman Khvaja-ughli, 87, 88, 92, 95, 97, 120, 127, 128, 130, 133, 142, 167, 176
Khusraw, Nasir, 17
Klem, V.O., 128
Klimovich, L., 22
Kobozev, 159, 161, 163
Kolchanov, General, 135
Kolesov, F., 149, 154-9
Korovnichenko, General, 149

Kuropatkin, A.N., General, 120, 122, 123, 125, 127, 128, 129, 144, 145
Kursavi, Abu Nasr, 59, 61, 68

Lapin, Shir 'Ali, 123, 150
Lenin, V.I., xvi, 149, 150, 159, 162, 164, 188
Levin, 101
Lilienthal, General, 89
Logofet, D., 13-14, 16, 28, 52, 90
Lyapovskii, 122
Lyubimov, 175

Mahmud Khvaja, 131
Maksudov, Sadri, 123
Malik Sinjar, 2
Mansurov, 171
Mansurov, Mirza Muhitdin, 46, 88, 92, 95, 101, 137, 142
Maragha'i Zayn al-'Abidin, 103
Marco Polo, 2
Marjani, Shihab al-Din, 59, 61
Masal'skii, V.I., 16
Mende, G. von, 190
Miller, A.J., 125-6, 127, 128, 129, 130, 131, 132, 135, 136, 137, 138, 139, 146
Milyukov, 131, 135, 136
Mir Baba, 134
Mirbedelev, Haydar Khvaja, 101
Mir Salih, 45-6
Mirza Habib, Shaykh, 97-8
Mirzashah Mawlana Shirazi, 33
Muhammad 'Ali, 66, 67
Muhammad 'Anis Beg, 157
Muhammad 'Azim, 98
Muhammad Rahim, 17
Muhitdinov, Mirza 'Abd al-Qadir Muhyi al-Din-ughli, 164, 167, 177
Muhyi al-Din Makhdum, 177
Mukammil al-Din Makhdum, 97, 167
Mukhtar Khan, 167
Muqimiy, Muhammad 'Ali Khvaja Mirzakhvaja, 64
Murad, Shah, 20, 30
Muteferriqa, Ibrahim, 58
Muzaffar al-Din, Emir, 3, 18, 35, 37-8, 48-50, 89

Nadir Shah, 29
Naim Ahmad, 133
Nalivkin, V.P., 79, 123, 149
Namaz, 73
Naqshband, Baha al-Din, 34, 108

Narbutabekov, 165, 166
Nasrallah, Emir, 3, 10, 15, 24, 25, 28, 35, 38, 89, 174
Nasrallah, Qush-begi, 130, 141
Nava'i, 'Ali Shir, 114
Nicholas II, Tsar, 76
Nizam al-Din Khvaja, 137, 141, 157, 161
Nobel, 43

Olufsen, A., xiii, 7, 16, 20
Ossipov, 161
Ostroumov, N., 71

Pahlavan, Niyaz, 120
Pershin, 149
Peters, Y., 163, 188
Poltoracky, P.G., 125, 138
Pozdhyshev, A., 171, 183, 184
Preobrazhenskii, 122, 139
Pulatov, Qari Juldash, 98, 167

Qari Kamil, 120
Qutayba b. Muslim, 1

Rafat, Muyhi al-Din, 127, 142
Rida, Rashid, 108
Ryskulov, Turar, 161, 162

Sabitov, Mulla Niyaz Sabir-ughli, 82-3
Safarov, G., 148
Sahbabe, Mirza, 134
Saizhanov, Musa, 127, 128
Samoilovich, A., 94, 96
Schepkin, N.N., 122, 123, 139
Seignobos, C., 110
Semenov, A., 17, 18
Shaumian, S., 160
Shaybani Khan, 2

Shaykh Safa, 34
Shcherbakov, General, 160
Shkapskii, 122
Shulga, 131, 137
Stalin, J., 160, 162, 181-3
Stolypin, P.A., 149
Sultan Galiev, 161, 181, 182

Tanyshbaev, Muhammad, 123
Tarzi, Mahmud, 102
Taymur, 178
Terent'ev, M.A., 67
Tereshchenko, 144
Tobalin, 149
Tomilin, 149
Tomskii, M., 188
Tura Khvaja Sudur, 141

Umnyakov, I., 97, 98
Uspenskii, 149
Utkin, 155

Vafa, Mulla, 97, 98, 99
Vahidov, Mirza 'Abd al-, 84, 85, 86, 87, 88, 92
Vahidov, mulla-nur, 161
Valiallah, Shah, 61
Validov, Ahmad Zeki (Togan), 162
Vambéry, A., 7, 16, 18, 20, 21, 23-4
Vazhaev, 45
Vezirov, 104
Vvedenskii, 131, 137, 139, 140
Vyatkin, V.L., 79, 135

Weinstein, 149

Yassawi, 114
Yusufzada, Mirza Chalal, 101, 134, 143